Unveiling Deception

Unveiling Deception

Understanding Truth and Lies in Spiritual Warfare

JONATHAN K. CORRADO
Foreword by Paul Covert

WIPF & STOCK · Eugene, Oregon

UNVEILING DECEPTION
Understanding Truth and Lies in Spiritual Warfare

Copyright © 2026 Jonathan K. Corrado. All rights reserved. Except for brief quotations in critical publications or reviews, no part of this book may be reproduced in any manner without prior written permission from the publisher. Write: Permissions, Wipf and Stock Publishers, 199 W. 8th Ave., Suite 3, Eugene, OR 97401.

Wipf & Stock
An Imprint of Wipf and Stock Publishers
199 W. 8th Ave., Suite 3
Eugene, OR 97401

www.wipfandstock.com

PAPERBACK ISBN: 979-8-3852-6180-2
HARDCOVER ISBN: 979-8-3852-6181-9
EBOOK ISBN: 979-8-3852-6182-6

01/14/26

Unless otherwise indicated, all Scripture quotations are from the New King James Version®. Copyright © 1982 by Thomas Nelson. Used by permission. All rights reserved. Italics and other citation indicators have been removed to avoid confusion.
Scripture quotations marked (ESV) are from the ESV® Bible (The Holy Bible, English Standard Version®), © 2001 by Crossway, a publishing ministry of Good News Publishers. ESV Text Edition: 2025. The ESV text may not be quoted in any publication made available to the public by a Creative Commons license. The ESV may not be translated in whole or in part into any other language. Used by permission. All rights reserved.
Scripture quotations marks (KJV) are from the King James Version. Public domain.
Scripture quotations marked (NET) are from the NET Bible® copyright ©1996–2017 All rights reserved. Build 30170414 by Biblical Studies Press, L.L.C.
Scripture quotations marked (NIV) are from THE HOLY BIBLE, NEW INTERNATIONAL VERSION®, NIV® Copyright © 1973, 1978, 1984, 2011 by Biblica, Inc.® Used by permission. All rights reserved worldwide.
Scripture quotations marked (RSVCE) are from The Revised Standard Version of the Bible: Catholic Edition, copyright © 1965, 1966 the Division of Christian Education of the National Council of the Churches of Christ in the United States of America. Used by permission. All rights reserved.

This book is dedicated to Earth's Creator.

For by Him all things were created that are in heaven and that are on earth, visible and invisible, whether thrones or dominions or principalities or powers. All things were created through Him and for Him. And He is before all things, and in Him all things consist.
—Col 1:16–17

> In war, truth is so precious that she should always be attended by a bodyguard of lies.
> —Winston S. Churchill

> Error is never so dangerous as when it is lightly sprinkled with truth.
> —John MacArthur, *Reckless Faith*

> Beware lest anyone cheat you through philosophy and empty deceit, according to the tradition of men, according to the basic principles of the world, and not according to Christ.
> —Col 2:8

Contents

Foreword by Paul Covert — ix

Preface — xi

List of Abbreviations — xvii

1. Deception Begins with Truth — 1
2. Why God's Word Is True — 83
3. What Are Truth and Falsehood? — 148
4. Strategic Deception Buries Lies in Truths — 235
5. Satan's Fall, His Ambitions, and His Power — 270

About the Author — 317

Bibliography — 319

Subject Index — 339

Scripture Index — 363

Foreword

IN THE PAGES THAT follow, you are invited into a profound exploration of one of the most pressing spiritual challenges of our time: the pervasive and insidious nature of deception. The human heart yearns for truth—a truth anchored in the eternal word of God. Yet, we live in a world where truth is constantly under siege, manipulated and obscured by an adversary who seeks to lead us astray. The author of this three-volume series has taken up the call to expose the strategies of deception that the enemy wields with such precision, offering believers a clear and actionable path toward spiritual fortification.

As someone deeply immersed in the ministry of prayer and spiritual leadership, I have witnessed firsthand how deception can erode the foundations of faith, leaving individuals and communities vulnerable to confusion and despair. Satan, the master deceiver, understands all too well that a divided, uncertain heart is fertile ground for his schemes. Yet, we are reminded in John 8:32, "And you shall know the truth, and the truth shall make you free." It is this freedom, grounded in God's truth, that this series seeks to illuminate and safeguard.

The strength of this series lies not only in its scholarly depth but also in its practical wisdom. Drawing from a unique blend of military experience and biblical insight, the author has crafted a field guide for modern-day spiritual warfare. The parallels drawn between military psychological operations and Satan's tactics are both striking and enlightening, equipping readers with the tools to recognize and resist the subtle distortions that can so easily ensnare us.

Each volume in this series builds upon a foundation of truth: uncovering the nature of deception, analyzing its manifestations throughout Scripture, and, ultimately, empowering believers to stand firm through countermeasures rooted in God's word. This journey is not merely theoretical—it is a call to action, a clarion wake-up call to the spiritual battle

FOREWORD

in which we are all engaged. As Eph 6:11 exhorts us, "Put on the whole armor of God, that you may be able to stand against the wiles of the devil."

As you read, I encourage you to approach these pages with an open heart and a prayerful spirit. Allow the insights within to deepen your discernment, sharpen your spiritual vision, and renew your commitment to the Great Commission. Together, let us embrace the challenge of living as ambassadors of truth in an age of profound deception. In doing so, we align ourselves with the heart of God, who desires for all his children to walk in freedom, clarity, and purpose.

I commend this work to you as a valuable resource for the journey ahead. May it inspire, strengthen, and equip you to fulfill your God-given calling with courage and conviction.

Paul Covert,
Threshold Ministries Founder,
Author of *Threshold: Transformational Prayer, Transformational Prayer Ministry* and *52 Creative Ways to Pray: Ideas for Individuals, Small Groups and Prayer Gatherings*

Preface

> All warfare is based on deception. Hence, when we are able to attack, we must seem unable; when using our forces, we must appear inactive; when we are near, we must make the enemy believe we are far away; when far away, we must make him believe we are near.
>
> —Sun Tzu, *The Art of War*

Deception is one of the most formidable forces shaping our world. It infiltrates culture, erodes truth, and operates with relentless precision—both spiritually and intellectually. For Christians, this battle is not only about living out their faith—it is about defending it.

Satan's tactics of manipulation, distortion, and psychological warfare are designed to undermine biblical truth, making vigilance and discernment more essential than ever. In such times, apologetics—the systematic defense of the Christian faith—becomes an indispensable tool, enabling believers to stand firm against deception, articulate their convictions with confidence, and engage in meaningful discussions that lead others toward the gospel.

You may also notice that certain concepts and themes are repeated throughout this book and these volumes. This is not an oversight but a deliberate method of emphasis. Just as a commander drills essentials into his troops until they become second nature, the repetition here is designed so that the most critical truths remain deeply ingrained in your heart and mind. Psychologists call this the *repeated exposure effect*—the principle that familiarity breeds acceptance and retention. And yes, you could even say it's a bit of deception on my part—sneaking the same truths past you in different uniforms. But since this whole book is about exposing deception, let's just call it strategic irony.

PREFACE

THE CALL TO DEFEND TRUTH

As Christians, we are commanded to fulfill the Great Commission, as laid out in Matt 28:19–20: "Go therefore and make disciples of all the nations, baptizing them in the name of the Father and of the Son and of the Holy Spirit, teaching them to observe all things that I have commanded you; and lo, I am with you always, even to the end of the age."

This divine charge calls us to spread the gospel, live out the teachings of Christ, and engage thoughtfully in defending the faith. Yet, despite this calling, we often find ourselves hindered by the influence of Satan and his masterful strategy of deception. Just as military psychological operations (PSYOP) are carefully crafted to manipulate and control, Satan's spiritual PSYOP strategically misleads, creating confusion and doubt, causing believers to question the truth of God's word.

Throughout history, skeptics, critics, and cultural influences have sought to erode the foundation of Christian doctrine. Recognizing these threats, reasoned apologetics emerges as a vital response—not only to reinforce faith but to equip believers with clarity and conviction.

A UNIQUE PERSPECTIVE ON DECEPTION AND WARFARE

Throughout this series, I reference Roman Catholicism, Mormonism, Jehovah's Witnesses, and several other religions as examples to illustrate broader points. This is not intended as a critique of any specific religion but rather as case studies among many possible examples. The themes discussed apply more broadly to various religious institutions and belief systems, emphasizing the universal nature of spiritual deception. However, I firmly believe that there is only one way to heaven, and that is through Jesus Christ alone (John 14:6, Acts 4:12, 1 Tim 2:5, John 10:9). For this reason, Scripture exhorts us to "contend earnestly for the faith which was once for all delivered to the saints" (Jude 3). In an age of competing voices and counterfeit gospels, our task is not merely to analyze error but to defend and proclaim the unchanging truth of Christ.

Having spent two decades as an officer in the US Navy, I have witnessed the intricacies of military deception and psychological operations firsthand. However, my studies in Scripture revealed something far more profound: the same strategic principles used in military PSYOP mirror Satan's spiritual tactics against believers.

PREFACE

Admiral Hyman Rickover, the father of the Nuclear Navy, understood this dynamic with relentless clarity. He insisted that truth, no matter how uncomfortable, must be faced without evasion. "Responsibility is a unique concept," he warned. "You may delegate it, but it is still with you. . . . If responsibility is rightfully yours, no evasion, or ignorance, or passing the blame can shift the burden to someone else."[1] For Rickover, a hidden flaw or a convenient half-truth could sink a submarine and cost lives. For Christians, a half-truth about God's word can just as surely shipwreck faith. The same vigilance demanded in nuclear engineering is required in spiritual warfare: no compromise, no illusion, no excuse.

This realization ignited my mission—to equip Christians with the knowledge and spiritual armor needed to stand firm against deception, both in their personal faith and in defending it against skepticism.

This work engages many apologetics arguments—addressing common objections and misconceptions about Christianity—but it cannot hope to cover them all comprehensively. My aim, instead, is to equip readers with core reasoning tools and examples that can be applied broadly across the varied questions believers encounter.

It is from this vantage point that I have crafted this three-volume series—an expansion and in-depth exploration of my previously published work, *Defying Deception: A Field Guide to Understanding and Countering Satan's Strategy of Deception*. This series is written for those engaged in the spiritual battle "in the thick of the fight."

By breaking down the core concepts of the original field guide, I provide a comprehensive road map to recognizing and countering Satan's deceptive tactics. In doing so, this series equips believers with the ability to defend their faith through both spiritual discernment and faith grounded, apologetic reasoning.

ROAD MAP OF THE THREE VOLUMES

Although this series is designed as a three-volume exploration, each book has been intentionally written to stand alone. Whether you begin with volume 1, 2, or 3, you will find a complete and self-contained discussion that does not require reading the others to grasp its main arguments—though together they form a fuller picture of the battle against deception.

---

1. Rockwell, *Rickover Effect*, 341.

PREFACE

Volume 1: Foundations of Deception

This opening volume examines the very nature of deception—how falsehoods are embedded within fragments of truth, making them appear credible and persuasive. It explores why God's word is the ultimate truth, defining the nature of truth and falsehood while exposing how Satan strategically buries lies within truths.

Additionally, this volume provides an in-depth look at Satan's fall, his ambitions, and the extent of his power, equipping readers with the knowledge to recognize spiritual deception and engage in apologetics that uphold Scripture's authority.

Volume 2: Deceptive Psychological Operations in Scripture

This volume takes readers on a journey through biblical history, revealing the profound influence of deceptive PSYOP throughout Scripture. From Adam and Eve's temptation to the cunning strategies of biblical enemies, it illuminates timeless lessons on discernment, truth, and resilience.

By examining these biblical narratives, readers gain a deeper understanding of the psychological battles they face today, and the spiritual fortitude required to stand firm against deception. Furthermore, this volume illustrates how Scripture itself serves as the foundation for apologetic reasoning, reinforcing the believer's ability to defend their faith against deception.

Volume 3: Countermeasures to Deception

The final volume equips readers with the knowledge and tools necessary to resist and overcome Satan's deceptive PSYOP. Through a combination of scriptural wisdom, psychological insights, apologetics-based reasoning, and practical applications, this volume provides a comprehensive guide to fortifying the mind and spirit against deception.

By mastering counter-PSYOP methods, believers can stand strong in their faith, confidently defend their beliefs, and prevail in the battle for truth and righteousness.

PREFACE

VIGILANCE AND DISCERNMENT IN A DECEPTIVE AGE

In an age where truth and deception often intertwine, it is crucial for Christians to be vigilant and discerning. This three-volume series aims to provide the insights and tools necessary to navigate the spiritual battlefield with confidence. Equipped with biblical truth and faith-grounded logic, believers will not only stand firm against deception but also engage in discussions that lead others toward the gospel.

The intellectual battle is just as critical as the spiritual battle, making apologetics an essential tool in the defense of biblical truth. Recognizing deception is only the first step—responding wisely, remaining anchored, and engaging thoughtfully are the marks of a well-equipped believer.

My prayer is that this series will inspire and strengthen you in your journey toward discernment and spiritual resilience, enabling you to fulfill the Great Commission and live out the life God has intended for you.

The battle between truth and deception is not theoretical—it is deeply personal, playing out in everyday life, shaping beliefs, decisions, and destinies. But as deception intensifies, so too must our commitment to God's unshakable truth.

Victory has already been secured through Christ. It is now our responsibility to stand firm, be vigilant, and wield truth as both our defense and our weapon in this ongoing spiritual war. With this assurance, we now turn to *Unveiling Deception: Understanding Truth and Lies in Spiritual Warfare*, volume 1 of the series, to expose how deception begins and how God's truth endures.

List of Abbreviations

1–2 Cor	1–2 Corinthians
1–2 Kgs	1–2 Kings
1–2 Macc	1–2 Maccabees (from the Apocrypha)
1–2 Pet	1–2 Peter
1–2 Sam	1–2 Samuel
1–2 Thess	1–2 Thessalonians
1–2 Tim	1–2 Timothy
AD	Anno Domini
AI	Artificial Intelligence
ARCINT	Architectural Intelligence
ATF	Bureau of Alcohol, Tobacco, Firearms and Explosives
BC	Before Christ
BDAG	Bauer, Danker, Arndt, and Gingrich's *Greek-English Lexicon*
BLUF	Bottom Line Up Front
c.	circa
CCC	*Catechism of the Catholic Church*
Col	Colossians
Dan	Daniel
Deut	Deuteronomy
DNA	Deoxyribonucleic Acid
DOCEX	Document Exploitation

LIST OF ABBREVIATIONS

Eccl	Ecclesiastes
EMCON	Emissions Control
Eph	Ephesians
Esth	Esther
ESV	English Standard Version
Exod	Exodus
Ezek	Ezekiel
Gal	Galatians
Gen	Genesis
GEOINT	Geospatial Intelligence
Hab	Habakkuk
Heb	Hebrews
HQ	Headquarters
HUMINT	Human Intelligence
Imago Dei	Latin for "Image of God"
IMINT	Imagery Intelligence
INT	Intelligence
Isa	Isaiah
Jas	James
Jer	Jeremiah
KJV	King James Version
LDS	Latter-day Saints
LGBTQ+	Lesbian, Gay, Bisexual, Transgender, Queer or Questioning, plus other sexual and gender identities (e.g., Intersex, Asexual, Nonbinary, Pansexual).
LSJ	Liddell, Scott, and Jones's *Greek-English Lexicon*
LXX	Septuagint
Mal	Malachi
Matt	Matthew
MILDEC	Military Deception

LIST OF ABBREVIATIONS

NIV	New International Version
NKJV	New King James Version
NPNF[1]	*The Nicene and Post-Nicene Fathers*, series 1
NPNF[2]	*The Nicene and Post-Nicene Fathers*, series 2
NT	New Testament
NWT	New World Translation (2013 revision)
OODA	Observe–Orient–Decide–Act loop
OT	Old Testament
Phil	Philippians
Prov	Proverbs
Ps	Psalms
PSYOP	Psychological Operations
Rev	Revelation
ROE	Rules of Engagement
Rom	Romans
SCRIPTINT	Scriptural Intelligence
SIGINT	Signals Intelligence
STR	Short tandem repeat
Strong's	*The New Strong's Expanded Exhaustive Concordance of the Bible*
TDNT	*Theological Dictionary of the New Testament*
TTPs	Techniques, Tactics, and Procedures
UK	United Kingdom
UN	United Nations
US	United States
VMI	Virginia Military Institute

1

Deception Begins with Truth

After orchestrating a brilliant flanking maneuver at Chancellorsville—one of his most celebrated victories—Confederate General Thomas "Stonewall" Jackson was tragically shot by his own troops while scouting ahead after dark. His wounds, including a shattered left arm, ultimately led to his death on May 10, 1863.[1] His legacy was honored at the Virginia Military Institute (VMI) where his statue once stood proudly in front of the barracks. In front of the monument sat four red cannons—the very artillery pieces cadets trained on under Jackson's instruction.[2] Beneath his likeness, the inscription read: "The [Virginia Military] Institute be heard from today"[3]—a rallying call reflecting his deep connection to the institution and its cadets.

1. Robertson, *Stonewall Jackson*, 762–84.

2. Image: Mukhranov, "VMI Battery," CC BY-SA 4.0 (https://creativecommons.org/licenses/by-sa/4.0/). No modifications were made to the image..

3. Gibson, *Virginia Military Institute*, 124–26.

Unveiling Deception

A man may imagine things that are false, but he can only understand things that are true, for if the things be false, the apprehension of them is not understanding.

—Sir Isaac Newton, *Opticks*

Deception has long shaped history—not just on battlefields but in the hearts and minds of those who trust too easily. In war, perception is everything. Manipulating an enemy's expectations—making them see what isn't there and ignore what is—can mean the difference between victory and defeat. Few understood this better than General Robert E. Lee, commander of the Army of Northern Virginia during the American Civil War.

This opening picture is more than military history—it is a living parable of how deception operates at every level. Every psychological operation (PSYOP) begins with a kernel of truth, and spiritual deception works the same way—twisting reality just enough to redirect behavior. This chapter is the baseline of the entire book, showing how the enemy shapes perception as the first move in a broader campaign.

General Lee's tactics at Chancellorsville illustrate the same principle that volume 1 as a whole seeks to uncover: deception begins by twisting fragments of truth into powerful illusions. Lee reshaped battlefield reality to gain advantage; Satan twists spiritual truth to make error look plausible. This first chapter lays the foundation for all that follows, showing how deception always begins by hiding lies within truth.

A twenty-first-century battlefield of perception is our newsfeed. Consider the viral spread of misinformation online: a headline slightly twisted, an image subtly altered, or a video edited to mislead. Millions accept it without question, and behavior follows. These digital illusions echo the same principle demonstrated at Chancellorsville: what people believe directs what they do. Spiritual deception works no differently.

Later chapters will expand this principle—examining why God's word is the only unshakable truth (chapter 2), how truth and falsehood are defined (chapter 3), and how Satan systematically buries lies in truth (chapter 4). But before tactics can be unmasked, we must see the strategy itself: deception framed as PSYOP, designed to influence perception and direct behavior.

DECEPTION BEGINS WITH TRUTH

DECEPTION: THE ART OF MISDIRECTION

In the spring of 1863, deep within the pine forests of Virginia, Lee faced his greatest challenge at Chancellorsville. His Confederate forces were vastly outnumbered by Union troops, yet he refused to play defensively. Conventional wisdom would have dictated a cautious approach—a desperate attempt to hold the lines to cling to survival against impossible odds. But Lee saw beyond the numbers. He understood that victory wouldn't come from brute strength—it would be won through cunning and misdirection.

In a move that defied military logic, he divided his army. Lee split his forces because he recognized the Union army was overconfident, spread out, and slow to react. By taking the initiative, he sought to keep his enemy off balance, forcing them into confusion rather than allowing them to exploit their overwhelming numbers. Under normal circumstances, dividing one's army in the face of a superior foe was reckless because it weakened defenses, exposed flanks, and risked total annihilation if the enemy struck swiftly. To his enemies, it must have seemed reckless—suicidal, even. But to Lee, it was calculated. It was audacious. It was the key to turning the tide of war.

At the heart of his strategy was General Thomas "Stonewall" Jackson, his most fearless commander.[4] Jackson wasn't just a soldier—he was an instrument of devastation. He struck like a phantom in the woods, unseen until it was too late. Yet Jackson was also different: a man of devout Christian faith whose ambition was not for rank or recognition but for obedience to God. He believed that true affirmation came only from his Master, and this conviction gave him a calm resolve even in the chaos of war.

While Lee held the Union forces in place, Jackson led a stealthy flanking maneuver, his troops moving like ghosts through the dense Virginia terrain. Union commanders, blind to the threat creeping toward them, had no idea what was coming. As the sun dipped below the Virginia pines, Union soldiers sensed an unease they couldn't shake. The forest

---

4. Before the war, Jackson served as a physics instructor at VMI, where he was known for his strict discipline and methodical teaching style, before answering Robert E. Lee's call to war. He was equally defined by deep Christian devotion, with an unwavering commitment to prayer and a conviction that success was measured not by promotion but by faithfulness to Christ. His life—like the Chancellorsville campaign itself—is noted here for its historical insight into character and conviction, not as an endorsement of the Confederate cause. See Robertson, *Stonewall Jackson*.

was silent—too silent. Then, like specters emerging from the shadows, Jackson's troops erupted in a fury of gunfire and chaos. Men shouted, scrambled, and fell. Their confidence shattered in an instant.

Then, with explosive force, Jackson's concealed army descended upon the Union's exposed right flank, catching them in chaos and confusion. Lines crumbled. Soldiers scattered. The tide of battle turned in an instant. Chancellorsville, against all odds, became a stunning Confederate victory—won not by sheer numbers but by the artistry of deception.[5]

In military doctrine, this is textbook PSYOP: perception shaped, confidence eroded, behavior redirected. The battle was not won by weapons alone but by controlling what the enemy believed to be true.

Deception, however, is not confined to war; it extends into everyday life. It operates in shadows, whispering lies disguised as truth, influencing decisions, shaping beliefs, and quietly shaping entire generations.

And here is the critical shift: what military strategists call psychological operations, Scripture identifies as Satan's ancient craft of deception. Both operate on the same principle—win the mind, and you win the battle.

Military deception shows the ingenuity of mankind—the ability to craft illusions and exploit weaknesses. But in the spiritual realm, deception is far more insidious. It does not come as an obvious falsehood but cloaks itself in half-truths, wrapping itself in familiarity to lure the unsuspecting.

John MacArthur (1939–2025), a renowned pastor, theologian, and author known for his unwavering commitment to biblical truth, captures this concept succinctly: "Deception rarely comes as an outright lie; it is often a subtle distortion of truth, designed to mislead even the most discerning."[6] His words remind us that deception rarely roars—it whispers. It weaves shadows into truths, wrapping falsehoods in a shroud of believability.

The Union generals at Chancellorsville were not defeated by force but by the elegance of illusion. They trusted what they saw. They believed what their eyes told them. And it cost them dearly.

History offers another reminder from the modern age. Admiral Hyman Rickover, father of the Nuclear Navy, was infamous for interrogating officers mercilessly—not to humiliate them but to expose any hint

---

5. Sears, *Battle of Chancellorsville*, 200–250.
6. MacArthur, *Truth War*, 12.

of bluff, vagueness, or deception. He knew that illusions tolerated in the classroom could turn fatal under the sea. In testimony before Congress he emphasized that "good ideas are not adopted automatically. They must be driven into practice with courageous impatience."[7] His conviction was simple: survival depended on absolute honesty and clarity. Chancellorsville was lost to illusion; Rickover's Navy endured by rejecting it. The same is true in the Christian life. Satan does not need to win by force if he can win by distortion. The moment believers accept appearances over reality, or comfort over truth, the battle is already lost.

The same principle holds true today. Deception shaped that battlefield, and it still twists our understanding of truth—blurring the line between reality and illusion. Leaders, ideologies, and entire movements have risen—and fallen—on the back of deception. This is why the first step in this book is not apologetic argument or cultural analysis, but a deep recognition of Satan's PSYOP: the reshaping of perception through half-truths. Only by exposing this pattern at the start can we prepare to trace its effects across history, doctrine, and daily life in the chapters ahead.

FROM CULTS TO CLICKS: MODERN MANIFESTATIONS OF SPIRITUAL DECEPTION

Just as deception shaped the battlefield at Chancellorsville, where illusion and misdirection determined victory, it has also influenced leaders beyond the realm of war. The manipulation of perception—whether through military strategy or spiritual doctrine—reveals how deeply deception permeates human history.

This is the very nature of PSYOP—planned manipulation of perception to shape emotions, reasoning, and behavior. Whether orchestrated through a general's feint, a cult leader's distortion of Scripture, or a tech company's invisible algorithms, the same principle applies: what people believe determines how they act.

This same pattern appears in our own time—not only in cults or algorithms but even in emerging technologies. Another modern example is the rise of artificial intelligence (AI) "hallucinations." These occur when a machine learning model—designed to provide helpful answers—confidently produces information that is entirely false. The deception lies

---

7. Rockwell, *Rickover Effect*, 210.

not in silence but in certainty: a fabricated citation, a fictitious quote, or a made-up event presented with the same tone of authority as genuine truth. This happens because such models are not reasoning agents but statistical pattern matchers, trained to predict the next most likely word based on enormous datasets. When gaps appear in the data or when the model is prompted beyond its training, it improvises—filling in blanks with plausible-sounding but unfounded material. The result is a confident illusion of knowledge without the underlying reality, a form of error that mimics conviction but lacks substance.

In PSYOP terms, this is "false confidence"—an illusion crafted so seamlessly that the audience lowers its guard. Much like Satan's strategy in the garden, the AI does not shout an obvious falsehood but cloaks fiction in the appearance of knowledge. A statement may feel trustworthy because of its polish, yet it leads the reader astray unless tested against reality.

The lesson is clear: not every answer that sounds authoritative is true. Authority without accuracy is still deception—whether it comes from a pulpit, a propaganda office, or a computer program. Discernment remains our shield because in every age—even the digital one—the battle is for perception.

This pattern is not limited to machines; history shows the same deceptive dynamic in human leaders. A striking modern example is the Branch Davidians. Charismatic leader David Koresh wielded deception not through armies but through ideology, twisting Scripture to claim messianic status while isolating followers and creating an environment of fear and control.[8] His followers, much like misled commanders on the battlefield, believed they understood the truth—only to be led astray.

Under his leadership, the Branch Davidians stockpiled weapons and prepared for an apocalyptic confrontation, believing they were fulfilling divine prophecy.

This led federal authorities to suspect illegal firearms possession, prompting the Bureau of Alcohol, Tobacco, Firearms and Explosives (ATF) to attempt a raid on the group's compound in Waco, Texas, on February 28, 1993. The operation quickly escalated into a violent gun

---

8. Even Koresh's chosen name was part of his deception. Born Vernon Wayne Howell, he legally changed his name in 1990 to "David Koresh"—a calculated messianic claim. "David" invoked the royal line of King David, and "Koresh" is the Hebrew form of "Cyrus," the Persian king in Isaiah 45 whom God calls "His anointed." The name itself was crafted to imply he was a divinely appointed deliverer with biblical authority.

battle, resulting in casualties on both sides and triggering a tense fifty-one-day standoff between the Davidians and federal agents. As negotiations stalled, the FBI launched a final assault on April 19, deploying tear gas to force the group's surrender. Instead, a devastating fire engulfed the compound, killing seventy-six people, including Koresh and over twenty children.[9]

The tragic siege serves as a solemn reminder of the vulnerability of untaught believers to deceptive doctrines. It illustrates how quickly manipulation can masquerade as faith and end in catastrophe. Koresh's campaign was essentially a spiritual PSYOP—shaping a narrative of "chosenness," controlling information, and cloaking deception in familiarity until it was too late.

Today, deception continues this pattern of adaptation. While Koresh led his followers into ruin through direct manipulation, the digital age accomplishes similar distortions through algorithms—guiding beliefs subtly but powerfully, shaping worldviews without notice. Social media algorithms, for example, deliver tailored content that reinforces bias. While seemingly harmless, these mechanisms can distort our perception of truth, drawing us into echo chambers that emphasize convenience over critical reflection.

Modern influencers follow the same pattern—reshaping beliefs under the guise of relatability. Deception doesn't require spectacle to be effective; it often flourishes in quiet manipulations of the ordinary.

Today's cultural currents mirror PSYOP tactics, normalizing lies not through open attack but through slow repetition, framing, and selective emphasis. The battlefield has shifted from compounds to comment sections, but the enemy's strategy is the same: capture perception, and the rest will follow.

From Chancellorsville to Waco, and now in digital culture, deception proves its reach—not just military or ideological but spiritual. In PSYOP doctrine, this is called "controlling the battlespace of perception." In spiritual warfare, it is Satan seeding illusions until they appear indistinguishable from reality.

Whether on battlefields or within belief systems, deception has dictated destinies—shaping victories, seducing minds, and capturing hearts. Military commanders have long wielded deception as a tactical weapon, misleading their enemies with calculated falsehoods. Likewise, spiritual

---

9. Newport, *Branch Davidians of Waco*, 45. Responsibility for the fire is disputed—federal reports blame Davidians, critics contest this.

leaders such as David Koresh have weaponized it for control, embedding manipulation within faith to exploit the trust of their followers.

Yet spiritual deception rarely arrives with fanfare. It operates subtly—threading half-truths into familiar convictions until we lower our guard. Just as Union forces once misread what seemed obvious on the battlefield, we too can be lured into error by what feels comfortable, traditional, or culturally affirmed. Familiarity is not the same as truth; discernment requires more than intuition—it demands vigilance and scriptural clarity.

Another modern illustration of this is the Hebrew Israelite movement, where salvation is reframed in terms of ancestry rather than grace.[10] While appealing as a source of heritage and belonging, it distorts the gospel's universal scope. Scripture declares that Christ purchased people "from every tribe and tongue and people and nation" (Rev 5:9), and that in him "there is neither Jew nor Greek . . . for you are all one in Christ Jesus" (Gal 3:28). By shifting belonging from the cross to ethnicity, this teaching replaces the gospel with tribalism cloaked in religious zeal.

These historical and modern strategies reveal the patterns of spiritual warfare—and how to resist them through discernment rooted in God's word. Deception rarely appears obvious; it slips quietly into our assumptions. Just as tactical misdirection shaped Chancellorsville, deception today continues to shift spiritual and cultural landscapes. But truth endures when paired with vigilance. History makes plain that deception thrives only when we fail to question the narratives before us.

This is why the rest of this volume—and each of the two that follow—takes the shape of a counter-PSYOP manual: first unmasking deception's reliance on truth, then dissecting its tactics, and finally equipping believers with countermeasures rooted in God's word.

Are we paying attention?

R. C. Sproul (1939–2017), a respected theologian, pastor, and founder of Ligonier Ministries, dedicated his life to helping believers understand and defend biblical truth. He insightfully warned, "Satan does not come to us with horns and a pitchfork. He comes as an angel of light, using deception to lead us away from the truth."[11] Sproul's reflection urges

---

10. While not monolithic, many sects within this ideology teach that true covenant identity is reserved for a particular ethnic lineage—often those of African descent—while others are excluded from God's promises.

11. Sproul, *Truth of the Cross*, 123; See also Sproul, *Holiness of God*, 113.

discernment, showing how lies often masquerade as wisdom, bypassing our defenses through quiet persuasion.

Such deception may appear in the form of a well-meaning friend misinterpreting Scripture or in our own rationalizations to justify actions we know are wrong. Just as deception thrives on the battlefield, it infiltrates our daily lives—quiet, unnoticed, disguised as reason or good intentions. A small compromise, a softened truth, or an unchallenged assumption can each lead us further down a path we never intended to walk. Yet, like those misled at Chancellorsville, we must ask, Are we truly seeing reality, or simply believing what is comfortable?

This quiet erosion of truth doesn't always arrive in grand deception—it often starts small, imperceptible. Consider the soft tug of a "white lie" told to spare someone's feelings, only to discover that the unintended consequences are far-reaching. What seems harmless—or even kind—can ripple into long-term distortion. We must ask ourselves, Are these compromises leading us closer to truth or further away from it?

Contemporary examples further demonstrate how self-deception can masquerade as spiritual truth. The widespread embrace of the "prosperity gospel," for instance, distorts Scripture to align with materialistic desires. This theology teaches that faith, positive declarations, and financial generosity will result in guaranteed material wealth and physical health, promoting the idea that God's favor is measured by financial success. Verses like Phil 4:13, "I can do all things through Christ who strengthens me," are taken out of context to support the notion that personal ambition and prosperity are divine rights, rather than focusing on perseverance through hardship.

As a result, many prioritize worldly success at the expense of genuine faith, equating financial blessing with spiritual favor while neglecting the biblical emphasis on humility, sacrifice, and dependence on God.[12]

This emphasis on the self is not unique to the prosperity gospel. Many religious systems revolve around the individual: refining the self, attaining enlightenment, achieving moral perfection, or escaping suffering. In Buddhism, the goal is to extinguish desire and reach Nirvana through disciplined meditation and moral living. Hinduism offers liberation (*moksha*) through karma, ritual, and spiritual ascent. Islam emphasizes submission and moral obedience to earn favor with Allah. New Age spirituality promotes inner harmony, self-actualization, and cosmic

---

12. Bowler, *Blessed*, 78.

alignment. Even secular philosophies elevate personal growth, wellness, and authenticity as ultimate ends.

The common thread? The self is central. These systems speak to the flesh—appealing to our desire to be elevated, admired, and in control. They place the individual on a pedestal, encouraging spiritual pride, moral arrogance, and a subtle form of self-worship (Rom 8:5–8). Even noble pursuits like discipline and virtue can become self-serving when the ultimate goal is personal advancement.

Christianity turns that paradigm inside out. Its central call is not self-improvement but surrender (Luke 9:23). Not elevation of the self but exaltation of God (John 3:30). The Christian life begins not with striving but with dying—dying to self, to pride, to autonomy (Gal 2:20). It is not a ladder to climb, but a cross to carry (Matt 16:24).

This contrast is not only theological but profoundly practical. The enemy's lie that the self is supreme often masquerades as identity and worth, and when that deception takes root, it destroys. Keith Emerson, famed keyboardist of the band Emerson, Lake & Palmer, was deceived into believing his entire value was measured by his ability to perform. When health issues and performance anxiety robbed him of that gift, he saw no reason to live, and in 2016 he tragically took his own life.[13] His story illustrates with heartbreaking clarity the futility of anchoring identity in anything other than Christ.

The aim is not to become better for our own sake but to become vessels for God's glory (2 Cor 4:7). We are not the heroes of our story; we are servants in his (Rom 12:1). The gospel does not say, "Fix yourself so you can reach God." It says, "God reached down to rescue you—now live for Him" (see Eph 2:8–10).

And why do we need rescue? Because we are all infected. Not with a virus of the body but with a condition of the soul. Scripture delivers the test result with sobering clarity: every human being is SIN positive (Rom 3:23). Like being HIV positive, it is universal, terminal, and inescapable apart from intervention. No amount of moral effort or spiritual discipline can cure it. The only remedy is a Savior (John 14:6).

Unlike Ethan Hunt, we're not assigned to the IMF to attempt a "mission impossible." Left to ourselves, salvation really is impossible. No strategy, no clever scheme, no human effort can achieve it. The truth is humbling: we cannot save ourselves. We need a Savior.

---

13. Ratliff, "Keith Emerson."

This is the scandal and beauty of Christianity: it is not about us. It is about him.

GOSPEL COMPROMISERS AND MAN-PLEASERS

One of the enemy's most subtle strategies is to dilute the gospel by overemphasizing certain truths while ignoring others. Just as the prosperity gospel twists God's promises into a materialistic formula, so too many leaders today reshape the message of Christ to make it more palatable to the culture. They speak often of God's love yet remain silent about his holiness, justice, and hatred of sin. In doing so, they present a half-gospel that comforts people in their rebellion rather than calling them to repentance and faith. This too is a form of spiritual PSYOP: emphasizing part of the message while suppressing the rest until the "whole gospel" is replaced with a carefully constructed illusion.

The apostle Paul warned against such distortion when he wrote, "For do I now persuade men, or God? Or do I seek to please men? For if I still pleased men, I would not be a bondservant of Christ" (Gal 1:10). Those who soften the exclusivity of Christ's gospel in the name of popularity, unity, or tolerance follow in the footsteps of man-pleasers, not apostles.

Tragically, this compromise extends even into efforts to embrace false systems as though they were valid expressions of Christianity. Some seek to reverse the Reformation by granting legitimacy to doctrines that deny justification by grace alone through faith alone. Others give platforms to those who proclaim "another gospel" without offering correction or warning. Such actions are not compassion but capitulation, leaving entire congregations vulnerable. Jesus himself declared that on the last day many will hear the words, "I never knew you; depart from Me, you who practice lawlessness!" (Matt 7:23).

This capitulation is also evident in Rome's ecumenical movement, which seeks to gather all professing Christians under papal authority. Once Protestants were branded heretics; now, according to Catholic ecclesiology, they are welcomed as "separated brethren"—a subtle rebranding that conceals an unchanging claim to supremacy. Roman Catholic ecumenical strategy can be discerned in practice, threefold: (1) seduce prominent Evangelicals to validate Catholicism as Christian, (2) urge "separated brethren" to return to "Holy Mother, the Church" through the Eucharist, and (3) beguile Protestants with high-profile Catholics who preach "another Jesus" unable to save completely.[14] This pattern is not hypothetical. Swedish pastor Ulf Ekman, once a leading charismatic Evangelical, shocked many when he converted to Catholicism and began commending Rome as the true church.[15] In Detroit, Pentecostal minister Alex C. Jones not only embraced Catholicism but led a portion of his congregation into the fold, citing the supposed "fullness" of faith found in Rome.[16] Former Anglican bishop Michael Nazir-Ali likewise entered the Catholic Church through the ordinariate, an arrangement designed specifically to reabsorb separated brethren under papal authority.[17] Yet not all such attempts go unchecked: the 1994 "Evangelicals and Catholics Together" statement, which sought to unite leaders from both camps in a shared witness, was met with strong evangelical resistance and produced a wave of critiques warning that it compromised the gospel itself.[18] These examples demonstrate that Rome's ecumenical strategy inevitably leads to "another gospel" of works, sacraments, purgatory, indulgences, and the blasphemous offering of a Eucharistic Christ as a propitiatory sacrifice.[19] Such strategies must be unmasked, for they are not the gospel once for all delivered to the saints but a counterfeit unity. Believers are called instead to remain sanctified by the truth and to contend earnestly for the faith (Jude 3).

The fruit of such compromise is plain. This concern is not merely theoretical; recent surveys confirm how deeply deception has infiltrated even the evangelical church. For example, the 2022 State of Theology Survey conducted by Ligonier Ministries and LifeWay Research revealed that over 73 percent of respondents with evangelical beliefs (as defined by the survey's doctrinal criteria) agreed with the statement that Jesus

---

14. See *Unitatis Redintegratio*, §3, in Vatican II, "Decree on Ecumenism," which first called Protestants "separated brethren" and affirmed that the fullness of salvation resides in the Catholic Church; *CCC*, §816 (teaches that the church of Christ subsists in the Catholic Church and that outside of it there is no salvation).

15. Ekman and Ekman, *Great Discovery*, is the testimony of a prominent charismatic pastor whose conversion validated Rome in the eyes of many Evangelicals.

16. Jones, *No Price Too High*.

17. Caldwell, "Dr. Michael Nazir-Ali."

18. See Horton, "Evangelicals and Catholics Together," for a contemporary evangelical response exposing the dangers of the ECT document as a compromise of the gospel.

19. Session 22, canon 3 from the Council of Trent explicitly declares the Mass to be a true propitiatory sacrifice for the living and the dead. However, calling the Mass "propitiatory" is contradictory, since propitiation means Christ's once-for-all sacrifice (Rom 3:25; Heb 2:17; Heb 10:10–14).

was "the first and greatest being created by God" the Father. While many likely answered out of doctrinal confusion rather than deliberate heresy, the result nevertheless echoes the ancient error of Arianism—a heresy condemned since the Council of Nicaea in AD 325, which affirmed Christ's eternal deity. Likewise, more than half of Evangelicals (55 percent) affirmed that the Holy Spirit is a force, not a personal being.[20] In other words, a majority of those identifying as Bible-believing Christians deny or distort the very doctrine of the Trinity that defines historic orthodoxy.[21]

Those survey results help explain why groups like Jehovah's Witnesses can gain traction at the margins of evangelical life. When significant numbers within the evangelical fold already entertain Arian-like ideas—however inadvertently—the doctrinal terrain is weakened. The theological confusion revealed by the survey creates an opening for Jehovah's Witnesses arguments: if the Trinity is misunderstood or reduced, the claim that Jesus is a created being sounds less foreign and can even appear plausible to readers who lack a firm grounding in Christ's deity.

This is no small doctrinal slip—it is the equivalent of a breach in the defensive line. In warfare, once the perimeter is compromised, the enemy does not need to win every battle; he simply exploits the opening until the entire position collapses. Yet even more decisive is the center of gravity—the source of strength or influence an opponent depends on; shift it, and the entire system can collapse. Satan works the same way. By sowing confusion about who God is—by blurring Christ's eternal Godhead and reducing the Spirit to an impersonal force—he attacks the center of gravity in Christian theology. From there, every downstream doctrine—salvation, sanctification, and worship—becomes vulnerable to distortion.

Scripture itself provides a striking illustration of this center of gravity in the resurrection of Christ. At different points the New Testament

---

20. The statements that "Jesus was the first and greatest being created by God the Father" and that "the Holy Spirit is a force, not a personal being" are core theological positions of Jehovah's Witnesses. The fact that such views were affirmed by a majority of self-identified Evangelicals in the survey highlights the extent to which heterodox beliefs have penetrated the church.

21. Carter, "State of Theology." Respondents categorized as holding "evangelical beliefs" met four criteria defined by the National Association of Evangelicals: (1) the Bible is the highest authority for faith, (2) personal evangelism is important, (3) Christ's death is the only sacrifice that removes sin, and (4) salvation comes through faith in Jesus Christ alone. The survey results reflect broad self-identification rather than doctrinal alignment. Ligonier cautions that many respondents who claim the label "evangelical" do not affirm historic theological essentials.

declares that the Father raised Jesus from the dead (Gal 1:1), that the Spirit raised him (Rom 8:11), and that Jesus himself declared, "Destroy this temple, and in three days I will raise it up" (John 2:19–21), referring to the temple of his body. The resurrection, in other words, is attributed to all three persons of the Godhead. Far from being a contradiction, this is the Bible's own testimony to the triune nature of God.[22] Jehovah's Witnesses, however, insist that "Jehovah God"—by which they mean the Father alone, excluding the Son and the Spirit—raised Jesus. Yet such a claim cannot reconcile the full biblical witness. For historic Christianity, this is precisely the point: the Father, Son, and Spirit act in perfect harmony, revealing one divine essence. The empty tomb is not just the vindication of Jesus but the revelation of the Triune God who saves.

Jehovah's Witnesses illustrate where this doctrinal confusion leads when left unchecked. Claiming to restore biblical truth, they distribute literature and conduct door-to-door evangelism with an appearance of sincerity. Yet beneath this veneer lies a fatal distortion: the denial of Christ's eternal deity. By reducing Jesus to a created being—"the first and greatest created one of God," according to Watch Tower teaching[23]—they revive the same ancient heresy first rejected at Nicaea.

Consider just a few biblical facts that directly contradict Watch Tower claims:

As previously quoted, Jesus himself affirmed that he would raise his own body in three days (John 2:19–21), claiming divine power over his own resurrection. The very disciple who had doubted the resurrection worshiped him as "My Lord and my God" (John 20:28)—literally in Greek, *ho kurios mou kai ho theos mou*, "the Lord of me and the God of me"—a declaration Jesus accepted rather than rebuked. In John 8:58, he declared, "Before Abraham was, I am" (*egō eimi*), echoing the divine

---

22. The same triune pattern appears elsewhere, unmistakably affirming the Trinity and the deity of all three persons: at creation, where the Father speaks, the Word creates, and the Spirit hovers (Gen 1:1–3, John 1:1–3); at the baptism of Jesus, where the Father speaks from heaven, the Son is baptized, and the Spirit descends like a dove (Matt 3:16–17); and in the Great Commission, where disciples are baptized "in the name of the Father and of the Son and of the Holy Spirit" (Matt 28:19).

23. John 1:1 from the New World Translation (NWT). See also Watch Tower Bible and Tract Society of New York, *Truth That Leads*. The NWT, first published in 1950 by the Watch Tower Bible and Tract Society, was deliberately revised to support Jehovah's Witnesses doctrines, especially by obscuring texts affirming Christ's deity and the Trinity. Most scholars view it as a sectarian translation that distorts the original languages to reinforce Watch Tower theology.

name revealed to Moses in Exod 3:14, which is why his hearers picked up stones to kill him for blasphemy.

But Scripture not only affirms his deity; it also bears witness to the nature of his resurrection. The New Testament testifies that Jesus rose bodily, not as a mere spirit (Luke 24:39–43), demonstrating that the resurrection was not symbolic or spiritualized but the triumph of God over death itself—something a created being could never accomplish. And because his resurrection was bodily, believers can look forward with confidence to their own resurrection in glorified bodies, a blessing Scripture holds out as our sure and joyful hope (1 Cor 15:20–23, Phil 3:21). Each of these truths dismantles the Watch Tower's claims and shows that their theology is not biblical Christianity but a revival of ancient heresy. Their approach shows how deception embeds itself in familiar language: Christ may be given lofty titles, but without his true deity the cross is robbed of saving power and the gospel collapses.

The aforementioned 2022 State of Theology Survey's finding—that many who call themselves Evangelicals hold views consonant with Arian tendencies—makes the Jehovah's Witnesses example more than an external oddity; it becomes a diagnostic indicator of internal vulnerability. Congregations that do not robustly teach the Trinity risk hearing Jehovah's Witnesses literature and thinking "this fits" because the defenses are not in place.

Tragically, the rank-and-file members are not usually willful heretics but captives, sincerely believing they are serving God while being held in place by a system that will not allow them to leave. They are simply doing what their religion expects of them, unaware that their allegiance is to an institution rather than to the risen Lord. Here the enemy's PSYOP is unmistakable—wrapping a lie in the vocabulary of truth until people can no longer tell the difference.

This illustrates the broader pattern: the enemy's long-game PSYOP is to erode confidence in the Trinity so that all other truths fall like dominoes. What appears to be "Evangelical" in name may already be spiritually neutralized in reality because deception has succeeded where it matters most—the knowledge of God himself.

And what is true of Jehovah's Witnesses holds true in every other guise of compromise: once the center is compromised, deception rarely stops there. It often dresses itself in cultural virtues—words like *inclusion* or *tolerance*—to disguise compromise as compassion. What appears to be inclusion or tolerance is, in reality, a calculated distortion designed to redirect allegiance away from the true gospel. The danger is not hypothetical. When believers put up with "another gospel" (2 Cor 11:4), they surrender the very treasure entrusted to them. Just as in military strategy a breach can open the way for the enemy, so in spiritual warfare a small compromise can undermine the church's witness. The next generation depends on our vigilance. Paul refused to yield "even for an hour, that the truth of the gospel might continue with you" (Gal 2:5). We must be no less resolute.

The stakes are generational. In PSYOP terms, this is the "long game": if one generation's perception of truth is shifted, the behavior of the next generation can be entirely redirected. Satan understands this principle, which is why Paul's uncompromising stand must be our own. His warning was not confined to the first century; it speaks directly into our moment, where the same tactics of deception now appear in cultural and philosophical disguise.

DEFENDING TRUTH IN A POSTMODERN AGE

In the spiritual realm, deception thrives on blending truth with lies—a distortion that mirrors broader philosophical challenges in today's postmodern era.

The Rise of Cultural Relativism

Postmodern relativism, much like spiritual falsehoods, fosters doubt and confusion by rejecting absolute truths. Rooted in the belief that reality, knowledge, and morality are subjective and shaped by individual perspectives or cultural contexts, postmodern relativism denies the existence of universal truths. It challenges the idea that objective knowledge is attainable, arguing instead that truth is fluid and constructed by societal narratives. This mindset, while appearing open-minded, can lead to moral ambiguity and intellectual skepticism, making it difficult to discern deception from genuine truth. In both spheres, recognizing and confronting deception requires vigilance, discernment, and unwavering adherence to foundational principles.

In modern terms, cultural relativism functions like an ongoing information campaign—an environment saturated with narratives designed to make absolutes appear arrogant and conviction appear intolerant. As cultural critic Neil Postman observed, our age is not so much hostile to truth as it is distracted from it—amusement and image replace reflection, leaving society vulnerable to illusion.[24] Such cultural conditioning is not accidental; it mirrors the objectives of PSYOP, which aim not simply to inform but to reshape what entire populations perceive as normal.

Understanding the tactics of deception—whether in military strategy or spiritual warfare—is essential for navigating this battlefield. Just as General Lee's masterful misdirection at Chancellorsville shifted the course of battle, Christians face similar challenges in the spiritual realm, contending with an adversary who thrives on distraction and deceit. Preparation and discipline, vital in combat operations, mirror the believer's call to readiness in confronting spiritual threats.

This vigilance is especially critical today, as some churches compromise foundational doctrines to adopt secular ideologies under the banner of inclusivity. Moral relativism—a philosophy that denies absolute truth and claims morality is shaped by culture or personal preference—has led congregations to waver on core tenets like the sanctity of marriage and the exclusivity of salvation through Christ. By treating truth as fluid, they risk diluting Scripture, sowing confusion among believers, and diminishing the church's witness in a world starving for truth.[25]

In such times, believers must remain spiritually alert—discerning truth amid cultural noise and holding fast to Scripture as their unshakable guide. Faith is not passive; it is a battle stance, a shield raised against the storm of deception. Even in a culture that blurs truth, God's word remains a lamp to our feet and a light to our path (Ps 119:105). For those anchored in Christ, relativism cannot silence the Spirit's voice. The Good Shepherd promises his sheep will hear his voice and not follow a stranger (John 10:27). When uncertainty strikes, God's word is the lifeline, anchoring the soul to the immovable foundation of divine truth.

Those who hesitate risk being swept away by the tide of lies, but those who stand resolute, anchored in Scripture, wield the unwavering strength of divine wisdom. Armed with discernment, they cut through deception, exposing falsehood and advancing the kingdom of God with unshakable conviction.

---

24. Postman, *Amusing Ourselves to Death*, 107.
25. Trueman, *Rise and Triumph*, 112.

Unveiling Deception

Deception, after all, is the art of cloaking falsehood in familiarity—of presenting illusion as truth. Scripture repeatedly warns of Satan's mastery of deception, using subtle distortions to lead people astray. This same principle is reflected in military PSYOP, where perception is shaped through controlled narratives rather than brute force. PSYOP are "planned operations to convey selected information and indicators to foreign audiences to influence their emotions, motives, and objective reasoning, and ultimately the behavior of foreign governments, organizations, groups, and individuals."[26]

Whether in warfare or spiritual battles, deception thrives where vigilance is weak and truth is compromised. By naming this parallel explicitly, this chapter shows that whether the target is a nation, a congregation, or a single soul, the method remains the same: distort perception to direct response.

Just as military strategists analyze PSYOP to counter enemy tactics, Christians must recognize the deceptive strategies used against them in spiritual warfare. Understanding these methods allows believers to resist manipulation and stand firm in truth. Military deception relies on blending truth with lies to control perception. Satan operates similarly—not through outright falsehood but by distorting what is familiar, credible, and persuasive. This awareness is crucial, as deception will only intensify. As Paul warns in 2 Tim 3:13, "But evil men and impostors will grow worse and worse, deceiving and being deceived."

This recognition is what positions the entire series: volume 1 lays the groundwork by defining truth and exposing deception, volume 2 will track PSYOP through Scripture itself, and volume 3 will equip believers with counter-PSYOP strategies to resist deception in daily life. Together, these books provide a comprehensive understanding of deception from its origins to its real-world applications, equipping readers to discern and resist manipulation.

To move forward, we must first be anchored in what we mean by truth—because without a clear grasp of truth, every claim of error or correction is merely opinion. Before diving into the tactics of PSYOP in the second book and the remedies in the third book in this series, it is crucial to first lay the foundation by examining deception itself. Just as a shadow cannot exist without light, deception is only possible when truth is first established. This initial book focuses on defining truth and deception,

---

26. Joint Chiefs of Staff, *Joint Publication 3-13.2*, vii.

exploring how falsehoods—especially those wielded by Satan—have shaped history, influenced individuals, and distorted reality.

Truth is not fleeting but foundational—it shapes reality, informs discernment, and stands as a pillar of understanding. Its depth and permanence are reflected in biblical languages. The Greek word *aletheia* conveys the idea of truth as "unconcealedness"—a reality that cannot be hidden, often associated with divine revelation. Similarly, the Hebrew word *'emeth* expresses not only truth but also firmness, constancy, and faithfulness—suggesting that truth is not merely conceptual but an enduring force we can trust.[27]

It is precisely this permanence that makes truth the primary target of deception. In both military PSYOP and spiritual warfare, the enemy knows that if he can distort the perception of truth, he can control every subsequent decision.

While the meaning of truth can be defined linguistically, its real challenge lies in how it is perceived and applied. Across cultures and eras, truth has been debated, reshaped, and even weaponized, making it more elusive than ever. It is easy to discuss the lexicographical nature of "truth"—that is, its formal definition and linguistic origins—but the concept itself remains widely contested. The issue is not a lack of desire to understand truth but rather that society's evolving perspectives have fractured conventional definitions.

As a result, the question of truth has grown more urgent than ever in modern discourse. Before examining the truth of the Bible, we must first establish the existence and necessity of absolute (or universal) truth.[28]

Because deception can only exist in contrast to truth, this chapter begins where every PSYOP analysis begins—with the baseline. A shadow exists only where light is present, and so before we can study deception, we must first establish what truth is.

In everyday conversation, truth is often treated as a straightforward concept—something that aligns with fact or reality. Yet beneath this simplicity lies profound philosophical tension. Perspectives on truth vary widely: while some assert that absolute reality governs the universe, others insist that truth is merely a construct shaped by perception, culture, and power.

---

27. *Strong's* (1996), s.v. "ἀλήθεια (aletheia)," G225, and s.v. "אֱמֶת (emeth)," H571.
28. Geisler, *Christian Apologetics*, 562–66.

Postmodern thinkers champion this latter view, rejecting universal principles in favor of relativism.[29] This is how "truth" is viewed, according to postmodernism:

- Truth is invented, not discovered.
- Truth is relative, defined by each individual or culture.
- No universal or transcultural truth exists.
- Truth is fluid, evolving with social change.
- Truth is shaped by personal mindset and communal consensus.
- Objective knowledge is ultimately unknowable.[30]

Such claims dismantle moral absolutes and foster skepticism. Ethics, once grounded in timeless values, become situational—subject to momentary emotion or social pressure. This is cultural PSYOP at work—not through a single leader like David Koresh but through systems that normalize relativism until absolute truth itself feels intolerant.

This erosion leads to moral inconsistency. Situational ethics argues that context determines right and wrong, allowing flexibility but often lacking stability. For example, lying to protect someone's safety may seem justified, while theft might even be deemed acceptable depending on community norms. Yet these compromises, while appearing compassionate, can ultimately cloud judgment.

Feel-Good Ethics and Their Philosophical Roots

Postmodernism's influence doesn't stop there. It gives rise to "feel-good" ethics reflected in noncognitive theories like emotivism and expressivism:

- *Emotivism* views moral claims as emotional expressions (e.g., "Stealing is wrong" = "I dislike stealing").
- *Expressivism* treats ethical language as a call to action rather than a statement of fact.

---

29. It is important to recognize that postmodernism is a complex worldview with many facets, influencing perspectives on morality, knowledge, and truth itself. Understanding its implications is key to discerning deception and navigating the ever-shifting landscape of contemporary thought. It is difficult to succinctly encapsulate this viewpoint, as there are many nuances. For a more thorough exposition of this topic, see Sire, *Universe Next Door*.

30. Holtz, "Postmodernism."

Both reject objective morality, separating feelings from foundational truth. In this landscape, truth is no longer discovered—it's personalized, improvised, and unstable.[31] As comedian Ricky Gervais—himself a staunch atheist—once quipped, "Just because you are offended, doesn't mean you are right."[32] It is striking that one who openly rejects Christianity can still articulate a principle that exposes the emptiness of relativism. His remark highlights that offense proves nothing—feelings cannot establish truth.

These frameworks are not neutral—they function as narrative control, teaching people to interpret morality as nothing more than mood or preference. In PSYOP terms, this is "influence through framing"—where the way questions are asked and categories are defined dictates the conclusions that people reach.

Contrast this with the conviction that absolute truths do exist. In this worldview, right and wrong are judged by unchanging standards, offering clarity and consistency. Consider the law of gravity—an undeniable reality—or mathematical principles like $2 + 2 = 4$. If these absolutes weren't fixed, science, logic, and even daily life would unravel. Commerce, technology, and justice systems depend on certainty.

Amid cultural relativism, Scripture stands firm. It doesn't shift with the winds of opinion—it anchors us in unwavering truth. As Ps 119:160 declares, "The sum of Your word is truth, and every one of Your righteous rules endures forever."

This raises the central challenge for every believer: Why do you believe what you believe? Is it shaped by cultural trends, the shifting impulses of your own heart (Jer 17:9), or the eternal word of God that endures forever? Only Scripture offers a foundation that remains unshaken when every other authority collapses.

Contemporary voices continue to warn against this cultural drift. The late Charlie Kirk (1993–2025), founder of Turning Point USA, observed that relativism is not merely a philosophical misstep but a calculated weakening of cultural foundations, leaving individuals vulnerable to manipulation. His critique echoes Scripture's warning: when objective truth is dismissed, deception gains a foothold. In this sense, Kirk's cultural analysis parallels the Bible's spiritual warning—truth must be guarded or society itself begins to unravel.[33]

31. Marturano, "Non-Cognitivism in Ethics."
32. Katsidou, "Ricky Gervais."
33. Kirk, *Christian Response*, 45.

In a culture saturated with competing narratives, God's word is not one more opinion in the information war—it is the immovable reference point, the ultimate counter-PSYOP.

The pursuit of truth—in philosophy, faith, or daily life—ultimately converges in the timeless wisdom of God's word. While postmodern philosophies promote skepticism and relativism, Scripture provides clarity, discernment, and moral direction. It cuts through deception and aligns our hearts with reality as defined by the Creator.

In a world spinning with uncertainty, believers must anchor their understanding in this firm foundation. For without absolute truth, even compassion can become confusion, and ethics dissolve into emotional whims. But with God's word as our compass, we navigate not by shadows—but by light.

Although it is illogical to assert that there is no absolute truth, many individuals today embrace a cultural relativism that denies its existence. In addition to the problem of inherent contradictions, many logical obstacles must be surmounted to accept that there are no absolute or universal truths. One is that because all humans have limited knowledge and finite minds, it is logically impossible for them to make absolute negative statements. A person cannot logically assert, "There is no God" (although many do so) because to do so would require absolute knowledge of the entirety of the universe's existence, spanning from its beginning to its end. Since this is impossible, the most anyone can logically assert is, "Based on my limited knowledge, I do not believe in God."

Another issue with the denial of absolute or universal truth is that it contradicts what we know to be true from our own consciences, experiences, and observations of the actual world. If there is no such thing as absolute truth, then nothing is right or wrong in the final analysis. What is "right" for you does not necessarily make it "right" for me. On the surface, this type of relativism is appealing, but it actually means that everyone establishes their own rules and does what they believe is right.

Taking all of this together, we can see why it is important that there is no neutral position. The Bible clearly conveys this concept:

> Enter by the narrow gate; for wide is the gate and broad is the way that leads to destruction, and there are many who go in by it. (Matt 7:13)

> Therefore whoever hears these sayings of Mine, and does them, I will liken him to a wise man who built his house on the rock:

> and the rain descended, the floods came, and the winds blew and beat on that house; and it did not fall, for it was founded on the rock. But everyone who hears these sayings of Mine, and does not do them, will be like a foolish man who built his house on the sand. (Matt 7:24–26)

> He who is not with Me is against Me, and he who does not gather with Me scatters abroad. (Matt 12:30)

> "The just shall live by faith." For the wrath of God is revealed from heaven against all ungodliness and unrighteousness of men, who suppress the truth in unrighteousness, because what may be known of God is manifest in them, for God has shown it to them. (Rom 1:17–19)

Habakkuk had first declared centuries earlier, "Behold the proud, his soul is not upright in him; but the just shall live by his faith" (Hab 2:4). This Old Testament affirmation of faith over pride and works became a cornerstone for Paul's theology of justification by faith, later quoted in Rom 1:17, Gal 3:11, and Heb 10:38. In its original context, Habakkuk contrasts the arrogance of Babylon with the steadfast trust of the righteous remnant, highlighting that genuine life and endurance come only through faith in God.

The clarity of Scripture on this point cannot be overstated. Neutrality is not an option. Hebrews reminds us, "By that will we have been sanctified through the offering of the body of Jesus Christ once for all" (Heb 10:10). Salvation rests on a single sacrifice—Christ's death—not on repeated rituals or human striving. Jesus himself illustrated this with sobering simplicity in Matt 7. He described two roads, two gates, and two destinies. The broad way, entered by default, is crowded, comfortable, and ultimately destructive. The narrow way, entered by repentance and faith, is difficult but leads to life. God does not blur the lines—he makes the issue black and white. There is no third option.

Christ pressed the contrast even further: there are two kinds of trees—good and bad. A good tree bears good fruit; a corrupt tree produces decay and is cut down. Likewise, there are two kinds of disciples—those who do the will of the Father and those who merely say, "Lord, Lord." On the day of judgment, Christ will reject hollow profession with the chilling words, "I never knew you; depart from Me" (Matt 7:23). Again, God leaves no middle ground. His truth is black and white—life or destruction, truth or deception, divine accomplishment or human effort.

The wide road is not neutral—it represents every human attempt at salvation apart from Christ: religious works, moral scorekeeping, ritual sacrifices, or self-improvement schemes. Every world religion shares this impulse: do enough, climb high enough, purge long enough, and perhaps God (or karma, or fate) will accept you. But this is nothing more than human achievement dressed in spiritual clothing. Its end is death, for sin's debt is unpayable by human effort. God keeps perfect record of every word, thought, and deed. Every sin demands justice. Left to ourselves, we pay forever in hell because the cost is infinite.

By contrast, the narrow way rests wholly on divine accomplishment. It is entered not by striving but by new birth—by repenting, renouncing self-sufficiency, and trusting Christ's finished work. Our sins are paid in full by another. Works cannot supplement grace any more than a dollar bill can settle a hundred-dollar debt; to offer our merit is not only insufficient but offensive to the sufficiency of the cross. As Isaiah declared, "All our righteousnesses are like filthy rags" (Isa 64:6). To add human effort is to nullify grace. Salvation is black and white: either Christ pays it all, or we pay forever.

Yet human nature continually resists this simplicity, searching for visible assurances to lean on. Across history, people have reached for substitutes—rituals, works, and even sacred objects[34]—hoping to supplement or confirm what Christ has already finished. This misplaced confidence is not new; it is simply another form of the same deception. Just as works cannot earn salvation, neither can relics add to it. Which raises the question: if relics disappeared tomorrow, would true faith be diminished?

Scripture never calls us to trust in objects but in the Savior himself. According to Roman Catholic teaching, relics are not worshiped but venerated, serving as tangible reminders of God's work through the saints. Yet even granting that distinction, Scripture nowhere presents relics as aids to faith. At best, they stir sentiment; at worst, they invite misplaced confidence.

Consider the Shroud of Turin, believed by many to be the burial cloth of Christ, or the Holy Nails, said to have pierced his hands and

---

34. Some elevate relics or physical artifacts as though faith depends on them. But even if no relics existed, Christianity would stand unchanged. As Gary Habermas emphasizes, the foundation of faith is not in religious objects but in the historical reality of Christ's resurrection, which alone secures salvation and validates the gospel message. To confuse relics with the substance of faith risks superstition, not salvation. See Habermas and Licona, *Case for the Resurrection*, 43–49.

feet—of which dozens of "authentic" versions exist worldwide. There's the Veil of the Virgin Mary, the Tooth of Saint Apollonia, and even the incorrupt body of Saint Catherine of Bologna, preserved in a seated position. Some churches claim fragments of the True Cross, while others house the blood of Saint Januarius, which is said to miraculously liquefy. These relics, though historically fascinating, risk becoming spiritual distractions when elevated beyond their symbolic value.

In reality, God has gone out of his way to protect his people from misplaced confidence in relics. When Moses—Israel's greatest prophet—died, "[the Lord] buried him . . . but no one knows his grave to this day" (Deut 34:6). Jude 9 even records a spiritual conflict between Michael and Satan over Moses' body, underscoring its significance. Why would God hide the body of his servant? One reasonable conclusion is that God was guarding Israel against their tendency toward idolatry. If relics were essential to build faith, we might expect God to display Moses' body as a permanent shrine. Instead, Scripture presents his concealment as a reminder that faith must rest not on sacred remains but on God himself. Relics cannot add to salvation any more than works can; to elevate them, even as "helps," is to risk shifting confidence away from Christ's finished work and toward symbols that cannot save.

The human impulse to seek assurance in physical tokens is not unique to relics. Scientology, for example, employs the "E-meter" in its auditing process, claiming this device can measure spiritual burdens and chart a path toward freedom.[35] Like medieval relics, the E-meter functions as a tangible prop—a visible object that promises access to hidden realities. In both cases, confidence is redirected from the sufficiency of Christ to the spectacle of signs or objects.

Deception outside religion demonstrates the same principle. In 1835, *The New York Sun* published a series of articles describing life on the moon: bat-winged humanoids, crystalline temples, and lush lunar landscapes—all supposedly verified by scientific observation.[36] The "Great Moon Hoax" captivated readers, boosting circulation and convincing thousands, until it was exposed as fiction.[37] In the same way, relics can function as perceived "proofs" when presented with the sheen of authority, enticing the imagination while obscuring where true faith

---

35. Hubbard, *Dianetics*, 171–74.
36. Goodman, *Sun and the Moon*, 85–102.
37. Zielinski, "Great Moon Hoax."

should rest. The comparison is not about relics being a hoax but about how both rely on appearance and authority to gain credibility.

The craving for tangible proof—whether in ancient relics or modern inventions—has not disappeared. Where relics tie faith to the past, eucharistic miracles attempt to validate it in the present. Where relics tie faith to sacred remains from the past, eucharistic miracles attempt to validate faith through supernatural signs in the present. Both appeal to the senses, but in doing so they risk shifting confidence away from Christ's once-for-all work and onto experiences or objects that cannot save.

For example, according to Roman Catholic teaching, at consecration the substance (or inner essence) of bread and wine is changed into the literal body and blood of Christ, while the outward accidents (taste, smell, appearance) remain unchanged. This distinction between "substance" and "accidents," drawn from Aristotelian philosophy rather than Scripture, was officially defined as *transubstantiation* at the Fourth Lateran Council (1215).[38] The Roman Catholic catechism states, "The whole Christ is truly, really, and substantially contained" in the Eucharist, his presence continuing "whole and entire" in each element.[39] The Council of Trent went further, pronouncing anathema on anyone who denied this claim.[40] Roman Catholic teaching presents miraculous hosts that bleed or remain incorrupt as divine confirmation of the doctrine. Yet the New Testament leaves no ambiguity: Christ's sacrifice was once for all (Heb 10:10–14). No philosophical distinction and no miraculous phenomenon—however dramatic—can add to the finality of Calvary.

This conviction matters all the more today because eucharistic miracles are not only historical but have been curated and promoted in modern times. Carlo Acutis (1991–2006), a teenager canonized by the Roman Catholic Church in 2025, gained recognition for compiling a website and exhibition of eucharistic miracles worldwide. His devotion and technological skill were celebrated as evidence that these signs still inspire faith in a digital age.[41] Yet the question remains: What do they

---

38. Tanner, *Nicaea I to Lateran V*, 230.

39. *CCC*, §§1374–77.

40. Schroeder, *Canons and Decrees*, 73. The Council of Trent (1545–1563) was the Roman Catholic Church's major ecumenical response to the Protestant Reformation, defining Catholic doctrine and establishing reforms related to Scripture, tradition, salvation, and church authority.

41. Walcott, "God's Influencer."

actually prove? If faith rests on miracles, it is fragile; if it rests on Christ's once-for-all death and resurrection, it is unshakable.

This raises the deeper question: Do we need eucharistic miracles, relics, or sacramental claims to build faith? Scripture answers with clarity, "Faith comes by hearing, and hearing by the word of God" (Rom 10:17). Jesus himself declared, "Blessed are those who have not seen and yet have believed" (John 20:29). Signs may confirm truth, but they cannot create saving faith. Even those who witnessed Jesus' miracles hardened their hearts (John 12:37).

In PSYOP terms, the enemy does not need to deny Christ outright; he only needs to redirect confidence away from him and onto substitutes. Whether relics, eucharistic miracles, or philosophical claims of transubstantiated essence, each shifts assurance from the cross to the system. Scripture grounds faith in Christ alone, whose once-for-all sacrifice requires no repetition, confirmation, or supplementation.

And here is the beauty: God has made the gospel simple. Humans complicate it with layers of ritual, philosophy, and performance, but Christ presents it in terms even a child can grasp. That is why he said, "Assuredly, I say to you, unless you are converted and become as little children, you will by no means enter the kingdom of heaven" (Matt 18:3; see also Luke 18:17). The way of salvation is not intellectual mastery or religious achievement—it is simple, childlike trust in what Christ has already accomplished.

Thus salvation is received, not earned. Faith comes by hearing God's word, repentance turns us from the broad road, and faith places us on the narrow path where Christ has already borne the cost. Good works follow as fruit, never as root. In this way, salvation is entirely divine revelation and accomplishment—a message not born of human instinct but one that confronts human pride and self-sufficiency. It is counterintuitive to our natural impulses yet beautifully simple in its divine origin—a gift of grace. Those who trust in Christ are born again, forgiven, and secure; those who remain in their natural state continue on the broad road that ends in destruction. God himself has drawn the line in stark, black-and-white terms, and he has made the way of life so simple that even a child can believe.

Yet this simplicity is precisely where the battle rages. Humanity resists it, proving that people are not neutral: "all have sinned" (Rom 3:23) and "the heart is deceitful above all things, and desperately wicked; who can know it?" (Jer 17:9). Out of this rebellion flows a cultural vulnerability:

younger generations, untethered from God's truth, are increasingly exposed to atheistic indoctrination. In the absence of an anchor, they are taught to measure truth by feelings, popularity, or political power rather than by God's word. This opens the door for them to be conditioned into accepting moral relativism as they are propagandized to conform to the world's non-biblical worldviews. Such worldviews include the LGBTQ+ movement that redefines identity and sexuality apart from God's design. The very language of sexual identity has multiplied in only a few decades, and Gallup polling shows the share of Americans who self-identify as LGBTQ+ doubled from 3.5 percent in 2012 to 7.1 percent in 2022, with nearly one in five members of Generation Z describing themselves this way.[42] This sharp increase reflects a cultural shift in identity and self-understanding rather than a timeless reality, underscoring how ideology can shape perception when untethered from biblical anthropology.

Other false frameworks include the justification of abortion as a matter of personal choice rather than the taking of life, critical race theory that interprets human worth and justice through power struggles instead of the image of God, the teaching of atheistic evolution that denies divine creation, and the ideological absolutism often attached to man-made climate change, which can elevate human regulation of the environment into a kind of secular religion. While Earth has always experienced natural cycles of warming and cooling—such as ice ages long before industrialization—most scientists attribute present warming trends largely to human activity, though significant aspects of the interpretation and certainty remain debated. My concern here is less about the science itself than about the way climate discourse is framed as a quasi-religious system that displaces biblical stewardship with human autonomy.[43] Each

---

42. Hall et al., "Sexual Orientation Identity Development"; Jones, "LGBT Identification." The expansion of sexual identity terminology is striking. Where older generations typically recognized only heterosexuality and homosexuality, today's landscape features a proliferating catalog: lesbian, gay, bisexual, transgender, queer, intersex, asexual, pansexual, nonbinary, gender-fluid, demisexual, and many more, with new labels regularly coined in online subcultures and activist literature. A systematic review of identity development milestones among LGBTQ+ individuals confirms how rapidly terminology and self-identification have shifted in youth populations over the past few decades.

43. Plimer, *Heaven and Earth*. Climate change is often framed as settled science, with dissenters quickly labeled "anti-science" or dismissed as "deniers." Yet Pew Research Center reports that while a strong majority of Americans acknowledge climate change, a significant subset rejects that it is happening at all, and many others express skepticism about scientists' findings or motivations. Levels of trust in climate scientists vary, with only about a third of Americans saying they have a great deal of confidence in

of these positions rejects God's authority and substitutes a counterfeit framework that exalts human autonomy above divine truth.[44]

This is the conditioning effect of deception at scale: repeated narratives shape perception until entire generations assume that what is popular must also be true. It is no accident—this is Satan's long-term PSYOP, and the only defense is to anchor in the unchanging truth of God's word. When that defense is abandoned, the fallout is inevitable: once absolute truth is undermined, chaos rushes in to fill the vacuum.

One of the most effective instruments in this deception is music—a medium uniquely crafted to bypass reason and stir affections. It is no coincidence that Satan exploits this channel with surgical precision. In times of trial and uncertainty, many young people instinctively turn to songs for solace, only to find themselves drawn less to God and more into a counterfeit refuge. Much of today's popular music saturates the airwaves, streaming platforms, and social media feeds with lyrics that exalt sensuality, despair, rebellion, and self-centered ideals—messages cloaked beneath irresistible melodies, hooks, and rhythms. This is a special kind of spiritual danger because music touches the heart before reason can intervene.

Yet not all music is inherently bad. God himself designed music as a vehicle for worship, joy, and truth (Ps 150; Eph 5:19; Col 3:16), and Scripture repeatedly commends singing and psalms as means of glorifying him. At times it serves as celebration, refreshment, or even wholesome entertainment—as when David's harp refreshed Saul (1 Sam 16:23) or when God's people danced with joy (Ex 15:20; 2 Sam 6:14; Ps 149:3). The same medium Satan distorts can, when aligned with God's word, become a powerful force for encouragement, holiness, and spiritual formation

---

them to provide accurate information (Pasquini et al., "Why Some Americans"). Critics also stress that Earth's climate has always been cyclic, with ice ages and warming periods (e.g., the "Little Ice Age," c. 1300–1850) occurring long before industrialization. These natural fluctuations highlight that climate shifts are not new phenomena, raising legitimate questions about how much current changes stem from human activity versus natural variability. In a notable—and ironic—shift, Bill Gates, who for years warned of catastrophic, near-apocalyptic climate outcomes, has recently moderated his stance. After long reinforcing doomsday-style projections in public interviews and writings, Gates now argues that climate change, while serious, is "not the end of the world" and should be approached as a manageable global challenge rather than an unavoidable catastrophe. He emphasizes innovation, adaptation, and improved human welfare over fear-based messaging, asserting that many projected harms are ultimately "tolerable" or can be substantially mitigated through technological and practical measures. How can this be if we were previously near distinction?

44. For more on this, see Ham, *Divided Nation*.

(John 10:10). This contrast—between God's design and Satan's distortion—sets the stage for why music is such a contested battlefield.

What makes this particularly insidious is that Christian tradition has long suggested Satan once held a role in worship in heaven. Though Scripture does not explicitly call him the "choir director," many preachers and theologians have observed that he twisted worship into pride and rebellion, even amid the heavenly courts.[45] It is no surprise, then, that he continues to pervert music as one of his prime instruments of influence on earth. A medium once connected with heavenly praise has become a battlefield. Because humans respond emotionally and physiologically to rhythm, harmony, and melody, songs can sink deep into our emotions, betraying us into sin while our minds remain oblivious.

The nefariousness of this tactic is often hidden behind a catchy tune. Consider the long-running "What Happens Here, Stays Here" campaign for Las Vegas. Set to upbeat music and paired with glamorous visuals, the slogan became a cultural mantra—celebrating secrecy, indulgence, and moral compromise as entertainment. The jingle didn't just promote tourism; it normalized escapism, lust, and lawlessness under the guise of fun and freedom. The hook disarms resistance while the message takes root. This is precisely the sort of subtlety that makes music such a potent weapon of deception—sin dressed in song, evil smuggled in melody.

This same dynamic plays out not only in advertising but in the classic, nostalgic songs that define generations. Take, for example, the Eagles' classic rock ballad "Hotel California." Its smooth guitar lines, haunting harmonies, and unforgettable refrain—you can check out at any point, but you can't ever really leave—make it musically captivating.[46] Yet the lyrics describe a luxurious but sinister hotel, widely interpreted as an allegory for hedonism, addiction, and spiritual bondage. Beneath the artistry lies a chilling reality: the "welcome" of indulgence quickly becomes a prison of enslavement. The beauty of the melody and arrangement masks the despair of the message. What millions sing with delight is, at its core, a parable of damnation packaged as entertainment.[47] The brilliance of the music conceals the darkness of the words—illustrating

---

45. See Ezek 28:13–17, Isa 14:12–15. For the view that Satan held a role in heavenly worship before his fall, see Morris, *Long War Against God*, 63–65.

46. The Eagles, "Hotel California."

47. Don Henley and Glenn Frey of the Eagles both described "Hotel California" as "a metaphor for the excesses of American culture" and "a journey from innocence to experience." Eliot, *To the Limit*, 256–58.

how Satan disguises destruction with beauty, just as Scripture warns that he "masquerades as an angel of light" (2 Cor 11:14).

Another example is the album *Tommy* (1969), the rock opera by the band The Who, often heralded as one of the greatest albums of all time for its ambitious score and string of classic, catchy hits. The musical brilliance of the record propelled it to legendary status, yet its storyline centers on Tommy Walker, a traumatized boy rendered deaf, mute, and blind after a childhood shock. He becomes a pinball prodigy, rises as a messianic cult figure, briefly regains his senses, and ultimately collapses back into isolation and disillusionment when his followers abandon him. The tale mixes themes of idolatry, false worship, abuse, and hollow promises, showing how people seek transcendence in human leaders only to be left empty.[48]

Its most famous track, "Pinball Wizard," is both musically electrifying and lyrically absurd, praising Tommy's supposed savant-like skills as though they were grounds for worship. Other songs reinforce the cult-like devotion of his followers and the futility of their faith in a flawed savior. Yet someone casually listening—captivated by the sheer musical brilliance—may never pause to consider the twisted storyline or the non-God-honoring substance beneath the surface. Worse still, the narrative often seeps in unnoticed: themes of false worship, spiritual emptiness, and misplaced hope take root without deliberate reflection. The melodies captivate, the rhythms impress, and the lyrics slip past unexamined, embedding confusion beneath sonic brilliance. Research confirms this dynamic: repeated exposure to musical content—especially when paired with emotionally resonant melodies—can shape mood, memory, and even moral frameworks, often without conscious awareness.[49]

In this way, *Tommy* intertwines some of rock's most celebrated compositions with a storyline that normalizes disordered worship and despair. Critics hail the album as a cultural triumph, yet at its heart it is a portrait of spiritual emptiness. Once again, dazzling artistry conceals darkness, luring listeners with melody while normalizing despair and false hope. What may appear to be only one album in rock history is in fact representative of a broader reality: music's capacity to shape the soul runs deeper than most realize. These cultural patterns and scientific findings point to the same truth: music is never neutral.

---

48. The Who, *Tommy*.

49. Barradas and Sakka, "When Words Matter"; Balestrieri, "Music Lyrics"; Zhang et al., "Effects of Lyrics."

Research underscores this danger. Hodges summarizes studies showing that as many as 75 to 80 percent of adolescents report using music as their primary coping strategy during times of stress, ranking it above talking with parents, friends, or engaging in religious practices. In one survey, nearly two-thirds of teens said they "couldn't get through the day without music."[50] These numbers highlight how easily music displaces spiritual disciplines, subtly shaping where young people turn for comfort and identity. One study on Christian youth found that secular songs could either challenge their faith or redirect gratitude toward God, illustrating how music powerfully shapes spiritual perception.[51] Neuroscientific research has likewise demonstrated that religious songs tend to engage the emotions more deeply than secular songs when the listener intends to encounter the divine, highlighting music's capacity to either draw one closer to God or away from him.[52] Analyses of youth culture show that most teenagers fill every spare moment—commutes, study breaks, and downtime—with music, while prayer and Scripture intake diminish.[53] Thus, music is not neutral: it either reinforces devotion or undermines it, depending on its content and the spirit behind it.

Because of its divine origins in worship and its profound emotional reach, music demands more vigilance from believers than nearly any other medium. A malicious lyric or cynically crafted hook can slip past our defenses while embedding seeds of falsehood in our hearts. For this reason, Christians must approach music with discernment, testing what they hear against the word of God and intentionally filling their lives with worship that glorifies Christ. When music is co-opted as propaganda, the path from deception to destruction is already paved—one of Satan's most effective PSYOPs. But when surrendered to the Lord, music remains one of God's greatest gifts—able to lift weary hearts, unite his people in praise, and provide holy joy and even wholesome refreshment. In God's hands, what the enemy meant for harm becomes a means of grace. But this example simply illustrates the broader danger we discussed earlier: once truth becomes relative, deception spreads into every area of life.

50. Hodges and Sebald, *Music in the Human Experience*, 325–28. Hodges surveys research showing that adolescents often use music as a primary coping mechanism in times of stress.

51. Bist et al., "Music and Spirituality."

52. Koelsch, "Towards a Neural Basis." Koelsch reviews evidence that religious songs evoke stronger emotional responses when participants expect transcendent experience.

53. Twenge et al., "Decreases in Psychological Well-Being," 768.

The Consequences of Rejecting Absolute Truth

Eventually, one person's sense of justice will collide with another's. If there is no absolute truth and no universal standard of right and wrong, then we can never be certain of anything. People would be free to do whatever they want, including murder, rape, theft, lying, and cheating, and no one could object. There would be no government, no laws, and no justice because it would be impossible to claim that the majority has any authority to impose standards on the minority. A universe devoid of absolutes would be the most horrifying universe imaginable.

This is the logical conclusion of a successful PSYOP: when truth itself is undermined, chaos fills the vacuum. Without a standard, perception becomes the only reality—and whoever controls perception controls society.

Spiritually, this type of relativism leads to religious confusion as there is no one true religion and no way to have a proper relationship with God. Therefore, all religions would be false because they all make absolute claims about the afterlife. Increasingly, people hold the contradictory belief that two religions with fundamentally opposing doctrines could both be true—even when each asserts exclusivity as the only way to heaven. Such contradictions are not merely intellectual mistakes—they are evidence of deception at work, cloaking irreconcilable claims in the language of tolerance and "inclusivity."

People who do not believe in absolute truth disregard these assertions and embrace a more tolerant universalism that teaches that all religions are equal and that all roads lead to heaven. People who hold this worldview fiercely oppose evangelical Christians who believe that Jesus is "the way, the truth, and the life" (John 14:6) and that he is the ultimate manifestation of truth and the sole means of salvation.

Tolerance has become the sole cardinal virtue of postmodern society—the only absolute—and intolerance is deemed its greatest vice. As a result, any dogmatic belief, particularly a belief in absolute truth, is regarded as the ultimate sin of intolerance. Those who deny absolute truth often assert that it is permissible to believe whatever you want, as long as you do not attempt to impose your beliefs on others. However, this view itself represents a belief about what is right and wrong, and those who hold it inevitably attempt to impose it on others. By setting a behavioral standard for everyone else, they contradict the very principle they claim to uphold. This inherent contradiction highlights their unwillingness to accept responsibility for their actions.

If absolute truth exists, then there must also be absolute standards of right and wrong, for which we are accountable. When individuals deny absolute truth, they reject this accountability in favor of moral relativism.

And this is where deception achieves its greatest victory: not only are people misled about what is true, they are also shielded from the weight of accountability. Like a battlefield enemy convinced to lower his guard, entire cultures are persuaded that judgment is an illusion—until the reality of God's standard breaks through.

The Evolutionary Foundation of Relativism

In politics, candidates campaign on promises about the future, but their credibility hinges on the past. Voters examine both ends—what has been and what is yet to come—because these extremes reveal character, consistency, and vision. The same dynamic plays out in theology.

It's no mystery why the Bible's bookends—Genesis and Revelation—draw the fiercest scrutiny. The beginning and the end are where worldviews collide, where assumptions are laid bare, and where the stakes feel highest. These are the claims that shape everything else.

While this book does not address eschatology or end-times doctrine, it does confront the foundational question of origins. What we believe about the beginning—about creation, design, and purpose—sets the trajectory for how we interpret science, Scripture, and human identity. If Genesis is merely myth, then the rest of the Bible becomes suspect. But if it speaks with truth and authority, then its implications ripple through every discipline and domain.

This section explores that beginning. Not as a relic of ancient imagination but as a revelation that still challenges modern assumptions. The goal is not to win a debate but to clarify the stakes—and to show why the Bible's account of creation deserves serious, thoughtful engagement.

At first glance, the discussion of evolution in this context may seem unexpected. However, it is precisely at the root of the issue. The rejection of absolute truth and the rise of moral relativism are not isolated phenomena; they stem from a worldview that removes objective moral standards and replaces them with subjective interpretations of existence. This shift finds one of its strongest ideological foundations in the widespread acceptance of naturalistic evolution. If evolution is true, then life is the product of random processes rather than intentional design, eliminating any inherent purpose or objective moral standards. Without a Creator establishing absolute truth, morality becomes subjective, shaped by cultural and individual preferences rather than fixed principles. As a result, the same relativistic mindset that dismisses moral absolutes finds its roots in a framework that denies a higher authority governing human existence. This is more than a philosophical drift—it is the success of a cultural PSYOP, a coordinated information campaign aimed at reframing assumptions and behavior. By recasting existence as the product of chance, the narrative severs accountability to a Creator and reshapes humanity's perception of origin and, by extension, of morality. In such a frame, life has no inherent meaning, and moral "oughts" collapse into preference—further eroding accountability and clarity.

In PSYOP doctrine, this is "reframing the environment"—altering the starting assumptions so thoroughly that every conclusion drawn afterward leads away from the truth.

The debate over absolute truth extends beyond philosophy and morality—it fundamentally shapes how Scripture is understood. This divergence between evolution and creationism lies in the interpretation of Gen 1 and 2. If these chapters are viewed as symbolic or poetic rather than a literal, historical account of creation, the question becomes, how should the rest of Genesis, and ultimately the Bible, be interpreted? The answer to this question becomes subjective and open to individual determination. However, examining Genesis through the lens of Hebrew narrative—not poetry—underscores the inerrancy of the creation account and affirms a young Earth. By reading Genesis as a literal historical record, we preserve the integrity of Scripture and uphold the concept of absolute truth that provides the foundation for moral and spiritual accountability.[54]

If the opening chapters of Genesis can be redefined, then every doctrine downstream can be redefined as well. In strategic terms, this is "attacking the center of gravity." Once the foundation is destabilized, the rest of the structure collapses.

Multiple scientific lines of argument are marshaled in defense of the Genesis account. Alternate theories, such as the day-age theory, theistic evolution, and progressive creationism, were developed outside the biblical text from a modern (and ever-changing) scientific worldview.

---

54. Johnson, "Genesis Is History."

A significant amount of research and scholarship (both scientific and theological) indicates that a young Earth is the most straightforward, conservative way to interpret God's word. The book of Genesis says God made everything in six days and that genealogy commences with Adam. The entire universe was formed with functional maturity, including Earth and its creatures. In addition, God created everything "very good" (Gen 1:31), and there was initially no death. The fact that death doesn't exist until the third chapter of Genesis (the curse) precludes any kind of evolution (e.g., theistic evolution). There couldn't have been any "evolutionary selections" because nothing died; therefore, nothing replaced it. Ultimately, believing in an old Earth not only implies an acceptance of evolutionary processes but also contradicts the biblical truth that death did not enter the world until Gen 3.

This highlights again that Satan's oldest deception—"You will not surely die" (Gen 3:4)—is echoed in evolutionary frameworks that require death before the fall. It is not merely science at stake but the authority of God's word.

Given the importance of preserving absolute truth, how Scripture is interpreted plays a crucial role in maintaining theological consistency. The most unambiguous way to interpret the Bible is according to its grammatical-historical sense, or the intended meaning of the authors.[55] A literal interpretation accounts for all figures of speech in the text, providing the most straightforward method of interpreting Scripture. To this point, when Jesus quoted the Old Testament, it was always clear that he considered its passages as factual. In Luke 4, for example, Jesus responds to Satan with Scripture:

> You shall fear the LORD your God and serve Him, and shall take oaths in His name. . . . You shall not tempt the LORD your God as you tempted Him in Massah. (Deut 6:13, 16)

> So He humbled you, allowed you to hunger, and fed you with manna which you did not know nor did your fathers know, that He might make you know that man shall not live by bread alone; but man lives by every word that proceeds from the mouth of the LORD. (Deut 8:3)

Jesus' use of these historical texts presumes their factual referents; his hermeneutic models ours.

---

55. International Council on Biblical Inerrancy, "Chicago Statement," article 15.

Many people attempt to explain the words, phrases, or paragraphs in a Bible verse or passage according to their own interpretations, disregarding key elements like context and the author's purpose.[56] That's not what God intended, however, which is why he instructs us to handle the word of truth correctly (2 Tim 2:15).

Additionally, the disciples took Christ's (Bible-based) directives literally. After Jesus commands them in Matt 28:19–20 to "make disciples of all the nations," they begin preaching the gospel across the then-known world, telling people to "believe on the Lord Jesus Christ" and be saved (Acts 16:31).[57]

Literal obedience flows from a literal word. Once the word is reduced to metaphor or cultural artifact, obedience becomes optional. That is exactly how deception infiltrates—by reframing God's commands as suggestions.

When we make ourselves the final arbiters of which sections to read plainly, we exalt ourselves above God. Who, then, can claim that one person's interpretation of a biblical event or truth is more or less accurate than another's? As a result of the inevitable confusion, Scripture would be rendered essentially invalid. The Bible is God's inspired, written revelation to us, and he intended for it to be taken completely at its word—including the literal, six-day creation of Genesis. This exegetical foundation matters deeply: how we interpret Genesis determines whether we uphold God's authority or reinterpret it through modern assumptions. We will return to this theme later from another angle—how these debates themselves are used strategically to reshape worldviews.

Although we interpret the Bible literally, it contains some literary devices that are meant to be taken figuratively; however, these are readily apparent (e.g., Ps 17:8). In fact, Scripture uses 217 different figures of speech.[58] For example, in John 10:9, Jesus says, "I am the door." Clearly, this doesn't mean he has hinges or a doorknob—it's a powerful metaphor illustrating his message.

This distinction matters. Understanding how Scripture uses both literal language and figurative expression affirms its richness—but it also raises a critical question: What happens when this interpretive balance is lost? If we begin reinterpreting foundational texts like Genesis based on external influences rather than biblical context, we risk reshaping

---

56. Corrado, "Importance of Context."
57. White, *Scripture Alone*, 200–213.
58. Bullinger, *Figures of Speech*.

theology to suit modern preferences. This subtle shift doesn't just affect doctrine—it influences culture, ethics, and worldview. The way we interpret Scripture directly impacts how we understand origin, purpose, and morality. Earlier, we considered how naturalistic evolution erodes absolute truth by replacing divine design with randomness. But its influence doesn't stop at philosophical abstraction—it infiltrates biblical interpretation itself. When foundational texts like Genesis are reimagined through an evolutionary lens, the ripple effect impacts theology, morality, and spiritual accountability.

Here deception functions like a cascading PSYOP: shift the starting assumptions and the downstream worldview bends with it—until entire cultures and churches are reshaped without ever realizing how the drift began.

When evolution replaces creation in the public imagination, it does more than reinterpret science—it dismantles the very concept of divine accountability. A worldview shaped by random processes naturally rejects moral absolutes, allowing each person to define meaning for themselves. Over time, this foundation leads to moral chaos, spiritual confusion, and cultural decay.

This is not just an intellectual debate but a spiritual campaign of disinformation—one that rewrites origins to erase accountability and, in doing so, prepares hearts to reject the gospel itself. Pastoral voices have long warned about these downstream effects. David Jeremiah, a well-known American evangelical Christian pastor, Bible teacher, author, and radio/television broadcaster, warns of evolutionism's far-reaching consequences—not just in theology but in everyday life:

> Many layers of error have been built on the faulty foundation of evolutionism. Humanism is the natural result. If God is not central in all our thinking, then man must be. Atheism is humanism's twin brother, and consistent evolutionists cannot logically believe in the personal God of the Bible, the God who is the Creator of all life. Abortion, infanticide, and euthanasia are logical behaviors for those who have so easily disposed of the image of God in the eternal soul of man. The concept of a resurrected body and eternal life is also a casualty of this evil philosophy. The average person neither knows nor cares much about the error of evolution, and yet their life is constantly being influenced by it. Pornography, adultery, divorce, homosexuality, premarital sex, the destruction of the nuclear family—all are weeds that have grown from Satan's big lie about the universe.

We are now on the verge of adopting full-fledged animalism in human practice—promiscuity, vandalism, hedonism, even incipient cannibalism. Even the Holocaust is "explained" by evolution. Hitler's extermination of the Jews grew out of his desire to speed up the evolutionary process.[59]

The scope of Nazi evil underscores this point with chilling clarity. At the 1942 Wannsee Conference, officials not only confirmed the policy of the "Final Solution"—a calculated program of systematic, continent-wide extermination of the Jewish people—but also cloaked their intentions in euphemism. For years, Nazi leaders had spoken of the so-called "Jewish Question," a phrase that reduced millions of lives to an abstract "problem" requiring a political answer. The "Final Solution" was presented as the definitive resolution of that question, yet the language itself served as deception: genocide disguised as policy, mass murder veiled as administration. Such terminology reveals that the perpetrators knew the moral weight of what they were doing, yet deliberately chose to obscure it.

At the conference, they presented detailed statistical tables. These figures accounted for Jewish populations across Europe—both in territories already occupied and in nations they had yet to conquer, including Great Britain. The lists included country-by-country tallies: 3.9 million in the Soviet Union, 2.3 million in the General Government (occupied Poland), 865,000 in Romania, 275,000 in France, 330,000 in Hungary, 131,000 in England, and many more. In total, the Nazis calculated over eleven million Jews marked for extermination.[60] Underlying these figures was a delusion: they assumed they would win the war, conquer every one of these nations, and carry out their plans on a global scale. Worse still, they portrayed their exterminationist ideology as if they were doing humanity a favor. Hitler himself, in *Mein Kampf*—his political manifesto written in the 1920s that outlined his ideology and future plans for Germany—cast the elimination of Jews as a cleansing of society and a service to the world.[61] This chilling mixture of meticulous planning and self-deceived justification demonstrates the depth of their evil: genocide rationalized as progress, mass murder rebranded as moral duty. This was no improvised violence but a systematic, research-driven plan—ministries and bureaucrats coordinating census data, rail timetables, and deportation logistics.

59. David Jeremiah is quoted in Morris, *Long War Against God*, 9.

60. Longerich, *Wannsee Conference*, 98–101; Browning, *Origins of the Final Solution*, 410–12.

61. Hitler, *Mein Kampf*, 60–61.

Unveiling Deception

The infamous Wannsee protocols reveal a chilling reality: genocide was treated as an administrative problem to be solved with precision. Such deception-driven ideology illustrates how far men will go when truth is abandoned and human life reduced to expendable matter.

Jeremiah's warning highlights how evolution functions not only as a scientific claim but as a cultural PSYOP—an ideological narrative designed to reframe man as an accident, thereby eroding accountability to God and normalizing behaviors once universally condemned.

Regardless of how much sinful men and women deny the existence of God and absolute truth, they will one day face his judgment. As Rom 1:19–22 states,

> Because what may be known of God is manifest in them, for God has shown it to them. For since the creation of the world His invisible attributes are clearly seen, being understood by the things that are made, even His eternal power and Godhead, so that they are without excuse, because, although they knew God, they did not glorify Him as God, nor were thankful, but became futile in their thoughts, and their foolish hearts were darkened. Professing to be wise, they became fools.

Here Paul describes the same process PSYOP strategists recognize: truth is visible yet suppressed; reality is plain yet reframed. The result is not enlightenment but futility.

In moments of moral questioning or spiritual searching, many wrestle with a foundational question: Does absolute truth actually exist—or are all convictions simply relative? Yet compelling evidence points to a deeper reality, beginning with something every person experiences: the human conscience.

And even if skeptics dismiss the evidence of beginnings and design, they cannot escape the law written on their hearts. Every human being instinctively knows there is such a thing as right and wrong. Love is better than hate, justice better than injustice.

One of the most powerful evidences for absolute truth is this internal compass—a "something" within us that tells us the world ought to be a certain way. It affirms that suffering, starvation, and injustice are wrong, while love, generosity, and compassion are inherently good. C. S. Lewis (1898–1963) described this as the "Law of Human Nature"—a universal moral law that stands above individual preference and cultural custom.[62]

---

62. Lewis, *Mere Christianity*, 17.

This reality also refutes John Locke (1632–1704), who, in the spirit of Enlightenment optimism, advanced the notion of the *tabula rasa*—the belief that the human mind begins as a blank slate.[63] Enlightenment thinkers often exalted human reason while dismissing divine imprint, but conscience remains a stubborn reminder that we are not morally neutral at birth. A higher law is already etched into the heart, whispering to every soul what ought to be.

Without such a standard, how could history have judged the atrocities of the Nazi regime? The Nuremberg trials themselves only made sense because the world recognized that there exists a higher moral law to which even nations and rulers are accountable.

General of the Army George C. Marshall (VMI Class of 1901), America's highest-ranking active officer during World War II and one of only five men ever to hold the five-star rank, echoed this same clarity when he unveiled the Marshall Plan at Harvard in 1947: "Our policy is directed not against any country or doctrine but against hunger, poverty, desperation, and chaos."[64]

As the architect of America's postwar recovery strategy, Marshall identified the true enemies not in political ideologies or national rivalries but in universal human conditions. In a world fractured by ideology, his words remind us that truth must name reality plainly rather than be lost in deceptive narratives. These moral impressions transcend culture and era, suggesting a universal standard written on the heart.

The American Founders also understood this truth. In his 1796 "Farewell Address," George Washington warned the young Republic that morality and religion are "indispensable supports" of political prosperity. He declared, "In vain would that man claim the tribute of patriotism who should labor to subvert these great pillars of human happiness—these firmest props of the duties of men and citizens." Washington cautioned that national morality could not long survive apart from religious principle, asking pointedly, "Where is the security for property, for reputation, for life, if the sense of religious obligation desert the oaths which are the instruments of investigation in courts of justice?"[65] His words, once revered as a kind of civic Scripture, remind us that a society cut free from transcendent morality will eventually consume itself.

---

63. Locke, *Essay Concerning Human Understanding*, bk. 2, ch. 1; Olson, *Journey of Modern Theology*, 53–54, 83.

64. Marshall, "Marshall Plan Speech."

65. Washington, "Farewell Address."

Paul affirms this in Rom 2:14–16:

> For when Gentiles, who do not have the law, by nature do the things in the law, these, although not having the law, are a law to themselves, who show the work of the law written in their hearts, their conscience also bearing witness, and between themselves their thoughts accusing or else excusing them in the day when God will judge the secrets of men by Jesus Christ, according to my gospel.

This passage confirms that even those without Scripture intuitively recognize moral standards—a reflection of God's law etched into the human heart. Conscience itself is God's internal countermeasure against deception. By contrast, evolutionary naturalism attempts to reduce morality to instinct—a survival mechanism.[66] But if morality is nothing more than instinct, then no atrocity can be truly condemned. Genocide would be no worse than generosity; both would be equally amoral survival strategies. This is relativism's endgame: truth reduced to preference, morality collapsed into utility, and deception triumphant in silencing the voice of conscience.

Yet our very outrage at injustice proves the opposite: morality is objective and comes from the holy Lawgiver. No matter how thoroughly culture reframes truth, conscience bears witness against the lie.[67] And beyond this internal witness, external evidence also points beyond materialism—reinforcing the reality of absolute truth rooted in God himself.

Alongside the witness of conscience and Scripture, one striking area is the study of near-death experiences. For over four decades, Christian philosopher and apologist Gary Habermas has compiled and analyzed thousands of these reports from medical records, eyewitness accounts, and personal testimonies.[68] What makes many of these cases so compelling is the presence of verifiable data—individuals accurately reporting conversations, objects, or medical procedures occurring while they were clinically dead and had no measurable brain activity.[69]

---

66. Lewis, *Abolition of Man*, 708–14.

67. While Scripture affirms the witness of conscience, it also warns that the human heart is "deceitful above all things, and desperately wicked" (Jer 17:9). This means conscience is a genuine moral indicator but must be shaped and corrected by God's Word rather than trusted as an autonomous guide.

68. Habermas and Moreland, *Beyond Death*, 36–60.

69. Habermas, "Near-Death Experiences," 287–303.

Habermas argues that such evidence undercuts naturalistic assumptions that consciousness is merely the by-product of neurochemistry. If people can perceive accurately while their bodies are nonfunctional, then materialism cannot explain the fullness of human existence. Instead, these phenomena cohere with Scripture's claim that humans are more than physical matter—we are embodied souls destined for eternity (Eccl 12:7, 2 Cor 5:8).

For the atheist, the implications are profound: if consciousness persists beyond death, then life is not followed by annihilation but accountability before a Creator.[70] If even death itself cannot silence the evidence of consciousness, then the atheist assumption of a purely material world collapses under the weight of reality. This raises the next critical question: not only whether life continues after death, but whether life itself began by chance or by design.

Religion inherently supports absolute truth. Across the world's major faiths, people seek meaning, hope, forgiveness, and understanding through their beliefs, demonstrating that humans are more than just highly evolved animals. This desire for something beyond a mere existence points to a personal and purposeful Creator who instilled within humanity the longing to know him. If such a Creator exists, then he is the standard for truth, and his authority establishes it.

Across religions, this search for truth reflects a universal longing that transcends biology or survival—it suggests a divine imprint. And for Christians, that longing is answered in Scripture.

Thankfully, this Creator has graciously revealed his truth through the Bible, which serves as an unwavering anchor amid cultural relativism and deception. Scripture affirms God's unchanging truth, guiding believers to discern righteousness and eternity in a world where ideologies constantly shift. Jesus himself declared, "I am the way, the truth, and the life. No one comes to the Father except through Me" (John 14:6). The existence of absolute truth not only affirms a sovereign God who created the cosmos but also reveals his desire for a personal relationship with us through his Son, Jesus Christ. But Scripture also warns that some will reject this truth—trading the Creator for creation, embracing lies in place of his glory (Rom 1:25).

Even outside the realm of faith, the structure of reality itself bears witness to fixed truths. Scientific inquiry, for instance, presumes that the

---

70. Habermas, *Risen Jesus*, 85–110.

universe is governed by laws—patterns that do not shift with opinion or culture. Science depends on the existence of observable, consistent truths. While it doesn't always claim to reveal absolute truth in the philosophical sense, it does rest on the assumption that the universe operates according to fixed, discoverable laws. This pursuit of knowledge depends on reality being knowable, measurable, and predictable—making investigation possible in the first place. Without objective patterns or reliable principles, science would collapse into chaos, rendering experimentation meaningless. In other words, even science itself depends on what relativism denies: the existence of absolutes. Here again, Satan's PSYOP works by making people forget the very truths their daily lives depend on.

How else could one verify the accuracy of scientific findings? The laws of science presume the existence of consistent, demonstrable truths—principles that remain fixed regardless of opinion or culture.

This foundational understanding of truth directly influences worldviews on origins. A key aspect of the creation versus evolution debate is that many proponents of evolutionary theory are agnostics or atheists, believing that life developed purely through natural processes. Others hold a deistic view, acknowledging God's existence but seeing him as uninvolved in the details of creation. Some assess the data with sincerity and conclude that evolution best explains life's complexity. However, the prevailing position remains that evolutionary theory, in its naturalistic form, is incompatible with faith in God and Scripture. This divergence over origins reflects more than scientific debate—it reveals a deeper spiritual conflict between a worldview grounded in divine authority and one that insists on self-defined truth. That is the essence of the battle: Who defines truth—God, or man? Every PSYOP hinges on this question, and every deception thrives where man places himself as the arbiter of reality. Philosopher Charles Taylor calls our era the "immanent frame," where transcendence is pushed aside and human voices compete for authority.[71]

This charge has even been used against Christians themselves. Critics often accuse Christians of being "anti-intellectual," yet history tells another story. Thomas Aquinas (1225–1274), one of the most influential Christian philosophers and theologians in history, wrote far more about biblical prophecy and theology than about physics, and the giants of the Scientific Revolution, such as Isaac Newton (1642–1727), Johannes Kepler (1571–1630), Robert Boyle (1627–1691), and Blaise

---

71. Taylor, *Secular Age*, 539.

Pascal (1623–1662), were mesmerized by the wisdom of Scripture, often viewing their scientific pursuits as acts of worship. Likewise, Galileo Galilei (1564–1642), though often misrepresented in modern retellings, remained deeply committed to the belief that nature was a book written by the same God who authored Scripture. Nicolaus Copernicus (1473–1543) dedicated his heliocentric work to the church, framing it as a deeper glimpse into God's orderly creation. Later, pioneers such as Michael Faraday (1791–1867), James Clerk Maxwell (1831–1879), and Louis Pasteur (1822–1895) openly testified that their discoveries were inseparable from their Christian convictions. In more recent years, John C. Sanford, a Cornell University geneticist and co-inventor of the "gene gun," has argued from genetics for the reality of a recent creation, contending that mutation accumulation is consistent with the biblical account of humanity's fall.[72] Far from stifling inquiry, faith in a rational Creator provided the very foundation for modern science—and continues to inspire discovery today.

The Bible itself commands us to "give a reason" for our faith (1 Pet 3:15) and invites us to "come, let us reason together" (Isa 1:18). Far from being anti-intellectual, Christianity grounds the very possibility of reason.

By contrast, a purely materialistic worldview—especially as expressed through philosophical naturalism and Darwinian reductionism—struggles to account for rational thought. Materialism holds that everything, including human consciousness, is reducible to physical processes. If our minds are merely the accidental by-products of blind evolutionary forces—mutations built on mutations, shaped by survival rather than truth—then our thoughts are not truly rational but simply the result of neurochemical reactions. In such a system, beliefs are not formed because they are logically valid but because they happen to be advantageous for reproduction or survival. This undermines the trustworthiness of reason itself.

C. S. Lewis—once a staunch atheist, later a devout Christian—powerfully exposed this contradiction in his "argument from reason," especially in *Miracles* and *The Weight of Glory*. He wrote, "Unless Reason is an absolute—all is in ruins. Yet those who ask me to believe this world picture also ask me to believe that Reason is simply the unforeseen and unintended

---

72. See Aquinas, *Summa Theologica*; Boyle, *Christian Virtuoso*; Copernicus, *On the Revolutions*; Faraday, *Life and Letters*; Galilei, *Letter to the Grand Duchess*; Kepler, *Harmonices Mundi*; Maxwell, *Life of James Clerk Maxwell*; Newton, *Religion of Nature*; Pascal, *Pensées*; Dubos, *Louis Pasteur*; and Sanford, *Genetic Entropy*.

by-product of mindless matter at one stage of its endless and aimless becoming."[73] In other words, if materialism were true, we would have no basis for trusting reason itself. And if reason cannot be justified, then the charge that Christians are "anti-intellectual" collapses under its own weight. Lewis's observation cuts to the heart of deception: when reason itself is undermined, the enemy no longer needs to win the argument—because the very tools for discernment have been disarmed. This is PSYOP at the deepest level: dismantling the capacity to recognize truth at all.

Lewis's defense of reason not only dismantles the foundations of materialism—it also reframes the way we approach questions of origins. If rational thought cannot emerge from blind, purposeless processes, then the idea that life itself arose by accident becomes deeply suspect. This philosophical insight leads us directly into one of the most contested arenas of modern thought: the doctrine of creation.

While discussions about the age of the Earth often dominate creation debates, it's important to recognize that this issue, though significant, is not necessarily the central concern. A literal six-day creation affirms the authority and clarity of Scripture and serves as a vital theological pillar—but it is not the most foundational question in the origins discussion. The deeper issue is whether life was the result of design or chance. Elevating the dating dispute above the core conflict of intentionality can distract believers from the greater reality: Are we here by purpose or accident? Whether one affirms a young Earth or an old Earth, the unmistakable evidence of design—in physics, cosmology, and biology—points to an intelligent Creator. What matters most is not *when* he created, but *that* he created. This distinction is crucial: while the age of the Earth matters for biblical interpretation, the larger battle is narrative. If the discussion can be reframed around chronology alone, the deeper question of design versus chance is sidelined—and the PSYOP succeeds in shifting the center of gravity.

Framed through the lens of PSYOP, this is the decisive question of "narrative priming": settle the audience on chance over design, and every downstream conclusion (meaning, morality, destiny) can be steered without further argument.

Interestingly, some scientists accept evolution while maintaining belief in God and the Bible, seeing no contradiction between the two. This has led to the rise of theistic evolution—also referred to as creation

---

73. Lewis, *Miracles*, 319.

evolution or evolutionary creationism—which suggests that God designed nature in such a way that evolution progressed according to his plan. However, this perspective introduces deep contradictions across theology, philosophy, and science—such as reconciling death before the fall, undermining the historicity of Adam, and redefining divine intentionality in a process driven by randomness.

This is the classic "both-and" deception: preserve spiritual vocabulary while adopting naturalistic premises, producing a hybrid narrative that soothes the conscience even as it shifts allegiance away from biblical authority.

Theistic evolution undermines biblical authority by forcing theology to conform to an unstable scientific paradigm. Genesis presents creation as an intentional, immediate act of God—not a drawn-out evolutionary process characterized by mutation, suffering, and extinction. If life evolved over millions of years, then death and decay existed before sin, contradicting Scripture's teaching that death entered the world through Adam's transgression.[74] Further theological concerns arise when considering the implications of theistic evolution on biblical inerrancy. If Genesis is reinterpreted as allegory rather than historical narrative, this shift extends beyond creation and affects other foundational doctrines. The genealogies in Luke 3 and 1 Chronicles trace lineage back to Adam, affirming his historical existence, and Jesus himself references Adam and Eve in his teaching on marriage (Matt 19:4–6), reinforcing their reality. If Adam and Eve were merely symbolic figures rather than historical individuals, then the doctrine of original sin loses coherence, and Christ's redemptive work—tied to a literal fall—becomes theologically unstable. In this way, theistic evolution forces a reinterpretation of Scripture that undermines its authority, replacing divine revelation with human speculation.[75] These doctrinal consequences are not accidental; they are strategic. By reframing the fall, theistic evolution shifts the doctrinal "center of gravity"—if the fall is reframed, the need for a Redeemer is reframed, and the gospel itself is reinterpreted.

Beyond these theological and doctrinal concerns, another issue arises: theistic evolution attempts to reconcile an unguided evolutionary process with divine intentionality, creating a logical contradiction. Darwinian evolution is defined as an undirected mechanism, yet theistic

---

74. Moreland et al., *Theistic Evolution*, 123.
75. Moreland et al., *Theistic Evolution*, 785–810.

evolutionists claim that God guided it. If evolution is truly unguided, then it cannot be directed by God. Theistic evolutionists sometimes attempt to resolve this paradox by suggesting that God subtly guides evolutionary processes in ways that are scientifically undetectable.[76] Yet this raises further epistemological concerns—if God's role in creation is indistinguishable from naturalistic processes, then his creative power becomes functionally irrelevant. Scripture consistently portrays God as actively involved in creation, from forming Adam from dust (Gen 2:7) to sustaining all things by his word (Heb 1:3). To reduce his role to an invisible, undetectable force risks redefining creation as passive rather than intentional. This epistemological shift ultimately subordinates theological claims to prevailing scientific theories rather than affirming Scripture as authoritative revelation. The paradox remains: theistic evolutionists must either redefine evolution to include divine intervention—contradicting mainstream biology—or accept an unguided process, which undermines theological coherence. Furthermore, theistic evolution reinforces scientism—the idea that scientific consensus dictates truth—placing human reasoning above divine revelation.[77]

This is PSYOP by authority transfer, trust migration: move trust from revelation to consensus, and the standard of truth quietly relocates.

Scientifically, neo-Darwinism, the foundation of modern evolutionary theory, is a synthesis of Charles Darwin's theory of natural selection and modern population genetics. It asserts that evolution occurs primarily through genetic mutations, which are acted upon by natural selection to drive biological change over time. However, neo-Darwinism fails to account for biological complexity. Mutation and natural selection—often cited as the driving forces behind evolution—lack the creative power necessary to generate new anatomical structures or body plans. Leading evolutionary scientists at the 2016 Royal Society Conference on Evolutionary Biology openly questioned the adequacy of these mechanisms, acknowledging their explanatory deficits.[78]

Further challenges arise from the collapse of the "junk DNA" paradigm. For decades, evolutionary biologists pointed to noncoding DNA as functionless remnants of genetic history—supposed evidence of unguided evolution. Yet recent discoveries have overturned this assumption, demonstrating that so-called junk DNA plays essential roles in gene

---

76. Moreland et al., *Theistic Evolution*, 539–620.
77. See Gillespie, *Charles Darwin*.
78. See Bateson et al., "New Trends"; Müller, "Explanatory Deficits."

regulation, cellular communication, and disease prevention. Research from Stanford University has identified short tandem repeats (STRs) as critical regulators of gene expression, directly influencing neurodevelopmental processes. Likewise, pseudogenes—once dismissed as evolutionary leftovers—have been shown to actively participate in transcriptional regulation, contradicting the claim that they are nonfunctional.[79]

These findings expose a fundamental flaw in theistic evolution's reliance on outdated evolutionary assumptions. If junk DNA was once hailed as proof of purposeless processes but is now recognized as biologically essential, then the broader evolutionary framework built upon such assumptions becomes increasingly unstable. By aligning itself with these shifting paradigms, theistic evolution inherits their weaknesses, forcing theology to conform to a model that continues to be revised and questioned.[80]

Notice the tactic: keep the public narrative fixed even when expert conversations reveal cracks. That is "perception management," a hallmark of sustained influence campaigns.

Earlier we considered the exegetical case for a literal six-day creation. But there is also a strategic dimension often overlooked. In cultural PSYOP terms, the question of origins is not only about timing but about narrative priming: Is life the product of design or of chance? Debates over the age of the Earth, while significant, can sometimes overshadow this deeper issue. A literal six-day creation affirms biblical authority, but even more foundational is the truth that creation itself was intentional, not accidental.

Despite efforts to harmonize faith and science, theistic evolution weakens both. It compromises biblical authority, introduces philosophical contradictions, and relies on a scientific framework that is increasingly being questioned. If life required divine intervention at every stage of evolution, wouldn't the simplest explanation be that God spoke everything into existence just as Genesis records? Rather than bridging the gap between theology and science, theistic evolution deepens it, forcing believers to navigate an unstable synthesis that ultimately undermines both faith and reason.

History shows the consequences of rejecting a literal six-day creation. The Scopes trial, though legally won by the prosecution, was

---

79. Meyer, *Darwin's Doubt*, 275–90.
80. See Wells, *Myth of Junk DNA*.

strategically framed to undermine biblical authority in the public mind. Clarence Darrow, a committed humanist, recognized that Gen 1 clearly teaches six literal days of creation. Yet his true objective was to expose Christian inconsistency, persuading the world that believers did not truly adhere to Scripture. By placing William Jennings Bryan on the stand and leading him to concede that scientific claims about an old Earth could be trusted over a plain reading of Genesis, Darrow powerfully shaped public perception. Bryan's unintended message—that extra-biblical information could override God's word—allowed secularism to gain influence, reinforcing skepticism about the Bible's reliability and eroding foundational Christian doctrines.[81] When categories are blurred, discernment dulls. PSYOP thrives in the gray.

Departing from a six-day creation framework can introduce theological compromise and risk undermining the authority of Scripture. This is crucial because the Bible not only reveals Jesus as our Savior but also declares him the Creator (John 1:1–3, Col 1:16–17). Jesus is not only the Creator but also the living Word (John 1:1), the very embodiment of divine truth. The Bible, as God's inspired revelation, carries his authority and declares his plan from creation to salvation. This divine order is not just a theoretical concept—it is an essential foundation for life itself. Creation is more than the beginning of life—it testifies to Christ's divine authority and his central role in our redemption. If Genesis is merely metaphorical, where does the line between literal and symbolic interpretation end? The denial of absolute biblical truth invites deception, weakening theological foundations and allowing secular philosophies to take root. Once the foundation is treated as flexible, everything built upon it becomes negotiable—exactly the environment deception requires to prosper.

Just as spiritual deception operates quietly, leading individuals astray without notice, evolutionary ideology masks its contradictions under the guise of scientific progress. This pattern of manipulation isn't confined to overt philosophical declarations. It manifests quietly—even in scientific discourse—where misdirection cloaks historical facts and reframes ideas to serve ideological ends. The story of intelligent design offers a powerful example. The controversy surrounding intelligent design reveals more than a philosophical tension—it exposes the strategic misrepresentation of ideas that threaten prevailing worldviews. At its core, intelligent design proposes that certain features of life and the cosmos are best explained by

---

81. Ham, "Big Picture."

an intelligent cause rather than undirected processes like natural selection. This premise draws from observable phenomena—digital coding within DNA, microscopic machinery in cells, and the fine-tuning of the universe's physical constants—all of which exhibit purposeful design.

The pattern is consistent: rebrand design as "religion," restrict it from the conversation, then declare consensus. That is framing, not refutation.

Yet in public discourse, this theory has been deliberately recast as "faith-based," an alleged attempt to insert religious ideology into science classrooms. One flash point came in 2005 during the Dover, Pennsylvania, trial, where national media outlets framed intelligent design as creationism in disguise. *Time* magazine described it as a new theological movement—not a scientific theory grounded in empirical inquiry.[82] This depiction wasn't just misleading; it was a textbook example of cultural PSYOP—reframing truth through selective language to manipulate perception. Labeling is a powerful influence tool: change the label, and you steer the listener's conclusions before evidence is even considered.

In reality, intelligent design operates from the same inferential logic championed by Darwin himself: reasoning from observable data to the best causal explanation. Its roots stretch back to ancient philosophers and were pivotal during the Scientific Revolution. Founders of modern science—Kepler, Boyle, Newton—built their investigations upon the conviction that nature was ordered by a rational mind and therefore intelligible to human reason. Recovering this history restores the true frame: design inferences are not a retreat from science but one of its oldest engines.

This historical truth is frequently obscured. During a public hearing convened by the US Commission on Civil Rights in 1998 on science education and viewpoint discrimination, commissioners heard testimony from legal scholars, scientists, and education-policy advocates on how origins debates are treated in classrooms and public institutions. In that setting, a commissioner asked whether intelligent design echoed the philosophies of early scientists. When affirmed, one of the invited critics—speaking from the witness table—interjected, claiming Newton strictly separated faith from science to avoid testing God's existence.[83] This statement, though confidently delivered, was historically false. Newton, in his *Principia*, first published in 1687, specifically in the section known as the General Scholium, explicitly attributed the solar system's orchestration to

---

82. Lemonick, "'Intelligent Design' on Trial."
83. US Commission on Civil Rights, *Public Hearing on Creationism*.

"the counsel and dominion of an intelligent and powerful being," asserting that natural laws alone could not explain its order.[84] In other words, Newton's natural philosophy integrated empirical investigation with theological inference about design, not a wall of separation that banished God from scientific reflection. Confident misinformation is a hallmark of deception campaigns: say it often, say it forcefully, and many will accept it without scrutiny.

Such revisionist tactics—denying design despite overwhelming historical and empirical support—are more than innocent errors. They're sophisticated forms of deception, subtly shifting public understanding while undermining the credibility of Scripture and the rational pursuit of truth. This framing doesn't challenge the evidence; it controls the narrative. And narrative control, not neutral inquiry, is the operational objective.

But truth withstands deception—it requires discernment and unwavering adherence to God's word. The six-day creation account is not just plausible—it serves as a theological anchor, reinforcing Scripture's unshakable foundation in a world increasingly clouded by distortion. Anchoring to Scripture is the believer's counter-PSYOP: hold the line on the standard, and the fog of narrative warfare begins to clear.

Of course, there are spiritual motivators propelling some of these views. For atheism to be considered valid, an alternative explanation must exist for the origin of the universe and life, one that does not involve a Creator. Enter Charles Darwin, the nineteenth-century naturalist whose work revolutionized the scientific understanding of biological development. While evolutionary ideas existed before him, it was Darwin who introduced natural selection as the driving force behind the evolutionary process, offering a framework for how species adapt and diversify over time—though not addressing the origin of life itself. Darwin was raised in a Christian household and studied theology, but following a series of personal tragedies and philosophical shifts, he gradually distanced himself from orthodox belief. In later life, he described himself not as an atheist but as an agnostic.[85] When a narrative promises freedom from accountability, it will always attract converts. That is as true in ideology as it is in warfare.

The influence of Darwin's ideas extended far beyond scientific circles, shaping broader ideological movements. One such example is

---

84. Newton, *Principia*, 940–41.
85. Brooke, "Darwin and God."

Marxism, which built upon the framework of naturalistic evolution to support its philosophical foundations. D. James Kennedy (1930–2007), a renowned American pastor, author, and Christian apologist, often addressed the intersection of faith, science, and culture. In his book *Why I Believe*, he remarked,

> Karl Marx asked Darwin to write the introduction to *Das Kapital*, since he felt that Darwin had provided a scientific foundation for communism. Throughout this century, all over the world, those who pushed the communist conspiracy also pushed an evolutionary, imperialistic, naturalistic view of life, endeavoring to crowd the Creator right out of the cosmos.[86]

Ideologies seek scientific cover to amplify persuasion. Wrap a moral vision in "inevitability," and resistance can be painted as ignorance.

Many contemporary Bible believers oppose modern evolutionary theory, in part because it is often accompanied by an imposed atheistic worldview. While few evolutionary scientists would openly claim their ultimate goal is to provide an alternative explanation for the origin of life—one that eliminates the need for a Creator—the Bible suggests this is precisely why evolution is framed as it is today. Again, the operative word is *framed*: the battle is over assumptions long before it is over evidence.

One of the most outspoken proponents of this perspective is Oxford evolutionary biologist Richard Dawkins, a leading advocate for atheism who argues that evolution naturally leads to the rejection of religious belief. He reinforces this idea by stating, "The more you understand the significance of evolution, the more you are pushed away from an agnostic position and towards atheism. Complex, statistically improbable things are by their nature more difficult to explain than simple, statistically probable things."[87]

This is persuasion by inevitability—present atheism as the "mature" destination of science, and many will follow the current rather than test the claims.

As expressed in the Bible in no uncertain terms,

> The fool has said in his heart,
> "There is no God."
> They are corrupt,
> They have done abominable works,

---

86. Kennedy, *Why I Believe*, 38.
87. Fisher, *Logic of Real Arguments*, 84.

> There is none who does good.
> (Ps 14:1)

The Bible asserts that individuals have no justification for not believing in a Creator God: "For since the creation of the world His invisible attributes are clearly seen, being understood by the things that are made, even His eternal power and Godhead, so that they are without excuse" (Rom 1:20). Scripture defines a fool as one who rejects the existence of God—but not because they lack intelligence. Many evolutionary scientists are brilliant; however, foolishness in this context refers to the improper application of knowledge. As Prov 1:7 declares, "The fear of the LORD is the beginning of knowledge, but fools despise wisdom and instruction." Or, to borrow the words of the gruff, gold-chained, mohawked Mr. T of *The A-Team*, "I pity the fool" who ignores the evidence of God's creation and chooses instead to dismiss the foundation of true wisdom. Biblical wisdom restores the proper chain of authority: begin with the fear of the Lord, and the fog of competing narratives begins to lift.

Creation and/or intelligent design are often mocked by evolution-supporting atheists as devoid of merit for scientific investigation. They contend that for something to be classified as a science, it must possess "naturalistic characteristics"—principles rooted in empirical observation, repeatability, falsifiability, predictability, and reliance solely on natural causes. In other words, scientific inquiry must be limited to explanations derived from physical, chemical, or biological processes, excluding supernatural elements. Redefine the rules of the debate, and you predetermine the winner. That's not neutral refereeing; that's strategic gatekeeping.

Intelligent design challenges this framework by proposing that certain features of the universe and living organisms are best explained by an intelligent cause rather than an undirected process like natural selection. Proponents argue that biological structures exhibit complexity that cannot be accounted for by gradual evolutionary mechanisms alone, suggesting purposeful design.[88]

By definition, creationism transcends the rules of the natural universe, making it incompatible with scientific methodologies that require observable, testable, and repeatable phenomena. The controversy lies in the fact that since God cannot be subjected to scientific testing, critics argue that neither creation nor intelligent design can be regarded as

---

88. Dembski, *Intelligent Design*, 15.

scientific. However, supporters contend that the limitations of naturalistic science should not be mistaken for proof that a Creator does not exist. Limitation of method is often mistaken for limitation of reality—a subtle but potent sleight of hand.

From a strictly scientific standpoint and to the same extent, both evolution and intelligent design cannot be directly observed or tested. However, it appears that atheistic evolutionists do not consider this to be problematic. Consequently, all data are subjected to the filtering process of naturalism's preconceived, presupposed, and pre-accepted worldview without accommodating alternative explanations.

The investigation or firsthand observation of the origin of the universe or life is not possible. Acceptance of both creation and evolution necessitates a degree of faith. It is impossible to travel back in time to observe the origin of the universe or life. Individuals who vehemently oppose creation do so on the basis of arguments that would logically compel them to also reject evolution. Although both evolution and creationism require a degree of faith due to the inability to directly observe origins, only creationism is frequently labeled as pseudo-scientific—a term used to describe beliefs or practices that claim scientific validity but lack adherence to empirical testing and falsifiability. This classification stems from the fact that creationism invokes a divine Creator, which lies beyond the scope of empirical scientific testing. Meanwhile, evolutionary theory, despite its own assumptions and reliance on inference rather than direct observation, is widely accepted within scientific circles. Critics argue that this difference is less about strict scientific methodology and more about a philosophical predisposition toward naturalism, favoring explanations rooted in materialism while dismissing those that invoke a transcendent cause. When a worldview polices language and categories, it is not merely describing reality—it is directing it. That is the operational edge of cultural PSYOP.

The debate over origins is not merely a scientific or philosophical discussion—it carries profound implications for morality, purpose, and accountability. If naturalistic science is correct in rejecting any divine influence, then human existence is left without absolute meaning or objective moral standards. However, if a Creator does exist, then humanity is answerable to him, and life is imbued with purpose beyond mere chance or natural processes. This is why chapter 1 keeps returning to this fulcrum: who defines truth determines how we live.

A Creator exists to whom we are answerable. Evolution, in its contemporary form, facilitates an atheistic worldview, providing atheists an explanation for the development of life apart from a Creator God. William Provine (1942–2015) of Cornell University, an American historian of science and evolutionary biology, stated in a debate, "If Darwinism is true, then there are five inescapable conclusions: there's no evidence for God, there's no life after death, there's no absolute foundation for right and wrong, there's no ultimate meaning for life, people don't really have free will."[89] Provine names the stakes plainly: remove design, and you erase destiny, duty, and hope. That is not a side issue; it is the entire battlespace.

Douglas Axe, a molecular biologist renowned for his extensive research into protein structures and functional complexity, critiques the theory of evolution, stating, "[It's] what I consider to be one of the weakest, most pathetic scientific theories that has ever come out in the history of science."[90] As the author of *Undeniable: How Biology Confirms Our Intuition That Life Is Designed*, Axe champions intelligent design, arguing that biological systems exhibit complexity and functionality that point to purposeful design rather than random, unguided processes. While some proponents of evolution argue that natural selection operates as a directed process rather than a purely random one, critics contend that this distinction does not resolve the fundamental issue of information generation. Evolutionary algorithms may simulate adaptation, but they rely on pre-programmed information input by designers.[91] Serving as a professor at Biola University and holding the Rosa Endowed Chair of Molecular Biology, Axe presents compelling evidence challenging Darwinian evolution, urging both scientists and laypeople to critically examine its claims in light of alternative explanations rooted in design.

Voices like Axe's remind readers that the contest is not merely technical—it is spiritual, moral, and existential. This is why the rest of this book, and the volumes that follow, move from exposing deception to training discernment—a counter-PSYOP rooted in the unchanging word of God.

While motive, logic, and biblical compatibility have been examined, another question remains: how does scientific inquiry influence the debate? From a scientific standpoint, ten significant problems challenge the

---

89. Strobel, *Case for the Creator*, 26.
90. McDowell, "Debate over Evolution," 16:56.
91. Meyer, *Signature in the Cell*, 256.

evolutionary framework. These represent some of the most prominent critiques, though they are by no means exhaustive—many additional scientific, philosophical, and mathematical objections to evolution continue to be discussed among researchers and scholars.

Read these as "fault lines" where narrative pressure meets empirical resistance. In influence terms, Darwinism often advances by framing—PSYOP-style category-setting—while these ten points test the frame against stubborn facts.

1. *The Universe Had a Beginning*—The majority of contemporary scientists agree that the universe had a definitive beginning, often citing the Big Bang theory as a leading explanatory model. While the Big Bang remains a dominant framework in secular science, its assumptions and implications continue to be debated. Regardless of the model's accuracy, what matters most is the consensus: the universe is not eternal but had an origin. The first law of thermodynamics confirms that matter and energy cannot create themselves,[92] while the second law shows that the universe is winding down.[93] If the cosmos had always existed, it would already have reached complete disorder. These laws testify to a beginning—and therefore to a Beginner.[94] This is the essence of the *cosmological argument*: the universe's very existence points beyond itself to a necessary First Cause. Only the eternal God, outside of time, space, and matter, fits the description of the First Cause. To claim instead that the universe somehow sprang into existence from nothing, or that it caused itself, is not reason but deception. Out of nothing, nothing comes. As Heb 3:4 states, "For every house is built by someone, but He who built all things is God." When origins are acknowledged, the frame must account for a Cause—or work hard to distract from it.

2. *Fine-Tuning of the Universe*—Scientific discoveries increasingly affirm that the universe is fine-tuned for life in ways that defy mere

---

92. Morris, *Scientific Creationism*, 42.

93. Morris, *Scientific Creationism*, 47–48.

94. By contrast, the *ontological argument* for God's existence differs sharply from the cosmological argument, which reasons from the universe's beginning to a First Cause. Instead, it proceeds from the very *concept* of God: if God is "that than which nothing greater can be conceived" (Anselm of Canterbury, *Proslogion* 2 [Williams]), then his existence must be necessary rather than contingent. To deny his existence would be a logical contradiction since a God who exists in reality is greater than one who exists only in thought. Though highly abstract and often debated (notably by Thomas Aquinas, Immanuel Kant, and Alvin Plantinga), the ontological argument has remained a central strand in classical theistic reasoning. See Anselm of Canterbury, *Proslogion* 2–4.

chance. Yet God's fingerprints extend far beyond the beginning. The *teleological argument*—the reasoning that apparent design points to a Designer—finds one of its strongest applications in the phenomenon of fine-tuning. The precise values of fundamental constants (such as gravity, electromagnetism, and nuclear forces) fall within an incredibly narrow range necessary for life to exist. Even a slight deviation would render stars, planets, chemistry, and life impossible: "These numbers are precisely calibrated for the existence of intelligent life, and if any of them deviated by even a small amount, stars, planets, chemistry, and living things could not exist."[95] This is not vague impression but measurable fact.

Consider one famous example. Sir Fred Hoyle, a committed agnostic, studied the nuclear reactions necessary for carbon formation. Carbon is essential to life, capable of forming long chains and storing information. Hoyle predicted that an unusual resonance energy level must exist in the carbon atom for it to form in sufficient quantities. Against all expectations, experiments confirmed his prediction exactly. Shaken by this discovery, Hoyle concluded the universe looked as though "a superintellect has monkeyed with physics."[96] Or take Roger Penrose's calculation of how extraordinarily fine-tuned the universe's initial entropy had to be—one chance in $10^{10^{123}}$.[97] That number is so unimaginably precise that filling the universe with zeros would not be enough to write it down. These constants are not accidents but signs of deliberate order, pointing unmistakably to purpose.

This reality exposes a "chicken-and-egg" dilemma for naturalism. Evolutionary theory is often invoked as an explanation for life's complexity, but even if one grants evolution's assumptions for argument's sake, it cannot begin without preconditions established by fine-tuning. Evolution presupposes replicating molecules, information storage, and functional chemistry.[98] Yet those, in turn, depend on stable atoms, carbon bonding, and a universe finely tuned from the outset. Without the right gravitational strength, nuclear forces, or electromagnetic balance, there would be no stars, no carbon, no water—no stage at all on which

---

95. Corrado, "Is There Evidence."
96. Hoyle, *Religion and the Scientists*, 54.
97. Penrose, *Road to Reality*, 762. 1 in $10^{10^{123}}$ is a 1 followed by roughly a trillion trillion trillion trillion trillion trillion trillion trillion trillion trillion zeros (far more than could fit in the observable universe).
98. Meyer, *Signature in the Cell*, 74.

evolution could even attempt to play.[99] Fine-tuning is not the outcome of evolution; it is the indispensable foundation that makes even the idea conceivable. To overlook this is like insisting a novel wrote itself while ignoring the alphabet, paper, and ink required for any story to exist.

But a caution is necessary. Not all fine-tuning arguments are sound. Some versions rely on the Big Bang as their foundation, despite its biblical and scientific problems.[100] Christians must not smuggle in assumptions that undermine the very truth we defend. The validity of fine-tuning as an application of the teleological argument does not rest on secular cosmological models. Instead, it rests on the observable fact that the universe is deliberately organized to sustain intelligent life.

As Rom 1:20 declares, "For since the creation of the world, His invisible attributes are clearly seen." And as the psalmist affirms, "The heavens declare the glory of God; and the firmament shows His handiwork" (Ps 19:1). Fine-tuning is where data strains the chance narrative; the typical countermove is reframing through speculation such as the "multiverse" theory—countless unobservable universes where one, by blind luck, produces conditions for life—which is not science but philosophical conjecture dressed in scientific clothing.[101] This smokescreen buries truth under complexity to avoid the obvious: fine-tuning points to a Fine-Tuner.

3. *The Problem of Mutations*—Evolution relies on an extended sequence of beneficial mutations to drive complexity and adaptation. However, the overwhelming majority of observed mutations are neutral or harmful rather than advantageous. Beneficial mutations are rare, and even when they occur, they often involve minor modifications rather than the creation of entirely new biological structures. The lack of evidence for a sustained pattern of upward complexity presents a significant hurdle for evolutionary theory, especially in explaining the emergence of highly sophisticated biological systems. Signal vs. noise: the persuasive story spotlights the rare "wins," while the dataset is dominated by loss or neutrality.

4. *The Second Law of Thermodynamics*—Newton's second law states that in an isolated system, entropy (disorder) increases over time. Evolutionary theory, however, asserts that biological complexity and order have increased over billions of years. This presents a paradox: If

99. Meyer, *Signature in the Cell*, 81–82.
100. Morris, *Young Earth*, 93–96.
101. Davies, *Goldilocks Enigma*, 218.

the natural tendency of the universe is toward decay, how can intricate biological organisms emerge and thrive through purely undirected processes? The idea that matter and energy degrade over time directly contradicts the assumption that life evolves toward higher complexity. Here the narrative banks on exceptions and caveats—such as appeals to "open systems" with external energy sources—but the baseline physics still leans the other direction.

5. *Misuse of Microevolution to Support Macroevolution*—Evolutionists often cite small-scale adaptations (microevolution) as proof of large-scale biological transformation (macroevolution). While minor genetic variations occur within species, no definitive scientific evidence demonstrates that such changes result in entirely new species with fundamentally different anatomical structures. The assumption that small genetic shifts can accumulate into entirely new organisms requires a massive leap in logic, one that lacks direct empirical confirmation. Classic framing move: redefine terms so the observed (micro) is presumed to guarantee the unobserved (macro).

6. *The Origin of DNA and Information*—DNA contains highly complex, specified information necessary for life. Evolutionary mechanisms struggle to explain how this information originated in the first place. As Stephen C. Meyer—a Cambridge-trained philosopher of science and director of the Discovery Institute's Center for Science and Culture—has pointed out, random mutations and natural selection do not account for the emergence of the intricate coding system found in DNA, which resembles a sophisticated digital language. Information is the inconvenient category for materialism; the counter-PSYOP is to call it "chemistry" and move on.

7. *Irreducible Complexity*—Many biological systems, such as the bacterial flagellum and the human eye, exhibit irreducible complexity—meaning they require multiple interdependent parts to function. If any one part were missing, the system would fail. Evolutionary theory suggests that organisms develop gradually through small, beneficial mutations, but irreducibly complex structures challenge this idea, as they require all components to be present simultaneously for functionality.

Even Charles Darwin himself admitted this problem. In *The Origin of Species* he wrote, "If it could be demonstrated that any complex organ existed which could not possibly have been formed by numerous slight successive modifications, my theory would absolutely break down."[102] The eye provides exactly such a challenge. For vision to occur, the cornea, lens, retina, optic nerve, and neural processing centers must all work together from the start. If even one component is missing, the organ fails to function and provides no survival advantage. By Darwin's own criterion, the existence of irreducibly complex organs falsifies his theory. Rather than supporting unguided evolution, such systems point unmistakably to purposeful design.

When stepwise narratives meet all-or-nothing machinery, the usual play is to assert hypothetical pathways—another framing tactic.

8. *The Cambrian Explosion*—The fossil record reveals a sudden appearance of diverse, fully formed life forms during what secular scientists call the Cambrian period, rather than a gradual progression of evolutionary development. This rapid emergence of complex organisms contradicts the slow, incremental changes predicted by Darwinian evolution and raises questions about the sufficiency of evolutionary mechanisms to explain such a dramatic biological leap. Data surprise vs. story arc: when the record "jumps," narrative control must work overtime.

9. *The Lack of Transitional Fossils*—While evolution predicts a gradual transition between species, the fossil record does not consistently support this claim. Many supposed transitional forms remain highly disputed, and the gaps between major biological groups remain significant. The absence of clear, undisputed transitional fossils challenges the idea that species evolved through small, successive modifications over time. Gap management is itself an influence campaign: rename gaps as "expected," and the pressure eases without new evidence.

10. *The Problem of Consciousness and Human Uniqueness*—Evolutionary theory struggles to explain the emergence of human consciousness, abstract reasoning, morality, and self-awareness. While physical traits can be traced through evolutionary processes, the development of complex cognitive abilities and moral reasoning remains largely unexplained within a purely naturalistic framework.[103] C. S. Lewis warned of this contradiction in his argument from reason, observing that if our thoughts are merely the unintended by-product of blind evolutionary forces, we would have no reason to trust reason itself.[104] If reason is re-

---

102. Darwin, *Origin of Species*, 189.

103. Kampourakis, *Understanding Evolution*, 134; IDEA Center, "Primer"; Rogers, "Evolution," 846.

104. Lewis, *Miracles*, 311–21.

duced to firing patterns, discernment dissolves—and with it, the ability to test any narrative at all. Here the *moral argument* also comes into play: if objective moral values and duties exist, they cannot be grounded in material processes alone but point instead to a transcendent Lawgiver. That's deception's endgame.[105]

Scientific inquiry is not merely about collecting data—it is about how we interpret that data. While evolutionary theory dominates mainstream discourse, thoughtful critiques highlight its explanatory limitations. Questioning Darwinism does not equate to rejecting science; rather, it invites an honest assessment of which framework best accounts for the complexities of life. As expressed by G. K. Chesterton (1874–1936), an English writer, philosopher, Christian apologist, and literary and art critic, "It is absurd for the evolutionists to complain that it's unthinkable for an admittedly unthinkable God to make everything out of nothing and then pretend it is more thinkable that nothing should turn itself into anything."[106]

Chapter 1's thrust is exactly this: expose the framing, restore the standard. From here, the book moves from identifying deception's tactics to training countermeasures—anchored in truth, tested by reason, and grounded in Scripture.

PROPHECY, SCIENCE, AND THE BIBLE'S ENDURING ACCURACY

While secular interpretations of science often dismiss the role of a Creator, the question of truth extends beyond scientific inquiry alone. Scripture offers not only a theological foundation for understanding creation but also a compelling historical record of fulfilled prophecy—an aspect that strengthens its credibility in ways science cannot address. One of the most profound and unique proofs of the Bible's reliability is the fulfillment of prophecy. A striking example is Ps 22, written a thousand years before Jesus was born by a man who had never seen a crucifixion, as the practice had not yet been invented. Yet, the psalm describes crucifixion in remarkable detail. Prophecy functions as God's "anti-deception protocol." Where human narratives can be managed by perception, predictive

---

105. For resources on creation science, see Institute for Creation Research (https://www.icr.org); Creation Ministries International (https://www.creation.com); and Answers in Genesis (https://answersingenesis.org), among others.

106. Chesterton, *Everlasting Man*, 96.

specificity shatters propaganda: only the One who rules history can name it in advance and then fulfill it.

> My God, My God, why have You forsaken Me?
> . . . .
> All those who see Me ridicule Me;
> They shoot out the lip, they shake the head, saying,
> "He trusted in the LORD, let Him rescue Him;
> Let Him deliver Him, since He delights in Him!"
> . . . .
> Many bulls have surrounded Me;
> Strong bulls of Bashan have encircled Me.
> They gape at Me with their mouths,
> Like a raging and roaring lion.
> . . . .
> The congregation of the wicked has enclosed Me.
> They pierced My hands and My feet;
> I can count all My bones.
> They look and stare at Me.
> They divide My garments among them,
> And for My clothing they cast lots.
> . . . .
> All the prosperous of the earth
> Shall eat and worship;
> All those who go down to the dust
> Shall bow before Him,
> Even he who cannot keep himself alive.
> (Ps 22:1, 7–8, 12–13, 16–18, 29)

Many sacred texts—such as the Qur'an, Hindu Vedas, Bhagavad Gita, Book of Mormon, and Buddhist scriptures—contain passages that some interpret as prophetic. Yet upon closer examination, these so-called prophecies are often vague, symbolic, or retroactively applied, lacking the specificity, time-boundedness, and verifiability that define true predictive claims.[107] Unlike the Bible, which anchors its authority in detailed, historically fulfilled prophecy, these texts tend to veer away from concrete predictions—and for good reason. A prophecy that fails doesn't just discredit a passage; it undermines the entire theological structure built upon it. The risk is existential: if a sacred text makes a falsifiable claim

---

107. See Geisler, *Baker Encyclopedia*, 597–99, where Geisler compares the precision and historical verification of biblical prophecy with the symbolic or post-event nature of prophetic statements in texts such as the Qur'an, Hindu Vedas, and Buddhist writings.

and that claim is proven false, the religion it supports begins to unravel. This is why ambiguity is often preferred—deception thrives on vagueness and post-hoc reinterpretation. In contrast, Scripture stakes its credibility on verifiable fulfillment, inviting scrutiny rather than evading it. That is the opposite of a PSYOP.

As emphasized in Isa 41, prophecy functions as God's unmistakable signature—his sovereign means of authenticating his authority. Only he can declare the future with precision and bring it to pass.

In fact, prophecy constitutes a substantial portion of the Bible. Dr. J. Barton Payne, respected theologian and author of the *Encyclopedia of Biblical Prophecy*, calculated that approximately 27 percent of Scripture is predictive in nature, identifying 1,817 distinct prophecies. This remarkable concentration highlights the Bible's unique role in foretelling future events with accuracy and specificity.[108]

Volume 1's aim—to define truth against deception—finds its strongest exhibit here: God binds his revelation to history so his people are not captive to manipulated narratives.

This concept of prophecy aligns with Isa 41:21, where God directly challenges skeptics and false gods to present their case. He demands, "'Present your case,' says the LORD. 'Bring forth your strong reasons.'" In this passage, God exposes the inability of idols and false prophets to predict the future, proving that only he can declare events before they occur. Biblical prophecy serves as God's undeniable mark of authenticity, demonstrating his sovereignty and confirming his divine authority. Unlike human speculation or vague predictions, biblical prophecies are fulfilled in history, showcasing God's power to shape events according to his will.

Building on the undeniable uniqueness of biblical prophecy, mathematical analysis offers further compelling evidence of its authenticity.

Peter Stoner (1888–1980), a mathematician, applied the science of probability to biblical prophecy in his book *Science Speaks*. Stoner calculated the likelihood of just eight messianic prophecies being fulfilled in the life of Jesus—or in the life of any one individual—as one in one hundred quadrillion (100,000,000,000,000,000). But Jesus fulfilled not merely eight prophecies—he fulfilled 108. The probability of fulfilling sixteen rises to one in 10^{45} and fulfilling forty-eight escalates to one in 10^{157}—numbers so vast that they surpass comprehension, rendering

---

108. Payne, *Encyclopedia of Biblical Prophecy*, 674.

mere coincidence statistically impossible.[109] Numbers aren't the gospel—but they do unmask the myth that faith rests on wishful thinking. Probability here serves as a light that dissolves the fog of narrative control.

To put this into perspective, imagine covering the entire state of Texas in silver dollars two feet deep and marking just one of them. If a blindfolded person were to wander across the state, reach down, and randomly select the marked silver dollar on their first attempt, their odds would be approximately one in one hundred quadrillion—the same probability Stoner assigned to eight fulfilled prophecies. Now consider that Jesus fulfilled over a hundred, making the statistical certainty of divine orchestration all the more astounding.[110]

Such staggering probabilities demonstrate that biblical prophecy is not just an ancient tradition—it is a tangible, mathematical affirmation of the supernatural. For any thoughtful observer, this means that Scripture's prophetic accuracy stands unmatched, reinforcing the reliability of the Bible and its claims about Jesus Christ. The fulfillment of prophecy is not merely an abstract theological concept; it is a mathematical impossibility unless orchestrated by a divine hand.

Fulfilled prophecy is God's way of saying, "Test this." Deception avoids tests—revelation invites them. Even critics outside the faith acknowledge these events. Renowned atheist scholar Bart Ehrman concedes, "The crucifixion of Jesus by the Romans is one of the most secure facts we have about his life."[111] Similarly, agnostic historian Gerd Lüdemann writes, "Jesus' death as a consequence of crucifixion is indisputable."[112] Ancient non-Christian sources reinforce this: the Roman historian Tacitus (c. AD 56–120) records that "Christus, from whom the name [Christian] had its origin, suffered the extreme penalty during the reign of Tiberius at the hands of . . . Pontius Pilatus."[113] The Jewish historian Josephus (c. AD 37–100) likewise notes that "Pilate . . . condemned him to the cross."[114] Even when stripped of theological interpretation, the bare facts remain uncontested: Jesus lived in first-century Judea and was executed by crucifixion under Pontius Pilate.

---

109. Stoner, *Science Speaks*, 100–110.
110. Stoner, *Science Speaks*, 100.
111. Ehrman, *New Testament*, 162.
112. Lüdemann, *Resurrection of Christ*, 50.
113. Tacitus, *Annals* 15.44 (Grant).
114. Josephus, *Antiquities* 18.3.3 (Whiston).

Building on the astounding accuracy of biblical prophecy, these predictions can be divided into two key categories: those that have already come to pass and those awaiting fulfillment. This division is significant because fulfilled prophecies provide tangible evidence of Scripture's reliability, while those yet to be fulfilled point toward future events that shape theological expectations. Together, they reinforce the idea that biblical prophecy is not mere speculation but a consistent pattern of divine revelation unfolding across history. Examples of fulfilled prophecies include the following:

The first coming of Christ:

> The LORD your God will raise up for you a Prophet like me from your midst, from your brethren. (Deut 18:15)

> Daniel spoke, saying, "I saw in my vision by night, and behold, the four winds of heaven were stirring up the Great Sea. And four great beasts came up from the sea, each different from the other." (Dan 7:2–3)

> And the people of the prince who is to come
> Shall destroy the city and the sanctuary.
> The end of it shall be with a flood,
> And till the end of the war desolations are determined.
> (Dan 9:26)[115]

> Behold, He is coming with clouds, and every eye will see Him, even they who pierced Him. And all the tribes of the earth will mourn because of Him. (Rev 1:7)[116]

The restoration of Israel:

> Behold, the days are coming, says the LORD, when I will make a new covenant with the house of Israel and with the house of Judah. . . . For I will forgive their iniquity, and their sin I will remember no more. (Jer 31:31, 34)

> And so all Israel will be saved, as it is written:
> "The Deliverer will come out of Zion,

---

115. Dan 9:26 foretells the cutting off of the Messiah and the destruction of Jerusalem. The prophecy is widely recognized as fulfilled in Christ's crucifixion and the Roman destruction of the temple in AD 70.

116. Rev 1:7 is debated among scholars—some interpret this as fulfilled in the judgment on Jerusalem (AD 70), while others view it as a prophecy of Christ's second coming.

And He will turn away ungodliness from Jacob."
(Rom 11:26)

The new heavens and new earth:

> For behold, I create new heavens and a new earth;
> And the former shall not be remembered or come to mind.
> (Isa 65:17)

> Nevertheless we, according to His promise, look for new heavens and a new earth in which righteousness dwells. (2 Pet 3:13)

> Now I saw a new heaven and a new earth, for the first heaven and the first earth had passed away. Also there was no more sea. (Rev 21:1)

The role of fulfilled prophecy as compelling evidence supporting its divine authorship:

> And if you say in your heart, "How shall we know the word which the LORD has not spoken?"—when a prophet speaks in the name of the LORD, if the thing does not happen or come to pass, that is the thing which the LORD has not spoken; the prophet has spoken it presumptuously; you shall not be afraid of him. (Deut 18:21–22)

> But Micaiah said, "If you ever return in peace, the LORD has not spoken by me." And he said, "Take heed, all you people!" (1 Kgs 22:28)

> As for the prophet who prophesies of peace, when the word of the prophet comes to pass, the prophet will be known as one whom the LORD has truly sent. (Jer 28:9)

The Bible's prophetic accuracy serves as a testament to God's omniscience, affirming that his declarations of future events are fulfilled with precision. As Isa 46:9–10 states, "I am God, and there is no other; I am God, and there is none like me, declaring the end from the beginning and from ancient times things that are not yet done." This ability to foretell history underscores the divine nature of Scripture.

Prophecy is not a side feature of Scripture; it is God's built-in safeguard against the world's PSYOPs—his seal that truth is not merely argued but demonstrated.

Unveiling Deception

In the ancient world, medical knowledge was often a chaotic blend of superstition, ritual, and guesswork. Egyptian texts prescribed remedies involving crocodile dung, lizard blood, and incantations to drive out imagined spirits. Babylonian healers relied on astrology and magical rites to treat ailments. Even Greek physicians, revered for their intellect, subscribed to the humoral theory—believing that health depended on balancing bodily fluids through bleeding, purging, or bizarre dietary restrictions.[117]

These practices weren't fringe; they were mainstream. They filled the libraries of empires and shaped the health systems of entire civilizations. And yet, not one of these absurd remedies appears in the pages of Scripture.

This silence is not accidental. It points to a deeper authorship.

If the Bible were merely a product of its time—written by men echoing the cultural norms around them—it would inevitably reflect these flawed medical beliefs. But it doesn't. Instead, it presents principles that align with modern science: quarantine protocols, hygiene laws, and dietary guidelines that promote health and prevent disease.[118] These insights, recorded millennia ago, were not rediscovered until centuries later.

The absence of error is itself a form of evidence.

The Bible's restraint—its refusal to echo the medical nonsense of its age—suggests a source beyond human authorship. It speaks with timeless authority, not because it says everything but because it avoids saying what would later be proven false. In a world filled with ancient texts that now embarrass their originators, the Bible stands alone: untainted, uncontradicted, and unafraid of scrutiny.

Beyond prophecy, the Bible also aligns with observable scientific realities. Throughout the sixteen-hundred-year period during which it was written, every stated scientific fact has stood the test of time—even as we look back nearly three thousand five hundred years from today. Science, at its core, is the logical assembly of experimentally derived or observed information about the physical universe. Though the advancement of science and significant leaps made across the scientific disciplines over the last several centuries in and of themselves may seem substantial, in

---

117. For examples of Egyptian and Babylonian remedies, see Allen, *Middle Egyptian*, 328; Scurlock, *Ancient Mesopotamian Medicine*, 45–47. On humoral theory, see Nutton, *Ancient Medicine*, 154–59.

118. On biblical hygiene and quarantine practices, see McMillen and Stern, *None of These Diseases*, 9–15; Gabriel, *Culture of Conquest*, 77–81.

the context of the pursuit of unbiased truth, they have fallen short. Those with a human-centered worldview often make science the sole basis and definer of truth rather than a tool to pursue truth. When culture elevates method into a metaphysic, it turns a tool into a throne—an influence move that swaps the Giver of truth for a process that can only measure it.

This approach is inadequate. At any given moment in history, the scientific thought or discovery at that time would be considered truth, but scientifically acquired knowledge is ever-changing. What is considered scientific fact now may not have been so a decade ago.

In fact, science uses the term "half-life of facts" to explain that many things that we believe are factual get overturned over time. Knowledge, like radioactivity, decays over time. For example, lead-based paint was once widely used and considered safe. However, it was later discovered to cause severe health issues, particularly in children, including developmental delays and neurological damage. Today, its use is heavily regulated and strongly discouraged.

Much of scientific knowledge, particularly knowledge derived from measurements, can be classified as meso-fact. Meso-facts are pieces of information that evolve gradually over long periods—decades or even centuries—due to advancements in technology, improved methods of measurement, and ongoing research.

Christians have every reason to approach scientific inquiry with confidence, knowing that the truths of Christianity stand up to scientific interrogation. Science only becomes problematic when it is stretched beyond its limits—when scientists move beyond empirical investigation and make sweeping metaphysical claims about reality as a whole, straying into territory that science itself cannot validate. Deception often happens at this boundary—where empirical method ends and speculative metaphysics begins—yet the speculation is smuggled in as "settled science." Naming that shift is part of our counter-PSYOP.

Carl F. H. Henry (1913–2003), a prominent theologian and founding editor of *Christianity Today*, was instrumental in shaping modern evangelical thought alongside Billy Graham.[119] While Graham became the face of evangelical revival, Henry laid its intellectual foundation,

---

119. Billy Graham (1918–2018) was one of the most influential Christian evangelists of the twentieth century, known for his powerful preaching and worldwide crusades. Through his ministry, he reached millions, spreading the message of salvation and shaping Evangelical Christianity into a global movement. His partnership with thinkers like Carl F. H. Henry helped unify intellectual and revivalist traditions within modern Evangelicalism.

advocating for a faith that engaged both theological and philosophical discourse. He addresses the intersection of science and Christianity in his work *Theology and Science*, stating, "The fact is that empirical science has no firm basis whatever on which to raise objections to Christianity, not because scientific and historical concerns are irrelevant to revelation and faith, but because scientists must allow for possible exceptions to every rule they affirm, and for the empirical vulnerability of the rules themselves."[120] His words emphasize that true scientific inquiry remains open-ended, inherently unable to dismantle the faith that stands upon revelation and historical truths. Scientifically acquired information that is confirmed to be accurate will harmonize with the Bible. The Bible petitions man to learn from God's handiwork and to observe God's incredible characteristics as revealed in scientific pursuits:

> Lift up your eyes on high,
> And see who has created these things,
> Who brings out their host by number;
> He calls them all by name,
> By the greatness of His might
> And the strength of His power;
> Not one is missing.
> (Isa 40:26)

> For since the creation of the world His invisible attributes are clearly seen, being understood by the things that are made, even His eternal power and Godhead, so that they are without excuse. (Rom 1:20)

As science discovers more about our universe, more evidence of creation and design is revealed. As Christians, we welcome and support science that pursues truth but reject assertions by scientists beyond the realm of what scientific methodology can support.[121]

In short, Scripture sets the frame; honest science fills in the picture. When the frame is swapped, confusion reigns—exactly what deception intends.

This alignment between Scripture and science is beautifully illustrated in Job 26:7, which describes the Earth's positioning in space: "He stretches out the north over empty space; He hangs the earth on nothing." Scholars date the book of Job anywhere from the second millennium BC

---

120. This is noted in Olson, *Journey of Modern Theology*, 631.
121. Corrado, "Role and Realm of Science."

to the post-exilic period (sixth to fourth centuries BC). Regardless of its exact dating, this verse poetically reflects a truth that science would only later begin to uncover—that the Earth is suspended in space without visible support. In the sixteenth and seventeenth centuries, Nicolaus Copernicus proposed a heliocentric model, followed by Galileo Galilei, who defended it with telescopic evidence, and Johannes Kepler, who described planetary motion with mathematical precision. Their discoveries paved the way for a deeper understanding of celestial mechanics. Later, Isaac Newton mathematically formalized the concept of gravity in 1687, explaining how the sun's invisible force holds the Earth in orbit. Yet long before these scientific breakthroughs, Scripture offered a glimpse into the majesty of creation—affirming that divine wisdom precedes human understanding. Revelation anticipated observation—not to replace science but to guard us from worshiping it.

Unlike Scripture's poetic accuracy, ancient cultures devised imaginative theories to explain Earth's positioning—revealing the contrast between divine revelation and human speculation. Throughout history, various hypotheses have been proposed. Aristotle, in the fourth century BC, noted the early belief that Earth rested on water. Others imagined the Earth supported by a great sea turtle. Native American traditions, such as those of the Lenape and Iroquois, passed down creation myths in which Earth balances on a turtle's back—often calling the continent "Turtle Island" even today. Similarly, Hindu mythology teaches that the Earth rests atop four elephants standing on a turtle. These rich stories illustrate humanity's symbolic attempts to explain natural phenomena in the absence of divine revelation.[122]

In contrast to these mythical explanations, Matthew Fontaine Maury pursued truth anchored in biblical observation. A devout Christian and avid Bible student, he exemplified a deep commitment to exploring its scientific insights and accuracy. Maury joined the Virginia Military Institute faculty in 1868 as a professor of physics after an internationally acclaimed career as an oceanographer, astronomer, historian, meteorologist, cartographer, geologist, writer, and commander in the United States Navy. Accordingly, he is affectionately remembered as the "Pathfinder of the Seas," "Father of Modern Oceanography and Naval Meteorology," and "Scientist of the Seas." Maury was an uncompromising Christian and fervent believer in the truths of Scripture. He was struck by the reference

---

122. Yellowhorn and Lowinger, *Turtle Island*, 68–70.

in Ps 8:8 to "the paths of the seas." As a result, throughout his career, he sought these paths of the sea and ultimately found them. Maury models the posture this book commends: let Scripture set the hypothesis, then test it—truth welcomes examination because it does not fear exposure.

Amid his many successes, Maury never forgot his belief in Scripture. Physical geography is filled with references to the Bible, and Maury was fascinated by passages that mention the sea.[123] He wrote,

> We must look upon it as a part of that exquisite machinery by which the harmonies of nature are preserved, and then will begin to perceive the developments of order and the evidences of design . . . and thus will see bars and doors to stay its proud waves; and who gave the sea His decree that its waters should not pass His command. He laid the foundations of the world so fast they should not be moved forever.[124]

This idea aligns with the concept of general revelation—God's disclosure of himself through nature. Psalm 19:1–4 beautifully expresses this truth: "The heavens declare the glory of God; and the firmament shows His handiwork. Day unto day utters speech, and night unto night reveals knowledge. There is no speech nor language where their voice is not heard. Their line has gone out through all the earth, and their words to the end of the world."

Thirteen years before his passing, Maury delivered a speech that encapsulated both his scientific and Christian convictions, marking the culmination of an extraordinary career as one of the most influential creation scientists of the nineteenth century.

> I have been blamed by men of science, both in this country and in England, for quoting the Bible in confirmation of the doctrines of physical geography. The Bible, they say, was not written for scientific purposes, and is therefore of no authority in matters of science. I beg pardon! The Bible is authority for everything it touches. What would you think of the historian who should refuse to consult the historical records of the Bible, because the Bible was not written for the purposes of history? . . . And when your men of science, with vain and hasty conceit, announce the discovery of disagreement between them, rely

---

123. See, for example, Isa 43:16, Ps 107:23–24, and Eccl 1:7. Grady, *Matthew Fontaine Maury*; Major, "Honor to Whom Honor," 82–87; Johnson, "Matthew Maury's Paths," 21.

124. Maury, *Physical Geography of the Sea*, 295–96.

upon it, the fault is not with the witness of His records, but with the worm who essays to interpret evidence which he does not understand.[125]

That is a counter-PSYOP posture: refuse the false choice between faith and reason, and refuse the reframe that makes method the master.

Maury's words echo the biblical conviction that creation itself testifies to the wisdom and authority of God. As Job 12:7–9 declares, "But ask the beasts, and they will teach you; and the birds of the heavens, and they will tell you; or speak to the earth, and it will teach you; and the fish of the sea will declare to you. Who among all these does not know that the hand of the LORD has done this?" This idea—of nature as a testament to divine truth—finds further support in the theological reflections of Joshua Lapine, a theologian and scholar known for his deep insights into the relationship between faith and reason. Lapine emphasizes the interplay between Scripture and the natural world, highlighting how both sources of revelation contribute to a fuller understanding of God's design.

> Both sources of revelation are divinely given, but the former explicitly frames how we are to understand the latter. Scripture is . . . our magisterial authority. Nature is what saturates concepts, gives content to God's thoughts. Yet God's word is primary because his word brings into being all that is, nature included. Being (and epistemology) proceeds from his speech; what he says is. Humankind approaches nature within loving covenantal relationship with God through the regenerated gifts which we have been endowed, (embodied) reason and perception, following God's unfolding guidance through his prophets and apostles, his Son, and latterly, through the Scriptures which have been passed down and interpreted through his church and by the power of the Holy Spirit. The very words of God stand, while the ministers of his word, like our capacities and tradition, clarify and saturate the concepts.[126]

Lapine's point reinforces the thesis of this chapter: the battle for perception (PSYOP) is ultimately a battle over which authority frames reality—Scripture or shifting consensus.

In this excerpt, Lapine highlights that while both sources of revelation—nature and Scripture—are divinely given, Scripture provides the authoritative framework for understanding the world around us.

---

125. Quoted in Lewis, *Matthew Fontaine Maury*, 99.
126. Lapine, *Logic of the Body*, 8.

He explains that God's word brings all things into existence and gives meaning to what we observe, shaping humankind's pursuit of knowledge through reason, perception, and faith.

This dynamic between revelation and reality is more than philosophical—it's historically verifiable. The Bible doesn't merely proclaim eternal truths; it embeds them within a tapestry of real people, real places, and real events. It meticulously names cities, geographic landmarks, and the individuals who inhabited them—details that, time and again, align with archaeological discoveries. Archaeology is where narrative meets stone. Deception can spin theories; it cannot move inscriptions.

A striking example emerges in the work of Sir William Ramsay (1851–1939), a nineteenth-century Scottish archaeologist and New Testament scholar who initially approached Scripture with deep skepticism. Convinced that the book of Acts was historically unreliable, Ramsay set out to disprove its claims. Armed with his Bible, he traveled extensively through Asia Minor (modern-day Turkey), tracing Paul's missionary journeys and investigating cities that were, at the time, poorly documented or unknown to historians. What began as an effort to debunk Scripture became a transformative encounter with archaeological evidence—setting the stage for an extraordinary confrontation between skepticism and historical truth.

Ramsay followed the Roman road to Pisidian Antioch, a city perched on a high plateau and referenced in Acts 13 and 14. While the biblical text doesn't specify the duration of Paul's journey, scholars estimate it would have taken several days on foot through rugged terrain. Acts 14:21–26 records, "And when they had preached the gospel to that city and made many disciples, they returned to Lystra, Iconium, and Antioch. . . . From there they sailed to Antioch, where they had been commended to the grace of God for the work which they had completed."

Here, the first Antioch refers to Pisidian Antioch (v. 21) and the second to Syrian Antioch (v. 26). During one of Ramsay's early excavations, marble fragments inscribed with "Pisidian Antioch" were uncovered—confirming the city's identity and powerfully aligning with the biblical account.

Continuing along Paul's trail, Ramsay located Lystra, which Acts 14:6–8 and 14:21 describe as a place of ministry and healing:

> They became aware of it and fled to Lystra and Derbe, cities of Lycaonia, and to the surrounding region. . . . And in Lystra a certain man without strength in his feet was sitting, a cripple

from his mother's womb, who had never walked. . . . And when they had preached the gospel to that city and made many disciples, they returned to Lystra, Iconium, and Antioch.

From there, Ramsay proceeded to Derbe, the site of Paul's continued ministry and the meeting of Timothy, as referenced in Acts 14:20 and 16:1:

> When the disciples gathered around him, he rose up and went into the city. And the next day he departed with Barnabas to Derbe. (Acts 14:20)

> Then he came to Derbe and Lystra. And behold, a certain disciple was there, named Timothy, the son of a certain Jewish woman who believed, but his father was Greek. (Acts 16:1)

Such geographic detail, once questioned, was verified through Ramsay's excavations within the borders of modern-day Turkey—corresponding to the historical region of Asia Minor. His discoveries garnered global attention: the cities Paul referenced were confirmed to exist, and remarkably, the terminology Luke used to describe public officials matched inscriptions buried beneath the ruins. When Scripture's names match archaeology's stones, the noise of skepticism fades. Facts are stubborn things—deception hates that.

One especially striking term appears in Acts 17:6—*politarchs*, referring to the rulers of Thessalonica. This word was long assumed to be fictional, as it appeared nowhere else in known literature. But during Ramsay's team's excavation of Thessalonica, they uncovered a marble inscription bearing the word "politarchs," proving Luke's accuracy and reinforcing the historical reliability of the biblical text.[127] Evidence like this profoundly influenced Ramsay, ultimately leading him to embrace Christianity—not through emotional persuasion but by encountering truth carved into stone.

Thus, the chapter's through line comes full circle: God grounds his truth in history so his people can resist the siren song of managed perception. Prophecy, science rightly bounded, and archaeology together form a counter-PSYOP—arming believers to discern and to stand.

---

127. Ramsey and Wilson, *St. Paul.*

IMAGO DEI: TRUTH WRITTEN INTO HUMAN DESIGN

Yet, the Bible is more than a historical record; it offers profound insight into the nature of existence itself. Beyond geography and recorded events, it speaks to the very essence of humanity. One of its most foundational truths is that humans are made in God's image, setting us apart from every other part of creation. Despite this, many modern worldviews present distorted interpretations of human nature. Naturalism, rooted in evolutionary theory, views mankind as nothing more than a highly sophisticated biological machine, devoid of spirit. In this framework, emotions, thoughts, and inspirations are reduced to mere chemical reactions in the brain. This perspective not only contradicts biblical truth but also strips life of deeper meaning and purpose. This reduction is not value-neutral; it functions like a cultural PSYOP—reframing persons as processes so that dignity, destiny, and accountability can be negotiated away.

In contrast, the biblical account of creation affirms humanity's intrinsic worth, revealing that only God's design provides meaning, purpose, and hope—ultimately paving the way to eternal life. To be made in the image of God is to be destined for redemption. The *imago Dei* is thus God's built-in countermeasure to deception: identity precedes influence, and design defeats nihilism.

Building on the biblical truth that humanity is set apart as God's unique creation, Scripture reveals how this distinction was established from the very beginning. From the outset, God defines the frame—so that rival narratives cannot.

On days one through five of the creation week, God developed and populated the originally empty ("without form and void") Earth introduced in Gen 1:2. He did so with great precision and tact to form a magnificent backdrop on which to place his crowning creative achievement, humankind. Not only did God save the best for last, but he created humans distinctly different from animals. Human life was segregated in distinct relation to God, as Gen 1:26 explains: by the divine plan ("let us make man"), by the divine pattern ("in our image"), and by the divine purpose ("let them have dominion"). Being in the image of God (*imago Dei*) is not simply an attribute bestowed by God and retained by humans. It is also the essence of God's perfect attributes reflected in humankind, who were specifically designed to represent God on earth and reflect these attributes. More succinctly, being an image-bearer of God is what humankind is rather than something humankind has.

Deception targets these three clauses—plan, pattern, purpose—because if any are blurred, stewardship becomes self-rule and representation becomes self-invention.

Imago Dei, Latin for "the image of God," refers to humanity's unique role as reflections of God's character. Picture a mirror catching sunlight: while the mirror itself does not produce light, it faithfully reflects the sun's brilliance. Similarly, humans are created to embody God's essence, including attributes like love, reason, and creativity. This concept underscores humanity's inherent value and purpose, making it central to understanding what it means to be made in God's likeness.

Influence operations work by fogging the mirror; sanctification clears it.

As with the animals, God formed Adam from the dust: "And the LORD God formed man of the dust of the ground, and breathed into his nostrils the breath of life; and man became a living being" (Gen 2:7). Thus, humanity is unique and expressly set apart among God's creations, possessing both a material body and an immaterial soul. The breath of God marks a boundary materialism cannot cross—personhood is not an emergent illusion but a bestowed reality.

The material part of humans is not to be thought to directly resemble God as having flesh and blood. Nevertheless, it echoes the life of God as it was formed in perfect health and was not originally subject to death. The immaterial part of humans reflects the image of God morally because humankind was created in righteousness and perfect innocence that reflects God's holiness; mentally because humans have the ability to reason and choose, which reflects God's intellect and freedom; and socially because humanity was created for fellowship, reflecting God's triune nature and his love. Hence, these three attributes make a relationship between God and humans possible and endow humans with great capacity and its responsibility.

These capacities—moral, mental, social—are precisely where counter-truth narratives concentrate their fire because if you corrupt the faculties, then you compromise discernment.

Because humans have significant capacity, they are able to make free choices; however, these choices (and their consequences) are their responsibility.[128] Adam and Eve made a fatal choice of which all human-

---

128. The discussion of human responsibility and free will has long been explored within theological frameworks such as Calvinism and Arminianism. While Calvinism emphasizes God's sovereign ordination of events, Arminianism highlights the role

ity bears the scars and the responsibility. In so doing, they blemished the image of God within humankind. James 3:9 affirms that we still manifest the image of God, but we also exhibit the damage of sin: "With it we bless our God and Father, and with it we curse men, who have been made in the similitude of God."

The fall didn't erase the image—it introduced interference. Redemption is the restoration of signal clarity.

Wayne Grudem, a respected theologian and scholar known for his contributions to systematic theology, articulates this concept with clarity. He explains,

> Since man has sinned, he is certainly not as fully like God as he was before. His moral purity has been lost and his sinful character certainly does not reflect God's holiness. His intellect is corrupted by falsehood and misunderstanding; his speech no longer continually glorifies God; his relationships are often governed by selfishness rather than love, and so forth. Though man is still in the image of God, in every aspect of life some parts of that image have been distorted or lost.[129]

Grudem describes, in theological terms, what PSYOP engineers exploit: distorted perception, disordered loves, and disintegrated community.

Because humankind was designed specifically to be the image-bearer of God, if that characteristic were eliminated, humans would cease to be humans. Furthermore, by virtue of retaining God's image, blemished by sin as it is, humans are redeemable and worth redeeming by God's perfect love and abundant grace. Dignity is not a policy preference; it is ontological. That is why every anti-human narrative must first deny the image.

Thankfully, we have a perfect, omniscient Redeemer. He anticipated our fallen state and was therefore "slain from the foundation of the world" (Rev 13:8) to restore the original image of God in humanity. This action formed a "new man, which was created according to God, in true righteousness and holiness" (Eph 4:24). Faith in the redemptive act of Christ is the only way to restore humankind to its created *imago Dei* stature. As 2 Cor 5:17 states, "Therefore if anyone is in Christ, he is a new creation; old things have passed away; behold, all things have become new."[130] The

---

of human choice in moral accountability. Regardless of one's stance, Scripture affirms both God's authority and humanity's genuine responsibility for the choices we make.

129. Grudem, *Systematic Theology*, 444.
130. Corrado, "Imago Dei."

gospel is not motivational rhetoric; it is God's decisive counter-operation to undo deception and remake image-bearers.

This restoration is not merely theological—it is existential. Humanity was not only made by God but made for God. Our design is not autonomous; it is relational. Just as a mirror only fulfills its purpose when it reflects light, so too do humans only fulfill their purpose when they reflect the glory of their Creator. Where deception says "self-define," design says "reflect." Freedom is found in alignment, not in reinvention.

The creation narrative itself affirms this relational design. When God created fish, he spoke to the sea. When he created trees, he spoke to the earth. But when he created man, he turned inward and spoke to himself: "Let us make man in our image, after our likeness." This distinction is not incidental—it is foundational. Fish are sustained by water; trees, by soil. Remove them from their source, and they die. Likewise, humanity was created to live in the presence of God. When disconnected from him, we do not merely falter—we perish. God is our natural environment, the atmosphere in which human life was meant to thrive. Severing creatures from their source is the primal deception. Reconnection is the heart of redemption.

Water without fish remains water. Soil without trees remains soil. But fish without water are nothing, and trees without soil are nothing. In the same way, God remains God without man, but man without God loses all meaning, purpose, and life. This underscores the gravity of the *imago Dei*: we were not only made to resemble God; we were made to remain in him. Our identity is not just derived from God; it is sustained by him. Thus the ultimate influence war is about environment: dwell in truth and live; dwell in illusion and wither.

Having explored the nature of truth as the path to salvation, we now turn to its stark counterpart: deception, a force that seeks to pull us away. History is filled with falsehoods masquerading as truth, and the spiritual battlefield is no different, littered with half-truths that appear convincing yet lead astray. To stand firm, one must ask the crucial question, Why is God's word the ultimate anchor for absolute truth? Chapter 2 delves into this foundation, tracing the path from Scripture to unwavering certainty.

From Chancellorsville's battlefield illusions to Waco's twisted doctrines, from the relativism of postmodern thought to the denial of our design in God's image, the enemy's strategy has not changed: deception reframes truth until illusion feels more plausible than reality. This is the essence of psychological operations—planned campaigns to control perception, shape belief, and steer behavior. Chapter 1 has identified the target—truth, design, identity—and exposed the tactic—deception through reframing. Chapter 2 now begins the counter-PSYOP: anchoring perception to God's word, the immovable foundation that unmasks lies and steadies hearts. Only when truth is fixed can we resist the enemy's narratives and live as the image-bearers we were created to be.

PERSONAL APPLICATION: RECOGNIZING DECEPTION IN EVERYDAY LIFE

Deception is rarely loud—it whispers, weaving itself into truth until it becomes nearly indistinguishable. The story of deception at Chancellorsville remind us that misdirection often thrives in subtlety, shaping outcomes before anyone realizes its influence. In much the same way, deception in our own lives is rarely blatant; it masquerades as wisdom, logic, or even goodness, waiting for the perfect moment to mislead. Recognizing its subtlety is the first step in guarding against it. Just as deception shaped historical victories, it seeks to shape our beliefs and choices today. The key is discernment—an unwavering commitment to truth that allows us to identify falsehood before it takes root.

The battle against deception is not fought passively—it requires intentionality and spiritual preparedness. Here are a few ways to apply the lessons of this chapter:

1. *Be Watchful:* Just as military leaders studied their enemy's tactics, take time to examine the influences in your life. Ask yourself, What voices, messages, or beliefs am I allowing to shape my decisions? Are they rooted in God's truth, or do they contain elements of deception?

2. *Arm Yourself with Scripture:* God's word is the ultimate defense against deception. Memorize key passages, such as John 14:6 or Matt 7:24–26 to strengthen your discernment and fortify your spirit.

3. *Reflect on Shadows of Deception:* Think about areas in your life where you may have accepted "half-truths." Consider how you can align those aspects more closely with absolute truth as revealed in Scripture. Deception's greatest weapon lies in its subtlety—its ability to blend into the rhythms of everyday life, unnoticed until it

has taken root. Reflect on the stories shared here—the prosperity gospel's misuse of Scripture and the moral relativism disguised as tolerance. Each is a mirror through which we see our own vulnerabilities. By anchoring ourselves in Scripture and seeking God's wisdom, we can resist these quiet compromises and stand firmly in truth.

4. *Pray for Discernment:* Ask God for the wisdom to recognize truth from falsehood in every area of your life. Deception often operates beneath the surface, making it difficult to detect without divine guidance. Through prayer, we invite God to sharpen our understanding and align our hearts with his truth. Seek his wisdom daily, asking for clarity in moments of uncertainty and strength to stand firm against misleading influences. As Jas 1:5 reminds us, "If any of you lacks wisdom, let him ask of God, who gives to all liberally and without reproach, and it will be given to him." A posture of prayer keeps us rooted in truth and enables us to navigate life's complexities with spiritual discernment.

Much like the soldiers and strategies described in this chapter, navigating the battlefield of spiritual deception demands vigilance, preparation, and trust in our ultimate Commander. Just as deception on physical battlefields shaped victories at Chancellorsville, spiritual deception operates with similar cunning, thriving in subtleties. The enemy embeds falsehoods within truth, misdirecting even the most discerning. Military victories required preparation and discipline, and our spiritual victories depend on the same—readiness and trust in God's unwavering truth.

Picture life as a battlefield, and you as a soldier equipping yourself for unseen skirmishes. Scripture is your armor, prayer your shield, and faith your compass, guiding you through the fog of deception toward the light of absolute truth. Anchor your heart to God's word—it is the unshakable rock in a world prone to shifting sands.

Personal Reflection

1. Have you ever experienced a situation where a lie was hidden within a partial truth? How did you eventually recognize it?

2. In what ways has your understanding of truth been influenced by culture, media, or social norms? How does that compare to the biblical view of truth?
3. What role does Scripture play in helping you discern truth from deception in your daily life?
4. Can you recall a time when you justified an action because it "felt right" in the moment, but later realized it conflicted with God's truth?

Group Discussion

1. The chapter presents military PSYOP as a parallel to spiritual deception. How does this comparison help us better understand Satan's strategies?
2. Discuss how postmodernism and moral relativism affect our culture's understanding of truth. What are some ways the church can respond?
3. How can we, as a group, support each other in growing discernment and avoiding subtle forms of deception in our spiritual lives?
4. How do you reconcile the idea of absolute truth with the pluralism of today's world? What practical tools can help believers stand firm in biblical truth?

Scripture Connection

- Read John 14:6 and 2 Tim 3:13. What do these verses teach us about the nature of truth and deception?
- Matthew 7:24–26 talks about building on a firm foundation. How does this metaphor apply to your life when it comes to spiritual discernment?

Deception thrives where truth is neglected. But when Scripture becomes our foundation, discernment sharpens, and we stand firm against the forces that seek to lead us astray. Let us remain watchful, armed with truth, and committed to seeking God's wisdom in every aspect of life.

2

Why God's Word Is True

The gravestone of "Major William Martin" stands as a testament to the ingenuity of Operation Mincemeat—an audacious World War II deception that changed the course of history by blending truth with illusion.[1]

---

1. Image: Rufito, "William Martin Burial," CC BY-SA 4.0 (https://creativecommons.org/licenses/by-sa/4.0/deed.en). No modifications were made to the image.

> Every one who is seriously involved in the pursuit of science becomes convinced that a spirit is manifest in the laws of the Universe—a spirit vastly superior to that of man, and one in the face of which we with our modest powers must feel humble.
>
> —Albert Einstein, "Religion and Science"

In 1799, French soldiers digging a fort in Egypt uncovered a slab of black basalt carved with three scripts—hieroglyphics, Demotic, and Greek. For centuries, Egyptian hieroglyphs had been a mystery, their meaning lost to time. But the Rosetta Stone became the key. By comparing the known Greek with the unknown symbols, scholars unlocked an entire language.[2]

Just as the Rosetta Stone confirmed truth by cross-checking it against a reliable standard, Scripture is our Rosetta Stone for reality. In a world of shifting interpretations, God's word remains the unchanging key that makes sense of everything else.

But confidence can be as deceptive as it is empowering. History is full of generals, investors, and leaders whose "assurance" was built on illusions—only to collapse when appearances gave way to reality. Scripture warns of this danger: confidence not rooted in God's word is presumption, not faith. The Latin phrase *con fide*—"with faith"—reminds us that true confidence flows from trust in God's revelation, not from evidence twisted or perceptions manipulated.

This chapter turns from deception's distortions (seen in chapter 1) to the one secure anchor: the trustworthiness of God's word. Without Scripture as our reference point, every later example of deception would lack a standard by which to test falsehood.

DECEPTION AND THE RELIABILITY OF SCRIPTURE

In the early twentieth century, one of the most infamous financial deceptions in history unfolded—the Ponzi scheme. Named after Charles Ponzi, this fraudulent investment scheme promised extraordinarily high returns with little risk. Investors believed they were reaping rewards from lucrative foreign exchange transactions, but in reality, Ponzi was simply using new investors' money to pay earlier ones. The illusion of success fueled more investments until the deception collapsed, leaving thousands

---

2. Parkinson, *Rosetta Stone*, 12–15.

financially ruined. The entire system depended on misleading narratives wrapped in partial truths, proving that deception often flourishes when it appears convincing.[3]

This principle is not confined to finance. In military strategy, deception operations (i.e., PSYOP) often exploit half-truths to disorient an enemy, planting just enough credibility to make the lie believable. Operation Fortitude in World War II, for example, fed the Nazis a steady stream of fabricated reports and false troop movements to convince them that D-Day would strike at Calais instead of Normandy. The operation worked precisely because the false information was wrapped in layers of plausibility. Deception succeeds not by being outrageous, but by being almost true.

Today's digital world offers no shortage of examples. A viral post, a manipulated image, or an AI-generated video can circulate globally within hours, convincing thousands of something that never happened. Like Operation Fortitude's inflatable tanks, these modern "deepfakes" succeed not because they are absurd but because they feel plausible. The parallel is striking: deception in our age is less about outright lies and more about believable distortions. And just as with ancient or wartime propaganda, Scripture remains the only sure lens to separate reality from illusion.

Just as deception thrives when wrapped in partial truths, many today question the reliability of Scripture based on misconceptions rather than evidence of its divine preservation. Similarly, some argue that the Bible has been altered, manipulated, or distorted over time—believing misconceptions instead of examining the overwhelming evidence of its faithful transmission. However, unlike human plans that falter, God's word stands unshaken—divinely inspired, faithfully preserved, and entirely trustworthy. If military deception can reroute divisions and collapse empires, spiritual deception—unchecked—can misdirect souls for eternity. Scripture is therefore not optional background reading; it is the secure map that reveals truth amid enemy disinformation. While deception distorts facts to manipulate reality, Scripture remains God's unchanging truth, a foundation upon which faith is built.

---

3. Frankel, *Ponzi Scheme Puzzle*, 45–67.

THE INSPIRATION AND AUTHORITY OF GOD'S WORD

Jesus himself affirmed the verbal plenary inspiration of Scripture—that is, the belief that every word and every part of the Bible is fully inspired by God—confirming that all Scripture originates from him:

> Now we have received, not the spirit of the world, but the Spirit who is from God, that we might know the things that have been freely given to us by God. These things we also speak, not in words which man's wisdom teaches but which the Holy Spirit teaches, comparing spiritual things with spiritual. (1 Cor 2:12–13)

> All Scripture is given by inspiration of God, and is profitable for doctrine, for reproof, for correction, for instruction in righteousness, that the man of God may be complete, thoroughly equipped for every good work. (2 Tim 3:16–17)

Jesus further reinforced this truth, declaring, "Do not think that I came to destroy the Law or the Prophets. I did not come to destroy but to fulfill. For assuredly, I say to you, till heaven and earth pass away, one jot or one tittle will by no means pass from the law till all is fulfilled" (Matt 5:17–18). With this statement, Jesus confirms the accuracy and authority of Scripture—even down to the smallest details—affirming it as the very word of God.[4] In intelligence terms, the Bible is not just a "source" among many; it is the ultimate Signals Intelligence (SIGINT) feed—the uncorrupted signal amid all the enemy's noise. In a world where deception distorts reality, the Bible remains a steadfast foundation of truth, unaltered by human schemes or manipulation.

Word-for-Word vs. Paraphrase

Because every word of Scripture is inspired and without error, it is essential to distinguish between two types of Bible translations: word-for-word translations and paraphrases (also known as dynamic equivalence). Word-for-word translations function like photographs, preserving every detail precisely as it is. Paraphrases, on the other hand, resemble impressionist paintings—capturing the essence and emotion of the text while sacrificing precision for interpretation.

---

4. Geisler, *Christian Apologetics*, 56–58.

While paraphrases like the Living Bible can aid understanding, they cannot replace the authoritative, inspired word of God. This distinction matters because God inspired the exact words of Scripture, not merely their paraphrased interpretations. Like sermons, paraphrases can provide insight, but they must not be confused with Scripture itself.

Recognizing the difference between translation methods leads to a deeper appreciation of the Bible's reliability. Its authority stands apart from human traditions, religious institutions, or personal interpretations. As we explore its divine inspiration, it becomes clear that Scripture alone serves as the foundation for discerning ultimate truth. Just as translation accuracy shapes how we read God's word, so too does our approach to its interpretation. Misinterpretation distorts meaning, leading to theological confusion and doctrinal inconsistency. It is no accident that PSYOP doctrine stresses "plausibility" and "context"—a mis-framed message can redirect entire populations. In the same way, a mistranslation or misinterpretation of Scripture can redirect lives away from truth.

SOLA SCRIPTURA: SCRIPTURE ALONE AS FINAL AUTHORITY

This distinction leads to a crucial question: If Scripture alone is inspired by God, what does that mean for how it should function as the ultimate authority in matters of faith? This question could not be more pressing. Recent research reveals a startling erosion of biblical conviction among those who profess faith in Christ. According to the American Worldview Inventory 2024, conducted by the Cultural Research Center at Arizona Christian University, only 6 percent of self-identified Christians in the United States actually possess a biblical worldview.[5] That number is not a misprint—it's a symptom. While many claim allegiance to Scripture, the majority unknowingly embrace a fusion of beliefs pulled from incompatible sources: secular humanism, moralistic therapeutic deism (a feel-good pseudo-faith in which God exists to affirm personal happiness and moral niceness), postmodern relativism, and fragments of cultural morality. The result is theological confusion dressed in spiritual vocabulary. People believe that human nature is basically good—denying original sin. Others argue that all religions lead to God—dismissing the

---

5. Barna, *American Worldview Inventory 2024*, 12.

exclusivity of Christ. And still others assume that good deeds help earn salvation—undermining grace itself.

George Barna, the lead researcher, calls this a worldview crisis—not merely in culture but within the church. His conclusion? Without robust discipleship and deep biblical literacy, the drift will continue. That's precisely why *sola scriptura*—Latin for "by Scripture alone"—matters. It's not just an academic doctrine—it's a safeguard. Like the *Challenger* disaster in 1986, where NASA engineers had raised concerns about the O-rings' ability to withstand cold temperatures, yet their warnings were overlooked, even small compromises in biblical authority can produce catastrophic consequences. One overlooked weakness doomed the shuttle and its crew; one overlooked concession can endanger the church's witness. *Sola scriptura* is the fire wall against doctrinal sabotage, the counter-PSYOP that keeps the church oriented on truth. Roman Catholic teaching insists that the sacraments are channels of saving grace. Yet baptism and the Lord's Supper are signs that point to Christ's finished work, not mechanisms that dispense salvation. Grace flows not through ritual but directly from the one Mediator: "For there is one God and one Mediator between God and men, the Man Christ Jesus" (1 Tim 2:5). In a time when truth is regularly traded for trends, Scripture remains the anchor that holds firm.

Clarifying Misunderstandings

In light of this doctrinal drift, a proper understanding of *sola scriptura* becomes essential. Yet, this doctrine is often misunderstood—by both its critics and even some of its adherents. Some assume it means that Scripture is the only source of truth or authority, but this is not what the doctrine teaches. Instead, it asserts that Scripture is the highest and final authority—the standard against which all other teachings and traditions must be tested. This does not deny the value of church leadership, tradition, or reason, but it ensures that these never take precedence over God's revealed word. Recognizing this principle helps safeguard biblical truth from distortion, ensuring that interpretation remains anchored in the word rather than external influences. Notably, some Roman Catholic theologians claim the Bible never explicitly teaches *sola scriptura*, pointing to verses about "tradition" (2 Thess 2:15, 1 Cor 11:2).[6] But these refer

---

6. I engage Roman Catholic arguments because they help surface key errors in

to apostolic teaching—much of which became Scripture—ecclesial accretions (the layers of doctrine and practice added by the church over centuries). In contrast, 2 Tim 3:16–17 affirms Scripture as fully sufficient to equip the believer for every good work.

In clarifying what *sola scriptura* does and does not mean, it becomes clear why critics often distort the doctrine. Roman Catholic apologists, for example, frequently shift the discussion from the sufficiency of Scripture to the supposed chaos of Protestant diversity. The Roman Catholic Church often mischaracterizes Protestant diversity by citing inflated statistics—such as the popular claim that the Reformation spawned over forty thousand denominations—to suggest doctrinal confusion and undermine *sola scriptura*. However, this argument conflates structural variety with theological fragmentation. Many of these "denominations" share identical core beliefs and differ only in governance or geography. By portraying Protestantism as hopelessly divided, Roman Catholic apologists obscure the real issue: *sola scriptura* challenges centralized ecclesial authority by insisting that Scripture—not tradition or magisterial pronouncement—is the final standard of truth. This misrepresentation serves a rhetorical purpose: it shifts attention away from the Roman Catholic Church's own reliance on unwritten traditions and magisterial interpretations that often lack clear biblical warrant.

Moreover, this critique ignores the fact that doctrinal unity in Roman Catholicism is often maintained not by theological consensus but by hierarchical enforcement. Protestant diversity, by contrast, reflects the freedom of conscience and theological inquiry that *sola scriptura* protects. This difference is strategic: uniformity enforced from above resembles command-and-control in a military hierarchy, while *sola scriptura* trains believers more like a decentralized unit—each soldier equipped with the same field manual, able to test orders against higher command. The irony is that while Roman Catholics accuse Protestants of fragmentation, their own interpretive authority rests on a *magisterium*—the Roman Catholic Church's teaching authority—that has only infallibly interpreted a handful of verses, leaving vast theological terrain subject to internal debate. Another frequent objection is that *sola scriptura* opens the door to endless interpretive confusion. Yet, the Bible never teaches that believers must interpret in isolation, and the Reformers consistently

---

understanding biblical authority. While I do not believe core Roman Catholic theology aligns with Scripture, my concern is with doctrines, not necessarily with those who hold them.

rejected the idea as well. Scripture is clear on essentials, and the Spirit equips the church collectively to guard the truth. True unity arises not from silencing dissent but from submitting to God's word.

A second line of Roman Catholic critique focuses on the canon itself, as argued by Dr. John Bergsma, a former Protestant turned Roman Catholic scholar. He contends that Protestants are inconsistent because they rely on tradition to affirm the biblical canon—arguing that *sola scriptura* is self-defeating since the Bible does not establish its own canon, and the list of books was not formally codified until the Council of Rome in AD 382.[7]

This reasoning, however, is historically and theologically flawed. It confuses *recognition* with *creation*: the church did not invent the canon but acknowledged what was already authoritative and in wide use.[8] Early Christians were reading the Gospels, Acts, Pauline letters, and other New Testament writings long before any council met. The Muratorian fragment (c. AD 170), Athanasius's Easter Letter (AD 367), and widespread liturgical use show a functioning canon prior to Rome's formal affirmation.[9]

Put simply, the canon is not an authoritative list of books created by the church; it is a list of authoritative books the church recognized. The difference may sound subtle, but it changes the entire framework of the debate.

An analogy helps clarify this. Michael Jordan is not great because he appears on every "all-time greatest" list—he appears on the list because he was already great. The list merely recognizes his greatness; it does not create it. In the same way, the church did not give the biblical books authority by including them. They were included because they were already inspired by God and therefore authoritative.

Anglican theologian J. I. Packer made the same point: "The church no more gave us the New Testament canon than Sir Isaac Newton gave us the force of gravity. Newton did not create gravity, but recognized it."[10] The councils of Hippo (AD 393) and Carthage (AD 397)—regional gatherings of North African bishops that dealt with questions of doctrine and church practice—functioned in this same way, merely endorsing what had already been recognized. Athanasius's Easter Letter, written thirty

---

7. Bergsma and Pitre, *Catholic Introduction to the Bible*, xxiii–xxv.
8. Bruce, *Canon of Scripture*, 276–77.
9. Metzger, *Canon of the New Testament*, 191–95; Athanasius, *Festal Letters* 39.
10. Packer, *God Has Spoken*, 111.

years earlier, listed the same twenty-seven New Testament books we affirm today.

Thus, the real question is not whether the church gave us the canon, but whether it rightly discerned the canon God had already given. To mistake recognition for creation is to ascribe to the church a power it never possessed and to diminish the divine authorship that makes Scripture unique.

This same pattern of confusion appears in Bergsma's other critiques as well. For example, he faults Protestant translations for rendering the Greek word *paradosis* as "teachings" instead of "tradition" when Paul uses it positively.[11] Yet this ignores the word's context. Paul applies paradosis to apostolic tradition—a positive, authoritative handing down of instruction (2 Thess 2:15)—but Jesus uses the same term to rebuke the Pharisees for elevating human tradition—a negative, man-made set of rules—above God's word (Mark 7:13). Protestant translators are not obscuring meaning but applying common translation principles—drawing on *lexical semantics* and *functional* (thought-for-thought) *equivalence*—to render the word according to its contextual sense rather than forcing a uniform translation.

Most importantly, Bergsma's case conflates apostolic tradition with the later accretions of Roman Catholic doctrine. By claiming unwritten traditions bear equal authority with Scripture, Roman Catholicism opens the door to teachings without clear biblical grounding—such as papal infallibility, Marian dogmas, and purgatory (discussed in the next chapter).[12] Protestants resist not out of stubbornness but from fidelity to God's word, which is not one authority among many but the final court of appeal (2 Tim 3:15).[13] Thus, the canon is not the product of tradition but the measure by which tradition itself is tested. To suggest otherwise is to confuse historical transmission with doctrinal authority.

Roman Catholic apologists often argue that *sola scriptura* cannot be biblical since the exact phrase "Bible alone" does not appear in Scripture. Yet ironically, for instance, they defend the magisterium, consisting of the pope and bishops in communion with him, who claim the authority to infallibly interpret both Scripture and tradition—using the very same reasoning in reverse.[14] They acknowledge that the word *magisterium*

---

11. Carson, *Exegetical Fallacies*, 27–28; Sproul, *Scripture Alone*, 56–59.
12. King, *Biblical Defense*, 43–48; Allison, *Roman Catholic Theology*, 91–97.
13. Mathison, *Shape of Sola Scriptura*, 35–37.
14. *CCC*, §§85–100.

never appears in the Bible, just as the word *Trinity* does not, but claim the concept is implied. In other words, absence of a term is treated as fatal when Protestants appeal to Scripture, but excusable when Roman Catholics appeal to tradition. This inconsistency exposes the weakness of their objection. Protestants apply the principle consistently: even if a term is not explicitly named, the real question is whether the concept itself is taught by Scripture. The Trinity is; the magisterium is not.

This objection also overlooks how doctrine is normally recognized. The Bible never says, "Here is the doctrine of the Trinity," yet its teaching about God's nature—Father, Son, and Holy Spirit—both implicitly and explicitly allows us to affirm it. *Sola scriptura* follows the same pattern: while the terminology is absent, the principle is woven throughout Scripture.

An example of this comes from 2 Thess 2, where Paul warns believers not to be shaken by a spirit, a spoken word, or even a letter *seeming* to be from the apostles. He urges them to discern truth based on what they already know to be authoritative. If teachings arise that contradict the foundation already laid, they must be rejected. This idea—that believers must test teachings against an established divine standard—is central to *sola scriptura*. It affirms that God's prior revelation stands above later claims, requiring discernment from every Christian, not just those in leadership. In modern military terms, Paul is teaching "red teaming"—stress-testing every incoming message to ensure it aligns with known truth before acting on it. A forged signal, no matter how official it looks, must be discarded if it contradicts higher command. This directly opposes the Roman Catholic and Orthodox position that teachings outside of Scripture, declared by authoritative bodies, must be received as apostolic truth. Instead, Paul's statement implies that even something that *seems* to be apostolic must be tested against what was already established.

Having already appealed to the magisterium on lexical grounds, Roman Catholic apologists now appeal to it conceptually. They argue that while the word itself is not found in Scripture, the concept is, pointing to Exod 24 (with the pillars, elders, and high priest), Matt 18 (binding and loosing), and Acts (the formation of the *ekklesia*, or "assembly/church") as evidence of a hierarchical teaching office. But this reasoning is flawed. In the Old Testament, the authority of elders and priests was always derivative, never autonomous—they were subject to God's word and were often rebuked by the prophets when they strayed. In the New Testament, the apostles' authority was unique and unrepeatable, rooted in their eyewitness testimony of Christ and guaranteed by the inspiration of the Holy Spirit (John 14:26, 16:13). Their teaching authority culminated in the writings of the New Testament. Once Scripture was complete, authority resided not in successors to the apostles but in the word itself. When the Bereans examined Paul's teaching, they were commended for testing it against Scripture (Acts 17:11). Paul warned that even if an angel preached another gospel, it must be rejected (Gal 1:8). Such warnings make sense only if Scripture is the final authority, not an infallible human office.

Thus, while the Roman Catholic magisterium claims to safeguard and interpret truth through hierarchical succession, Scripture shows that the church's task is to preserve and proclaim the word already delivered "once for all to the saints" (Jude 3). Authority rests in Scripture, not in ecclesiastical hierarchy.

This principle extends beyond the New Testament. In Deut 13:1–3, Moses warns Israel that if a prophet performs signs yet leads people toward false gods, they must reject him. His validity is tested against what was already revealed, demonstrating that God's word is the measuring rod, even against seemingly authoritative voices. Jesus reinforces this principle in Matt 15:3–9 and Mark 7:6–13 when confronting the Pharisees. He acknowledges their position yet rebukes them for teaching traditions of men as though they were commands of God. This expectation that believers must discern between truth and error—even when taught by religious authorities—underscores the necessity of *sola scriptura*.

History is replete with examples where failure to test claims against reality led to catastrophe. In military intelligence, accepting false reports without cross-checking has cost armies battles and lives. Spiritually, accepting untested traditions as divine truth risks even greater losses—the souls of men and women.

A historical parallel can be drawn between the Pharisees and modern claims by Roman Catholic and Orthodox leaders regarding unwritten apostolic traditions. Just as Jesus expected his followers to distinguish between genuine commands from God and human traditions, Christians today must weigh doctrinal claims against Scripture itself. While Roman Catholicism locates authority in a centralized magisterium and Orthodoxy emphasizes conciliar authority expressed through Holy Tradition (the consensus of Scripture, the fathers, liturgy, and councils), both place unwritten traditions alongside Scripture.[15] Yet no human authority—whether hierarchical office or collective council—can override what is clearly revealed in God's word.

Understanding this doctrine is crucial because it ensures that faith remains anchored in God's revealed truth. Without it, believers risk elevating human traditions above Scripture, allowing external authorities to define truth rather than the word of God itself. *Sola scriptura* does not deny the role of pastors, church history, or tradition, but it insists that these must always be tested and corrected by Scripture, safeguarding the integrity of Christian belief. As seen throughout biblical history, God repeatedly calls his people to measure all teachings against his word—whether coming from prophets, religious leaders, or even supposed apostolic writings. The principle is unavoidable: what God has already spoken must take precedence over any new claims, ensuring that his truth remains the foundation of the Christian faith.

Because Scripture stands as the ultimate authority, how it is interpreted becomes a crucial issue. While *sola scriptura* affirms the necessity of measuring all teachings against God's word, improper interpretation can still distort its meaning. This is especially evident when individuals selectively interpret passages allegorically while insisting on a literal reading of others, subjecting the Bible to human whims rather than divine authority. Words have meaning. This approach risks distorting the intended message, leading to misinterpretation and undermining the credibility of Scripture as a cohesive and authoritative text.

Rome's claim to interpretive authority therefore becomes a practical example of this very inconsistency. While only a handful of verses—perhaps five or six—have ever been formally interpreted in an "infallible" sense, Roman Catholic teaching extends this authority more broadly, shaping doctrine through the interpretation of overarching theological themes.[16] A prime example is John 20:23: "If you forgive the sins of any, they are forgiven them; if you retain the sins of any, they are retained." Rome appeals to this text in support of their sacrament of confession, teaching that priests exercise judicial power to absolve sins. In this

---

15. Unlike the Roman Catholic model, Orthodoxy rejects the idea of a single infallible office. Instead, it understands the church's authority as dispersed through bishops acting in council, ideally reflecting the Spirit's guidance through consensus. The distinction is structural rather than functional, since in both cases the practical effect is to place tradition on the same level as Scripture—something the Reformers resisted because Scripture itself rejects placing tradition on equal footing.

16. Catholic Answers, "Magisterium"; Akin, "Limits of Scripture Interpretation."

view—formalized in the doctrine of absolution—the priest does not merely announce forgiveness but actively participates in granting it through Christ's authority.[17]

This interpretation is often reinforced by Rome's reading of Matt 16:19 and 18:18, where Jesus speaks of "binding and loosing." Catholic theology links these verses to the conferral of ecclesial authority, particularly through apostolic succession. The priesthood, in this framework, inherits the power to bind (retain) or loose (forgive) sins, functioning as a judicial office within the church. Yet this reading stretches the original context, which in its Jewish setting referred to permitting or forbidding actions—not mediating divine forgiveness. Scripture consistently emphasizes reconciliation with God through faith in Christ, not mediation through an earthly priesthood. As 1 John 1:9 declares, "If we confess our sins, He is faithful and just to forgive us our sins and to cleanse us from all unrighteousness." The New Testament portrays confession as directed toward God himself, not delegated to an institutional office. The authority to proclaim forgiveness belongs to the gospel itself, not to a clerical intermediary.

This misapplication of John 20:23 is just one example of how selective interpretation can create contradictions with the broader testimony of Scripture. And whenever Scripture is handled in a way that conflicts with its own teaching, the result is confusion and mistrust. Why should one trust any interpretation that undermines the very text it claims to explain? Various religious traditions have at times upheld interpretations that contradict their own sacred texts. This inconsistency is not unique to Roman Catholic doctrine. Similar contradictions arise in other religious traditions, further illustrating the risks of theological manipulation.

One example is found in Mormonism. Unlike the Bible, which is divinely inspired and carefully preserved, the Book of Mormon contains doctrinal shifts that contradict biblical truth. Regarded by members of the Church of Jesus Christ of Latter-day Saints as additional Scripture, the Book of Mormon lacks both the historical credibility and theological authority of the Bible, which remains the universally recognized foundation of Christian faith.

This becomes clear in the doctrinal tension between 2 Nephi 25:23—found in the Book of Mormon—and Eph 2:8–9. Second Nephi states, "For we labor diligently to write, to persuade our children, and

---

17. *CCC*, §§1461–63.

also our brethren, to believe in Christ, and to be reconciled to God; for we know that it is by grace that we are saved, *after all we can do.*" This verse implies that grace is applied only after human effort, introducing a works-based component to salvation. In contrast, Ephesians affirms the biblical doctrine of salvation by grace alone: "For by grace you have been saved through faith, and that not of yourselves; it is the gift of God, not of works, lest anyone should boast." Here, salvation is presented as entirely a gift—independent of human merit.

It is worth noting that this is not a new error. The Council of Nicaea in AD 325 confronted *Arianism*—an early heresy that denied the eternal deity of Christ by claiming he was a created being (briefly discussed in chapter 1).[18] In a similar way, Mormonism teaches that Jesus was conceived as the literal offspring of the Heavenly Father (whom LDS theology portrays as an exalted man who became God the Father) and Mary,[19] reducing him to a created figure rather than the eternal Son. Athanasius and other defenders of orthodoxy recognized that if Christ were less than fully God, his sacrifice could not provide true salvation. Thus, the Nicene Creed affirmed that Jesus Christ is "very God of very God, begotten, not made, being of one substance with the Father."[20] Mormonism repeats this same christological distortion and, by consequence, undermines the sufficiency of his saving work. The core theological missteps of Mormonism were answered by the church centuries before Mormonism ever existed. Truly, there is nothing new under the sun.

As noted earlier, the heart of the matter is grace—God's unearned gift—not human contribution. This truth is reinforced throughout Scripture: Rom 3:24, Rom 11:6, Gal 2:16, Titus 3:5, and John 1:12–13 (among others) all underscore that salvation comes solely through grace, apart from human effort. The contrast between these texts and Mormon teaching reveals a fundamental theological divergence—one rooted in the authoritative word of God and the other in later writings that lack divine inspiration and doctrinal consistency.

When religious institutions impose interpretations that diverge from the plain meaning of Scripture, it calls into question the reliability of their theological framework. If interpretation is not grounded in consistent hermeneutical principles, Scripture becomes vulnerable to

---

18. Kelly, *Early Christian Doctrines*, 223–25.

19. Smith, *Teachings of the Prophet*, 345; Church of Jesus Christ of Latter-day Saints, *Gospel Principles*, 9, 11.

20. "Nicene Creed" (325), in Leith, *Creeds of the Church*, 30.

manipulation, allowing theological positions to be shaped by tradition rather than textual integrity. In PSYOP language, this is the equivalent of "information operations"—using selective truth, omission, or reinterpretation to control perception. When applied to theology, the result is not just confusion but eternal misdirection.

A truly authoritative approach must respect the literary, historical, and theological context of each passage, ensuring that Scripture speaks for itself rather than being molded to fit institutional doctrines.

At the heart of this discussion lies the distinction between justification and sanctification. Justification is God's once-for-all declaration that sinners are made righteous in Christ through faith. It is not about living out our callings or doing good works but about Christ's finished work credited to us. Sanctification, by contrast, is the lifelong process by which believers, already justified, are transformed into Christ's likeness through the Spirit and enabled to live out holiness in their daily lives—including their unique callings within the body of Christ. Confusing these categories, even slightly, reshapes the gospel itself.

Why the Distinction Matters

To some, the debate over justification and sanctification may appear like theological hair-splitting. After all, Christ, grace, and good works are affirmed by all. In many ways, the fruit is visible in a more moral society—defending life, caring for the needy, pursuing integrity. Yet Scripture presses the question further: What difference does it make if the order is blurred?

In deception terms, this is the difference between a decoy and a target. If you confuse them in the fire-control sequence, you don't just miss—you create friendly fire. Likewise, when justification and sanctification are swapped, the church ends up "firing" at the wrong objective, mistaking the fruit for the root. This is why false gospels are so persuasive: they take something good—justice, creation care, family, health, discipline—and make it the root instead of the fruit. Each one provides its own "fall, redemption, and salvation" storyline, but all miss the true gospel. This confusion isn't limited to theological debate. It shows up in the instincts of ordinary people and public figures alike. President Donald Trump once quipped that if he could broker peace in Ukraine, "this will be one of the reasons [I get to heaven]."²¹ However lighthearted, the remark captures a universal instinct: justification by achievement. It assumes good works can tilt the scale toward salvation, when in reality any appeal to human merit displaces the sufficiency of Christ.

The difference is eternal. If justification rests in any measure on human effort, then the ground of salvation shifts from Christ's finished work to human contribution. Grace ceases to be grace (Rom 11:6). Paul's warning to the Galatians could not be clearer: to add anything to faith is to proclaim "another gospel" (Gal 1:6–9). The issue is not marginal; it strikes at the heart of the cross itself.

Satan's preferred PSYOP is subtle: he doesn't deny the cross; he dilutes it. He adds "just a little" human merit—enough to redirect trust from Christ to performance. A one-degree drift at the gun line (the point of aim) becomes a miss at the objective. That drift takes many forms today:

- The "woke gospel" reframes oppression as the fall and activism as salvation. Righteousness is measured not by faith but by protest, resistance, or advocacy. Its sacraments are activism, cancel culture, and "allyship." As Robin DiAngelo, known for her work on whiteness studies and critical discourse analysis and author of the bestselling book *White Fragility* on race and social justice, puts it, "The antidote to guilt is action"—not repentance, but perpetual works.²²

- The "environmental gospel" makes reconciliation not with God but with nature. Stewardship becomes salvation, and recycling or voting green becomes a sacrament of righteousness. Its prophets range from the UN (warning of a ten-year "point of no return" in 1989) to Greta Thunberg, who embodies a zeal that functions like religion. We are told we've sinned against "Mother Earth" and can atone only by recycling, carbon offsets, or lifestyle sacrifice.

- The "sexual gospel" declares that restraint is the problem and liberation through desire is the solution. Freedom is sought in breaking God's design, mistaking indulgence for redemption. Hugh Hefner's "Playboy Philosophy" championed this creed, arguing that true freedom required throwing off all sexual restraints.²³ The so-called "sexual revolution" of 1945 echoed the same lie: society's ills come

21. Jeyaretnam, "All the Times."
22. DiAngelo, *White Fragility*, 149.
23. Exemplified in Hefner's serialized essays in *Playboy*, from December 1962 to December 1965.

from repression, not sin. Eighty years later, broken homes, anxiety, and confusion about even what a man or woman is prove that this gospel enslaves rather than saves.

- The "grace-plus gospel" teaches that Christ's work was not enough—something must be added. Sometimes it is baptism, sacraments, or moral performance; sometimes it is social activism or humanitarian deeds. But Scripture is clear: salvation is "by grace you have been saved through faith ... not of works, lest anyone should boast" (Eph 2:8–9). Any system that requires human merit as a condition for acceptance before God contradicts the gospel of grace. Paul declared such mixtures "another gospel" (Gal 1:6–9). Grace plus anything is no gospel at all.

- The "prosperity gospel" likewise redefines Christ: he becomes a means to wealth, health, and success rather than the Savior from sin. Following him is sold as a pathway to comfort, not the cross. Many testimonies expose the hollowness: one youth pastor admitted, "I didn't become a Christian because I was a sinner in need of forgiveness; I became a Christian because I was hurting and told that Jesus would make me feel better."[24] That is no gospel at all, only a spiritualized self-help scheme.

- The "high-achievement parenting gospel" seeks justification in the success of children. Parents live vicariously through their children's grades, sports, or careers, measuring their own worth by their offspring's accomplishments. Club sports, SAT prep, piano lessons, and relentless tutoring often signal this shift. The temptation is not to bless children but to justify ourselves by their performance.

- The "political gospel" offers identity and hope through party or policy. Votes become badges of righteousness, and despair follows when power shifts hands. Tim Keller noted how extreme reactions to elections—despair, rage, even talk of leaving the country—reveal politics functioning as a god.[25] When political victory is the measure of salvation, hope crumbles whenever "our side" loses.

- The "fitness gospel" treats the body as the measure of worth. Health, diet, and discipline provide a sense of superiority, but age and sickness eventually expose its fragility. CrossFit has been called "the

---

24. Horton, *Christless Christianity*, 78.
25. Keller, *Counterfeit Gods*, 98.

new church" for many secular people: it is communal, ritualistic, and even evangelistic.[26] Yet as articles on health advocates show, the fittest still die young—marathoner Jim Fixx at fifty-two, juice-fasting guru Paavo Airola at sixty-four, and the author of *Younger Next Year* Henry Lodge at fifty-eight. Fitness cannot defeat death.

- The "legalism gospel" trusts in religious duty—church attendance, Bible reading, moral restraint—as if those acts themselves earn God's favor. It looks pious but replaces grace with pride. Like the older brother in the prodigal son parable, legalists boast, "I've never left; I've done my duty," yet miss the Father's heart of grace. Duty without delight leaves people just as lost as rebellion.

All of these confuse the fruit of sanctification with the root of justification. They cloak growth, discipline, or cultural concern in the clothing of salvation itself, and the result is ruin.

It also touches assurance. If good works are part of what secures our standing before God, then assurance can never be more than fragile, dependent on fluctuating performance. But if justification is God's declaration of righteousness through faith, then good works flow from that reality as its fruit, not its cause. The believer's confidence rests in Christ's completed work, freeing obedience to become a joyful response rather than an anxious striving. This explains why those who hope in politics despair when their candidate loses, why parents crumble when their children stumble, why the health-conscious fearfully chase longevity but cannot stop aging. False gospels collapse because they cannot give assurance. Only justification by faith produces unshakable confidence.

Assurance, then, functions like morale under fire: when your position rests on the finished work of a victorious King, your courage holds; when it rests on your last "performance," morale collapses with every setback. Every counterfeit gospel enslaves and disappoints both in this life and the next. The true gospel alone frees us from fear of death, gives us an identity rooted in Christ, and promises forgiveness and eternal life. Consider the story of Father Damien, who served faithfully among lepers in Molokai. For years the people respected him, but it was only when he himself contracted leprosy that they truly embraced his message. By sharing their suffering, he broke down barriers and won their hearts.[27] In a far greater way, Christ entered our condition—taking on flesh, sharing

26. Beck, "Church of CrossFit."
27. Englebert, *Hero of Molokai*, 112–14.

in weakness, and bearing our sin. His incarnation and suffering are the ground of our justification, not simply an inspiring example of sanctification. To confuse the two is to think our endurance or sacrifice could justify us, when only the Son's suffering secures our standing before God.

Finally, the distinction matters because of authority. If Scripture alone is God-breathed, then it alone defines salvation on his terms. To blur the line between grace and merit, however subtly, is to substitute human reasoning for divine revelation. The safeguard of *sola scriptura* ensures that the gospel remains what God has declared it to be—not what human systems reshape it to become. False gospels always elevate some other authority: ideology, activism, tradition, success, self-discipline, or cultural expectation. Each redefines salvation on human terms and supplants God's word with a man-made standard.

Think of *sola scriptura* as rules of engagement (ROE) from the Commander. Units may have techniques and Standard Operating Procedures (SOPs), but no field-expedient tradition can overrule the written ROE.

In the end, this is not about abstract categories but about fidelity to the message of Christ. As Jesus said, "Whoever is not with me is against me" (Matt 12:30). To preserve the line between justification and sanctification is to preserve the gospel itself. Roman Catholic apologists often raise Jas 2:24 as a counterpoint, claiming it undermines *sola fide* (faith alone): "You see then that a man is justified by works, and not by faith only." Yet James is not contradicting Paul; he is addressing a different issue entirely. He is not asking how a sinner is declared righteous before God but confronting a dead, fruitless "faith," not a rival gospel. Paul and James are answering different questions: Paul explains how someone is justified before God, while James shows how genuine faith is vindicated before people—demonstrated as real by its fruit. Both apostles agree: faith alone justifies, but the faith that saves is never alone—it inevitably produces works. This is the razor's edge between the true gospel and every counterfeit: justification first, sanctification second. To reverse them is to lose both.

And in spiritual warfare, preserving the gospel is the fortress wall—once it falls, the enemy pours in unchecked. Whether through cultural ideologies, different Jesuses (e.g., Mormonism, discussed prior), or Jesus-plus distortions, the tactic is always the same: confuse root and fruit, justification and sanctification. The only defense is to hold the line on *sola fide* and *sola scriptura*.

If Scripture alone guards the purity of the gospel, then confidence in Scripture itself becomes paramount. It is not only divinely inspired but also historically reliable. God has preserved his word, and time and again history confirms its truth. This assurance leads naturally to the question of preservation and historical confirmation.

PRESERVATION AND HISTORICAL CONFIRMATION

The essential truth remains: every word of Scripture is inspired by God and is without error. John Stott (1921–2011), a renowned British Anglican pastor, theologian, and leader in the global evangelical movement, profoundly captures this idea, stating, "The Bible is not man's word about God, but God's word about man."[28] Scripture is the trustworthy foundation for doctrine, correction, and instruction in righteousness, equipping believers to live in alignment with God's design. Historical confirmations of the Bible's accuracy, such as the discovery of the *Tel Dan Stele* in 1993—an ancient inscription from the ninth century BC that mentions the "House of David"—further silence skeptics by providing extra-biblical evidence of biblical figures like King David.[29]

From an intelligence standpoint, this is cross-verification—ARCINT (architectural intelligence, a tongue-in-cheek coined category describing the material and cultural "signatures" of faith in history, like artifacts, liturgy, and institutions) reinforcing what SCRIPTINT (scriptural intelligence, another illustrative coined category for the direct testimony of inspired Scripture) already reveals. These are not formal intelligence disciplines but analogies, borrowing the language of the intelligence community to help illustrate the point. SCRIPTINT functions like HUMINT (human intelligence)—direct reporting from the authoritative source—while ARCINT is closer to IMINT (imagery intelligence) or GEOINT (geospatial intelligence), the visible structures and patterns that corroborate what the text declares. These sources don't generate truth; they confirm it, much like how satellite imagery, intercepted signals, and human reports converge to verify a single target. Scripture remains the primary intelligence; tradition and historical artifacts serve as supporting sensors, strengthening confidence in what's already been identified.

28. Stott, *Understanding the Bible*, 14.
29. Shanks, *Mystery and Meaning*, 112.

While the Tel Dan Stele confirms the biblical existence of King David, another fascinating artifact found in Egypt may corroborate one of the most pivotal events in biblical history—the exodus. Again, the apologetic value here is not that "intel created the target," but that independent reporting aligns with what God has already revealed.

In a small, overlooked museum in Isma'ilya, northeast of Cairo, rests an artifact that may hold one of the most startling confirmations of the biblical exodus—the El Arish Stone. This massive slab of black granite, weighing two tons and spanning four feet in length, was unearthed in 1887 on a farm in El Arish. But instead of being preserved as a historical treasure, it was repurposed—lying on its side, serving as a simple water trough for cattle.[30]

That was until archaeologist Frances Llewellyn Griffith recognized its true significance.[31] The hieroglyphics carved into its surface told a story that defied expectations. By the writing, Griffith dated the stone to the Ptolemaic period, specifically the Thirtieth Dynasty (380–360 BC), when it was likely used as a shrine. But the events it recorded weren't contemporary—they seemed to describe something far older, reaching back twelve hundred years to around 1500 BC. And the most shocking part? It appeared to tell the story of the exodus—from Pharaoh's perspective.

Among the inscriptions is a unique hieroglyph: three waves and two knives. Egyptologist James Hoffmeier proposed that this symbol should be read plainly.[32] Taken literally, it translates as "the parting of the sea"—an undeniable parallel to the miraculous event recorded in Exod 14.

Due to its years exposed to the elements and used for livestock, some inscriptions have faded, but remarkably, seventy-four lines remain intact.[33] One passage appears to reference Moses, calling him the "Prince of the Desert," while his Israelite followers are labeled the "evil ones" or "evildoers"—an unmistakable echo of Pharaoh's contempt toward the departing Hebrews.[34]

Even more astonishing, the Egyptian text describes Pharaoh in pursuit of the Queen Mother, Tefnut, as she departs with the Israelites. This aligns with an ancient Jewish tradition recorded in the Talmud (b. Sotah 12a), which states that Pharaoh's daughter—the same woman who

---

30. Griffith, *Catalogue of the Egyptian Antiquities*, 17–22.
31. Hoffmeier, *Israel in Egypt*, 143–45.
32. Pinch, *Egyptian Myth*, 76–79.
33. Wilkinson, *Complete Gods and Goddesses*, 289–91.
34. See b. Sotah 12a.

raised Moses—chose to leave Egypt alongside the fleeing Israelites and ultimately married Caleb, son of Yefuneh.[35]

And it doesn't stop there. The stone also seems to reference the biblical plagues, including prolonged darkness and a violent tempest, reinforcing the catastrophic events that led to Egypt's downfall.[36] But perhaps the most striking confirmation comes from its mention of *Pekharti*—a location referenced right next to where the sea was parted.[37] This same place appears in Exod 14:2, 9, listed as *Pi-hahiroth*, where the Israelites camped just before witnessing one of the most defining miracles in history.

If all this weren't enough, the Torah—the first five books of the Bible, traditionally attributed to Moses and foundational to Jewish law and narrative—records one final connection to this extraordinary stone. In Gen 48:16, the dying patriarch Jacob blesses his son Joseph, praying that his descendants would "fishify"—a term he coined meaning "to increase in the land like fish."[38] The Hebrew word *idgu* appears nowhere else in Scripture—it was uniquely crafted for Joseph's blessing. Centuries later, when the Israelites prepared to leave Egypt, they carried Joseph's bones with them to the promised land (Exod 13:19).

Now, here's the shocker. The El Arish Stone describes the departure of the Israelites and states that when the "evildoers" fled Egypt, they took Dagai with them. *Dagai*—a word unmistakably close to the Hebrew term for fish—was the very nickname given to Joseph in the Torah.[39]

A forgotten stone, once used for feeding cattle, holds an Egyptian account that may confirm one of the most pivotal moments in biblical history. Coincidence? Or yet another hidden testament to God's providence?

Archaeology, then, serves as supporting fires—not the center of gravity. In military terms, supporting fires refer to indirect or auxiliary firepower (like artillery or air strikes) that assist the main force by shaping the battlefield, suppressing threats, or clearing obstacles. Likewise, archaeology supports the mission by confirming and illuminating Scripture, but it is not the driving force. The center is still the revealed word. External confirmation is helpful, but the mission orders come from Scripture itself.

---

35. Sarna, *Genesis*, 331.
36. Kitchen, *On the Reliability*, 412–14.
37. Hoffmeier, *Israel in Egypt*, 147.
38. Sarna, *Genesis*, 331.
39. Kitchen, *On the Reliability*, 412–14.

While archaeology provides tangible confirmations of biblical events, the most authoritative testimony comes directly from Jesus himself. Throughout his ministry, he affirmed not only the reliability of historical figures but also the divine truth preserved within Scripture.

And just as units authenticate messages with challenge-and-reply, believers authenticate all claims—ancient and modern—by Christ's voice in Scripture (John 10:27).

Archaeology and Jesus' Affirmation

The preservation of biblical truth extends far beyond archaeology—Jesus himself affirmed the historical accuracy of key figures and events recorded in Scripture. Throughout his ministry, he reinforced the reliability of the Old Testament, leaving no room for doubt regarding the reality of Adam, Noah, Abraham, and others. In intelligence terms, archaeology is corroboration, not command—and Jesus' own affirmations function as the primary source. Artifacts provide supporting fires; the Commander's word defines the mission.

During Jesus' ministry, he affirmed the historical reliability of many accounts:

Adam and Eve as the first two humans:

> And He answered and said to them, "Have you not read that He who made them at the beginning 'made them male and female,' and said, 'For this reason a man shall leave his father and mother and be joined to his wife, and the two shall become one flesh'?" (Matt 19:4–5)

Noah and the global flood:

> But as the days of Noah were, so also will the coming of the Son of Man be. For as in the days before the flood, they were eating and drinking, marrying and giving in marriage, until the day that Noah entered the ark. (Matt 24:37–38)

Abraham as a person who lived and who knew Christ as God the Son:

> Your father Abraham rejoiced to see My day, and he saw it and was glad. (John 8:56)

The righteous sacrifice of Abel:

> That on you may come all the righteous blood shed on the earth, from the blood of righteous Abel to the blood of Zechariah, son of Berechiah, whom you murdered between the temple and the altar. (Matt 23:35)

Moses and the burning bush:

> But concerning the dead, that they rise, have you not read in the book of Moses, in the burning bush passage, how God spoke to him, saying, "I am the God of Abraham, the God of Isaac, and the God of Jacob"? (Mark 12:26)

David's historical role as king and spiritual leader:

> Or have you not read what David did when he was hungry, he and those who were with him? (Matt 12:3)

Elijah's era of famine:

> But I tell you truly, many widows were in Israel in the days of Elijah, when the heaven was shut up three years and six months, and there was a great famine throughout all the land. (Luke 4:25)

Daniel's role as a prophet and his writings:

> Therefore when you see the "abomination of desolation," spoken of by Daniel the prophet . . . (Matt 24:15)

The sign of Jonah:

> For as Jonah was three days and three nights in the belly of the great fish, so will the Son of Man be three days and three nights in the heart of the earth. The men of Nineveh will rise up in the judgment with this generation and condemn it, because they repented at the preaching of Jonah; and indeed a greater than Jonah is here. (Matt 12:40–41)

Note the pattern: Jesus treats Scripture's people and events as historical and its claims as authoritative. In deception analysis, pattern recognition distinguishes signal from noise; here, the signal is that the Son of God validates the record as fact, not fable.

Additionally, by affirming miracles, Jesus reinforces their divine significance. Beyond validating biblical figures and supernatural events, his historical existence itself stands as one of the most well-attested occurrences in ancient historiography. Even the most skeptical historians acknowledge that Jesus of Nazareth lived, preached, and was crucified under Pontius Pilate. The notion that he was merely a myth—commonly known as the "Christ myth theory"—is overwhelmingly rejected among scholars.

Historical methodology, such as the criterion of multiple attestation, strengthens this conclusion. This criterion holds that an event or saying is more likely to be historically reliable if it is independently reported by multiple sources. In Jesus' case, his existence is confirmed through numerous independent accounts, including the Gospels; Tacitus, a Roman historian and senator whose *Annals* provide one of the earliest non-Christian references to Jesus and his execution under Pilate;[40] Josephus, a first-century Jewish historian whose *Antiquities of the Jews* offers additional testimony regarding Jesus, John the Baptist, and James, the brother of Jesus;[41] and the Babylonian Talmud, a foundational text of Jewish law and tradition compiled between the third and sixth centuries, which contains indirect references to Jesus within rabbinic discussions.[42]

Multiple attestation is the historian's version of multi-INT confirmation—Human Intelligence (HUMINT), Document Exploitation (DOCEX), and hostile-source acknowledgment all aligning on the same target. HUMINT refers to information gathered directly from people— eyewitnesses, informants, or participants—through interviews, debriefings, or interrogation. DOCEX involves the systematic extraction of data from written or digital records, such as ancient inscriptions, manuscripts, or official archives. Hostile-source acknowledgment occurs when even adversarial or skeptical voices inadvertently confirm key facts, lending unexpected credibility. Disinformation frays under cross-check; truth coheres.

Further evidence lies in the radical transformation of his disciples. Unlike other failed messianic movements—such as that of Simon bar Kokhba, a Jewish military leader who led a revolt against the Roman Empire in AD 132, claiming to be the Messiah, only for his movement to

---

40. Tacitus, *Annals* 15.44.
41. Josephus, *Antiquities* 18.3.3.
42. Ehrman, *Did Jesus Exist?*, 78.

collapse upon his execution AD in 135—Christianity flourished despite persecution, largely because his followers genuinely believed they had encountered the risen Christ.[43]

Early Christians willingly suffered persecution and even faced martyrdom, demonstrating an unwavering conviction that distinguished them from other movements. Their steadfast faith was grounded in a deep trust in the Gospel accounts; as Craig L. Blomberg, a New Testament scholar and Distinguished Professor Emeritus at Denver Seminary, explains, "The historical reliability of the Gospel accounts is consistent with what we expect from well-preserved ancient biographies."[44] Blomberg has extensively researched the historical trustworthiness of Scripture, particularly the Gospels, reinforcing the credibility of early Christian testimony.

In military terms, their behavior is an effects assessment: men do not charge machine-gun fire for a known lie. Willingness to suffer functions as a hard indicator that they believed the report.

This legacy of sacrificial faith continues today. Around the world, Christians still willingly endure persecution, imprisonment, and even death for their belief in the Gospel. Such resilience across centuries affirms not only the historical reliability of the biblical witness but also its transformative power—compelling believers to stand firm in the face of suffering, just as the earliest disciples did.

Satanic PSYOP aims to coerce recantation through fear; Spirit-born conviction resists coercion. Counter-PSYOP begins with truth lodged in the conscience.

Yet despite Christ's affirmation of biblical truth, modern liberal theology increasingly challenges the reality of miracles and the authority of Scripture. This skepticism is countered by the Bible's consistent presentation of historical and divine evidence. Doubt even extends to Jesus himself, as some critics argue that the Gospels offer a fragmented portrayal of his identity—depicting him at times as merely a prophet, and at other times as God incarnate. However, a closer examination of Jesus' own words reveals a consistent and deliberate claim to divinity, leaving no room for the notion that he was merely a wise teacher or moral messenger.[45]

---

43. Schiffman, *From Text to Tradition*, 230–35.
44. Blomberg, *Historical Reliability*, 112.
45. Meier, *Roots of the Problem*, 34.

Here's the deception frame: redefine terms, rebrand miracles as metaphors, and you've neutralized the target without firing a shot. Change the categories, and you change the conclusions.

For instance, when Jesus refers to himself as the Son of God, he does so in a way that equates him with God rather than differentiating himself. In John 10:33, Jewish leaders attempted to stone him, stating, "For a good work we do not stone You, but for blasphemy, and because You, being a Man, make Yourself God." His enemies understood his words perfectly—he was claiming equality with God. Furthermore, his favorite title for himself, "Son of Man," is not merely a reference to humanity, but rather a direct connection to Dan 7, where this divine figure is granted dominion, glory, and an everlasting kingdom.

Yet Jesus' words go even further, making explicit declarations that confirm his preexistence, his power over life, and his oneness with the Father. In John 17:5 (ESV), he prays, "And now, Father, glorify me in your own presence with the glory that I had with you before the world existed." This is no ordinary claim—Jesus is asserting that he shared divine glory with the Father before creation itself. This passage directly parallels Isa 42:8 (NIV), where God declares, "I am the LORD; that is my name! I will not yield my glory to another or my praise to idols." If Yahweh—the covenant name God reveals in the Old Testament, expressing his self-existence ('I AM WHO I AM')—does not share his glory with anyone, yet Jesus claims to have had it before the world existed, then Jesus must be coequal with the Father—eternally existent as God himself.

Even more striking is Jesus' role as the source of eternal life. He states in John 17:3 (ESV), "And this is eternal life: that they may know you, the only true God, and Jesus Christ, whom you have sent." Here, Jesus makes eternal life dependent not just on knowing the Father but also on knowing himself. This is a staggering claim—salvation itself hinges upon a personal relationship with Jesus. If he were merely a prophet or messenger, this statement would be blasphemous. But because he is Yahweh in human flesh, his words are a revelation of his divine authority.

This claim is further explained by the *hypostatic union*, the theological doctrine that Jesus is fully God and fully man, united in one person without division or mixture. While possessing the full attributes of deity—eternal existence, omniscience, and omnipotence—he also took on human nature, experiencing hunger, fatigue, suffering, and death. This doctrine clarifies how Jesus, while fully God, submits to the Father during his earthly ministry, not as one lacking authority but as one fulfilling his messianic mission. He does not speak as a mere servant but as the Son who possesses life within himself—a divine attribute belonging only to God. John 5:26 affirms, "For as the Father has life in Himself, so He has granted the Son also to have life in Himself." Jesus does not receive life from an external source—he is the source. Just as Yahweh alone sustains creation, Jesus possesses self-existent life, further proving his divinity.[46]

Yet perhaps the most direct affirmation of his identity as Yahweh comes from his own lips. In John 8:58, Jesus boldly declares, "Most assuredly, I say to you, before Abraham was, I AM." His audience immediately understood the gravity of his statement—they picked up stones to kill him, recognizing this as a direct reference to Exod 3:14, where God speaks to Moses from the burning bush. In that moment of divine revelation, God commissions Moses to lead his people out of Egypt and reveals his covenantal name: "I AM WHO I AM." This wasn't just an abstract title—it was a declaration of self-existent, eternal being. By invoking that same divine name, Jesus was clearly identifying himself with the God of Israel, claiming not just authority but eternal coexistence with the Father.

Jesus does not merely hint at his divine nature—he proclaims it with absolute clarity. Every claim he makes reinforces his identity as Yahweh in human flesh, fulfilling prophecy and offering eternal life. He does not describe himself as a messenger who carries God's words but as the very Word of God made flesh (John 1:1, 14). He does not speak of salvation as something provided through obedience to the law alone but as something found solely in him: "I am the way, and the truth, and the life. No one comes to the Father except through Me" (John 14:6). Jesus' words leave no ambiguity—he is Yahweh incarnate, eternal, self-existent, and the giver of life. His dual nature, fully divine and fully human, is the foundation of Christianity, and Scripture consistently upholds this truth. As Richard Bauckham explains, "Jesus' use of the title 'Son of Man' is a reference to His exaltation, not merely His humanity."[47]

Therefore, Jesus is not merely a prophet or wise teacher—he is Yahweh in human form, fulfilling prophecy and offering eternal life. Dismissing this is not neutral scholarship; it's a classic adversary technique: redefine the principal, then degrade the message.

---

46. Wellum, *God the Son Incarnate*, 173.

47. Bauckham, *Jesus and the Eyewitnesses*, 56. Bauckham's work on New Testament Christology highlights how the Gospel accounts reflect direct eyewitness testimony, reinforcing their credibility.

It is important to note that liberal theology often reinterprets or rejects traditional miracles, favoring metaphorical or ethical readings over supernatural claims. Theologians within this movement do not believe Jonah was actually swallowed by a fish for three days and survived, that Daniel survived the fiery furnace, that the burning bush was a real event, or that a global flood occurred—whereas Jesus did. Liberal theology, also known as liberal Christianity, is a movement that interprets Christian teachings by prioritizing modern knowledge, science, and ethics. It emphasizes reason and experience over doctrinal authority, viewing theology as an alternative to both atheistic rationalism and traditional interpretations of external authority. Liberal Christian teaching diverges significantly from traditional Christianity, as it places human reason above divine revelation, diminishing Christ's central authority. The objective of liberal theologians is to reconcile Christianity with secular science and contemporary thought, considering science to be all-knowing while viewing the Bible as a collection of myths and legends.

Strategically, this swaps the authority hierarchy: human reason becomes the "higher headquarters," Scripture the subordinate unit. But Jesus' own ROE places Scripture as the supreme directive.

While modern liberal theology challenges the authority and miraculous accounts of Scripture, the enduring testimony of the Bible and Christ himself reaffirms its truth and reliability. The miraculous events recorded in Scripture are not myths but divine acts that underscore God's power and faithfulness. Historical, theological, and divine evidence consistently uphold the Bible's authority, strengthening the foundation of Christian faith. Deception exploits ambiguity; Scripture's clarity closes those seams.

In essence, the Bible is historically trustworthy. Its accuracy and divine authorship are affirmed by Christ and have been consistently supported through centuries of archaeological discoveries and meticulous textual preservation.

Bottom line up front (BLUF): Jesus authenticates Scripture, and history keeps failing to debunk it. That's not coincidence; that's providence.

In addition to Jesus, there is a remarkable harmony of conviction among the more than forty authors of the Bible that the words they wrote were not their own but were given by God. This is what is meant by "inspiration"—the process by which God, through the Holy Spirit, guided these individuals to communicate his message while fully preserving their unique styles and personalities. For instance, 2 Sam 23:2 states,

"The Spirit of the LORD spoke by me, and His word was on my tongue." These authors consistently testified that they were not expressing their own ideas but delivering divine truth directly from God.[48]

Conversely, God did not inspire the Apocrypha—or the Pseudepigrapha, which are collections of writings falsely attributed to biblical or historical figures, such as 1 Enoch or Jubilees. For readers unfamiliar with the term, the Apocrypha (Greek for *apokryphos* meaning "hidden/obscure" or "concealed," originally referring to writings not publicly read) refers to books written during the intertestamental period—the roughly four hundred years between the end of Malachi (the final prophetic book of the Old Testament) and the beginning of the Gospel accounts in the New Testament. These books were included in the Septuagint (the ancient Greek translation of the Hebrew Bible made in the third century BC)[49] and in the Latin Vulgate (a fourth-century Latin translation prepared by Jerome at the request of Pope Damasus I, which became the standard Bible of the Western church),[50] but they were not part of the Hebrew Bible or the Protestant canon. These texts are considered deuterocanonical ("secondary canon") by the Roman Catholic Church but are viewed as noncanonical by Protestants. While not inspired Scripture, they provide valuable historical insight into Jewish thought, culture, and traditions during the intertestamental era. Additionally, the Apocrypha can be appreciated for its literary style, as it often reflects the language and themes of biblical writings, making it useful for understanding the linguistic and cultural backdrop of the Bible. For example, books like 1 Maccabees offer historical accounts of Jewish resistance against Hellenistic influence, while others, such as Ecclesiasticus (Sirach), contain moral teachings and wisdom literature.[51] The canon itself refers to the authoritative collection of books inspired by God and serving as the standard for faith and practice.

Although the Roman Catholic Church did not formally recognize the Apocrypha as Scripture until the Council of Trent (1545–1563), these texts had long circulated due to their inclusion in the Septuagint and the Vulgate. Jerome, the fourth-century translator of the Vulgate, explicitly

---

48. Geisler, *Christian Apologetics*, 51.

49. Salvesen and Law, *Oxford Handbook of the Septuagint*, 45–67. The LXX was produced for Greek-speaking Jews under Ptolemaic rule and was widely used in the early church, even shaping NT vocabulary.

50. Loewe, "Medieval History."

51. Geisler, *Christian Apologetics*, 51; Kelly, *Early Christian Doctrines*, 223–25.

distinguished these books from canonical Scripture, stating they were suitable for edification but not for establishing doctrine. Regarding Judith, Tobit, and Maccabees, Jerome wrote, "As, then, the Church reads Judith, Tobit, and the books of Maccabees, but does not admit them among the canonical Scriptures, so let it read these two volumes for the edification of the people, not to give authority to doctrines of the Church."[52]

This distinction raises a critical question: If these texts were truly authoritative, why did it take over fifteen hundred years for their canonization? It appears that Rome's decision was a direct response to Martin Luther and the Protestant Reformers, who rejected the Apocrypha and its teachings.

Even the Apocrypha itself suggests it is not Scripture. First Maccabees 9:27 states, "So there was great distress in Israel, the worst since the time when prophets ceased to appear among them."[53] This implies that prophetic revelation had ended, reinforcing the Jewish belief that the Holy Spirit departed after the ministries of Haggai, Zechariah, and Malachi—around 400 BC. Accordingly, the Apocryphal texts, written after this period, were never considered divinely inspired.

Moreover, these books contain theological and historical errors. For example:

- Wisdom of Solomon 11:17 suggests creation from preexisting matter: "Your all-powerful hand, which created the world out of formless matter." This contradicts the biblical doctrine of creation *ex nihilo* (out of nothing).
- Judith 1:5 incorrectly identifies Nebuchadnezzar as king of Assyria, when he was actually king of Babylon.

The New Testament further underscores the Apocrypha's lack of authority. Though it contains hundreds of Old Testament quotations—some 295 by one count—it never cites the Apocrypha as Scripture.[54] Jesus and the apostles consistently quote from the Hebrew canon, not the intertestamental additions.

---

52. Jerome, *Preface to Proverbs* (NPNF[2] 6:492).

53. Lumpkin, *Lost and Rejected Scriptures*, 717.

54. Willmington, "Old Testament Passages." The New Testament never cites the Apocrypha with a formula of authority ("It is written," "the Scripture says"), despite quoting the Old Testament nearly 300 times. While it occasionally echoes Apocryphal themes, it never treats these books as canonical.

Also, Jews have never recognized the Apocrypha as canonical Scripture. The Talmud, a central text of Rabbinic Judaism, is a compilation of Jewish civil and ceremonial law, as well as legend, comprising the Mishnah (an authoritative collection of oral Jewish law and tradition) and the Gemara (commentary on the Mishnah). According to the Babylonian Talmud, after the prophets Haggai, Zechariah, and Malachi perished, the Holy Spirit left Israel.[55] Malachi, the last book of the Old Testament, was written before the close of the prophetic era. After his death, Jews believed prophetic revelation had ceased. Thus, the Apocryphal texts, which were composed after Malachi, are not inspired by the Holy Spirit.

Roman Catholic apologists sometimes argue that the Reformers erred in adopting the Jewish canon for the Old Testament. They claim that the Jewish list of books was finalized only after the rise of Christianity, particularly after AD 70 (the destruction of the temple in Jerusalem), as a reaction to the church's growth. According to this view, Judaism became increasingly conservative after the destruction of the temple and deliberately restricted its canon in response to Christian claims. Does this make sense?

This narrative does not withstand closer examination. By the time of Jesus and the apostles, the Hebrew Scriptures were already well-defined. Christ himself spoke of "the Law, the Prophets, and the Psalms" (Luke 24:44), reflecting the tripartite division of the Hebrew Bible that Jews had recognized for centuries. The New Testament writers appeal consistently to this established canon, yet never once do they cite the Apocrypha as inspired authority—even though those books were readily available in the Greek Septuagint.

The oft-mentioned Council of Jamnia (a series of Jewish rabbinic discussions—not a formal council—estimated to have occurred around AD 90) did not establish a new canon but rather reaffirmed the books already received by the Jewish community. The discussions among rabbis show that the boundaries of the canon were already recognized; what remained was clarifying the status of a few books, not inventing Scripture. Far from being a reaction to Christianity, this was simply Judaism continuing to recognize what had long been understood as the inspired word of God.

By contrast, as previously stated the Roman Catholic Church did not officially declare the Apocrypha canonical until the Council of Trent

---

55. Babylonian Talmud, Yoma 9b:16. Of note, the Talmud is authoritative in Judaism but is not considered Scripture.

(1545–1563)—over fifteen centuries after Christ. If these books were truly inspired, such late recognition makes little sense. The Reformers were not subtracting from the Bible but returning to the Scriptures that Jesus and his apostles affirmed—the Hebrew canon recognized by God's covenant people.

In other words, the Protestant appeal to the Hebrew canon is not ironic, as critics suggest—it is faithful. It stands with Christ and the apostles, who affirmed the authority of the Law, the Prophets, and the Writings, rather than with a later church decision that expanded the canon beyond what God had revealed.

Thus, the Bible was penned by men but authored by God. In fact, writers in the Old Testament refer to their writings as the "words of God" over thirty-eight hundred times. New Testament writers quote the Old Testament as the word of God around 300 times and make reference to Old Testament passages about a thousand times. So, New Testament writers affirm the authority and divine inspiration and authorship of the Old Testament. As for the New Testament, the testimony of the writers about the New Testament is clear. Galatians 1:11–12 says, "But I make known to you, brethren, that the gospel which was preached by me is not according to man. For I neither received it from man, nor was I taught it, but it came through the revelation of Jesus Christ." In 1 Tim 5:18, Paul makes two references and calls them both "Scripture." One is from Deut 25:4, and the other is from Luke 10:7. So, Luke's writing is "Scripture" just as is the Old Testament. In 2 Pet 3:15–16, Peter calls Paul's writing "Scripture." In Jude 17 and 18, Jude refers to the Scripture and then quotes Peter, from 2 Peter. John writes the book of Revelation and repeatedly, in chapters 2 and 3, says, "The Spirit has said this to the churches." And so it goes. One can easily trace the reality that the Bible writers knew full well they were writing the word of God.

Not only did the biblical authors understand they were writing the word of God, but this recognition extended beyond them to the early church. While Scripture's divine inspiration originates from God himself, early Christian leaders affirmed its authority as well.

Church fathers such as Clement of Rome (c. AD 96), one of the earliest bishops of Rome, wrote extensively to encourage unity and doctrinal faithfulness. In his first epistle to the Corinthians—not to be confused with Paul's canonical 1 Corinthians—he referenced apostolic writings alongside the Old Testament. Clement's letter was publicly read in many churches and treated with near-canonical reverence, though it

Unveiling Deception

was never included in the New Testament canon. Ignatius of Antioch (c. AD 108), a bishop and martyr, emphasized doctrinal purity and church unity, frequently citing apostolic teachings and warning against heresies that contradicted them. Polycarp of Smyrna (c. AD 120), a disciple of the apostle John, quoted extensively from New Testament writings in his letter to the Philippians—citing or alluding to at least seventeen of the twenty-seven books.

Irenaeus (c. AD 180), bishop of Lyons, played a crucial role in defending Christian doctrine against heresies and explicitly affirmed the divine origin of the four Gospels, arguing that their number was divinely ordained and symbolically rooted in Scripture.[56] Origen (c. AD 250), a prolific theologian and biblical scholar, used nearly all of the books that now constitute the New Testament, though some (like Hebrews and Revelation) were still disputed in his time.[57] Finally, Athanasius of Alexandria (c. AD 367) provided the earliest known complete list of the twenty-seven New Testament books in his thirty-ninth Festal Letter, formally recognizing the canon that is accepted today.[58]

While their affirmations support the integrity of the New Testament, the authority of Scripture does not stem from human recognition but from God himself. The early church did not grant divine inspiration to these writings—it merely acknowledged the inspiration already present from the moment the apostles penned them.

To summarize, the Bible stands apart as the complete and inspired word of God, faithfully preserved through the ages. Martin Luther (1483–1546), a German theologian and the central figure of the Protestant Reformation, challenged the authority of the Roman Catholic

---

56. Irenaeus, *Against Heresies* 3.11.8–9.

57. These disputes did not arise because the church was inventing Scripture but because certain books faced questions of authorship or usage: Hebrews, for example, was debated due to its anonymous style, yet it was preserved because of its deep apostolic theology and widespread use in worship; Revelation was sometimes resisted because of its symbolic content and association with fringe sects, but it was retained for its apostolic origin through John and its consistent testimony to Christ; and 2 Peter was accepted later because of stylistic differences from 1 Peter, though its teaching clearly aligned with apostolic doctrine. Importantly, these debates were not signs of weakness but of careful discernment, and they never shook the foundation of Scripture's authority—rather, they confirmed that what the church recognized was truly inspired by God.

58. Metzger, *Canon of the New Testament*, 55–75; Baker, *New Testament Canon*, 14, 15. I cite these Fathers for their historical testimony regarding the canon, not as doctrinal authorities. The early Fathers, though influential, were not infallible and sometimes advanced positions I would not affirm.

Church by emphasizing *sola scriptura*. His teachings sparked a seismic shift in Christianity, leading to the formation of Protestantism.

Yet it is important to recognize that Luther was not without his flaws, nor do Protestants exalt him as an untouchable figure. He was a fallible man who, despite his shortcomings, became a catalyst for change. More importantly, Luther did not invent reform out of thin air. The Reformer inherited a long trajectory of dissent that preceded him by centuries.

For instance, John Wycliffe in England (c. 1320–1384) had denounced papal authority, translated Scripture into the vernacular, and insisted that the Bible, not the church, was the supreme authority for faith. Though he died of natural causes, the Council of Constance (1415) condemned his teachings, and in 1428 his remains were exhumed, burned, and scattered—an attempt to erase his influence.[59] Jan Hus of Bohemia (c. 1369–1415), influenced by Wycliffe, preached against clerical corruption and indulgences—eventually being condemned and burned at the stake for refusing to recant.[60] In Italy, Girolamo Savonarola (1452–1498) railed against the moral decay of the papacy, calling for repentance and renewal.[61]

What Luther did in 1517 was not the creation of protest but its culmination. He gathered these scattered streams of dissent, codified them, and nailed them to the church door in his *Ninety-Five Theses*. By doing so, he gave unified voice to concerns that had been smoldering for centuries, igniting the flame of the Reformation.

Roman Catholic apologists charge that Protestantism began in the 1500s, while Catholicism alone traces to Peter. Yet the Reformers saw themselves as recovering apostolic Christianity, not inventing a new faith. Long before Luther, men like Wycliffe, Hus, and Savonarola pointed back to Scripture—showing that Protestantism is a rediscovery, not an innovation. Luther aptly stated, "The authority of Scripture is greater than the comprehension of the whole of man's reason."[62]

Scripture's authority is unparalleled, allowing for neither additions nor subtractions—a conviction rooted in passages like Rev 22:18–19 and Deut 4:2. Roman Catholics often assert that the early church was

---

59. Wycliffe, *On the Truth*, 45.
60. Fudge, *Jan Hus*, 132.
61. Martines, *Fire in the City*, 88.
62. Brecht, *Martin Luther*, 112–30. As a note of clarification, in addition to the aforementioned reformers (among many others, less known), numerous social, political, and theological factors fueled the Reformation, and widespread dissatisfaction with corruption in the Roman Catholic Church led many followers to embrace change.

uniformly Roman Catholic. But history reveals diversity: Ignatius emphasized bishops; Irenaeus, apostolic preaching; Augustine, grace; Origen, speculation. The fathers were not proto-Catholics awaiting Rome's system but fallible men who themselves appealed to Scripture as the ultimate standard.

This enduring authority is not merely a relic of history but a reality that continues to transform lives today. Consider the story of Rosaria Butterfield, a former tenured English professor and LGBTQ+ activist at Syracuse University, who openly opposed Christianity. As a self-proclaimed atheist, she viewed Christian teachings with skepticism, yet through a thoughtful correspondence with a local pastor and years of studying the Bible, she experienced a profound transformation. Hebrews 4:12 explains, "For the word of God is living and powerful, and sharper than any two-edged sword." For Butterfield, this verse became her reality, as God's word dismantled her preconceived notions and led her to embrace a new identity in Christ. She later documented this journey in her memoir, *The Secret Thoughts of an Unlikely Convert*, highlighting how Scripture challenged her deepest convictions and reshaped her understanding of faith and truth.

Her testimony demonstrates how the Bible speaks into the deepest corners of the human heart, reshaping lives regardless of background or beliefs. Just as Butterfield's life was transformed by Scripture, the reliability of the Bible's preservation is further underscored by monumental historical discoveries.[63] One such example is the Codex Sinaiticus, a fourth-century manuscript containing nearly the entire Bible in Greek. Discovered in 1844 at St. Catherine's Monastery in Sinai by scholar Constantin von Tischendorf, it includes both the Old and New Testaments. Written in uncial script (large, rounded, all-capital Greek letters) on vellum (high-quality calfskin parchment) and comprising over 730 large-format leaves (individual sheets, each with two pages), the codex is one of the earliest and most complete biblical manuscripts ever found.[64]

Its close alignment with later manuscripts—such as the Masoretic Text and Byzantine tradition—confirms that Scripture was transmitted with extraordinary care across centuries. Marginal notes and corrections added by later scribes reflect a deep reverence for the text and a commitment to preserving its integrity, not altering its message.[65] The Codex

---

63. Butterfield, *Secret Thoughts*.
64. Nongbri, "Date of Codex Sinaiticus," 520.
65. Barrick, "Ancient Manuscripts," 27.

Sinaiticus stands as a testament to God's providential preservation of his word, reinforcing the conviction that the Bible we hold today faithfully reflects the original writings. In the end, that's the decisive counter-PSYOP: not louder spin but verified truth—Scripture authenticated by the Savior, conserved in history, and confirmed in changed lives.

THE TRANSFORMATIVE POWER OF SCRIPTURE

For centuries, the Bible has been more than a book—it has been a lifeline. Its words don't simply exist on the page; they breathe hope into the weary, strength into the struggling, and comfort into the brokenhearted. Consider the single mother clinging to Prov 31, a chapter that highlights the virtues of a godly woman—her strength, wisdom, and faithfulness—as she faces another day. The recovering addict finds new purpose in 2 Cor 5:17—"Therefore, if anyone is in Christ, he is a new creation"—and the grieving spouse reads Ps 34:18—"The LORD is near to those who have a broken heart"—and feels an unexplainable peace.

Transformation is where truth proves itself operational. In information operations terms, Scripture doesn't just inform the target audience; it produces effects on target—changing behavior, allegiance, and hope.

These aren't just verses; they are divine whispers, meeting people precisely where they are. Every changed life becomes a living proof that the Bible carries divine authority, not because of external arguments but because of its inner power to transform. This reality echoes the assertion of Charles Hodge (1797–1878), a Reformed Presbyterian theologian and principal of Princeton Theological Seminary: "The best evidence of the Bible's being the Word of God is to be found between its covers. It proves itself."[66]

The gospel's "self-authentication" functions like an internal checksum—a built-in test that verifies a message's integrity—truth that validates itself in the conscience (Rom 2:15) and in lived outcomes (Matt 7:24–25). This inner witness prepares us to trust the external evidences that further confirm Scripture's authority.

Christians can trust the Bible because it reveals everything God wants us to understand about our spiritual lives. If something is not revealed in his word, it remains a mystery known only to him—or is not essential to our growth at this time. As Deut 29:29 declares, "The secret

---

66. Hodge, *Way of Life*, 300.

things belong to the LORD our God, but the things revealed belong to us and to our children forever." This verse reminds us that while God's wisdom is infinite, he has graciously unveiled what we need for faith and life.

Counter-deception starts with scope control: cling to what God has revealed, refuse speculation drift.

His eternity is proclaimed in Ps 90:2:

> Before the mountains were brought forth,
> Or ever You had formed the earth and the world,
> Even from everlasting to everlasting, You are God.

His omniscience is revealed in Prov 15:3:

> The eyes of the LORD *are* in every place,
> Keeping watch on the evil and the good.

And his knowledge of the future is demonstrated in Jer 29:11:

> For I know the thoughts that I think toward you, says the LORD, thoughts of peace and not of evil, to give you a future and a hope.

These attributes underwrite Scripture's authority: an eternal, omniscient Author speaks, so the product carries unmatched reliability.

Even the most brilliant minds have wrestled with the nature of truth and divine revelation. In September 1931, C. S. Lewis took a moonlit walk along Addison's Walk at Magdalen College, Oxford, with J. R. R. Tolkien and Hugo Dyson. At the time, Lewis was a theist but not yet a Christian, and he expressed skepticism about the Gospels, viewing them as mythological. "Lies breathed through silver,"[67] he called them: beautiful, but ultimately false.

Tolkien and Dyson challenged this view. They argued that myths and fairy tales from diverse cultures often share a common narrative structure—creation, fall, redemption, and restoration—because they reflect deep truths embedded in the human experience. These stories resonate not because they are fabricated but because they echo a reality greater than ourselves. Tolkien proposed that Christianity is the "true myth"—a myth that entered history and became fact. Unlike the imaginative tales of other cultures, the gospel is the fulfillment of every longing

---

67. Lewis, *They Stand Together*, 425.

those stories hint at: the incarnation of God, the death that conquers death, and the resurrection that restores all things.[68]

Lewis was deeply moved. Within days, he wrote to a friend that he had come to believe in Christ, describing it as being "carried on the tide" of truth.[69] That walk became a turning point in his life—a moment when myth and reason converged, and the story of Christ emerged not as fiction but as the ultimate reality.

Tolkien would later expand this idea in his essay *On Fairy-Stories*, explaining that fairy tales resonate because they reflect the ultimate story written by the Author of life. Christianity, he argued, is the eucatastrophe—the "good catastrophe"—of human history: the sudden and joyous turn that brings redemption out of despair.[70]

The Bible is not merely a beautiful story—it is the true story of God's pursuit of humanity. It is the myth become fact, the Word made flesh, the divine whisper that transforms lives.

Apologetically, this bridges imagination to incarnation: Scripture answers the heart's archetypes with historical reality.

Human understanding is limited, bound by time and experience, while God's knowledge is infinite and eternal. We cannot fully grasp his plans or comprehend all that he knows. Yet he does not leave us in ignorance. As the Creator and Sustainer of all things (Col 1:16–17), God has graciously unveiled truths that guide us in faith and life—truths revealed through "the words of this law" (Deut 29:29).[71] The more we immerse ourselves in Scripture, the more we grasp what truly matters.

Immersion is the antidote to narrative capture. Saturate in Scripture, and counterfeit scripts lose their stickiness.

This is not only an intellectual truth; it is also an existential one. The same word that persuaded Lewis of the gospel's reality has transformed countless ordinary lives. One of the clearest examples of this transformative power is the story of Nicky Cruz, a former gang leader in New York City. Born into a family steeped in occult practices, Cruz grew up with a hardened heart, trapped in a life of crime as the leader of the notorious Mau Maus, a violent New York street gang of the 1950s. His path seemed destined for destruction—until he encountered evangelist David Wilkerson, who courageously proclaimed the message of the Gospel. Through

---

68. Tolkien, *Letters*, 100–101 (letter 89).
69. Lewis, *They Stand Together*, 426.
70. Kohm, "What the Bird Said."
71. MacArthur and Mayhue, *Biblical Doctrine*, 193.

the power of God's word, Cruz's life was radically changed, becoming a testimony to redemption and grace. Lewis's journey shows how the gospel satisfies the mind; Cruz's story shows how it transforms the heart.

Romans 5:8—"But God demonstrates His own love toward us, in that while we were still sinners, Christ died for us"—pierced through his defenses and ignited a radical transformation. Leaving behind a life of violence and crime, Cruz embraced faith in God and became a devoted Christian and global evangelist. His testimony, detailed in his book *Run Baby Run*, serves as a powerful illustration of how Scripture can bring hope and redemption to even the most broken lives.

Nicky Cruz's journey exemplifies the life-changing power of trusting God's word. His story stands as a reminder that through the gospel, anyone can find the grace and purpose they need to navigate all that truly matters in life.[72]

That is effect on target—phase line advanced: the word moved a life from bondage to mission.

Jesus says, "Sanctify them by Your truth. Your word is truth" (John 17:17). Scripture declares that only God's true word can sanctify—setting believers apart as useful and pleasing to him. A genuine walk with God begins with a firm conviction of the Bible's truthfulness: "So then faith comes by hearing, and hearing by the word of God" (Rom 10:17).[73] God's word is unwavering in its truth; it speaks with divine authority, meaning exactly what it proclaims.

Sanctification here is not sentiment; it's reformation of loves, loyalties, and habits under revealed truth.

Voddie Baucham (1969-2025), an American pastor, author, and educator renowned for his Reformed theology and biblical apologetics, powerfully affirms the Bible's reliability. He describes Scripture as "a reliable collection of historical documents written down by eyewitnesses during the lifetime of other eyewitnesses. They report [of] supernatural events that took place in fulfillment of specific prophecies and claimed that their writings are Divine rather than human in origin."[74]

This assertion aligns with the testimony of Peter, who emphasizes the firsthand nature of the apostolic witness in 2 Pet 1:16–21:

---

72. Cruz, *Run Baby Run*, 45.
73. Drawn from Barnett, "Sober Minded."
74. Baucham, "Why I Believe the Bible," 7:55.

> For we did not follow cunningly devised fables when we made known to you the power and coming of our Lord Jesus Christ, but were eyewitnesses of His majesty. For He received from God the Father honor and glory when such a voice came to Him from the Excellent Glory: "This is My beloved Son, in whom I am well pleased." And we heard this voice which came from heaven when we were with Him on the holy mountain. And so we have the prophetic word confirmed, which you do well to heed as a light that shines in a dark place, until the day dawns and the morning star rises in your hearts; knowing this first, that no prophecy of Scripture is of any private interpretation, for prophecy never came by the will of man, but holy men of God spoke as they were moved by the Holy Spirit.

John, an eyewitness to Christ's ministry, declares with certainty the reality of the Word of life in 1 John 1:1–3:

> That which was from the beginning, which we have heard, which we have seen with our eyes, which we have looked upon, and our hands have handled, concerning the Word of life—the life was manifested, and we have seen, and bear witness, and declare to you that eternal life which was with the Father and was manifested to us—that which we have seen and heard we declare to you.

Eyewitness, prophecy, fulfillment—three lines of effort converging on one truth claim.

The Bible's remarkable unity offers compelling evidence of its divine origin. Written by more than forty authors—most of whom never met—across three continents, over approximately fifteen hundred years, it presents one integrated message. Despite the diversity of backgrounds, languages, and literary styles, a seamless theological pattern emerges across its pages, pointing to a singular divine Author. From Genesis to Revelation, the Bible consistently reveals one overarching theme: God's redemptive plan for humanity through Jesus Christ. It conveys a unified message, a coherent system of doctrine, and a singular path of salvation—testifying to its supernatural design and divine inspiration.

Only the one, true, and holy God could have given us such a flawless Bible with such an unparalleled message—his astounding love for his creation. Throughout history, various texts have sought to echo the Bible's authority—none more prominently than the Book of Mormon.

Unity across centuries is an anti-forgery marker, but counterfeits struggle to sustain coherence across time, authors, and cultures.

Despite living in the Victorian era (1830–1900), Joseph Smith (1805–1844), founder of Mormonism and the Latter-day Saint movement, deliberately styled the Book of Mormon (1830) in Jacobean English (1603–1625)—the same language used in the King James Version of the Bible (1611)—rather than the vernacular of his time.[75] This linguistic choice was intentional, mimicking the revered biblical style to lend his work an air of authenticity. Smith claimed to have experienced visions, including one in which God the Father and Jesus Christ appeared to him, directing him to restore true Christianity, which he said had become corrupted. He also reported that an angel named Moroni guided him to golden plates buried in the ground, which he translated into what became the Book of Mormon.[76]

Presented as a record of ancient American civilizations and their interactions with God, the Book of Mormon has no independent historical or archaeological confirmation. Despite extensive research, no verifiable evidence supports its civilizations, locations, or events, and non–Latter-day Saint scholars widely reject its historical claims.[77] Although many theories exist regarding Smith's linguistic choices, it is most likely that he adopted this antiquated form to enhance perceived authenticity. His contemporaries, steeped in the King James Bible, were more likely to accept a scripture written in that style as genuine. Thus, Smith intentionally modeled the Book of Mormon's language after the King James Bible, reinforcing its illusion of divine legitimacy.[78]

Style mirroring is a classic deception technique: borrow the cadence of authority to smuggle in alien content.

Just as the Book of Mormon falters under historical scrutiny, so too the Qur'an—though claiming final revelation—reveals deep textual and theological fault lines. It likewise claims divine origin and continuity with

---

75. Brodie, *No Man Knows My History*, 112–35.

76. Yet Scripture itself anticipates and refutes such claims: "But even if we, or an angel from heaven, preach any other gospel to you than what we have preached to you, let him be accursed" (Gal 1:8). Movements claiming to "restore" a supposedly corrupted Christianity are a common mark of false religions; this does not include Christian reform movements such as the Stone-Campbell Restoration Movement, which sought to restore biblical unity and New Testament practices within orthodox Christianity—not to introduce new revelation, deny essential doctrines, or establish a separate religion.

77. Fudge, *Jan Hus*, 132; Ehrman, *Did Jesus Exist?*, 78.

78. Abanes, *One Nation Under Gods*, 112–35.

earlier revelation, yet its historical and theological foundations invite equally serious examination. Islam's central religious text, the Qur'an, affirms the Torah and the gospel as revelations from God (Ali 'Imran 3:3, Al-Ma'idah 5:46) and presents itself as the final and complete message. Islam was founded by Muhammad (c. AD 570–632), who was born in Mecca and later migrated to Medina—two cities that remain the holiest sites in Islam. Mecca is revered as the birthplace of Islam and home to the Kaaba, the sacred shrine toward which Muslims pray. Medina is where Muhammad established the first Islamic community and is buried.

According to Islamic tradition, the Qur'an was revealed to Muhammad over a twenty-two-year period through the angel Gabriel, beginning in AD 610. After Muhammad's death, his followers compiled the Qur'an into a single volume, reportedly under the direction of Caliph Uthman (c. 644–656). However, unlike the Bible, the Qur'an's manuscript history poses significant challenges. The earliest surviving qur'anic manuscripts—such as the Samarkand and Topkapi codices—date from the late eighth century. That is more than a century after Muhammad's death. These manuscripts are written in Kufic script, which was not used in Mecca or Medina during his lifetime. And to this day, no archaeological evidence confirms the existence of the original codices allegedly compiled under Uthman.[79]

In contrast, the Bible is supported by thousands of manuscripts, some dating centuries before Muhammad's time, including the Dead Sea Scrolls and early Greek papyri. These historical gaps in qur'anic transmission raise questions about its textual preservation and contrast sharply with the Bible's well-documented manuscript lineage.[80]

Another striking contrast lies not only in manuscript history but in message. The Qur'an proclaims in Surah Al-Hadid 57:3 that Allah is "the First and the Last."[81] Yet Rev 1:17–18 records Jesus declaring the very same title: "Do not be afraid. I am the First and the Last. I was dead, and now I am alive forevermore, holding the keys of death and Hades."

This creates an unavoidable dilemma for Muslims. If "the First and the Last" is a name for Allah alone, then why does Jesus claim it for himself? Worse yet, he adds, "I was dead and now live forevermore." When did Allah ever die? The Qur'an denies Jesus' death, but history and Scripture testify to it. Thus either

79. Déroche, *Qur'an Manuscripts*, 45–52.
80. Wallace, *Revisiting the Corruption*, 25–27; Déroche, *Abbasid Tradition*, 15–22.
81. Quotations from the Qur'an are from the Abdel Haleem translation.

1. Jesus blasphemed by taking Allah's title (which would disqualify him from being a true prophet, as Islam claims), or
2. Jesus spoke the truth—that he is God Almighty, one with the Father and the Spirit.

This is not to disparage Muslims, many of whom sincerely seek God, but to expose the deception that obscures Christ's true identity. Either way, the Qur'an's teaching collapses: if Jesus is God, the Qur'an is wrong for denying his deity; if he is not, the Qur'an is still wrong for affirming him as a true prophet since a true prophet cannot commit blasphemy.

Moreover, the Qur'an's ethical content presents further contradictions. While many Muslims assert that Islam is a religion of peace, a literal reading of certain verses reveals troubling commands. Surah Al-Anfal 8:12 states, "I will cast terror into the hearts of those who disbelieve. Therefore, strike off their heads and strike off every fingertip of them," and Surah At-Tawbah 9:5 commands, "Then, when the sacred months have passed, kill the polytheists wherever you find them." Though some argue these verses are context-specific to early Islamic warfare, the doctrine of abrogation (*naskh*) often elevates these later militant verses above earlier peaceful ones (e.g., Surah Al-Baqarah 2:256: "There is no compulsion in religion"). This creates a theological inconsistency: if violent verses override peaceful ones, then literal adherence to the Qur'an entails accepting and potentially enacting violence. If a Muslim rejects these verses or interprets them metaphorically, they are not following the Qur'an to the letter but engaging in selective theology—contradicting Surah Al-Baqarah 2:85: "Do you believe in part of the Scripture and reject the rest?"

Muslims often respond by claiming, "Your Bible has been corrupted." Yet this objection collapses as well because the Qur'an itself affirms the Torah and the gospel as God's uncorrupted word (Al-Ma'ida 5:47, Yunus 10:94). To deny the Bible's reliability is to deny the Qur'an's own testimony.

The Bible reveals Jesus not as a mere messenger but as the eternal God who died and rose again—the "First and the Last" who alone holds the keys of death and Hades. Unlike the Qur'an, which creates contradictions it cannot resolve, Scripture consistently testifies to the eternal Christ whose death and resurrection bring life, truth, and transformation.

Strategic takeaway: competing revelations cannot both be final when they contradict at first principles. Scripture's Christology holds its line under textual, historical, and theological scrutiny.

GOD'S COVENANT PROMISES AND ENDURING WORD

An example of the unity of Scripture is found in God's covenants, which emphasize the consistent and unchanging nature of God's relationship with humanity throughout the Bible. Wayne Grudem provides a helpful definition of a covenant. He describes it as "an unchangeable, divinely imposed legal agreement between God and man that stipulates the conditions of their relationship."[82] These covenants, spanning from Abraham to Christ, reveal God's unwavering commitment to his people and the cohesive truth of his word. Covenants are Scripture's spine—threading Genesis to Revelation—so they function as an internal anti-forgery mark: one Author, one plan, unfolding through time.

But while God's promises form a seamless thread, human promises unravel. Human society is marked by broken promises—a painful consequence of living in a fallen, depraved world. Treaties are violated, leading to bloody wars. Families fracture as marriages fail to uphold the pledge "to love and to cherish till death us do part." Financial overextension leads to unpaid debts and broken contracts. Yet, amid this human frailty, God always perfectly upholds his end of the agreement. He is a "covenant-keeping" God. Wholly reliable, he possesses ultimate, unwavering truth through his word, which "cannot be broken" no matter what challenges come against it (John 10:35). The best part is that God's covenant promises are freely available to anyone.

When everything human wobbles, covenant steadies the soul—truth you can stake your life on.

One of the greatest examples of God's unbreakable promises is the Abrahamic covenant, a foundational agreement between God and man, discussed in Gen 12:1–3:

> Now the LORD had said to Abram:
> "Get out of your country,
> From your family
> And from your father's house,
> To a land that I will show you.

---

82. Grudem, *Systematic Theology*, 515.

> I will make you a great nation;
> I will bless you
> And make your name great;
> And you shall be a blessing.
> I will bless those who bless you,
> And I will curse him who curses you;
> And in you all the families of the earth shall be blessed."

Further, Gen 15:4–5 states,

> And behold, the word of the LORD came to him, saying, "This one shall not be your heir, but one who will come from your own body shall be your heir." Then He brought him outside and said, "Look now toward heaven, and count the stars if you are able to number them." And He said to him, "So shall your descendants be."

Notice the cadence: "I will . . . I will . . . I will." Salvation history rests on God's promises, not man's performance—an antidote to every works-based distortion.

Uniquely, the Abrahamic covenant is unconditional—God alone binds himself to its fulfillment, and mankind does nothing to earn its blessings. In fact, six times in Gen 12 God declares "I will." Further, this covenant applies to all people for all time. Through this covenant, God reveals his gracious love for humanity, his most cherished creation, despite its fallen state. The Abrahamic covenant remains true today, offering the enduring promise of blessing and redemption for all generations.

The scope is global ("all the families of the earth"), foreshadowing the gospel's reach in Christ (Gal 3:8).

As part of the Abrahamic covenant, God made a foundational promise—a specific plot of land for Abraham's descendants:

> On the same day the LORD made a covenant with Abram, saying: "To your descendants I have given this land, from the river of Egypt to the great river, the River Euphrates—the Kenites, the Kenezzites, the Kadmonites, the Hittites, the Perizzites, the Rephaim, the Amorites, the Canaanites, the Girgashites, and the Jebusites." (Gen 15:18–21)

Place matters in God's plan; promise is concrete, not nebulous—anchored in geography and history.

Not only was the land given, but it was declared to be forever. Through Abraham's son Isaac, to his son Jacob, the children of Israel became heirs to this land, despite enduring wars, rebellion, captivities, dispossessions, and long periods of exile—the last of which continued for two thousand years.

Throughout centuries of displacement, the Jewish people remained steadfast in their hope for restoration. Then, on May 14, 1948, David Ben-Gurion—using Ezek 37's "dry bones" prophecy as a guiding inspiration—officially announced the modern state of Israel.[83] His declaration marked a significant moment in Jewish history, as a homeland was reestablished following the horrors of the Nazi-run Holocaust. While some theologians see this as a fulfillment of biblical prophecy, others believe Israel's full restoration—both spiritually and territorially—is yet to come.

However one reads 1948 in prophecy, the takeaway is constant: God's promises outlast empires.

Despite Israel's long history, it has never fully possessed all the land promised by God. Many scholars believe that in the future, Israel will turn back to God, receiving full covenant blessings in accordance with his redemptive plan. Some hold that this final restoration is tied to the return of Christ, when God will fulfill his ultimate promises to Israel. At that time, the Lord will establish his throne, and under his perfect rule, the world will experience the fullness of peace, love, and divine prosperity as his plan reaches its completion.[84] Covenant hope points forward—truth with a horizon line.

Because the Abrahamic covenant is both unconditional and everlasting, it extends to the future kingdom of Christ. All the earth would be blessed through Abraham, and, as per John 3:16–17, all people have access to this blessing through Jesus. This promise achieves fulfillment in the new covenant prophesied in Jer 31:31–34:

> Behold, the days are coming, says the LORD, when I will make a new covenant with the house of Israel and with the house of Judah—not according to the covenant that I made with their fathers in the day that I took them by the hand to lead them out of the land of Egypt, My covenant which they broke, though I was a husband to them, says the LORD. But this is the covenant that I will make with the house of Israel after those days, says the LORD: I will put My law in their minds, and write it on their

---

83. Ben-Gurion (1886–1973) was a Polish-born Zionist leader who became the primary founder and first prime minister of Israel. As head of the Jewish Agency, he led the political and diplomatic efforts that culminated in Israel's independence, and he is widely regarded as the "Father of the Nation."

84. Corrado, "God Perfectly Keeps."

hearts; and I will be their God, and they shall be My people. No more shall every man teach his neighbor, and every man his brother, saying, "Know the LORD," for they all shall know Me, from the least of them to the greatest of them, says the LORD. For I will forgive their iniquity, and their sin I will remember no more.

The same covenant declared in Luke 22:20:

> Likewise He also took the cup after supper, saying, "This cup is the new covenant in My blood, which is shed for you."

Promise blossoms into Person: the new covenant is cut in Christ's blood, writing grace on hearts—not tablets.

Jesus Christ, a descendant of Abraham and the promised Redeemer, fulfilled God's covenant and will one day bring about the "restitution of all things" (Acts 3:21). Hebrews 2:16 affirms that those who inherit salvation through Christ (Heb 1:14) are the "seed of Abraham," making them beneficiaries of God's promise to him. Jesus fulfills God's covenant faithfulness by bringing believers "to glory" (Heb 2:10), just as God brought his people to the promised land.[85]

Union with Christ makes covenant blessings personal and present—already and not yet.

As God's covenant promises have remained steadfast, so has his word, preserved through extraordinary efforts and divine custodianship over centuries. Despite being targeted by rulers and empires, the Bible has endured through the ages under God's protection. He entrusted the Old Testament to prophets and priests and the New Testament to Christ and his apostles.

Covenant-keeping God → Scripture-keeping God. Same faithfulness, different arena.

In the Old Testament, priests served as mediators between God and his people. They were responsible for offering sacrifices, maintaining the sanctuary, and teaching the law to the Israelites. The priesthood was established through Aaron and his descendants, with the high priest holding a unique role in making atonement for the sins of the people.

Unlike priests, who mediated between God and his people through sacrifices and temple service, prophets were directly called by God to proclaim his truth—often urging repentance, warning of judgment, and offering hope. They were God's spokespersons, conveying his will during

---

85. Corrado, "God Perfectly Keeps."

times of moral and spiritual decline. Figures like Isaiah, Jeremiah, and Ezekiel played pivotal roles in guiding the nation of Israel.

In the New Testament, the apostles were the original messengers and witnesses of Jesus Christ's life, death, and resurrection. The term *apostle* means "one who is sent," and they were entrusted with spreading the gospel and establishing the early church. The apostles, including Peter, John, and Paul, played a foundational role in spreading the gospel, establishing churches, and shaping Christian doctrine through their teachings and writings.

In this way, the apostolic office joined the long line of covenant messengers—priest, prophet, apostle—each carrying, teaching, and inscripturating the covenant word, until it all culminated in Christ, our final Prophet, Priest, and King. Yet this entrusted word soon came under fierce attack.

The closest the Bible (and Christianity) came to extinction was AD 303–311, during the rule of Roman Emperor Diocletian. He was upset by the growing detachment of Christians from society, as they refused to take part in Roman culture due to its paganism, bloodshed, and immodesty. In AD 303, Diocletian decreed the return of Rome to its greatness, and in doing so, he ordered the destruction of every church building, the imprisonment or execution of every pastor and church leader, and the eradication of every copy of the Bible.[86]

Under Diocletian's iron grip, the faithful faced unimaginable peril. In the shadow of Rome's wrath, early Christians risked everything to preserve fragments of Scripture, ensuring that God's word endured even as emperors sought to extinguish it. To evade detection, they tore apart their cherished manuscripts, scattering the fragments in secret.[87] This act was both strategic and symbolic—destroying the completeness of the physical texts to ensure the enduring power of their divine message. Each fragment represented a thread of hope, carried by the persecuted in their flight from oppression.

These fragments became more than relics of Scripture; they transformed into beacons of faith and resilience. Hidden within homes, caves, and marketplaces, they fostered secret gatherings and whispers of worship. For those who risked their lives to safeguard them, these fragments became tangible reminders of God's presence, bolstering their resolve in

---

86. Eusebius, *Ecclesiastical History* 8.2.4–5.

87. Eusebius, *Ecclesiastical History* 8.2.4–5; see also Lactantius, *Death of the Persecutors* 12–13.

the face of persecution. Against all odds and the wrath of an empire, God's word emerged triumphant—restored and unbroken.

Diocletian's campaign against Christianity was so effective that few surviving church structures pre-date his reign, and no complete Bible survives from before AD 303.[88] Yet what looks like loss was actually gain: persecution sifted out casual scribes and careless copies. Those who preserved Scripture did so with costly devotion, ensuring remarkable accuracy. The stress test of suffering forged a transmission line that was both purified and multiplied. The resilience of the Bible speaks to something far greater than physical preservation—it reflects the unyielding determination of faith and the divine promise of its message. The fragments that survived those dark times continue to inspire and transform lives around the world, proving that God's word endures through the ages, untouched by the forces that sought to destroy it.[89]

Persecution stress-tested transmission. The result? An even stronger documentary chain and a church more certain of the word it cherished.

Throughout history, believers have clung to the Bible even under the harshest persecutions. Consider the underground churches of modern-day China, where believers risk their lives to own and share copies of Scripture. As 2 Cor 4:8–9 says, "We are hard-pressed on every side, yet not crushed; we are perplexed, but not in despair; persecuted, but not forsaken; struck down, but not destroyed."

These stories—from the era of Diocletian's persecution to the hidden churches of today—reflect the indomitable hope the Bible brings. Its message sustains faith even in the darkest times, proving again and again that neither persecution nor attempts at eradication can extinguish its truth.

So how do we still have the Bible? Because generation after generation, believers counted it more precious than life itself. They smuggled it, memorized it, copied it by hand, and passed it on—often at great cost. That is why today we possess over five thousand eight hundred Greek New Testament manuscripts, along with more than nineteen thousand in other ancient languages—over twenty-five thousand in total. This far exceeds the documentary evidence for any other work of antiquity.[90] Far from being compromised, the Bible's integrity was preserved through both suffering and devotion, ensuring its message endured.

88. Chadwick, "Diocletian."
89. Chadwick, "Diocletian."
90. Metzger and Ehrman, *Text of the New Testament*, 52–53.

Bottom line: God's covenants and God's word stand or fall together—and both stand. The same God who swore, "I will," also said, "Scripture cannot be broken."

TRUSTING THE BIBLE

Scholars specializing in ancient manuscripts agree that the Bible has been astonishingly well maintained over the years.[91] Through the tireless work of scribes and the unrelenting devotion of believers, the Bible stands as an unparalleled testament to its own truth. Unlike other ancient texts that succumbed to corruption and decay, Scripture's clarity and consistency endured against the odds. Its resilience mirrors the unwavering commitment of those who cherished its divine message, ensuring its survival through centuries of turmoil. Textual criticism (the discipline that compares manuscript copies to determine the original wording) doesn't rescue a broken book; it reveals a robust one. The more witnesses we have, the harder wholesale distortion becomes—and the Bible has more witnesses than any work of antiquity.

This remarkable preservation is evident in the comparison of biblical texts from the third century AD to those from the fourteenth century AD, which are remarkably consistent in content.[92] Such consistency underscores the meticulous efforts of those who safeguarded its accuracy, ensuring its transmission across generations. Beyond its textual reliability, the enduring preservation of Scripture highlights its profound spiritual significance and historical impact, inspiring trust and faith in the divine message it carries.

Where differences appear, they are overwhelmingly minor—spelling, word order—never touching doctrine.

One of the most compelling confirmations of Scripture's preservation came in 1947 when a young Bedouin shepherd stumbled upon clay jars in a cave near Qumran, about twenty miles east of Jerusalem. Over the next decade, eleven caves yielded tens of thousands of fragments representing nearly nine hundred manuscripts—now collectively known as the Dead Sea Scrolls. These texts, preserved in clay jars and protected by the arid climate, date from the third century BC to the first century AD and represent an estimated eight hundred distinct works. The discovery

---

91. Metzger and Ehrman, *Text of the New Testament*, 178.
92. Metzger and Ehrman, *Text of the New Testament*, 52–53.

let scholars test a thousand-year jump in the Hebrew Bible's transmission—an unprecedented control sample.

The scrolls include portions of every book of the Hebrew Bible except Esther, although recent claims suggest a possible fragment may exist.[93] Remarkably, these manuscripts were composed nearly a thousand years earlier than any previously known biblical texts. Some were written in ancient Paleo-Hebrew, others in Aramaic and Greek, and one was even engraved on copper.[94] Different scripts; same Scriptures—underscoring breadth of use across communities.

The scrolls fall into two main categories: "biblical" manuscripts—copies of texts now found in the Hebrew Bible—and "non-biblical" manuscripts, which include sectarian writings—texts that articulate the unique doctrines, communal regulations, and eschatological worldview of separatist Jewish groups such as the Qumran sect—alongside apocalyptic visions, legal texts, and the earliest known extant biblical commentary (on Habakkuk). These documents reflect the beliefs and practices of Jewish communities during the Second Temple period, prior to the destruction of the temple in AD 70.[95] This context explains minor textual streams (e.g., proto-Masoretic, Septuagintal), without threatening the core message.

The discovery of the Dead Sea Scrolls initially stirred excitement among skeptics, some of whom hoped it would disprove the reliability of the Bible. However, the scrolls overwhelmingly confirmed the remarkable preservation of Scripture. In fact, their close alignment with later manuscripts, especially the Masoretic Text, astonished both scholars and believers. Among the most famous finds is the Great Isaiah Scroll, which contains all sixty-six chapters of the book and aligns over 95 percent with the Masoretic Text. Minor discrepancies—such as spelling variations or alternate word choices like "sons of Elohim" instead of "sons of Israel" in Deut 32:8—do not affect the meaning or theological content. These

---

93. Esther's absence from the Dead Sea Scrolls does not indicate its rejection from the Hebrew canon. Several other canonical books (such as Nehemiah) are sparsely represented, likely due to the Qumran community's theological emphases rather than doubts about authenticity. The book of Esther was widely accepted in Jewish and Christian circles, included in the Septuagint (Greek OT) and later affirmed at the Jewish Council of Jamnia (c. AD 90). Its inclusion in the Hebrew Bible and Christian Old Testament reflects consistent recognition of its canonical status, despite its omission at Qumran. See Bruce, *Canon of Scripture*, 29–32; McDonald, *Biblical Canon*, 199–202.

94. VanderKam and Flint, *Meaning of the Dead Sea Scrolls*, 27.

95. Vanderkam and Flint, *Meaning of the Dead Sea Scrolls*, 27.

differences reflect the diversity of ancient textual traditions, including the Septuagint and Samaritan Pentateuch, but they do not undermine the Bible's core message.[96] In fact, it is striking—even ironic—that the very community which preserved Isa 53, a passage that so plainly foreshadows Jesus as the suffering Messiah, did not recognize him when he came. The scroll that prophetically testifies to Christ's redemptive work lay hidden for centuries in their caves, awaiting discovery as a witness to the continuity and reliability of God's word.

In short, preservation is the rule; variation the exception—and the exceptions are transparent.

Far from disproving Scripture's reliability, the Dead Sea Scrolls have become a cornerstone of biblical scholarship. They demonstrate that the Old Testament was transmitted with extraordinary care, even across centuries of political upheaval and cultural change. Rather than silencing Scripture, the scrolls silenced the critics, showing God's word preserved not only through human diligence but under divine custodianship.[97] Providence worked through pens.

By contrast, other religious texts claiming divine origin have undergone extensive revisions over relatively short periods. For example, the Book of Mormon has experienced nearly four thousand documented changes since its original printing in 1830—including grammatical corrections, stylistic updates, and significant doctrinal adjustments.[98] Notably, 1 Nephi 11:18 originally referred to Mary as "the mother of God," but was changed in the 1837 edition to "the mother of the Son of God." Similarly, 1 Nephi 11:21 was altered from "the Eternal Father" to "the Son of the Eternal Father" (an edit consistent with Joseph Smith's developing, non-Trinitarian theology). Another appears in Mosiah 21:28, which originally named King Benjamin as the recipient of divine revelation—despite his death earlier in the narrative. Later editions corrected this to King Mosiah. Early editions also carried racialized language: 2 Nephi 30:6 described the Lamanites as becoming "white and delightsome," a phrase revised by Joseph Smith himself in the 1840 edition to read "pure

---

96. Vermes, *Complete Dead Sea Scrolls*, 1–5.

97. The legends surrounding the Dead Sea Scrolls are greatly exaggerated. They did not reveal lost books of the Bible but consisted mainly of Old Testament manuscripts copied between 250 and 150 BC, with fragments from nearly every biblical book. Alongside these were some apocryphal and extra-biblical texts, yet the majority were Hebrew Scriptures. Their significance lies in their remarkable preservation, having been hidden for over two thousand years.

98. Tanner and Tanner, *3,913 Changes*.

and delightsome." Beyond textual edits, Mormon teaching itself shifted: for more than a century Black members were denied priesthood and temple ordinances, a ban only lifted in 1978 by "Official Declaration 2."[99] These revisions reflect evolving theological concerns and raise important questions about textual consistency and divine inspiration.

Despite these changes, Joseph Smith declared, "The Book of Mormon was the most correct of any book on earth, and the keystone of our religion, and a man would get nearer to God by abiding by its precepts, than by any other book."[100] This statement emphasized its spiritual reliability rather than its textual perfection. Yet that distinction is itself misleading. Scripture's authority rests not only on its ability to inspire but also on the integrity of the words transmitted. To claim divine revelation while repeatedly altering the text undermines both. What makes this even more inconsistent is that many Latter-day Saints question the Bible's trustworthiness because of its transmission history and multiple translations, yet they rarely apply the same standard to the Book of Mormon—even though it has undergone thousands of documented revisions, including doctrinal changes. In contrast, the Bible's reliability rests on providential preservation through manuscripts that demonstrate remarkable consistency across centuries, confirming both its spiritual power and textual trustworthiness.

Contrast: the Bible's vast manuscript base exposes variants; it doesn't require doctrinal retrofits.

Even the most adamant critics and skeptics of the Bible acknowledge that it has been preserved more accurately over the centuries than any other ancient manuscript. Despite this, Ricky Gervais—an English comedian, actor, and writer known for his sharp wit and outspoken atheism—argues that the existence of many religions suggests Christianity is merely one choice among thousands of gods.[101] However, the presence of competing beliefs does not invalidate truth. Just as a courtroom examines evidence to determine the guilty party among multiple suspects, reason and historical analysis must guide religious inquiry, distinguishing fact from fiction. Plurality doesn't cancel veracity; evidence adjudicates it.

In the same way, Christianity stands apart from other religious claims by offering verifiable historical, moral, and theological evidence.

---

99. Skousen, *1 Nephi–2 Nephi*, 55–58; 1 Nephi 11:18, 2 Nephi 30:6, Mosiah 21:28; Official Declaration 2 can be found in the church's *Doctrine and Covenants*.

100. Smith, *History of the Church*, 4:461.

101. Gervais, "Why I'm an Atheist."

The fine-tuning of the universe, the existence of objective morality, and the historical resurrection claims set Christianity apart from mythological figures like Zeus or Thor, whose narratives lack historical foundation.

As Gary Habermas and Michael Licona, a Christian apologist and professor of New Testament studies, argue, "The historical case for Jesus' resurrection remains one of the strongest arguments in religious scholarship today."[102] If the resurrection stands, Christianity stands; if it falls, Christianity falls (1 Cor 15:14). The manuscript record keeps that claim in view.

Not only do the manuscript quantities affirm the Bible's preservation, but its early translations further demonstrate its widespread transmission and influence. For just the New Testament, as previously stated, there are approximately five thousand eight hundred Greek manuscripts, with over twenty-five thousand total manuscripts when including translations into Latin, Syriac, Coptic, and other languages.[103] Some of these manuscripts date as early as AD 125, making the New Testament one of the most well-documented ancient texts.[104] Add the early versions and patristic quotations, and you gain a multilane highway of textual cross-checks.

While the New Testament enjoys unparalleled manuscript preservation, many other revered ancient works have far fewer surviving copies:

- Julius Caesar's *Gallic Wars*: Around 251 manuscripts, with the earliest copy dating nine hundred years after the original. Written as both a historical account and political propaganda, *Gallic Wars* offers firsthand insight into Rome's military expansion and Caesar's leadership, shaping perceptions of Roman strategy and governance for centuries.

- Aristotle's *Poetics*: Around fifty-one manuscripts, with the earliest copy dating four hundred and fifty years after the original. As one of the most influential works on literary theory, *Poetics* laid the foundation for Western thought on drama and storytelling, impacting everything from Greek tragedies to modern cinema.

- Herodotus's *Histories*: Around 109 manuscripts, with the earliest copy dating five hundred and fifty years after the original. Often

---

102. Habermas and Licona, *Case for the Resurrection*, 45.
103. Bauer, "Biblical Preservation."
104. Wallace, "Reliability," 182; Kruger, "Early Christian Manuscripts," 5.

considered the first true work of history, *Histories* chronicles major events such as the Greco-Persian Wars and offers a rich tapestry of cultural traditions, shaping how civilizations remember and interpret the past.

- Homer's *Iliad*: Over eighteen hundred manuscripts, with the earliest copy dating four hundred to five hundred years after the original. A cornerstone of classical literature, *Iliad* captures themes of heroism, fate, and divine intervention, profoundly influencing philosophy, ethics, and storytelling for millennia.[105]

If the study of manuscripts feels technical, remember this: these details matter because they prove the Bible you hold today is the same one God inspired. By any fair comparison, the New Testament sits in a different evidential galaxy. While these works have shaped literature, philosophy, and historical thought, the Bible transcends them—it has molded faith, morality, law, and civilization itself. Its extensive manuscript evidence far surpasses that of other revered ancient texts, underscoring both its historical reliability and profound cultural significance.

The Bible's extensive manuscript evidence is only part of the story. Its early translations into Syriac, Coptic, Latin, and Aramaic ensured its transmission across cultures, further solidifying its lasting influence. Additionally, the early church fathers extensively quoted the Bible, providing further textual continuity. Scholars note that patristic quotations are so extensive that, even if other sources were lost, they would be sufficient for the reconstruction of practically the entire New Testament.[106] Multiple streams, one message—that's how you detect fidelity, not fabrication.

Despite human error and historical opposition, the Bible has endured. Christianity stands apart from traditions lacking textual and historical continuity. While figures like Julius Caesar, Aristotle, and Homer

---

105. Metzger and Ehrman, *Text of the New Testament*, 26–28. The summaries of Julius Caesar's *Gallic Wars*, Aristotle's *Poetics*, Herodotus's *Histories*, and Homer's *Iliad* are included not only to compare manuscript quantities but to underscore the enduring importance of these texts. Each has profoundly shaped Western thought—whether in governance, literary theory, historical method, or epic storytelling. By highlighting their thematic significance, the contrast with the NT's manuscript preservation becomes more compelling. This framing invites readers to recognize that the NT, while a religious text, also stands as one of the most historically robust and widely transmitted documents of antiquity.

106. Metzger and Ehrman, *Text of the New Testament*, 126.

left behind a handful of surviving manuscripts, the New Testament boasts tens of thousands, some dating within a century of Jesus' life.[107]

As textual scholar Bruce M. Metzger (1914–2007) explains, "The overwhelming number of New Testament manuscripts makes significant alteration of its text virtually impossible."[108] A longtime professor at Princeton Theological Seminary and leading expert in New Testament textual criticism, Metzger's works—especially *The Text of the New Testament: Its Transmission, Corruption, and Restoration*—have profoundly shaped modern understanding of the Bible's reliability. In short, more manuscripts = more transparency = more confidence.

We can be confident that the Bible today remains true to its original form. Though the original manuscripts have been lost to time, their message has been faithfully preserved. The Old Testament was composed between 1400 BC and 400 BC, and the New Testament between AD 50 and AD 100. Modern translations are not based on previous versions but on thousands of ancient manuscripts in the original Hebrew, Aramaic, and Greek.

Of course, copies of the manuscripts cannot claim inerrancy; only the original manuscripts can. No scribe is flawless, no matter how meticulously they copied the Scriptures. However, the many manuscripts of the Bible changed little over the centuries. As noted earlier, most discrepancies involve minor textual differences, such as word order shifts (one manuscript reads "Christ Jesus," whereas another reads "Jesus Christ") or slight spelling variations (the equivalent of using the American "neighbor" vs. British "neighbour"). Readily recognizable missing words account for the bulk of these differences.[109]

Ancient codices such as the Codex Sinaiticus (mentioned before) and Codex Vaticanus, both from the fourth century, further affirm the consistency of the biblical text across centuries.[110] Translation itself does not corrupt Scripture; rather, faithful translations are grounded in the best available evidence and guided by rigorous linguistic scholarship. As languages evolve, updated translations help convey the original meaning more clearly—without altering the message. This reflects reverence for

---

107. Turner, *Greek Manuscripts*, 54.
108. Metzger and Ehrman, *Text of the New Testament*, 89.
109. Metzger and Ehrman, *Text of the New Testament*, 249–50.
110. Pratte, "Bible Preservation."

the text, not revisionism.[111] Good translation is the servant of inspiration, not its rival.

Skeptics often ask, "Can we still trust the Bible?" The answer is unequivocally, "Yes!" The Bible is inerrant because it was inspired by God: "All Scripture is given by inspiration of God, and is profitable for doctrine, for reproof, for correction, for instruction in righteousness, that the man of God may be complete, thoroughly equipped for every good work" (2 Tim 3:16–17).

In short, Scripture remains fundamentally unchanged—its message intact and unaltered over two millennia. We can trust the Bible because it is God's word, as Scripture itself declares:

> For assuredly, I say to you, till heaven and earth pass away, one jot or one tittle will by no means pass from the law till all is fulfilled. (Matt 5:18)

Internal claim + external corroboration = a uniquely credible witness.

Just as Scripture's absolute truth shines through its careful preservation and divine inspiration, history offers a striking counterpoint: Operation Mincemeat, a blueprint for deception through forged documents. In 1943, British intelligence planted falsified military plans on a corpse disguised as a Royal Marine, "Major William Martin," to mislead Nazi forces about the Allied invasion site. The ruse worked—German troops were diverted, and thousands of lives were saved.

This historical episode underscores a profound truth: documents shape destinies. In Mincemeat, a single forged letter redirected armies. In Scripture, thousands of faithfully preserved manuscripts have guided souls across millennia. Where Mincemeat relied on fabrication to deceive, the Bible's transmission relied on accuracy to reveal. The contrast is stark: one manipulated history through lies; the other has transformed history through truth.

Operation Mincemeat reminds us that the credibility of a message depends on the integrity of its transmission. The Bible's unmatched manuscript evidence ensures that its message remains intact, uncorrupted, and trustworthy. As F. F. Bruce observed, "The evidence for our New Testament writings is ever so much greater than the evidence for many writings of classical authors, the authenticity of which no one dreams of questioning."[112]

---

111. Turner, *Greek Manuscripts*, 54.
112. Bruce, *New Testament Documents*, 15.

The success of Operation Mincemeat was later confirmed through Ultra decrypts, which showed Hitler had diverted significant forces away from Sicily, leaving it vulnerable to the real Allied invasion. Ultra, the Allies' top-secret codebreaking project, enabled planners to anticipate enemy moves with precision—decisively shaping the war's outcome.[113]

The operation's brilliance lay in its ability to embed deception within an otherwise credible narrative. British intelligence crafted a story so convincing that it reshaped enemy perception without a single shot fired. This historical episode illustrates the power of strategic misinformation—how a well-placed lie, wrapped in truth, can alter the course of history.[114]

But deception is not confined to wartime tactics. Scripture warns that spiritual warfare is marked by similar strategies. Just as the Allies masked their true intentions to mislead their adversary, Satan cloaks lies within fragments of truth to distort perception and divert humanity from salvation. His tactics exploit human vulnerabilities—fear, pride, desire—offering plausible half-truths that lead to spiritual ruin.

Recognizing and resisting deception requires vigilance and discernment. Just as Allied planners safeguarded their mission through careful strategy, believers must fortify their faith by anchoring themselves in God's word. Operation Mincemeat underscores the necessity of discernment—an essential principle in recognizing and trusting the absolute truth of Scripture. As Jesus declared, "Sanctify them by Your truth. Your word is truth" (John 17:17) (Jesus praying to the Father for his disciples).

The reliability of the Bible as God's word is affirmed not only through manuscript preservation but also through archaeology, prophecy, science, and its transformative power. Each of these threads weaves into a coherent Christian worldview, offering clarity in a world clouded by confusion. This becomes especially clear when we consider the real reasons many people resist faith.

Frank Turek, a Christian apologist and author best known for *I Don't Have Enough Faith to Be an Atheist*, often frames the matter pointedly when he asks skeptics, "If Christianity were true, would you become a Christian?" More often than not, he receives silence in response. This hesitancy highlights that disbelief is frequently less about evidence and more about the will. As previously mentioned, Scripture declares in both

---

113. Macintyre, *Operation Mincemeat*, 142.
114. Montagu, *Man Who Never Was*, 85–86.

Ps 14:1 and Ps 53:1: "The fool has said in his heart, 'There is no God.'" The Hebrew word for "fool" (*nabal*) refers not to intellectual deficiency but to moral rebellion—a deliberate rejection of ethical and spiritual reality.[115] Scripture does not suggest that unintelligent people fail to believe in God; rather, sinful people suppress the truth. Their denial is not rooted in ignorance but in resistance to moral accountability.

Rejection of faith is rarely about reason alone—it often stems from a desire to avoid the implications of divine authority. Some will grant the possibility of a Creator, provided he remains distant and uninvolved. But they reject a God who demands righteousness. Rather than confront their conscience, they choose denial over conviction. Psalm 14:1 therefore calls such a person a "fool," not as an insult but as a moral and spiritual diagnosis.

A sense of accountability naturally follows belief in a Divine Being. To escape this, some suppress the inner voice of conscience—telling themselves, "There is no global overseer. No day of judgment. I am free to live as I wish." In doing so, the moral pull of conscience becomes easier to ignore. Yet attempting to persuade oneself that God does not exist is not only unwise—it is spiritually perilous. A heart steeped in sin leads one to deny God's existence, even in the face of overwhelming evidence—from the intricacies of creation to the moral compass within.

The absence of belief is often not due to lack of evidence but to a desire to escape moral constraints. As C. S. Lewis wisely observed, "There are only two kinds of people in the end: those who say to God, 'Thy will be done,' and those to whom God says, in the end, 'Thy will be done.' All that are in Hell, choose it. Without that self-choice, there could be no Hell."[116]

Romans 1:18–25 vividly illustrates how humanity has exchanged divine truth for deception. Paul writes,

> The wrath of God is revealed from heaven against all ungodliness and unrighteousness of men, who suppress the truth in unrighteousness, because what may be known of God is manifest in them, for God has shown it to them. For since the creation of the world His invisible attributes are clearly seen, being understood by the things that are made, even His eternal power and Godhead, so that they are without excuse, because, although they knew God, they did not glorify Him as God, nor were thankful, but became futile in their thoughts, and their foolish

---

115. *Strong's* (2010), s.v. "נָבָל (nabal)," H5036.
116. Lewis, *Great Divorce*, 506.

hearts were darkened. Professing to be wise, they became fools.
... Therefore God also gave them up to uncleanness, in the lusts of their hearts, to dishonor their bodies among themselves, who exchanged the truth of God for the lie, and worshiped and served the creature rather than the Creator.
(Rom 1:18-21, 24-25)

Truth is not just discovered; it is resisted or received. Scripture names both dynamics—and offers rescue. God's word not only reveals absolute truth but equips believers to discern deception—a skill vital for spiritual resilience. Through its divine inspiration, historical accuracy, and unified message, Scripture remains the foundation of truth for all generations.

As deception intertwines with fragments of truth, believers must grapple with a critical question: What are truth and falsehood, and how does one discern between them?

The reliability of God's word is not merely a theological assertion—it is a lifeline. The battle between truth and deception is not passive; it is a daily challenge that shapes how we think, act, and believe. To navigate this battlefield, believers must stand firm on the foundation of Scripture, resisting doubts and distortions that threaten faith. When faced with deception, biblical truth is our shield—guarding against subtle distortions that obscure reality.

This principle is seen vividly in the military realm. In warfare, secure communications are not peripheral—they are the nervous system of operations. Without them, even the most advanced weapons and strategies are inert. Orders must be authenticated, encrypted, and delivered without distortion; a single breach—a spoofed signal, a jammed frequency, a corrupted transmission—can cost lives and fracture trust down the chain of command.

That is why we build hardened networks, use advanced encryption to guard against evolving threats, and design systems that are difficult to detect or intercept. These are not conveniences; they are survival mechanisms. Secure communications protect operational integrity, preserve command and control, and enable synchronized action across domains. Without them, the mission fails before it begins.

When I consider the transmission of Scripture—God's word carried across millennia—I see a communication system far more resilient than any tactical network. The Bible is not a fragile signal bouncing between vulnerable nodes. It is a sovereign transmission, initiated by the

Commander of heaven, authenticated by prophecy, encrypted in truth, and preserved through persecution, translation, and time. Despite skeptics' jamming, cultural drift, and the spoofing of false teachers, the core message endures: God is holy, man is fallen; Christ is sufficient, grace is available.

This is not coincidence. It is divine communications discipline. God's word has moved through hostile regimes, survived underground churches, and bypassed censors. For those tuned to its frequency, the signal is unmistakable. Just as a battlefield commander ensures his orders are relayed without distortion, our Lord has ensured that his operational directive for redemption reaches us securely. When we open the Bible, we are not merely reading ancient literature; we are receiving a mission-critical transmission. In that moment, the line is secure.

Call to action: Test every signal you receive, but trust every word God has spoken, and let Scripture calibrate your discernment.

Chapter 3 explores these distinctions further, equipping readers with tools to uncover lies hidden within truths and to stand confidently in the light of God's word.

PERSONAL APPLICATION: TRUSTING THE BIBLE AS YOUR FOUNDATION

Chapter 2 highlights the divine inspiration, historical accuracy, and unchanging truth of God's word—principles that form a powerful foundation for spiritual growth and resilience. Yet, every believer must actively choose: Will you stand firmly on the eternal truths revealed in Scripture, or rely on human traditions, interpretations, and teachings that often diverge from God's word? This decision shapes the trajectory of your faith and commitment to God.

1. *Strengthen Your Conviction in God's Word*—Make it a daily habit to reflect on the Bible's reliability and historical accuracy, as affirmed by Jesus. Trusting Scripture isn't just an intellectual exercise—it is a transformative step toward living with unwavering confidence. When you embrace the Bible's divine inspiration and unified message, you equip yourself to navigate life's challenges with hope. Let this trust in God's word shape how you think, act, and relate to others. Meditate on 2 Tim 3:16–17, which declares that all Scripture is inspired and equips you for every good work.

I once met a young believer who nearly abandoned his faith after encountering online claims that the Bible had been "rewritten countless times." Instead of walking away, he began to compare manuscripts, study commentaries, and read the Bible with fresh eyes. What shook him at first became the very path to deeper trust: the so-called contradictions dissolved, and he found that Scripture's unity was stronger than ever. His story echoes what many discover—the Bible does not collapse under scrutiny; it proves itself.

2. *Anchor Your Decisions in Scripture*—In a world where values constantly shift, commit to evaluating your choices through the lens of God's word. The Bible is a steady foundation in a changing world. Before making key decisions, ask yourself, Does this align with the eternal principles revealed in Scripture? Turn to passages like Prov 3:5–6, which remind us to trust in God's guidance in both daily choices and life's crossroads. Applying biblical truth is more than knowledge—it is the difference between living by conviction or conforming to cultural trends. This isn't abstract theology—it's where you anchor your hope tomorrow morning.

3. *Deepen Your Understanding of Biblical Unity*—The Bible is not just a collection of disconnected writings; it is a masterfully woven tapestry that presents a unified message of redemption and grace. As you study themes from Genesis to Revelation, explore how biblical covenants—such as the Abrahamic covenant—reveal God's continuing promises to his people. Recognizing this overarching unity strengthens your trust in Scripture as a cohesive and divinely inspired revelation.

4. *Guard Against Modern Doubts and Liberal Theologies*—We live in an age where Scripture is often questioned, reinterpreted, or disregarded. Rather than simply rejecting opposing perspectives outright, equip yourself to discern truth by engaging with Scripture firsthand. Instead of merely reacting to doubts, prepare yourself by immersing in biblical truth and its prophetic fulfillment. Romans 12:2 reminds us, "Do not be conformed to this world, but be transformed by the renewing of your mind." Let the word reshape your thinking and refine your discernment so you can stand firm against interpretations that compromise biblical authority.

5. *Pray for a Heart of Trust and Reverence*—Spiritual strength comes not just from studying Scripture but from communing with God. Spend intentional time in prayer, asking him to deepen your faith and cultivate a greater love for his word. The Bible has stood the test of time, remaining unshakable despite human attacks and doubts. When your faith is rooted in God's truth, you will find peace, wisdom, and clarity in life's uncertainties.

As you trust and apply the truths revealed in Scripture, you will find that God's word truly is sufficient for every aspect of life. In practical terms, this means leaning on the Bible not only as a source of knowledge but as the foundation of your identity and purpose. Take time each day to reflect on how its theological pillars—divine inspiration, historical accuracy, and unified truth—actively shape your walk with God. In doing so, you align your life with the enduring wisdom and promises of his word. Its divine inspiration and unwavering accuracy provide a solid foundation on which you can build your faith, character, and purpose.

Personal Reflection

1. What convinced you (or challenges you) most about the claim that the Bible is the ultimate source of truth?
2. The word *confidence* comes from the Latin *con fide*, meaning "with faith." How does understanding confidence as rooted in faith reshape your trust in Scripture when facing deception or doubt? What evidence—or faith—strengthens that confidence?
3. In what ways has Scripture shaped your ability to recognize deception—in media, culture, or even personal thought? How does trusting its authority impact your daily decisions and worldview?
4. Consider the contrast between cultural narratives and biblical truth. Which biblical insight from this chapter most challenged or deepened your understanding of reality, and how might it influence your conversations with others?

Group Discussion

1. This chapter (as well as chapter 1) presents fulfilled prophecy as a key indicator of the Bible's divine authorship. How does this strengthen (or challenge) your faith?
2. How would you respond to someone who claims that the Bible is outdated or culturally irrelevant today?
3. What are the dangers of interpreting Scripture based on personal opinion rather than authorial intent? How can we guard against this?
4. In a culture that often elevates personal experience over objective truth, how does Scripture serve as a reliable anchor for discerning reality? What are the spiritual and practical consequences of rejecting biblical truth in favor of relativism?

Scripture Connection

- Reflect on Isa 46:9–10 and 2 Tim 2:15. What do these verses reveal about God's sovereignty and our responsibility in handling his word?
- Read Rom 1:18–25 and John 17:17. How do these passages contrast the suppression of truth with the sanctifying power of God's word, and what does this reveal about the believer's role in discerning deception?

As you meditate on these passages and engage in reflection and discussion, let Scripture not only inform your understanding but actively shape your faith and daily walk with God. Trust in his word as your foundation, and let its truth guide your every step.

In a world saturated with competing voices, discerning truth requires more than intellect—it requires *confidence with faith*. The Latin *con fide* captures this beautifully. Trust in God's word doesn't demand blind belief; it rests on divine authorship and enduring preservation. Confidence rooted in Scripture is not naïve—it is courageous, rational, and eternal.

3

What Are Truth and Falsehood?

United States forces dropped this PSYOP leaflet in Iraq, caricaturing al-Qaeda's al-Zarqawi as a rat caught in a trap. Its caption—"This is your future, Zarqawi"—not only mocked an enemy but exposed the futility of terrorism and sought to erode morale. More than propaganda, it illustrated how perception can be shaped by blending truth and symbolism.[1]

1. Image: US Military, "Your Future al-Zarqawi." Public Domain.

WHAT ARE TRUTH AND FALSEHOOD?

> In war, the truth is so precious that she should always be attended by a bodyguard of lies.
>
> —WINSTON CHURCHILL

History has shown that deception often lurks beneath the surface, hidden in plain sight, waiting to entangle the unsuspecting. From the Trojan Horse to modern intelligence warfare, manipulation has rewritten destinies, shattered lives, and even shifted the course of nations. Yet deception is not just a tactic of war or political intrigue—it is a fundamental strategy of spiritual warfare.

In military terms, this is the essence of PSYOP: shaping what an opponent believes to be true in order to influence how they act. A PSYOP leaflet, a false radio transmission, or even an inflatable "army" as used in Operation Fortitude during World War II all share the same DNA—truths and falsehoods interwoven to mislead, distract, and control. Satan's methods mirror these tactics, only with eternal stakes.

This chapter considers how such deception surfaces within the church itself. Before proceeding, it is important to clarify the purpose of this chapter. The examples that follow—including Roman Catholicism—are presented as case studies, not attacks. Many Roman Catholics deeply love Jesus, and their devotion is not in question. Roman Catholicism is highlighted because its long history and well-developed framework of tradition provide a clear illustration. Any system can drift when human authority is elevated alongside—or above—Scripture. The same principle applies across Protestant sectarianism—defined here as rigid allegiance to denominational identity or theological distinctives that foster division and elevate tradition or leadership above biblical authority—as well as prosperity gospel movements and modern cults. The goal is discernment, not condemnation; reflection, not rejection. At stake is nothing less than "the faith which was once for all delivered to the saints" (Jude 3). To examine these patterns is not to denounce individuals but to heed Scripture's call to contend earnestly for the truth entrusted to the church.

Having established in chapter 2 that God's word alone is the sure foundation of truth, this chapter now turns to the battlefield terms: What exactly is truth, and what is falsehood? Without these categories, discernment collapses, and deception gains the advantage. This is why volume 1 pauses here, before turning to Satan's specific tactics, to clarify the nature of the very thing under attack—truth itself.

This dynamic is not theoretical; history shows how quickly institutional authority, once elevated above Scripture, can obscure the gospel.

In this sense, the analysis functions much like a military after-action report: identifying where perception was manipulated, where the "narrative" gained power over reality, and how truth was compromised in the process.

As with all spiritual matters, the standard of truth is the word of God. When truth is displaced by institutional authority or tradition, it is comparable to a battlefield commander trusting enemy misinformation—building a strategy on faulty intelligence that guarantees eventual defeat.

The call to discernment stretches across every arena. Deception thrives when the familiar is weaponized, whether in theology, culture, or politics. It does not matter whether the delivery system is a pulpit, a political broadcast, or a covert military channel—the mechanics of misdirection remain constant.

If anything taught here is true, may it resonate; if it is in error, may it be tested against the plumb line of Scripture (Acts 17:11). For truth, by nature, welcomes examination. A skilled military unit trains by running "red-team" exercises—stress-testing their assumptions against deception scenarios. In the same way, believers must continually stress-test every teaching against Scripture, refusing to accept appearances at face value.

Satan's most effective weapon has never been brute force; it is illusion—distorting truth so convincingly that many embrace lies without realizing it. False teachings creep in, wrapped in familiarity, sounding just close enough to truth to deceive even well-intentioned believers. Scripture warns us repeatedly of this danger: "Be sober, be vigilant; because your adversary the devil walks about like a roaring lion, seeking whom he may devour" (1 Pet 5:8). The battlefield is perception. Just as armies can be routed not by superior firepower but by believing a false narrative, so too can believers be overrun when illusion is mistaken for reality. Discernment is not only for scholars. It is for parents guiding children, students facing pressure, and believers scrolling their newsfeeds.

Whenever human authority rivals or displaces God's word, confusion and distortion inevitably follow. The danger lies in the pattern, not the people. Carl R. Trueman—an English-born Reformed theologian, church historian, and professor at Grove City College—argues in his cultural analysis that once narratives of identity are redefined apart from Scripture, even sacred traditions bend to new authorities.[2]

History offers sobering confirmation. In 1633, Galileo Galilei stood before the Roman Catholic Inquisition, forced to recant his support for a heliocentric universe—the view that the Earth revolves around the sun. This stood in contrast to the church's long-held geocentric model, which placed the Earth at the center of the cosmos. The tragedy was not that Scripture had been disproved but that tradition and human authority had misinterpreted it, insisting on reading it through the lens of power—a kind of misinformation elevated to law. The Roman Catholic Church eventually admitted its error, but the damage was done—truth was obscured by misplaced authority.[3] This episode reminds us that whenever tradition or hierarchy displaces Scripture, distortion follows, even when intentions are sincere.

THE NATURE OF DECEPTION

Throughout history, deception has reshaped kingdoms, altered narratives, and led millions astray. One haunting example unfolded in nineteenth-century France: *the Dreyfus Affair*, a web of lies so corrosive it nearly tore the nation apart.

The crowd in Paris roared with fury. It was January 5, 1895, and Captain Alfred Dreyfus, dressed in his immaculate French military uniform, stood rigid before thousands of spectators. He was about to be publicly disgraced—his sword broken, his insignia stripped from his chest. The charge? Treason against France.

But there was one glaring problem: he was innocent.

Dreyfus had been framed, accused of passing military secrets to Germany—an act he had never committed. Yet, the military court manufactured evidence, forged documents, and manipulated public opinion to ensure his conviction. He was exiled to Devil's Island, a remote penal colony where he endured brutal isolation for years.

The true traitor? Major Ferdinand Esterhazy—a man the military chose to protect rather than expose. Even when evidence surfaced that exonerated Dreyfus, the government refused to admit its deception. It took years of relentless advocacy, most notably from Émile Zola, whose

---

2. Trueman, *Rise and Triumph*, 29–32.
3. Finocchiaro, *Retrying Galileo*, 45–47.

famous open letter *J'Accuse!* tore through the lies and forced France to confront its corruption.

But why did so many believe the lie?

Because deception, when wielded strategically, becomes more than just falsehood—it becomes reality to those who accept it. It distorts justice, rewrites history, and turns truth into a shadow lurking beneath propaganda. The Dreyfus Affair wasn't just a scandal; it was a national betrayal.[4]

Military strategists would recognize this dynamic immediately. In PSYOP terms, the French command executed a "narrative control operation": suppressing contradictory intelligence, amplifying selective evidence, and repeating a false message until it became the accepted reality. The effectiveness of the deception did not lie in its plausibility—it lay in its repetition and authority. The same pattern can be seen in operations like the Soviet Union's Cold War disinformation campaigns, where forged documents and planted stories shaped international perception for decades. In every case, truth was not destroyed by argument but buried under layers of controlled narrative.

The same danger confronts the church. When deception is institutionalized, it can masquerade as sacred truth. Religious systems that elevate tradition above Scripture risk perpetuating error that feels holy simply because it is old. As with Dreyfus, the evidence may be clear, but the cost of admitting error often proves too high for those invested in the system.

Now, consider this: What happens when spiritual deception operates in the same way? When false doctrine is accepted so widely that people no longer recognize truth? The enemy works not with force but with manipulation, slowly leading people into ruin while convincing them they are walking in the light.

Just as deception has reshaped history, spiritual deception has eternal consequences. Satan's tactics are strategic—he takes pieces of truth, distorts them, and convinces people that lies are harmless or even beneficial. His ultimate goal is to shift authority away from Scripture and lead souls astray. In this sense, Satan is the ultimate PSYOP commander: his battlefield is the human mind, his weapon is perception, and his objective is obedience to a false authority.

And yet, deception doesn't only spring from external false religions—it infects even those who sit in pews and carry Bibles. The greatest

---

4. Whyte, *Dreyfus Affair*, 45–67.

danger isn't atheism—the outright denial of God's existence—or paganism—the worship of false gods, idols, or nature in place of the Creator; it's professing Christians who no longer submit to Scripture as final authority. When only 6 percent of self-identified Christians in America hold a biblical worldview, we're not just witnessing cultural decline—we're watching spiritual collapse from within.[5] The shift isn't overt rebellion but quiet compromise: a slow replacement of divine revelation with therapeutic slogans and borrowed philosophies. This is how deception thrives—not by denial of Scripture but by dilution of it. And as the authority of God's word weakens in hearts and pulpits, the door opens for spiritual confusion, doctrinal drift, and emotional manipulation cloaked in sincerity.

Military history offers parallel warnings. As noted earlier, Operation Fortitude (1944) provides a chilling example: the Allies constructed entire fake armies—complete with inflatable tanks, false radio chatter, and double agents—to convince Hitler that D-Day would strike at Pas de Calais instead of Normandy. The purpose of this deception was to pin down German forces away from the real landing site, buying the Allies precious time to secure a foothold in France. The genius of the ruse was not in outright lies but in burying those lies within believable truths. The deception succeeded not because it was flawless but because it exploited what the enemy already wanted to believe. In the same way, Satan cloaks spiritual poison in familiar language, feeding illusions that reinforce existing assumptions until falsehood tastes like truth and the truth is hidden in plain sight.

The battle isn't fought with swords or creeds, but with the plumb line of truth held against every teaching that dares speak in God's name. The call to test every teaching against Scripture is no longer optional—it's a matter of spiritual survival.

This is precisely what we see in religious traditions that claim divine authority while contradicting the word of God. When institutions assert that salvation is mediated through rituals, sacraments, or ecclesiastical offices, they subtly replace Christ's finished work with human systems of control. This is not merely theological error; it is a spiritual deception campaign—a carefully orchestrated PSYOP that redirects trust away from Christ's sufficiency and toward institutional authority.

---

5. Barna, *American Worldview Inventory 2024*.

BY GRACE ALONE: THE BIBLICAL CASE AGAINST MERIT-BASED SALVATION

Many religious systems throughout history have taught that salvation must be earned—whether through ritual, moral achievement, or spiritual discipline. From ancient pagan rites to modern legalistic sects, the idea persists: divine favor must be merited, not received. This merit-based framework appeals to human pride, offering a sense of control and accomplishment. But it stands in stark contrast to the biblical message that salvation is a gift, not a wage (Rom 6:23).

Among the most subtle and influential distortions of the gospel is found in Roman Catholic doctrine. The catechism itself teaches that "justification is conferred in baptism, the sacrament of faith. It conforms us to the righteousness of God . . . and it is granted us through the co-operation of charity."[6] In this view, grace initiates salvation but must be infused through the sacraments and sustained by ongoing cooperation and obedience. The Council of Trent declared that "if anyone says that by faith alone the impious is justified . . . let him be anathema"[7]—meaning formally cursed or excommunicated from the church.

Scripture, however, declares plainly that we are "justified by faith apart from works of the law" (Rom 3:28). Any teaching that ties assurance of salvation to sacramental performance or human cooperation rewrites the gospel—turning Christ's finished work into a process mediated by ritual and reinforced by obedience. It shifts the anchor of assurance from Christ's sufficiency to personal striving, binding the conscience and confusing the heart.

Yet for those in Christ, assurance rests not on what we sustain but on what he has completed. The Spirit steadily trains believers to discern error, turning obedience from anxious striving into joyful response. As Paul declared, "He who began a good work in you will complete it until the day of Jesus Christ" (Phil 1:6).

"And if by grace, then it is no longer of works; otherwise grace is no longer grace. But if it is of works, it is no longer grace; otherwise work is no longer work" (Rom 11:6).

This redefining of grace strikes at the heart of salvation. Few distortions are more dangerous than those that tamper with the question of salvation itself. What happens when false teaching manipulates eternal

---

6. *CCC*, §1992.

7. Session 6, canon 9 in Schroeder, *Canons and Decrees*, 43.

destiny? The debate surrounding salvation—who receives it, how it is accessed, and whether Christianity is exclusive—reflects the greatest spiritual battle of all.

Military deception offers a striking parallel. The Soviet doctrine of *maskirovka*—a strategy of camouflage, disinformation, and staged maneuvers—regularly concealed troop movements and intentions from their enemies.[8] Before the Battle of Kursk in 1943, Soviet commanders used dummy tanks, false radio traffic, and concealed fortifications to convince German forces that their defenses were weaker than they really were. When the offensive came, the Red Army was far better prepared than the Germans expected, and the largest tank battle in history ended in Soviet victory.[9] By blending truth with illusion, they could project strength where there was weakness, or hide an offensive behind a screen of false security. The danger wasn't that the enemy lacked intelligence—it was that the intelligence they trusted had been subtly distorted. In the same way, Satan manipulates the doctrine of grace: institutionalizing distortion, mixing truth with ritual, and reshaping assurance until believers act on a false picture of reality.

The Exclusivity of Christ

False teachings often distort the reality of salvation, misrepresenting grace and eternal destiny. At the heart of Christianity, Jesus makes an exclusivist claim: "No one comes to the Father except through me" (John 14:6). This assertion challenges both religious pluralism and deception itself. The tension between inclusivity and exclusivity sparks some of the most debated discussions in theology: Is salvation reserved solely for believers in Jesus? What about those who have never heard the gospel? How does Christianity reconcile mercy with judgment?

Spiritual deception does not merely twist ideas—it alters eternal destinies. Satan's tactics are strategic—he takes pieces of truth, distorts them, and convinces people that lies are plausible, even attractive. His ultimate goal is to shift authority away from Scripture and lead souls astray. Truth liberates; deception enslaves. And the most dangerous lies are those that sound almost right.

---

8. Glantz, *Soviet Military Deception*, 47.
9. Glantz, *Soviet Military Deception*, 202.

This is why doctrines that teach salvation through sacraments or ecclesiastical mediation are spiritually perilous—they shift the focus from Christ to the church, from grace to ritual, from faith to works. In Scripture, *works* often refers to human efforts to obey the law in order to earn righteousness. Paul uses *law* (e.g., Rom 3:28) not merely to describe the Old Testament ceremonies or rituals but every form of human effort—whether Mosaic regulations, moral striving, or ecclesiastical requirements.[10] Whether through Jewish ordinances or church sacraments, the principle is the same: attempting to gain favor with God through performance. But as the apostle Paul warned, "If righteousness could be gained through the law, Christ died for nothing!" (Gal 2:21 NIV). To add works to grace is to nullify grace entirely—it's to say that Christ's death was insufficient, that the cross needs a supplement.

A modern illustration is found in the rise of Seventh-day Adventism. Emerging from the Millerite movement in the nineteenth century, this system blended an emphasis on end-times prophecy with renewed insistence on Old Testament law. Though many within the movement genuinely profess faith in Christ, the system itself has often treated Sabbath-keeping and dietary restrictions as boundary markers of the "true remnant church." By elevating such practices as tests of loyalty, Adventism risks turning assurance away from Christ's finished work and toward human compliance. This echoes the Galatian crisis: "Having begun in the Spirit, are you now being made perfect by the flesh?" (Gal 3:3). Satan's deception here is subtle, for he does not deny Christ outright but suggests that his work must be supplemented by law. This is works-based legalism dressed in religious zeal, and Paul's warning remains clear: "Christ will profit you nothing" if you add law to grace (Gal 5:2).

Isaiah illustrates this vividly: "But we are all like an unclean thing, and all our righteousnesses are like filthy rags" (Isa 64:6). The Hebrew phrase translated "filthy rags" (*beged 'iddîm*) refers to garments so defiled—stained by impurity and uncleanness—that they are rendered worthless and repulsive.[11] The image is not of slightly soiled clothing but of something ceremonially unclean, unacceptable in the presence of a holy God. Even the best human efforts, apart from his grace, are polluted by sin. By invoking this imagery, Isaiah reminds us that human works

---

10. Grudem, *Systematic Theology*, 722–23.
11. Oswalt, *Chapters 40–66*, 644.

cannot measure up to divine holiness; only Christ's righteousness can cover and cleanse.

The parallel in warfare is clear: once an army believes it must fight on two fronts, its strength is divided, its focus distracted. Satan's "Jesus-plus" gospel works the same way—it divides faith between God's gift and human effort, ensuring spiritual exhaustion without victory.

Viewed more broadly, this is the same distortion that has shaped parts of Roman Catholic doctrine as well. Not all Roman Catholic practices are equally problematic. Some doctrines—such as indulgences, purgatory, and the veneration of Mary—are explicitly unbiblical, directly contradicting the clear teaching of Scripture. Others, like liturgical forms or the church calendar, may be extra-biblical but not inherently heretical. This distinction matters. The concern is not with every tradition but with those that obscure or replace the gospel of grace with systems of human mediation.

At the heart of this distortion lies a deeper question: What does it mean to reject grace? Salvation is not imposed—it must be received. Scripture affirms that God does not coerce belief or force anyone into heaven. As C. S. Lewis insightfully observed, "The gates of hell are locked from the inside,"[12] implying that hell is not merely a punishment imposed by God but the natural consequence of rejecting him.

This rejection takes many forms. Some religious traditions—including Hinduism—attempt to harmonize Jesus with their beliefs, often portraying him as a spiritual teacher rather than the exclusive pathway to God. While such views may appear inclusive, they ultimately distort the biblical message—substituting a universal teacher for a crucified Savior and, in doing so, rejecting both the exclusivity of Christ and the redemptive path God has revealed.

Here again, religious deception mirrors PSYOP. Just as propaganda leaflets in Vietnam promised safety and prosperity to those who defected, false religions promise enlightenment or acceptance without the cross. Both appeal to human desire for an easier path, but both are lies crafted to divert allegiance away from the true source of freedom.

All religions contain elements of exclusivity because truth itself is exclusive. If salvation comes through Christ alone, then any teaching that denies this leads to spiritual deception. In a world where relativism

---

12. Lewis, *Problem of Pain*, 115.

promotes multiple paths, Christianity's exclusivity stands as a direct challenge—affirming that truth, by nature, cannot be flexible.

Christianity presents a unique dynamic: while salvation is offered to all, the pathway remains exclusive. Jesus invites everyone to come as they are, yet he does not leave them unchanged.

Some struggle with this paradox—how can murderers receive forgiveness while morally good individuals who reject Jesus may not? Yet, Scripture defines sin not just as immoral acts but as anything contrary to God's design. The Bible declares, "None are righteous, not even one" (Rom 3:10).

False teachings often misrepresent salvation as a system of moral achievement rather than a gift of grace. Deception encourages self-righteousness, leading people to believe they can secure eternal life apart from Christ. This is the heart of the Roman Catholic error: while affirming that grace is necessary, it teaches that grace is infused through sacraments, sustained by human cooperation, and mediated by the church. Scripture, however, declares that salvation is not a wage but a gift: "The wages of sin is death, but the gift of God is eternal life in Christ Jesus our Lord" (Rom 6:23).

A similar distortion appears in Islam, where salvation is tied to sincere belief, righteous deeds, and submission to Allah's will. While Islam affirms divine mercy, it denies the necessity of Christ's atoning sacrifice, offering conditional pardon based on obedience and ritual rather than the free gift of grace. Like Roman Catholicism, it presents a path of moral striving rather than a Savior who bore the penalty of sin.

Both examples function like classic deception operations: they offer "partial truths" wrapped in familiar language—mercy, faith, obedience—yet conceal the critical absence of substitutionary grace. In military PSYOP, this is the tactic of *maskirovka* discussed above: never deny everything outright, but hide the fatal flaw within an otherwise convincing picture.

In both cases, the gospel is obscured by systems that elevate human effort over divine grace. But the message of Scripture is clear: "For by grace you have been saved through faith, and that not of yourselves; it is the gift of God, not of works, lest anyone should boast" (Eph 2:8–9).

This emphasis on grace—not ritual, merit, or understanding—raises a profound and often painful question: What about those who cannot respond? One of the most difficult theological challenges is the fate of those who die in infancy, those unable to comprehend faith, or those who never encounter Christianity. In PSYOP terms, these "edge cases" expose whether a system's claims are genuinely benevolent or merely transactional. A counterfeit gospel tends to show its hand here by imposing human gatekeepers and procedures; the true gospel reveals the Giver's character.

While Scripture provides no exhaustive explanation, it does offer glimpses—affirming God's justice, mercy, and sovereignty—ensuring that his judgments are rooted in righteousness, not arbitrary condemnation.[13] This truth stands in stark contrast to systems that insist salvation must be mediated through religious rituals. Such beliefs not only limit God's freedom to extend grace but also misrepresent the nature of salvation itself. That's the logic of control operations: relocate authority from the King to the clerks, from Christ's proclamation to institutional process.

Doctrines like baptismal regeneration or the necessity of the Eucharist for salvation must therefore be tested against Scripture. If salvation depends on ritual, then grace is no longer grace—it becomes a transaction rather than a gift. Operationally, that's the shift from "gift-message" to "pay-to-play narrative"—the classic hallmark of deceptive influence, where compliance is purchased with assurances that only the institution can authorize.

This distortion is not limited to sacramental traditions. Another common deception is the reduction of God to an impersonal force—a concept found in many false religions. Eastern mysticism, for example, often portrays the physical world as illusory and advocates enlightenment through detachment from reality.[14] Deception loves disembodiment because it removes tangible checks: if reality is merely a fog, then any story can be sold.

Christianity counters this with the resurrection: a restoration of both physical and spiritual existence. It affirms that God's engagement with humanity is deeply personal. Unlike doctrines that suggest salvation comes through mystical awareness or inner awakening, Christianity teaches that Jesus entered history in flesh and blood to offer redemption.

---

13. Several passages suggest God's mercy and justice toward those unable to respond: David's hope of reunion with his child (2 Sam 12:22–23), the exemption of children "who have no knowledge of good or evil" (Deut 1:39), Jesus' welcome of children into his kingdom (Matt 19:14), and the assurance that "the Judge of all the earth" always does what is right (Gen 18:25; see also Ps 145:17).

14. Flood, *Introduction to Hinduism*, 86–91; Rahula, *What the Buddha Taught*, 51–58.

This is the ultimate counter-PSYOP: truth incarnate. The message is not an inner technique but a historical act—public, verifiable, embodied.

Whether through ritual or mysticism, one of the greatest deceptions is the idea that humanity can earn salvation—through morality, enlightenment, or spiritual discipline. Scripture paints a very different picture: humanity is deeply flawed yet profoundly loved. The enemy's playbook rarely denies love outright; it merely redefines it as something we must purchase.

False teachings often reject the doctrine of original sin, focusing instead on self-improvement or moral refinement. But Christianity teaches that sin is not merely the violation of moral laws—it is the rejection of God's design, whether through active rebellion or passive neglect. That's why "almost-truths" are so potent: they retain moral language while removing dependence on the Savior.

In every age, deception adapts its form—but its goal remains unchanged: to obscure the sufficiency of Christ and the authority of Scripture. Whether through mysticism, moralism, or institutional tradition, the enemy's strategy is to replace divine truth with human invention. Different uniforms, same mission profile: displace the Commander, elevate the intermediaries, control the story.

Grace is not earned. It is freely given. It is such a wonderful gift—we don't have to do anything, and in fact we can't, for "there is none righteous, no, not one" (Rom 3:10). We should be ecstatic over this incredible blessing, so plainly described in Scripture and so simple: grace is not achieved; it is received. Unlike philosophies that emphasize self-transformation as the path to salvation, Christianity teaches that salvation precedes transformation—not the other way around. Transformation is fruit, not currency.

Christianity offers a paradox that is both beautiful and challenging: salvation is radically inclusive in its invitation yet profoundly exclusive in its means. Grace is extended to all—regardless of background, status, or sin—but it is received only through faith in Christ. This is not "narrowness" as propaganda claims; it's specificity. A rescue radio frequency is exclusive by design—it saves precisely because it is clear.

Even so, those who affirm salvation by grace alone must guard against forgetting it. We may rightly reject sacramentalism yet subtly live as if our standing with God rested on our theological precision, devotional consistency, or moral performance. But the gospel is not "Jesus plus." It is Jesus—period. Self-reliance can masquerade as orthodoxy; performance can impersonate piety.

Alistair Begg illustrates this with a striking image:

If you were to ask the man who was crucified next to Jesus, "How did you get here?" he might say, "I don't know."

"What do you mean you don't know?"

"I mean, I don't know."

"Well, did you go to a Bible study?"

"No."

"Did you get baptized?"

"No."

"Did you understand justification by faith?"

"I've never heard of it."

"Then on what basis are you here?"

And he would say, "The Man on the middle cross said I could come."

Begg uses this story to underscore that salvation is not earned by theological knowledge, religious rituals, or moral performance, but by trusting in Christ alone. He urges believers to resist the temptation to answer the question "Why are you saved?" in the first person—"Because I . . ."—and instead answer in the third person, "Because he . . ."[15]

This is the daily reminder every Christian needs: our salvation rests not on our grasp of doctrine, our record of obedience, or our emotional experience, but on Christ's finished work and his invitation. We must preach this gospel to ourselves as often as we proclaim it to others. This is spiritual discipline as counterintelligence: rehearse the true story until counterfeit narratives lose their power.

Yet, when we forget the simplicity of grace, we become vulnerable—not only to false doctrine but to subtle distortions that masquerade as truth. These deceptions don't merely misstate doctrine; they misalign authority and redefine salvation. Influence ops do not always need new lies; they only need to move the center of trust.

Over time, such error infiltrates religious structures, shaping traditions that contradict Scripture and enslave rather than liberate. That's why it's vital to understand what constitutes false doctrine—and to recognize misinterpretations of Scripture—so we can faithfully discern truth from deception. Train like a unit that expects deception: red-team your assumptions, and return to Scripture as the mission order.

---

15. Begg, "Power and Message."

Unveiling Deception

In 1957, a man named Frank Abagnale Jr. began impersonating professionals—pilots, doctors, and lawyers—without ever holding a license or formal training. He forged credentials so convincingly that even experts believed him. Airlines let him fly jump seat. Hospitals let him supervise medical staff. His story later gained pop-culture fame when Leonardo DiCaprio portrayed him in the 2002 film *Catch Me If You Can*. His deception was so effective because it mimicked legitimacy. It wasn't the outlandishness of his claims that fooled people—it was how closely they resembled the truth.[16]

Spiritual deception works the same way. False doctrine doesn't always arrive in the form of blatant heresy. It often comes dressed in orthodoxy, quoting Scripture, using familiar language, and cloaking itself in tradition. That's what makes it so dangerous. It doesn't deny truth outright—it distorts it just enough to mislead. Think Operation Mincemeat: forged documents placed on a dead courier led Nazi planners to trust what looked impeccably official. The paperwork was wrong precisely because it looked so right.

False doctrine often masquerades as sacred tradition, cloaked in centuries of repetition and institutional endorsement. But longevity does not equal legitimacy. As Jesus warned, "In vain they worship Me, teaching as doctrines the commandments of men" (Matt 15:9). Repetition is a PSYOP multiplier; only revelation is a safeguard.

In this chapter, we will expose the subtle ways deception infiltrates faith, misleads believers, and undermines the power of God's truth. We will examine what makes false teachings so persuasive, why they often go unnoticed, and how Scripture serves as our strongest defense against spiritual manipulation. Three rules of discernment mirror three rules of counter-deception: verify sources (Acts 17:11), confirm context (2 Tim 2:15), and test outcomes (Matt 7:16).

The question is not if deception will come—it is already here. The real challenge is this: Will you recognize it?

To answer that question, we must examine how Scripture portrays deception—not as a distant threat but as a present and active force. The Bible does not merely warn of deception; it exposes its tactics, its agents, and it's devastating consequences. Scripture gives you the adversary's playbook in advance—use it.

---

16. Abagnale and Redding, *Catch Me If You Can*, 1–25.

WHAT ARE TRUTH AND FALSEHOOD?

Scripture warns us repeatedly of deception's dangers, highlighting Satan's use of falsehood to lead people astray. Three powerful examples illustrate this truth:

> Then I saw an angel coming down from heaven, having the key to the bottomless pit and a great chain in his hand. He laid hold of the dragon, that serpent of old, who is the Devil and Satan, and bound him for a thousand years; and he cast him into the bottomless pit, and shut him up, and set a seal on him, so that he should deceive the nations no more till the thousand years were finished. (Rev 20:1–3)

> The coming of the lawless one is according to the working of Satan, with all power, signs, and lying wonders, and with all unrighteous deception among those who perish, because they did not receive the love of the truth, that they might be saved. And for this reason God will send them strong delusion, that they should believe the lie, that they all may be condemned who did not believe the truth but had pleasure in unrighteousness. (2 Thess 2:9–12)

> Be sober, be vigilant; because your adversary the devil walks about like a roaring lion, seeking whom he may devour. (1 Pet 5:8)

These passages reveal how deception operates as a weapon against truth. But to understand its full impact, we must define what "false" truly means—especially in the realm of faith. Note the pattern: authority claimed (power, signs), perception shaped (lying wonders), behavior altered (devour, deceive). That's the full PSYOP cycle.

Falsehood takes many forms, depending on the context in which it appears. In science, it contradicts evidence. In relationships, it manifests as betrayal. In education, it distorts taught principles. But in matters of faith, falsehood is far more dangerous—it leads believers away from the saving truth of God's word.

For Christians, "false" refers to anything that does not accord with Scripture or lead to salvation in Christ. As Samuel Chadwick (1860–1932), Wesleyan minister and principal of Cliff College renowned for his Spirit-filled preaching and fervent prayer life, aptly stated, "The man who thinks he can know the Word of God by mere intellectual study is greatly deceived. Spiritual truth is spiritually discerned."[17] False teaching offers guidance that cannot save, often leading people astray. False

---

17. Chadwick, *Way to Pentecost*, 38.

teachings, like shadows cast by dim light, often blend just enough truth to mask their poisonous core—misleading people into spiritual peril. The countermeasure is simple: increase the light, not the shadow. Read more Scripture, not more speculation.

The rise of televangelists who preach the "health and wealth gospel" illustrates the dangers of false teachings. Figures like Benny Hinn, a theatrical televangelist known for his global "Miracle Crusades" and promotion of prosperity theology, have faced criticism for promoting doctrines that prioritize material prosperity over spiritual growth. Such messages often exploit vulnerable believers, diverting them from the true gospel and causing spiritual confusion.[18]

But deception is not limited to fringe movements or prosperity preachers—it also thrives in institutionalized religion. When churches elevate human authority above Scripture, when they tie salvation to denominational loyalty, or when they teach that grace is dispensed through sacraments or salvation is mediated by priests, they obscure the simplicity of the gospel. The same distortion appears when ritual performance is treated as a substitute for faith, when mystical experience is prized over Christ's finished work, or when legalistic moral codes are portrayed as the pathway to God. In every case, human tradition replaces divine truth.

In Eastern Orthodoxy, for example, salvation is often portrayed as a mystical process tied to participation in the sacraments and *theosis*—a doctrine of spiritual transformation in which believers are gradually conformed to the likeness of God through union with Christ.[19] While theosis rightly emphasizes holiness and union with God, it can risk blurring the clarity of justification by faith alone—especially when sacramental participation is elevated above personal faith.

In some mainline Protestant denominations, theological liberalism has led to the rejection of core doctrines—such as the resurrection, substitutionary atonement, or the authority of Scripture—replacing gospel truth with moralism or cultural accommodation.

Even within evangelical circles, legalism that elevates rules or denominational distinctives above Christ's finished work can distort the message of grace.

---

18. Bowler, *Blessed*, 78. The prosperity gospel recasts Christianity around self-interest—"What can God do for me?"—rather than faithful obedience to God. Scripture shows that God's good plan for His people often includes suffering, as seen in the martyrdom of Stephen (Acts 7).

19. Veniamin, *Orthodox Understanding of Salvation*, 13–27.

Whether through ritualism, relativism, or rigid moralism, institutionalized religion often complicates what God has made clear: salvation is by grace alone, through faith alone, in Christ alone.

"If you abide in My word, you are My disciples indeed. And you shall know the truth, and the truth shall make you free" (John 8:31–32).

This conviction echoes through the early church. Hippolytus of Rome (c. AD 170–235), a theologian known for opposing doctrinal error and defending biblical authority, clarifies this further:

> There is, brethren, one God, the knowledge of whom we gain from the Holy Scriptures, and from no other source . . . so all of us who wish to practice piety will be unable to learn its practice from any other quarter than the oracles of God. Whatever things, then, the Holy Scriptures declare, at these let us look; and whatever things they teach, these let us learn.[20]

The church fathers didn't treat Scripture as one voice among many; they treated it as the operational order. Every other signal was secondary traffic.

The Question of Authority

When seeking truth, the critical question becomes, Where does authority lie? Is it rooted in a person, a group of people, traditions, or the Bible? In military terms, this is a command-and-control question: Who has the right to issue orders, set the ROE, and define the mission? In PSYOP, the first move is often to transfer perceived authority from the rightful source to a substitute—so that the substitute's "orders" feel binding.

This question is not theoretical—it is foundational. If Scripture is sufficient, then no pope, council, or tradition can override its authority. But if tradition is elevated to equal footing with Scripture, then the door is opened to doctrines that contradict the gospel itself. That elevation is a classic legitimacy operation: build an alternative center of gravity and then compel compliance through reputation, ritual, and repetition.

Deception most often arises when truth is mixed with tradition, emotion, or logic. Satan rarely discards Scripture outright—he distorts it. At the heart of doctrinal discernment, therefore, lies the "square"—the word of God. It is the central, immovable standard by which every theological development must be measured. The square is not merely a reference point; it is the fixed boundary of divine truth, revealed in Scripture

---

20. Hippolytus, *Noetus* 9.

and sufficient for faith and practice. It is perfect in shape, unyielding in structure, and incapable of accommodating error without distortion. Think of the square as your grid square on the map: if your navigation points drift off-grid, your whole operation goes astray no matter how confident the convoy feels.

Throughout church history, movements have risen around this square. Each one claims a corner—anchoring part of its theology within the word of God, while at times extending beyond its bounds into human reasoning, ecclesiastical tradition, or emotional experience. These corners represent partial alignments: some teachings remain inside the square, rooted in biblical fidelity; others protrude outward, introducing elements foreign to Scripture. Partial alignment is precisely where MILDEC (short for military deception) thrives: deliberate actions designed to mislead an adversary's decision-making by presenting a believable pattern with a concealed deviation. The fairest countermeasure is ruthless map-checking—returning to coordinates (Scripture) rather than following convoy chatter (tradition).

Not everything outside the square is necessarily harmful. Some practices may be culturally useful or spiritually enriching—as long as they are recognized for what they are: human expressions that must remain subordinate to divine revelation. But the danger arises when such practices are elevated to the same level as Scripture. At that point, they compete with truth and begin to reshape the gospel itself. That is escalation from TTPs to doctrine. In military terms, TTPs—short for techniques, tactics, and procedures—are the common ways operations are carried out before being codified as binding doctrine. In the same way, when spiritual preferences and customs harden into "musts," they no longer serve the gospel but start to supplant it. PSYOP exploits that shift, converting preferences into creeds and customs into commandments.

The longer one gazes at truth, the clearer it becomes. Yet when anything supersedes Scripture—whether papal decree, denominational tradition, emotional fervor, or logical construct—clarity gives way to confusion, and the gospel becomes vulnerable to distortion. The square must remain the supreme authority. Doctrine that cannot fit wholly within its lines must be reformed or rejected, while practices outside it must always bow to Scripture rather than claim its authority. Practically, every claim should be treated like a radio transmission: authenticate the call sign (source), verify the message against the operations order (Scripture), and reject spoofed traffic (traditions claiming equal rank). In military usage, an operations order (or op-order) is the authoritative plan that directs how a mission is to be carried out; in the same way, Scripture functions as the believer's op-order, the binding directive for faith and practice.

From this vantage point, the early church can be traced into what became Roman Catholicism. To be fair, much of Roman Catholic doctrine remains biblically consistent, especially in areas such as Christology, Trinitarian theology, and the preservation of the canon.[21] Indeed, God in his providence used the Roman Catholic Church to preserve the Scriptures, articulate the doctrine of the Trinity, defend the deity of Christ, and withstand heresies such as Arianism.[22]

Yet within the remaining fraction lies a deadly admixture: a works-based system that denies the once-for-all sufficiency of Christ's atoning death (Heb 10:10). This was formally codified at the Council of Trent (1545–1563), which convened over twenty-five sessions and produced seventeen dogmatic decrees (formal statements of doctrine) and more than one hundred canons (authoritative rules condemning specific errors and prescribing church practice). Among them was the declaration of "anathema" (formal condemnation) on those who hold to justification by faith alone.[23] In session 4, the council further proclaimed, "No one, relying on his own skill, shall—in matters of faith and morals pertaining to the edification of Christian doctrine—presume to interpret the said sacred Scripture contrary to that sense which holy mother Church . . . has held and does hold."[24]

Rome argued this restriction preserved unity, but in practice it suppressed the biblical pattern of Berean verification (Acts 17:11). The Bereans were commended because they eagerly received Paul's message and diligently tested it against Scripture to confirm its truth—carefully comparing teaching to God's word rather than blindly submitting to human authority.

Such teaching is not merely error but what Paul called "another gospel" (Gal 1:6–9). By anathematizing justification by faith alone as articulated by the Reformers and forbidding private interpretation of Scripture,

---

21. CCC, §1992. The catechism affirms that justification is "conferred in Baptism, the sacrament of faith," through grace. Protestants agree salvation is by grace but reject Rome's sacramental system, arguing it conflates faith with ritual and undermines the sufficiency of Christ's once-for-all work (Heb 10:10).

22. Kelly, *Early Christian Doctrines*, 223–25.

23. See session 6, canon 9 in Schroeder, *Canons and Decrees*, 43.

24. Session 4 ("Decree Concerning the Canonical Scriptures") in Buckley, *Canons and Decrees*, 18.

Trent replaced grace with merit, faith with ritual, and the gospel with a system of earned righteousness—baptizing infants into presumed salvation, confirming unregenerate hearts, and perpetuating spiritual death under the guise of tradition. By elevating tradition to equal authority with Scripture—and asserting apostolic origin for those traditions—Trent institutionalized a framework in which individual discernment is subordinated to ecclesiastical decree. From an information-warfare lens, Trent centralized interpretive authority and restricted decentralized verification—the opposite of Berean fieldcraft, where believers independently tested every teaching against Scripture. It made the "authorized narrative" the single source of truth and labeled rival signals as hostile.

This drift did not remain confined to Rome. In 1054, five hundred years before Trent, the Great Schism divided the church into Eastern Orthodoxy and Western Catholicism. Each branch claimed to represent the true church, yet both had already departed from the square of God's word. Tensions over the addition of the *Filioque clause*—an alteration to the Nicene Creed that changed the procession of the Holy Spirit from "who proceeds from the Father" to "who proceeds from the Father and the Son"[25]—deepened the divide. This modification, made unilaterally in the West, was rejected by the East as unauthorized and theologically misleading. Disputes about papal supremacy and differences in liturgy and practice added further strain. The East emphasized mystical tradition, sacramentalism, and the veneration of icons, while the West elevated papal authority and codified works-righteousness.[26] In both cases, tradition was placed alongside—or above—Scripture.

The result was a fractured church: two branches preserving elements of truth yet mingling them with distortions that obscured the gospel. The schism underscores the danger of shifting authority from God's word to human structures: division and deception inevitably follow. Strategically, this is what happens when coalitions—alliances of nations or factions formed for a common cause—fight over who writes the operation order rather than what the op-order says. Authority detached from the text yields competing narratives and enduring fragmentation.

---

25. The *Filioque* ("and the Son") controversy was significant because it altered the Nicene Creed without an ecumenical council's consent, raising questions of authority as well as theology. Theologically, the East argued that the Spirit proceeds eternally from the Father alone (John 15:26), while the West emphasized the unity of Father and Son in sending the Spirit (John 16:7). To the East, the unilateral change distorted the Trinity; to the West, it safeguarded the Son's full divinity.

26. Pelikan, *Spirit of Eastern Christendom*, 173–79.

WHAT ARE TRUTH AND FALSEHOOD?

In God's providence, the Protestant Reformation arose as a necessary reset—a doctrinal return to the authority of Scripture and the purity of the gospel. Reformers like Martin Luther, John Calvin, and Huldrych Zwingli courageously reclaimed justification by faith alone and the supremacy of the word of God.[27] Yet even they were not immune to error, for all humans are fallible. Though overwhelmingly biblical, their theology retained remnants of Roman Catholicism, such as covenantal assumptions and infant baptism. These were not "damnable" errors like Rome's sacramentalism, but they introduced theological drift—constructs that seemed logical yet lacked biblical mandate. Infant baptism, modeled after Jewish circumcision, is nowhere prescribed in the New Testament.[28] Sabbath observance and other law-retaining elements likewise echoed Israel rather than the freedom of the new covenant. Such errors did not destroy the gospel, but they divided Christ's church. Still, despite their flaws, the Reformers were God's instruments in recovering gospel clarity, showing that he uses imperfect vessels for his purposes. Even successful counteroffensives carry battlefield friction; reforms can overcorrect or retain legacy procedures—holdovers from past operations that no longer fit the mission. That's why after-action reviews (Acts 17:11 discipline) never end.

In the centuries that followed, Evangelicalism emerged, centered on personal conversion and gospel proclamation. Leaders like D. L. Moody and Billy Graham emphasized that all are born lost and must be regenerated—a message consistent with Jesus (John 3:3), Paul (Rom 3:23), and Peter (Acts 2:38).[29] Yet even this movement, built on the Bible, introduces traditions of its own. Sunday school, begun in 1789 by Robert Raikes, coinciding with the ratification of the US Constitution, was not instituted by Christ or his apostles, yet many equate it with church health.[30] Morning services, now standard, were not the pattern of the early church, which often gathered in the evenings. More concerning is the rise of decisionism—the belief that raising a hand, walking an aisle, or repeating a prayer secures salvation. This practice produces countless false assurances, echoing Jesus' warning, "Not everyone who says to me, 'Lord, Lord,' will enter the kingdom of heaven" (Matt 7:21–23). Just as sacramentalism offers false assurance through ritual, decisionism offers it through emotional response. True regeneration is not marked

---

27. Bainton, *Here I Stand*, 143–55.
28. Calvin, *Institutes* 4.16.
29. Marsden, *Fundamentalism and American Culture*, 56–63.
30. Boylan, *Sunday School*, 22.

by a momentary act but by a transformed life: a new heart, a hatred of sin, and a desire to obey God (Ezek 36:26–27, 2 Cor 13:5). Emotion is a powerful PSYOP amplifier; when untethered from Scripture, it creates the illusion of commitment without conversion—strong signal, wrong content. As Jeremiah reminds us, "The heart is deceitful above all things, and desperately wicked" (Jer 17:9).

The charismatic renewal marked another development in the church's story. Many within it are sincere believers who love Christ, yet the movement has often emphasized emotionalism and supernatural signs, particularly tongues and healing. This emphasis, however well-intentioned, can reveal dissatisfaction with the sufficiency of Scripture and the indwelling Spirit. The biblical gift of tongues was a Spirit-given ability to speak unlearned human languages for gospel proclamation (Acts 2, 1 Cor 12–14), a sign "for unbelievers" (1 Cor 14:22).[31] Modern tongues, for the most part, take the form of patterned syllables or private prayer language—not the miraculous gift given at Pentecost. Similarly, modern healing claims are selective and orchestrated, often resembling staged spectacles—far removed from apostolic healings where even shadows brought recovery (Acts 5:15). Paul himself urged Timothy to take wine for his ailments (1 Tim 5:23), showing that even in the apostolic age sickness was often met with ordinary means rather than miraculous healing. He also testified that his own "thorn in the flesh" remained despite prayer (2 Cor 12:7–9).[32] The craving for signs easily opens the door to counterfeit miracles, for Satan eagerly mimics the supernatural (Matt 24:4–5). Counterfeit signs function like decoys on the battlefield—attention magnets that pull focus from the Commander's clear orders.

Across every phase of church history—Roman Catholicism, Eastern Orthodoxy, the Reformation, Evangelicalism, and the charismatic renewal—the pattern remains the same: each has built on the Bible in part, yet each has introduced error. This recurring pattern reflects the strategy of syncretism—the blending of biblical truth with foreign elements, producing a hybrid that feels familiar yet distorts the gospel. Satan rarely replaces truth outright; he dilutes it, mixing the signal with interference until the message is scrambled. Some errors are fatal, others merely divisive, but all remind us of the devil's oldest strategy: to distort God's word. The antidote is not tradition, emotion, or theological logic,

---

31. Fee, *God's Empowering Presence*, 892–95.
32. Schaff, *Apostolic Christianity*, 399–401.

but Scripture alone. We must examine ourselves (2 Cor 13:5), test our doctrines, and continually return to the square—the word of God—as our sole authority. Only then can we discern truth from tradition, regeneration from ritual, and the true gospel from its counterfeits. Make this your ROE: "No claim outranks Scripture." If it conflicts with the op-order, it's noncompliant traffic.

At this point, the most pressing question emerges: Why do you believe what you believe? Is your trust anchored in what church tradition has told you, in the inclinations of your own heart (Jer 17:9), or in the unchanging word of God? Only Scripture stands as the final authority.

This tension between Scripture and tradition is not abstract—it has shaped entire religious systems. Roman Catholicism, for example, builds its framework not solely on the Bible but on what it defines as the single "deposit of faith," comprised of Scripture, tradition, and magisterial authority.[33] In practice, this means that doctrines such as papal infallibility, transubstantiation, and purgatory—though Catholics cite biblical texts, their connection depends on interpretive traditions developed over time—emerged through ecclesiastical development rather than a plain reading of Scripture.

At Trent, this framework was codified: Scripture was declared subject to the church's official interpretation, and private judgment contrary to ecclesiastical decree was forbidden. Catholics argue this preserves unity, but it stands in stark contrast to the Bereans, who were commended for testing every teaching by Scripture itself (Acts 17:11). By elevating tradition to equal authority with Scripture, Trent institutionalized a system in which human decree can displace divine revelation. That is narrative dominance by design—an authority architecture that privileges centralized messaging over distributed verification.

A plain reading of the Bible, however, points consistently to salvation by faith in Christ alone, apart from hierarchy, sacraments, or human intermediaries. As 2 Tim 3:16–17 affirms, Scripture alone is sufficient to equip believers for every good work. The issue of authority remains the hinge: Will we cling to man-made structures, or submit to God's word as

---

33. *CCC*, §82. The catechism states, "As a result the Church . . . does not derive her certainty about all revealed truths from the holy Scriptures alone. Both Scripture and Tradition must be accepted and honored with equal sentiments of devotion and reverence." See also Vatican II, *Dei Verbum*, §§9–10, which affirms that "Sacred tradition and Sacred Scripture form one sacred deposit of the Word of God, committed to the Church," and that the task of authentic interpretation "has been entrusted exclusively to the living teaching office of the Church" (the Magisterium).

final? This is the decisive point in the OODA loop: observe the claims, orient by Scripture, decide against counterfeits, act in obedience. Speed and clarity here prevent capture by misinformation.

The same manipulation of authority appears in modern forms as well. The New Age movement, cloaked in enlightenment, offers seekers spiritual fulfillment while distorting biblical truth. Concepts like "Christ consciousness" reduce Jesus to a spiritual archetype rather than the divine Savior.[34] As with ancient traditions, fragments of truth are fused with error to lure seekers away from the gospel. The enemy's strategy is unchanged: undermine Scripture, mix truth with falsehood, and divert trust from Christ to counterfeit authorities. Different uniforms, same op. The counter is unchanged too: authenticate every voice by the voice of Scripture.

The modern worship song "Make Room" echoes this call for spiritual renewal, urging believers to release empty traditions and rigid forms of religion in order to embrace God's better way.[35] When believers confront institutional teachings or cultural assumptions with Scripture, they discover that God's word is sufficient, requiring no external tradition or human system to reveal truth. This anthem echoes the heart of the Reformation and the witness of the Bereans—it is a call to clear away every rival authority so that Christ alone stands as Lord. For the word of God still stands firm. It is the square—perfect, unyielding, and sufficient. Only by submitting wholly to its authority can the church guard the gospel and shine as a beacon of truth in a world of deception. Hold the square. Keep the signal clean. Let Scripture be the only net that catches every message before it reaches your heart.

SCRIPTURE: OUR FINAL AND SUFFICIENT AUTHORITY

Having exposed the dangers of spiritual deception, we now turn to the unshakable authority of Scripture—our anchor in the storm and compass in the confusion. In the fog of war, units survive by their true compass and the authenticated op-order; every other voice is treated as potential spoofing. So it is with the Christian: Scripture is the authenticated order; everything else is chatter.

---

34. Groothuis, *Confronting the New Age*, 112.
35. The Church Will Sing, "Make Room."

WHAT ARE TRUTH AND FALSEHOOD?

Amid the cacophony of competing voices, Scripture stands resolute, an unwavering beacon that guides believers through the fog of spiritual confusion. As Ps 119:105 affirms, "Your word is a lamp to my feet and a light to my path"—illuminating the way forward when all other lights fail. Electronic warfare tries to blind and jam; the lamp of the word cuts through the jamming with a fixed signal that doesn't drift.

This is not merely a doctrinal claim—it is a divine guarantee. Scripture is not one authority among many but the final authority: the voice of God, preserved for his people. Unlike human wisdom, which is flawed and subject to error, Scripture is God-breathed—fully sufficient to perfect the believer. Paul emphasizes this in 1 Thess 2:13: "For this reason we also thank God without ceasing, because when you received the word of God which you heard from us, you welcomed it not as the word of men, but as it is in truth, the word of God, which also effectively works in you who believe." Final authority is a command decision, not a committee suggestion. Soldiers don't vote on the ROE—they obey it.

This contrast remains vital today. If a teaching is not rooted in God's word, it is merely human opinion. The Bible alone holds the power to transform lives and lead believers to truth. Consider the journey of Lee Strobel, a former atheist and investigative journalist. Determined to disprove Christianity, he embarked on a deep examination of the faith—only to encounter the compelling, undeniable truth of Scripture. His journey, documented in *The Case for Christ*, highlights the Bible's ability to confront skepticism and awaken genuine faith.[36]

Strobel's transformation is a testament to the Bible's power—not merely a book but the ultimate, unshakable authority for discerning truth. Scripture is divinely inspired, timeless, and wholly sufficient to guide believers in faith and daily living. No other source of authority can rival the supremacy of God's word.

The Bible is complete and unchanging. Jude 1:3 declares, "Beloved, while I was very diligent to write to you concerning our common salvation, I found it necessary to write to you exhorting you to contend earnestly for the faith which was once for all delivered to the saints." The phrase "the faith" refers to the body of New Testament truths that the apostles communicated under the guidance of the Holy Spirit. "Once for all delivered" signifies that this revelation was given within a single time period and was completed. This directly affirms that Scripture is final and

---

36. Strobel, *Case for Christ*, 73.

refutes the notion that Christian doctrine is progressively transmitted by any individual, organization, or institution. There is no "living doctrine feed" to be patched later—no updates from a human headquarters. The package is complete, signed, and sealed.

This truth stands in direct contrast to the Roman Catholic claim that the magisterium can issue binding, authoritative teachings that carry the weight of divine authority. While Roman Catholic doctrine teaches that the Roman Catholic Church is the custodian and interpreter of truth, Scripture declares that the faith has already been delivered—once for all. Christianity is founded solely on the authority of Scripture, not on evolving traditions that develop beyond the divinely inspired word. PSYOP seeks to relocate trust from the fixed text to the living interpreter; Scripture anchors trust in the Author, not the narrator.

Scripture itself warns against any alteration. Revelation 22:18–19 solemnly declares that those who add to or take away from God's word will face judgment. Like a compass even slightly misaligned, doctrinal error may seem small at first, but over time it leads generations far from the truth. A one-degree error at launch produces a miss at impact; small textual edits become strategic drift.

The authority of the Bible does not originate from the church—it comes directly from God himself. Yet, throughout history, religious institutions have established traditions that extend far beyond Scripture, sometimes offering assurances that contradict biblical truth. One striking example of this can be found at St. Peter's Basilica in the Vatican, where the Holy Door (*Porta Sancta*)—opened only during Jubilee Years (special Holy Years declared by the pope)—serves as a powerful symbol of forgiveness, reconciliation, and spiritual renewal.

According to Roman Catholic tradition, walking through the Holy Door during a Jubilee Year can be part of receiving a plenary indulgence— the remission of temporal punishment due to sin, not the forgiveness of sin itself.[37] To obtain it, the faithful must also go to sacramental confession, receive the Eucharist, and pray for the Pope's intentions.[38] While framed as an act of pilgrimage, this practice raises profound theological concerns. Nowhere does Scripture tie forgiveness or reconciliation to a physical doorway. Instead, Jesus makes it clear that redemption comes solely through faith in him (John 14:6).

---

37. See *CCC*, §§1471–79, which define indulgences as "the remission before God of the temporal punishment due to sins whose guilt has already been forgiven."

38. Francis, *Misericordiae Vultus*, §22.

WHAT ARE TRUTH AND FALSEHOOD?

The idea that passing through a specific entrance could contribute to absolution stretches tradition beyond biblical boundaries, reinforcing a system of religious authority that dictates spiritual access rather than relying on God's grace alone. This exemplifies how institutionalized religion, rather than preserving Scripture's authority, often introduces traditions that subtly shift the focus from God's word to human rituals. This is the mechanics of influence: create a visible rite, attach promises, and route conscience through the institution. The sign replaces the substance.

Such traditions, though cloaked in reverence, risk replacing repentance with ritual and grace with works. They illustrate how spiritual deception can be embedded in sacred spaces, leading sincere seekers away from the simplicity of the gospel. Sacred décor can function like camouflage: it hides the position of error inside the silhouette of piety.

This example highlights a broader issue within institutionalized religion: when tradition supplants biblical truth, it risks leading believers to trust in ritual rather than repentance. Rather than safeguarding Scripture's authority, religious institutions often introduce practices that subtly redirect focus from God's word to human customs. Countermeasure: ROE for the soul—"If it cannot be demonstrated from Scripture, it cannot bind the conscience."

Yet biblical authority was never dependent on institutional endorsement. The early church, under the guidance of the Holy Spirit, recognized the apostolic writings as divinely inspired and equal in authority to the Old Testament. These texts were circulated, embraced, and affirmed by God's people—not through ecclesiastical decree but through spiritual discernment. The church did not bestow authority on the Bible; it bowed to the authority the Bible already possessed. Authority recognition is like target identification: the church didn't manufacture the signature—it confirmed it.

As these patterns reveal, traditions—no matter how long-standing—must be tested against Scripture. Jesus rebuked the Pharisees for elevating man-made rituals above God's commandments (Matt 15:3-9), demonstrating that religious authority is never a substitute for divine truth. This reality is not confined to Roman Catholic traditions; throughout history, various religious systems have introduced practices and teachings that subtly redefine salvation and distort God's word. Test every signal: authenticate the call sign (Christ, the apostles), check the content (context and canon), and disregard spoofed traffic (traditions claiming coequal authority).

For this reason, God has placed strict boundaries on his word.

Warnings Against Additions

Because Scripture is complete, God issues a solemn warning in Rev 22:18–19: "If anyone adds to these things, God will add to him the plagues that are written in this book; and if anyone takes away . . . God shall take away his part from the Book of Life." Those who claim to possess new revelations or traditions on equal footing with the Bible are subject to this judgment. The canon is closed. The word is complete.

Guided by the Holy Spirit, early Christian leaders recognized the authenticity of the apostolic writings, affirming them as Holy Scripture long before later councils made formal declarations. This acknowledgment was not a delayed decision but a response to the Spirit's guidance, allowing the church to embrace the divinely inspired word without hesitation. Among the many passages that illustrate this reality are 1 Thess 2:13, quoted above, and two passages from John:

> However, when He, the Spirit of truth, has come, He will guide you into all truth; for He will not speak on His own authority, but whatever He hears He will speak; and He will tell you things to come. (John 16:13)

> For I have given to them the words which You have given Me; and they have received them, and have known surely that I came forth from You; and they have believed that You sent Me. (John 17:8)

This pattern of recognition continued beyond the apostolic era, as the early church fathers consistently treated these writings as authoritative Scripture. Irenaeus (AD 125–192), a Greek bishop of Lyon and an early Christian theologian, quoted the New Testament over eighteen hundred times in his writings, using them "in such a way as to imply that they had for some time been considered as of unquestioned authority."[39] His extensive references demonstrate that the apostolic texts had long been regarded as authoritative—not because of later ecclesiastical ratification but because the early church, under the Holy Spirit's guidance, recognized their divine origin. He firmly accepted the four Gospels as Scripture—only those four. Clement of Alexandria (AD 150–217), a

---

39. Miller, *General Biblical Introduction*, 140.

Christian philosopher and theologian who led the Catechetical School of Alexandria, similarly cited and acknowledged the four Gospels and the majority of other New Testament books, referring to them as "divine Scriptures."[40] Tertullian (c. AD 150–220), an early Christian apologist from Carthage and the first theologian to write extensively in Latin, quotes the New Testament thousands of times. In fact, about two-thirds of his scriptural citations come from the New Testament.[41] He regarded these writings as authoritative Scripture.

Alongside these patristic testimonies, the manuscript tradition also confirms the early recognition of the canon. Early Old Latin translations of the Bible, produced in the late second century, likewise contained most or all of the writings that now make up the New Testament—further evidence that the canon was embraced by the believing community well before formal ecclesial pronouncements.[42] In 1740, the Muratorian fragment—a late second-century list of New Testament writings—was discovered in the Ambrosian Library in Milan, Italy. Though damaged at the beginning and end, it includes most of the books now recognized as the New Testament canon, demonstrating that the majority of the canon was already acknowledged by the late second century.[43]

Some object that the canon was not finalized until Athanasius's Festal Letter (AD 367)[44] or the Councils of Hippo (AD 393) and Carthage (AD 397).[45] Yet these councils did not create the canon but confirmed what had long been recognized by the churches. Others note that certain books—such as Hebrews, James, 2 Peter, and Revelation—were disputed in some regions. But these debates were the exception, not the norm, and they reveal the church's careful discernment rather than widespread uncertainty.[46] Roman Catholic tradition further asserts that the church created the canon and therefore holds authority over it. In reality, the church did not bestow authority on the canon—it acknowledged the authority

---

40. Clement of Alexandria, in his *Stromata* ("Miscellanies"), a wide-ranging theological work written around AD 200, refers to the canonical writings as divine Scriptures, treating them as authoritative (*Stromata* 7.16).

41. See Tertullian, *Apology* 21.

42. Metzger, *Canon of the New Testament*, 191–92.

43. Hentz, *History of the Lutheran Version*, 60.

44. Athanasius, *Festal Letters* 39.

45. See canon 24 from the Council of Carthage (AD 397); Hippo's canons survive only in summaries preserved by Carthage, so citing Carthage covers both.

46. Metzger, *Canon of the New Testament*, 155.

those writings already carried as inspired Scripture. This is similar to forward units authenticating an order before central command stamps it—the authority was inherent in the message, not dependent on later bureaucracy. This recognition underscores the Spirit's role in the canon's formation. Yet many modern scholars dismiss that role in shaping the canon. But the apostles did not record Christ's life by mere initiative, nor did the early church decide inspiration on its own. God actively guided the process, ensuring his word was preserved in its entirety. The New Testament contains the inspired words of the Lord Jesus Christ, and his followers recognize the voice of their Good Shepherd. As Jesus says in John 10:4–5, "When he has brought out all his own, he goes on ahead of them, and his sheep follow him because they know his voice. But they will never follow a stranger; in fact, they will run away from him because they do not recognize a stranger's voice." Likewise, John 10:27 affirms, "My sheep listen to my voice; I know them, and they follow me." In PSYOP, this is voice authentication: soldiers are trained to ignore spoofed commands and follow only the commander's true call sign.

Because of this, believers must be discerning, ensuring that the teachings they follow genuinely reflect Christ's voice rather than distortions created by men. What voices shape your faith? Are they leading you toward Christ or away from his truth? While the apostles passed down divinely inspired doctrine, history has shown that many religious leaders have introduced traditions that stray from biblical truth, elevating man-made customs over God's revelation.

This is the very danger Jesus warned against—a religious system that honors God with its lips but denies him through its traditions. When church leaders claim authority to define doctrine apart from Scripture, they risk becoming the very Pharisees Christ rebuked.

> Then some Pharisees and teachers of the law came to Jesus from Jerusalem and asked, "Why do your disciples break the tradition of the elders? They don't wash their hands before they eat!" Jesus replied, "And why do you break the command of God for the sake of your tradition? For God said, 'Honor your father and mother' and 'Anyone who curses their father or mother is to be put to death. But you say that if anyone declares that what might have been used to help their father or mother is 'devoted to God,' they are not to 'honor their father or mother' with it. Thus you nullify the word of God for the sake of your tradition." (Matt 15:1–6)

Paul echoes this warning in Col 2:8: "Beware lest anyone cheat you through philosophy and empty deceit, according to the tradition of men, according to the basic principles of the world, and not according to Christ." Jesus' rebuke continues with Isaiah's prophecy: "Hypocrites! Well did Isaiah prophesy about you, saying: 'These people draw near to Me with their mouth, and honor Me with their lips, but their heart is far from Me. And in vain they worship Me, teaching as doctrines the commandments of men'" (Matt 15:7–9).

This warning applies not only to first-century Judaism but to every religious system that elevates tradition above Scripture. When the Roman Catholic Magisterium claims the authority to define doctrine, interpret Scripture infallibly, and bind the consciences of believers, it places itself in the very position Christ condemned. This is an influence operation: displace trust from the Commander's orders to the interpreter's commentary. Once that shift happens, loyalty is rerouted.

This serves as a stark reminder that false authorities erode trust in God's truth, leading believers astray. Like cracks in a dam, false teachings weaken faith, allowing deception to flood in. Trusting anything other than Scripture opens the door to confusion and spiritual vulnerability. Deception works like water infiltration—small breaches become catastrophic over time if not sealed by returning to the blueprint.

Picture biblical authority as a lighthouse—firm, immovable, guiding lost souls through the storm. By contrast, human traditions are like drifting buoys—floating aimlessly, vulnerable to every wave. What will you anchor your faith to? The lighthouse never moves; the buoy goes wherever the tide pulls.

We are grateful that the Lord has provided his church with a complete and sufficient revelation. The Bible alone contains everything necessary for faith and practice. This is why the Reformers cried *Scripture alone*, not Scripture plus tradition, not Scripture filtered through a magisterial elite, but the word of God: accessible to all, sufficient for all, and authoritative over all. The Reformation's cry was a call to return to authenticated communications, not filtered traffic.

While some may describe the Bible as a tradition, it stands apart as the only God-breathed tradition—divinely revealed, inherently authoritative, and spiritually sufficient. That is what distinguishes it from all other written works. Scripture does not merely claim authority; it demonstrates it—containing nearly two thousand instances of phrases such as "Thus saith the Lord" (KJV). Therefore, the only tradition Christians are called to uphold is the inspired truth recorded in the word of God. This is not another signal—it is the source frequency. Every other channel must be tested against it.

Anchor in Scripture Alone

Indeed, Scripture always upholds itself as the absolute and sole standard for truth. Isaiah 8:20 warns, "To the law and to the testimony! If they do not speak according to this word, it is because there is no light in them." Those who speak contrary to God's word walk in darkness. This is the principle of signal authentication: if a transmission doesn't match the codebook, it's enemy traffic, no matter how confident the voice sounds.

At this pivotal moment, ask yourself, Will you place your trust in human traditions, religious systems, or teachings that distort and contradict the truth of Scripture—offering a salvation contrary to God's word? Or will you stand firmly on the inerrant, authoritative, and inspired word of the one true God? While some traditions may reflect biblical principles, the ultimate standard of truth is found only in Scripture.[47] As we uncover the flaws and inconsistencies of human traditions, the Bible's unchanging sufficiency emerges as the only unwavering foundation for faith, life, and eternal hope. False authorities function like counterfeit field manuals: they mimic the format but send units into ambush. Only the true manual—Scripture—keeps the force aligned to mission.

The Bible is not a product of the church but the divine word of God, God-breathed and self-authenticating. Second Timothy 3:16–17 (NIV) affirms, "All Scripture is God-breathed and is useful for teaching, rebuking, correcting and training in righteousness, so that the servant of God may be thoroughly equipped for every good work." That is full-spectrum equipping: doctrine for orientation, correction for misfires, training for readiness, and righteousness for mission conduct.

Think of the Bible's self-authenticating authority as a watermark from heaven—an invisible seal that marks it as divine. Just as a watermark secures a document's authenticity, Scripture carries the imprint of God's inspiration, validating its truth without needing human endorsement. In

---

47. While human traditions can distort Scripture, some align with it. The Apostles' and Nicene Creeds summarize biblical doctrine, and practices like baptism, the Lord's Supper, and moral teachings on justice and love reflect Scripture. Yet all traditions must be tested against God's word to uphold its sufficiency and salvation by faith in Christ alone (2 Tim 3:16–17, Eph 2:8–9).

intelligence terms, it carries the embedded encryption of divine authorship—unalterable, non-forgeable, impossible to counterfeit.

The apostolic writings further reinforce this truth. The apostles, under divine inspiration, were entrusted with recording the New Testament Scriptures, guided by the Holy Spirit. For example, 2 Pet 1:20–21 teaches, "Knowing this first, that no prophecy of Scripture is of any private interpretation, for prophecy never came by the will of man, but holy men of God spoke as they were moved by the Holy Spirit." The early church simply recognized this reality, submitting to the authority the Bible already possessed. They didn't "approve the comms"; they acknowledged the Commander's orders already stood.

The sufficiency of Scripture—God's word as the ultimate authority for faith and practice—stands as a central truth. Psalm 119:105 beautifully illustrates this sufficiency: "Your word is a lamp to my feet and a light to my path." Here, Scripture is portrayed as complete and capable of guiding believers as fully sufficient and carrying divine authority, requiring no external validation from human institutions. On the battlefield, illumination means survival—distinguishing friend from foe, safe path from ambush. Scripture is that illumination: not a flicker but a fixed light that refuses to be jammed.

DISTORTIONS IN PRACTICE

Distortions throughout church history are not listed here to merely rehearse past errors or to criticize institutions. They serve as warnings and reminders that point us back to Christ and his word. Every example—whether tradition, emotion, or human reasoning—shows what happens when anything is placed alongside or above the Bible. The goal of this section is not to magnify distortions but to magnify the truth: that Christ alone is the cornerstone, and Scripture alone is the immovable standard for faith and practice. The gospel is gloriously simple: salvation by grace through faith in Christ alone. Paul warned the Corinthians not to be led astray "from the simplicity that is in Christ" (2 Cor 11:3). Martin Luther echoed this truth when he wrote, "The gospel is the most simple doctrine there is, and it is also the most difficult, for it is opposed to reason and the wisdom of the world."[48] When that simplicity is burdened with layers of ritual or human authority, the clarity of the cross is obscured.

---

48. Luther, *Lectures on Galatians*, 29.

This is exactly how disinformation works: simplicity is concealed under layers of noise, until the central message is almost unrecognizable. In communications terms, the "signal-to-noise ratio" gets inverted—ritual and tradition become the loud broadcast, while the true signal of grace is drowned out.

At the same time, these examples are meant to train our discernment. By studying errors carefully—examining what was added, what was subtracted, or what was twisted—we learn how to "smoke out" distortions when they appear in our own day. This is red-teaming for the soul: stress-testing every claim, identifying where it deviates from the order, and spotting the weak point where manipulation slipped in. Military deception is often exposed not by the grand illusion but by the small inconsistency—the shadow that doesn't match the camouflage. So too with doctrine: it is in the details of addition, subtraction, and twisting that the counterfeit betrays itself.

Each case becomes a living lesson: why a teaching sounded persuasive, how it drifted from Scripture, and what consequences followed. The purpose, then, is not merely to review history but to train for discernment—developing the ability to test every doctrine and practice by the word of God and to recognize when something, no matter how compelling, has slipped outside the square of truth. This is field training, not museum study. History serves as the live-fire range where we learn to spot deception early, before it captures the high ground of our hearts and minds.

Headquarters Hijacked: Christ vs. the Papal Command

The pope—recognized by the Roman Catholic Church as the bishop of Rome and the supreme head of the universal church—claims a unique authority that places him above all other bishops. This office is known as the *papacy*, the Roman Catholic system that elevates the pope as Christ's vicar on earth and the visible source of unity for the church.[49] Yet the true foundation of the church rests on Christ himself, with Scripture as the authoritative record of his teaching and the apostles' witness. As Eph 2:20 declares, "Having been built on the foundation of the apostles and

---

49. The Catholic Church defines the papacy as the office of the bishop of Rome, who, as successor of Peter, "is the perpetual and visible source and foundation of the unity both of the bishops and of the whole company of the faithful." *CCC*, §882. See also Kelly, "Papacy."

prophets, Jesus Christ Himself being the chief cornerstone." Christ alone is the cornerstone—the one who holds the entire structure together. By divine inspiration, the apostles and prophets provided the foundation, which Scripture preserves as God's revelation of truth. Ultimately, Christ—not any man—is the source and sustainer of the church. In military terms, he is the fixed headquarters; every other "command" must authenticate back to him.

Matthew 16:18 is often cited in support of papal authority, yet its true meaning affirms Christ's centrality. When Jesus says, "You are Peter, and on this rock I will build My church," the rock is not Peter himself but the confession of faith in Christ's divine identity. The preceding verse, Matt 16:16 (NIV), records Peter's declaration: "You are the Messiah, the Son of the living God." Jesus affirms that his church is built upon this truth—his divinity and messianic role—not upon any human figure. The church is founded on Christ alone, and Scripture, as the inspired word of God, is inextricably linked to this foundation, serving as the means through which his truth is revealed, preserved, and rightly understood. To reinterpret this as Peter himself is to commit what PSYOP analysts call "narrative capture"—seizing a phrase, detaching it from its original context, and reprogramming it for institutional ends.

Though Jesus likely spoke in Aramaic, where the word *kepha* would have been used in both cases, the inspired Greek text preserves a meaningful distinction: *petros* (masculine, a stone) and *petra* (feminine, a massive rock or bedrock). While some argue this is only a grammatical necessity, the contrast in wording naturally draws the reader to see a difference.[50] Christ is not building his church on one man but on the unshakable reality Peter confessed—"You are the Christ, the Son of the living God."

This interpretation is not a Protestant invention. Several early church fathers interpreted the "rock" as the confession or as Christ himself. Chrysostom taught that the church rests upon the faith Peter expressed, not his person.[51] Augustine, after considering both views, explicitly concluded, "On this rock, which you have confessed, I will build My church"[52]—underscoring that the foundation is the truth about Christ, not Peter in isolation. Other fathers, such as Origen and Hilary,

---

50. Keener, *Gospel of Matthew*, 425–27. See also Carson, "Matthew," 375.

51. "Upon this rock; that is, on the faith of his confession." John Chrysostom, *Homilies on Matthew* 54.3 (*NPNF*[1] 10:336).

52. Augustine, *Retractations* 1.21.1 (Bogan).

likewise emphasized the confession. Thus, while Peter was given a unique role among the apostles, the New Testament consistently identifies the foundation of the church as Christ himself (Eph 2:20, 1 Cor 3:11).[53]

The patristic witness to Matt 16:18 is considerably more diverse than Rome often acknowledges. Early commentators offered three primary readings: some identified the "rock" with Peter himself, others with his confession of faith, and still others with Christ as the true foundation. The prevalence of the latter two interpretations shows that the fathers did not speak with one voice equating the rock exclusively with Peter.[54] This diversity undermines the claim that the early church uniformly recognized Peter as the first pope. When Catholic apologists highlight only the fathers who support their position while overlooking the many who read the passage differently, it represents a selective use of evidence. In intelligence terms, it is not the full SIGINT picture—it is curated, pre-screened traffic, not the raw feed.

Nevertheless, Rome presents a competing interpretation of this passage, claiming that Matt 16:18 establishes Peter as the first pope and provides the basis for apostolic succession. Such a reading, however, diverges from the biblical foundation and must be weighed by careful exegesis and faithful hermeneutics. Exegesis, which critically analyzes a text in its historical, literary, and grammatical context, seeks to uncover the author's intended meaning. Hermeneutics, the broader discipline of establishing principles for biblical interpretation, ensures that later doctrines are not imposed upon the text.[55] Yet Rome often departs from these standards, reading subsequent dogmas back into Scripture—for example, its appeal to Luke 22:32 where Jesus tells Peter, "Strengthen your brethren," as evidence for papal primacy.

No early church writer explicitly treated Matt 16:18 or Luke 22:32 as a papal mandate in the later Roman sense. While some fathers spoke of Peter's primacy or unique role, the idea of universal jurisdiction and infallibility attached to his successors in Rome was unknown in the patristic era. The first explicit move in that direction appears in the letter

---

53. Augustine, *Sermons* 26.

54. "Upon this rock; that is, on the faith of his confession" (John Chrysostom, *Homilies on Matthew* 54.3 [NPNF[1] 10:336]); "This faith is the foundation of the Church" (Hilary of Poitiers, *Trinity* 6.36 [McKenna]); "On this rock, which you have confessed, I will build My church" (Augustine, *Retractations* 1.21.1 [Bogan]); "For the rock was Christ" (Augustine, *Tractates on John* 124.5 [Rettig]). See also Kolyadyuk, "Patristic Interpretation."

55. Carson, "Matthew," 375; Grudem, *Systematic Theology*, 108–9.

of Pope Agatho to the Third Council of Constantinople (AD 680), where he grounded his own authority in Christ's words to Peter—an appeal that functioned as self-affirmation in the context of a theological crisis.[56] This was not the settled conviction of the early church but a retroactive justification, what in deception planning is called "backfilling the narrative": inserting new meaning into old texts to give present authority a veneer of inevitability. Centuries later, the First Vatican Council (1870) formalized papal infallibility in *Pastor Aeternus*, declaring that when the pope speaks *ex cathedra* ("from the chair," in his official teaching office) on matters of faith and morals, his pronouncements are irreformable. Rome then read this doctrine back into earlier passages, claiming they had always testified to papal supremacy. In reality, such an interpretation was not articulated in the fathers and only emerged as dogma at Vatican I—making it both historically novel and biblically indefensible.[57]

Luke 21 contains no explicit reference to a papacy, and nothing in the passage suggests a unique office of universal jurisdiction. Read in context, Jesus is addressing Peter's denial and graciously restoring him after his threefold failure—a restoration that mirrors his threefold confession of love (John 21:15–17). The plain sense is reconciliation and recommissioning, not the creation of a new hierarchical office. Moreover, the New Testament presents shepherding the church as the shared responsibility of all elders, not a prerogative reserved for Peter alone. Paul, for example, exhorts the Ephesian elders to "shepherd the church of God" (Acts 20:28), and Peter himself later urges fellow elders to "shepherd the flock of God that is among you" (1 Pet 5:2). The consistent pattern is collegial oversight among the apostles and elders, not the elevation of one apostle above the rest.

At the Jerusalem Council in Acts 15, the pattern continues. Peter speaks up and reminds everyone that salvation is by grace through faith, not by works of the law. But notice what happens next: James is the one who delivers the final judgment. "It is my judgment, therefore, that we should not make it difficult for the Gentiles who are turning to God" (Acts 15:19 NIV). That detail is crucial. If Peter truly held supreme authority, why doesn't he render the decision himself? Instead, the council's outcome is shaped by collective discernment, and James, as the leader of the Jerusalem church, presides over the ruling. This scene doesn't picture

---

56. Costigan, *Consensus of the Church*, 45–47.
57. Kerr, "Vatican I."

papal primacy; it reflects shared apostolic leadership—undercutting the claim that Peter functioned as the pope of the early church.

When the original Greek, the historical context, and the broader biblical narrative are considered together, the conclusion becomes clear: the foundation of the church is not Peter but Christ himself. Throughout Scripture, the rock metaphor consistently refers to God or Christ (e.g., Ps 18:2, 1 Cor 10:4), reinforcing that Jesus—not any human leader—is the unshakable cornerstone of the church.

Additionally, John 1:42 provides further clarity. When Jesus renames Simon as Cephas ("stone"), it signifies Peter's role as a disciple, not as the singular foundation of the church. Even among the early fathers there was no consensus on identifying Peter as the rock. Origen, Chrysostom, and Augustine each offered interpretations that pointed to Christ or Peter's confession—not Peter's person—as the foundation. This diversity undermines the claim of a clear, apostolic endorsement of papal primacy.[58]

Proper hermeneutics requires interpreting Scripture in light of other biblical passages. Ephesians 2:20 states that the church is built on the apostles and prophets collectively, with Christ as the cornerstone, affirming that no single apostle holds exclusive authority. And as I've already noted in earlier, Acts 17:11 provides a powerful example: the Bereans tested every teaching against the Scriptures. That pattern reinforces the principle that God's word—not human authority—is always the ultimate standard for discerning truth.

This principle of discernment is echoed in Jesus' own words in Luke 21:8: "And He said: 'Take heed that you not be deceived. For many will come in My name, saying, "I am He," and, "The time has drawn near." Therefore do not go after them.'" Christ's warning is not only about false messiahs but about spiritual deception in general—especially deception that comes cloaked in religious authority. Every generation of believers must weigh such claims carefully, testing them against the word of God. Should we not do the same with any claim of ecclesiastical supremacy?

The Roman Catholic Church's interpretation of Matt 16:18 has been historically leveraged to justify centralized authority under the papacy. Yet when read in context and through sound biblical interpretation, the passage does not mandate a papal office. Rather, it affirms that the true

---

58. Webster, *Church of Rome*, 37–45.

foundation of the church is Christ himself and the confession of his identity as the Son of God—not any human figure.

This reinterpretation of Matt 16:18 functioned as both a political and ecclesiastical tool: consolidating power in Rome and legitimizing hierarchical control. This is organizational PSYOP: manufacture continuity, cloak it in divine mandate, and centralize the flow of authority. The "rock" becomes not a confession of Christ but a rallying flag for institutional loyalty.

History offers sobering parallels. In medieval Europe, the doctrine of papal supremacy was not merely a theological stance—it was a tool of political dominance. Monarchs bowed to popes, and dissenters were silenced not with argument but with excommunication. The line between spiritual leadership and institutional control blurred, and the voice of Scripture was often drowned out by the voice of power. This is not just history—it is a warning.[59] Information dominance has always been as decisive as military dominance: when one institution monopolizes the narrative, it dictates not only behavior but conscience.

Beyond theological claims, historical scrutiny also challenges the assertion of an unbroken papal succession tracing back to Peter. While Roman Catholic tradition maintains this lineage, early church records do not support the idea that Peter served as the bishop of Rome or formally established an ecclesiastical succession.

In fact, the earliest lists of Roman bishops are inconsistent, and there is no clear evidence that Peter ever held an official episcopal office in Rome. The concept of a singular, supreme pontiff evolved gradually, shaped more by political necessity than apostolic mandate.[60]

The leadership structure of the first few centuries was far less centralized than later Roman Catholic claims suggest, reinforcing the need to distinguish historical reality from institutional doctrine.

This historical backdrop sets the stage for the modern-day display of papal authority—one that unfolded in dramatic fashion at the funeral of Pope Francis. The world watched as an extravagant display of religious pageantry filled St. Peter's Basilica. Gold-trimmed vestments adorned the clergy, crimson robes draped cardinals in solemn procession, and incense thickened the air, mingling with Latin chants that reverberated

---

59. Mihalache, "Institution of the Papal Legation," 45–60.

60. Siecienski, *Papacy and the Orthodox*, 46–49. See also Kelly, *Oxford Dictionary of Popes*, 6–12; Chadwick, *Early Church*, 25–29; Cullmann, *Peter*, 162–77.

through the towering cathedral. The weight of centuries of tradition rested upon the moment, offering a spectacle of reverence and authority.

But beneath the grandeur lay a sobering reality: *Pope Francis now knows the truth.*

Like the rich man in Jesus' parable who pleaded for Lazarus to warn his brothers (Luke 16:19–31), one can only wonder if Pope Francis—now beyond the veil of earthly power—would urge those still within the system to return to the authority of Scripture and the sufficiency of Christ.

Yet, as the church mourned, it did what it has always done—moved forward, ushering in its next supreme pontiff, perpetuating the same cycle of authority built on tradition rather than Scripture. A new pope steps forward, adorned with the same titles, the same regalia, and the same claims of divine appointment.

But the question remains: Is this authority biblical, or is it a legacy of human tradition? Does the new pontiff stand on the rock of Christ or on the scaffolding of centuries-old ecclesiastical invention?

But does he truly believe in the authority he now holds, or is he trapped in a system of power, tradition, and institutional legacy—blinded like the Pharisees whom Christ rebuked?

Roman Catholics, captivated by the spectacle, are led to believe this system is their path to salvation. But Scripture warns that religious systems offering false assurances can lead people away from the truth. While tradition dictates the process of papal succession, biblical truth remains unchanged: *Christ alone is the foundation of the church.* Tracing that tradition back, even the very title itself exposes its human origin.

The title *papa* ("father") was used for bishops as early as the third century and gradually became associated with the Roman bishop. Gregory I (590–604) did not invent the term but greatly expanded the authority of the Roman see, solidifying its supremacy in the West and shaping the foundations of the medieval papacy. The title "pope" would not become reserved exclusively for the bishop of Rome until the eleventh century under Gregory VII.[61]

Additionally, the title *Pontifex Maximus* ("Supreme Pontiff") was originally a pagan designation for the chief priest of the College of

---

61. Ullmann, *Growth of Papal Government*, 39–45; Tertullian, *On Modesty* 1. In *Registrum Epistolarum* 5.43, Gregory rejects the title "universal bishop," calling it "profane" and warning it undermines other bishops' dignity. Yet his papacy marked a turning point in consolidating Roman authority.

Pontiffs in ancient Rome.[62] Roman emperors, beginning with Augustus, adopted it as part of their imperial authority, uniting religious and political power. Many early Christians regarded it as blasphemous. Tertullian mockingly applied the title to Callistus I, the Roman bishop, criticizing his presumption and linking it to pagan priestly pride.[63]

In AD 382, Emperor Gratian renounced the title because of its pagan roots.[64] While some later writers speculated about a connection to Pope Damasus I, there is no evidence that it was formally transferred at that time. Only gradually did the designation become associated with the bishop of Rome, and it was not until the medieval era that it was widely embraced as a symbol of papal authority. What began as a pagan priesthood title—and even a term of rebuke in the early church—eventually became a badge of ecclesiastical supremacy.[65]

This transformation was more than symbolic—it revealed how cultural and political forces could reshape the very fabric of religious authority. What began as a title rooted in paganism, once rejected by Christians, was eventually absorbed into the papacy, blurring the line between spiritual leadership and imperial ambition. It is a warning of how tradition can sanctify what Scripture never affirmed, and how titles once linked with idolatry can be rebranded as sacred. This is reflagging—taking an old banner from a defeated system and flying it over new ground, hoping its prestige will carry forward even as its meaning is repurposed.

History bears witness that these titles were not mere semantics. The very office that claimed to represent Christ on earth often stood opposed to his ways. Under papal sanction, crusades shed innocent blood, inquisitions silenced dissent with torture, and indulgences preyed on the poor. Such atrocities reveal the inevitable outcome when human power cloaks itself in divine authority—truth is eclipsed, and Christ's gospel is obscured.

This irony should not be lost on us: the title once associated with idolatry and condemned by the early church now appears on papal coins, monuments, and documents—a monument to how far tradition can drift when it absorbs what Scripture never affirms. Like captured equipment repainted with friendly insignia, the old idol's title now parades as holy—yet its origin still testifies against it.

62. Ullmann, *Growth of Papal Government*, 39–42.
63. Tertullian, *On Modesty*.
64. Freeman, *AD 381*, 152–54.
65. Gibbon, *Decline and Fall*, 3:110–12.

This appropriation raises serious theological concerns. Can a title rooted in pagan priesthood—once used by emperors who persecuted Christians—rightly describe the servant-leader of Christ's church? The adoption of *Pontifex Maximus* reflects not biblical fidelity but a fusion of imperial power and ecclesiastical ambition.[66]

The appropriation of a pagan title and the historical claims surrounding apostolic succession reflect a larger pattern in which religious authority has been shaped by cultural and political forces, raising broader concerns about doctrine. The apostle Paul listed apostles, prophets, evangelists, pastors, and teachers as church offices (Eph 4:11), yet he never mentions a pope or cardinal, nor does he describe a monarchical bishop over the universal church.

If the papacy were divinely instituted, why is it absent from every description of church leadership in the New Testament? Scripture's silence on this office is not an oversight—it reflects a consistent pattern of collegial leadership under Christ, the one true Head of the church (Col 1:18).

Furthermore, Jesus explicitly forbade his followers from adopting hierarchical authority that mirrors worldly power structures: "You know that the rulers of the Gentiles lord it over them, and those who are great exercise authority over them. Yet it shall not be so among you; but whoever desires to become great among you, let him be your servant" (Matt 20:25–26). This strikes directly at systems of religious leadership that elevate individuals above their brethren in authority.

Another significant concern arises when examining prayer practices within Roman Catholic tradition. Pope Leo XIII (1878–1903) openly prayed to Mary and urged the faithful to do the same, despite Jesus' clear instructions to pray to the Father in his name (Matt 6:5–15, John 16:23).[67] This practice is not a harmless custom—it departs from Christ's command. Jesus never directed his followers to pray to anyone but the Father, through the Son, by the Spirit. To introduce another mediator is to undermine the sufficiency of Christ's intercession (1 Tim 2:5).

Finally, the titles and authority attributed to the pope raise theological questions, as they encompass names and roles that Scripture reserves for God alone. Titles such as "Holy Father," "Head of the Church," and "Vicar of Christ" position the pope in a role that belongs only to God. Jesus referred to the Father as "Holy Father" in John 17:11—a title

---

66. Grimes, *Papacy and the Petrine Texts*; Carson, "Matthew," 418–21; Sakr, "Peter, the Rock."

67. See *Supremi Apostolatus Officio* in Ihm, *Papal Encyclicals*, 27.

never applied to any human. Ephesians 1:22–23 declares that Christ is the head of the church, and John 14:26 identifies the Holy Spirit—not the pope—as Christ's true vicar on earth. To claim such names is what military doctrine calls an "unauthorized assumption of command." It is impersonating the Commander-in-chief.

Rome claims Peter's authority as its foundation, yet Peter's own words dismantle the papal model. In 1 Pet 5:1–4 he exhorts fellow elders to shepherd the flock with humility—not for dishonest gain, not lording authority, but serving as examples until the "Chief Shepherd" appears. This vision leaves no room for a man to exalt himself as the supreme head of Christ's church. In PSYOP terms, the source itself issues the counter-signal: Peter repudiates the propaganda.

This exposes the fundamental issue: true authority rests not in human office but in Christ and his word. Scripture, breathed out by God, is timeless and sufficient, equipping believers for every good work (2 Tim 3:16–17). The church is not the source of this authority but its steward—called to submit to it, never to redefine it. With this foundation in place, we can now examine how certain traditions diverge from Scripture and distort the gospel.

Rome's claim is not unique. Other movements have used the same tactic of exalting a leader's authority above Scripture. Sun Myung Moon, founder of the Unification Church, declared himself the Messiah sent to complete Jesus' mission. His followers treated his pronouncements as divine revelation, granting him an authority that eclipsed the Bible itself.[68] This is the same PSYOP pattern: redirect trust from God's word to a human office, and you control the flock.

Secular history provides a parallel in *The Protocols of the Elders of Zion*, a forged document published in Russia in 1903 that claimed to reveal a Jewish conspiracy for world domination. Though entirely fabricated, it carried the weight of official authority, fueling anti-Semitism and shaping Nazi propaganda.[69] Once a lie is cloaked in institutional legitimacy, entire nations can be steered by deception. So it is with the papacy—bestowing unquestioned authority on a man's words, even when they contradict God's revealed truth.

---

68. Chryssides, *Advent of Sun Myung Moon*, 42–47.
69. Cohn, *Warrant for Genocide*, 16–25.

Unveiling Deception

Decoy Devotion: Saints in the Spotlight, Christ in the Shadows

With the papacy exposed as a distortion of biblical leadership, it is necessary to examine related traditions such as Mariolatry (the excessive veneration of Mary), saint intercession, the priesthood, the Mass, and the concept of purgatory—all absent from the New Testament and contradictory to foundational biblical teaching. These practices matter because they demonstrate how deception embeds itself not only in leadership structures but also in worship and devotion. By shifting trust from Christ alone to rituals, relics, mediators, and traditions, the enemy's PSYOP gains ground—redirecting allegiance away from the sufficiency of Christ's work and toward systems that promise assurance while obscuring the gospel. Just as military deception rebrands old symbols to command loyalty, these traditions cloak human invention in divine language, creating powerful illusions that shape belief and behavior. To discern them rightly is to expose another layer of the enemy's strategy and reclaim the clarity of Scripture as the believer's true safeguard.

The tendency to displace Christ with another mediator is not confined to Rome. Christian Science, founded by Mary Baker Eddy in the nineteenth century, denies the full reality of sin and sickness, offering instead a "science of mind" in which healing comes through right understanding rather than through Christ's finished work.[70] By re-centering devotion on a method rather than the Mediator, Christian Science replays the same PSYOP: substitute something novel in place of Christ's sufficiency, and the focus of devotion shifts away from the only true Savior.

History itself shows how the craving for proof can be exploited. In 1912, scientists in England announced the discovery of the "Piltdown Man," hailed as the missing link in human evolution. For forty years this fabricated fossil—a human skull combined with an orangutan jaw—was enshrined in textbooks as scientific fact.[71] The Piltdown fraud succeeded because it told people what they wanted to hear, confirming their preconceptions while disguising deception as discovery. Veneration of saints operates similarly: stories and legends, however sincere, can obscure the sufficiency of Christ when they become the object of confidence.

Among the most prominent of these is Mariolatry and the veneration of saints, which stand in direct opposition to 1 Tim 2:5: "For there

---

70. Eddy, *Science and Health*, 372–75.
71. Weiner, *Piltdown Forgery*, 1–12.

WHAT ARE TRUTH AND FALSEHOOD?

is one God and one Mediator between God and men, the Man Christ Jesus." Think of Mariolatry as focusing a spotlight so brightly on a supporting actor that the lead role—Christ himself—is overshadowed. While Mary holds a revered place in Scripture as the mother of Jesus, excessive veneration risks distorting the central focus of Christian faith.[72] Some apologists even argue that Jesus' entrusting Mary to John proves he had no siblings, otherwise he would have broken the law. Yet this reasoning distorts both Scripture and Jewish custom.[73] This is the essence of diversionary PSYOP: flood the field with so much attention on a secondary figure that the true center of gravity is eclipsed. In military terms, it's like directing all reconnaissance toward a decoy force while the real maneuver unfolds elsewhere.

This concern is not novel. From the Reformers onward, countless Protestant theologians have recognized that the Roman Catholic system, however sincere, obscures the biblical gospel. Figures such as Martin Luther, John Calvin, and Charles Spurgeon all rejected Rome's additions as distortions of grace. In more recent times, R. C. Sproul, J. I. Packer, and John MacArthur, among many others, have likewise affirmed that salvation comes by grace alone through faith alone in Christ alone. To align with these voices is not to innovate but to stand within a great cloud of witnesses who have faithfully defended the gospel against every attempt to bind it with human traditions.[74]

Similarly, the elevation of saints as intercessors diminishes Christ's exclusive mediating role. The Roman Catholic Church attempts to distinguish Christ's mediation from the saints' intercession, claiming it is like asking fellow believers for prayer. The catechism states, "Being more closely united to Christ, those who dwell in heaven fix the whole Church more firmly in holiness.... They do not cease to intercede with the Father

---

72. Garcia, *Mariology*.

73. While some argue that entrusting Mary to John at the cross breached Jewish law (John 19:25–27), no biblical law required this, and Jewish custom allowed flexibility (see Exod 20:12, Deut 21:17, Ruth 4). Moreover, Jesus' brothers were unbelievers (John 7:5) and absent, making John the right choice. The Gospels also explicitly mention Jesus' siblings (Matt 13:55–56, Mark 6:3). Thus, Jesus ensured Mary's care while inaugurating a new family of faith. See Carson, *Gospel According to John*, 621–24; Keener, *Gospel of John*, 1147–50.

74. For Protestant critiques of Rome's distortions, see Luther, *Bondage of the Will*; Calvin, *Institutes* 4.7; Spurgeon, "Doctrines of Grace"; Sproul, *Faith Alone*; Packer, "Doctrine of Justification"; MacArthur, *Gospel According to Jesus*.

for us."[75] Yet this practice undermines Christ's sufficiency, for Scripture allows no heavenly intercessors apart from him, who "always lives to make intercession" (Heb 7:25). Unlike asking a fellow believer on earth to pray with you—a practice Scripture commends (Jas 5:16)—Scripture never authorizes addressing the dead. In fact, such attempts are explicitly forbidden (Deut 18:10–12). Throughout the New Testament, believers are called to approach God directly through Christ, who alone is the way, the truth, and the life (John 14:6). Saints may inspire by their faithful witness, but their purpose is to point beyond themselves—to Christ alone, who is worthy of prayer, worship, and trust. Moreover, Scripture clearly teaches that all who are in Christ are saints, not a select group elevated by human tradition. Romans 1:7 states, "To all who are beloved of God in Rome, called as saints." Likewise, 1 Cor 1:2 affirms, "To the church of God which is at Corinth, to those who have been sanctified in Christ Jesus, saints by calling." Similar greetings in Eph 1:1, Phil 1:1, and Col 1:2 confirm that "saints" refers to all believers, not a special class of intercessors.

The Bible does not define saints as a spiritually superior subgroup but rather as all who are sanctified in Christ. This distinction is crucial because it underscores that every believer has direct access to God through Jesus Christ, without the need for intermediaries. The enemy thrives by inserting middlemen—layers of bureaucracy in the spiritual chain of command—so that the soldier doubts whether they can go directly to the commander-in-chief. This is doctrinal "intercept and reroute." Roman Catholics sometimes counter with Paul's words in 1 Cor 4:15, where he calls himself a "father" in the gospel. Yet Jesus' command in Matt 23:9 warned against titles of spiritual supremacy that usurp God's role. Paul's usage was relational and pastoral, not hierarchical—whereas Rome's institutionalized "Father" title risks the very distortion Christ forbade.

Roman Catholic tradition later introduced the practice of canonization, formally declaring certain individuals as "saints" after their deaths. Official teaching insists this does not create saints but merely recognizes them. Yet in practice it elevates a select few to a special status, often associating them with miracles, intercessory roles, and veneration. Another tradition tied to canonization is the veneration of so-called incorrupt bodies—saints whose corpses did not decompose as expected. Catholic theology interprets these cases as signs of God's favor, though

---

75. *CCC*, §956.

not automatic proof of sanctity.[76] Scripture, however, never points to preserved remains as evidence of holiness but directs us to Christ as the sole marker of righteousness.

Similarly, the Catholic veneration of relics—whether body parts, garments, or objects linked to saints—is defended as honoring God's work in his people.[77] Yet in practice, such devotion often drifts into functional idolatry. Pilgrims travel to view, touch, or kiss these remains, treating them as conduits of grace,[78] though Scripture warns against placing confidence in objects (Exod 20:4–5, Isa 42:8). In PSYOP terms, relics are false indicators: tangible but misleading, drawing focus away from the true center of gravity, which is Christ's finished work.

One contemporary extension of this same pattern appears in the defense of icon veneration. Advocates often argue that bowing before images of Christ is not idolatry but merely "showing respect," appealing to episodes of persecution in Japan, where Christians were forced to trample images of Christ (fumie) to prove their renunciation, or to biblical accounts of bowing as cultural gestures. Yet such reasoning collapses under the weight of Scripture. To refuse to spit on an image of Christ under duress is not the same as worshiping that image—it is allegiance to Christ himself, not to the object. By contrast, kneeling, kissing, and praying before man-made icons transfers to the object the reverence God reserves for himself alone.

The commandment could not be clearer: "You shall not make for yourself a carved image—any likeness of anything . . . ; you shall not bow down to them nor serve them" (Exod 20:4–5). This prohibition does not carve out an exception for good intentions. When worship is directed through an image, even one meant to represent Jesus, it becomes the very thing God forbids. True worship is "in spirit and truth" (John 4:24), not mediated through pictures or statues.

Nor does the argument from cultural bowing resolve the problem. Abraham bowed before the Hittites (Gen 23), but he did not light incense to them, pray to them, or seek their mediation. Respect is not the same as devotion. Similarly, the claim that mental images in prayer justify physical icons is misplaced. When believers pray, they are not bowing to an imagined picture but directing their hearts toward the living Christ, risen

---

76. *CCC*, §828.

77. Session 25 ("On the Invocation, Veneration, and Relics of Saints, and on Sacred Images") in Schroeder, *Canons and Decrees*, 215–16.

78. Catholic Answers, "Relics."

and enthroned. Scripture warns that idolatry is precisely the exchange of "the glory of the incorruptible God for an image made like corruptible man" (Rom 1:23). Icon veneration does exactly that—reducing the infinite to the finite.

True worship requires faith, not sight. "Faith is the substance of things hoped for, the evidence of things not seen" (Heb 11:1). To substitute icons for faith is to trade reality for ritual. What seems a harmless aid to focus actually blurs the distinction between Creator and creation, luring the heart away from Christ himself.

This same pattern of misplaced devotion is evident in the elevation of saints themselves. While many of these figures lived honorable and faithful lives, their devotion was meant to lead others to Christ—not to themselves. As John the Baptist declared, "He must increase, but I must decrease" (John 3:30). Yet later traditions elevated him as an intercessor, contradicting his own humility. Peter and Paul likewise rejected veneration—Peter rebuked Cornelius for bowing before him (Acts 10:25–26), and Paul tore his clothes in protest when people tried to exalt him (Acts 14:11–15). Any tradition that reverses this order risks turning saints into stumbling blocks rather than signposts to the Savior.

These apostles understood their role: to point others to Christ, not to receive veneration. Their actions stand in stark contrast to later traditions that canonized them and encouraged practices of prayer and devotion that Scripture never affirms.

Mary, the mother of Jesus, was honored as a faithful servant of God, but she herself recognized her need for a Savior (Luke 1:46–47). Over time, Roman Catholic doctrine expanded her role, often building on Luke 1:28, where the Greek *kecharitōmenē* is translated "full of grace." Catholics argue this singular form sets her apart as uniquely endowed with permanent divine favor, yet the broader New Testament presents no hierarchy of mediators apart from Christ alone (1 Tim 2:5). This elevation of Mary introduces a spiritual hierarchy absent from biblical teaching, further entwining tradition with ecclesiastical authority.[79]

The Roman Catholic Church teaches that prayers to saints and to Mary are not worship but requests for intercession, asking them to pray on behalf of believers. According to Catholic teaching, the saints

---

79. On *kecharitōmenē* as a perfect passive participle of *charitoō* ("to endow with grace"), Roman Catholic theologians interpret the term as implying a completed action with lasting results (see *CCC*, §§490–91). Yet this interpretation rests on a single lexical occurrence, risking overreach, contextual isolation, and circular reasoning.

in heaven remain spiritually united to the faithful on earth as part of the "communion of saints" and therefore can intercede before God. Mary, regarded as the Mother of God (*Theotokos*) and the most exalted of saints, is believed to have a unique intercessory role because of her place in salvation history. Roman Catholics often cite Luke 1:28, where she is called "full of grace"; John 19:26–27, where Jesus entrusts her to the care of his disciple; and the Council of Ephesus (AD 431), which affirmed her as *Theotokos*—interpreted as extending her spiritual motherhood to all Christians.[80]

Roman Catholics argue that asking saints or Mary to pray for them is similar to asking a fellow believer on earth to pray for them, citing Rev 5:8, which describes saints in heaven offering prayers to God. Yet the passage depicts the elders presenting the prayers of believers as incense—it never portrays them as recipients of prayer.

Other texts are sometimes pressed into service. For example, David's lament for Jonathan in 2 Sam 1:26 is a poetic funeral dirge, not a request for intercession. Some claim 2 Thess 1:10–11 shows Paul praying even now from heaven, but his words clearly describe prayers during his earthly ministry, not postmortem activity. Likewise, Heb 12:1 speaks of a "great cloud of witnesses," but these are past heroes whose lives testify to God's faithfulness, urging us to fix our eyes on Jesus (v. 2)—not intercessors watching or praying for us.

In every case, Scripture emphasizes that the heavenly intercessor is Christ alone, who "always lives to make intercession" (Heb 7:25). The analogy of asking saints to pray breaks down when applied to the spiritual realm. Nowhere does Scripture instruct believers to initiate communication with the dead—even the faithful departed. In operational terms, it is "comms with a compromised channel." The traffic may feel familiar, but it is unauthorized and exploitable.

---

80. The title *Theotokos* ("Mother of God") was affirmed at the Council of Ephesus to defend Christ's full divinity, emphasizing that Mary bore the incarnate Son who is fully God and fully man. Roman Catholic theologians use the title to set Mary apart and support her intercessory role, but several concerns arise. It risks confusion by suggesting a creature precedes the Creator, though Mary bore Christ's humanity, not his divinity. Though originally christological, the term became a springboard for later Marian doctrines (e.g., Immaculate Conception, Assumption). Scripture never calls Mary "Mother of God"; the closest phrase—"mother of my Lord" (Luke 1:43)—affirms the incarnation without granting divine maternity. Finally, its basis lies more in conciliar authority and linguistic precision than in broad biblical support, making it vulnerable to critique.

Despite Roman Catholic teaching on intercession, the biblical witness is unambiguous. Deuteronomy 18:10-12 condemns "a medium, or a spiritist, or one who calls up the dead," calling such practices an abomination—without distinguishing between the righteous and the unrighteous dead. Leviticus 19:31 commands, "Do not seek after mediums and familiar spirits." And Isa 8:19-20 warns, "Should not a people seek their God? Should they seek the dead on behalf of the living?"

These passages are not vague—they are direct. Seeking spiritual contact with the dead, even under the guise of intercession, is forbidden. The biblical pattern is clear: believers are to pray to God through Christ, not to departed saints. This is why PSYOP doctrine warns against false authorities: the wrong voice, even if wrapped in familiar tones, can redirect the entire unit. The only secure channel is Christ.

The Counterfeit Sacrifice: When the Table Replaces the Cross

Just as the veneration of saints distorts Christ's role as the sole mediator, the Roman Catholic Mass introduces theological elements that differ from the remembrance and proclamation described in Scripture. Rather than viewing the Lord's Supper as a symbolic commemoration of Christ's finished work, Roman Catholic doctrine teaches that the Mass is a sacramental re-presentation of Christ's one sacrifice—made present in an unbloody manner. This concept, though framed as mystical rather than literal repetition and not claiming to repeat the crucifixion, still implies that Christ's atonement must be continually accessed through ritual—an idea that contradicts the finality of the cross (Heb 10:10-14).

Paul clearly establishes that communion is a memorial of Christ's sacrifice—not a repeated offering. He writes in 1 Cor 11:23-26,

> For I received from the Lord that which I also delivered to you: that the Lord Jesus on the same night in which He was betrayed took bread; and when He had given thanks, He broke it and said, "Take, eat; this is My body which is broken for you; do this in remembrance of Me." In the same manner He also took the cup after supper, saying, "This cup is the new covenant in My blood. This do, as often as you drink it, in remembrance of Me." For as often as you eat this bread and drink this cup, you proclaim the Lord's death till He comes.

These verses emphasize that the Lord's Supper serves as a proclamation of his death until his return—an act of remembrance rooted in faith, not a continual sacrificial offering. This distinction is essential because Scripture teaches that Christ's sacrifice was completed once for all, never to be repeated or re-presented (Heb 7:27, 9:24–28, 10:10). Commemoration is a signal flare pointing back to the decisive strike; it is not a new strike package.

When Jesus breathed his last on the cross, he declared, "*Tetelestai!*"—translated as, "It is finished" (John 19:30). This Greek word carries profound theological and historical weight. In Roman culture, *Tetelestai* was a term written on financial documents to signify that a debt had been fully paid. It was also marked on legal sentences to confirm that a punishment had been completely served—no further payment or imprisonment required.[81]

Earlier in John 19:28, John uses the same word in relation to the fulfillment of Scripture ("to fulfill the Scripture, He said, 'I thirst'"). There it clearly refers to a specific prophecy (Ps 69:21). But in verse 30, the context broadens: John does not add "to fulfill Scripture" but simply records Jesus' absolute declaration—"It is finished." This signals not only the closing of prophecy but the full completion of his entire redemptive mission.

Christ's final declaration was not a mere statement of completion—it was a victorious proclamation that the debt of sin had been paid in full, and the penalty for mankind's transgressions had been fully satisfied through his atonement. Unlike the repetitive offerings of the Old Testament sacrificial system—culminating each year on the Day of Atonement—Jesus' sacrifice was the final offering, once for all. As he himself said, "Do not think that I came to destroy the Law or the Prophets. I did not come to destroy but to fulfill" (Matt 5:17). In him, the law's demands were fully met and the sacrificial system brought to its intended fulfillment. Nothing remained unfinished or requiring continuation. A commander's "mission accomplished" order isn't followed by the same mission flown again each morning.

From a Protestant perspective, this truth stands in tension with the Roman Catholic understanding of the Mass as a sacrificial memorial. Catholic theology insists that the Mass does not re-crucify Christ but "makes present" his one sacrifice in a mystical way,[82] often citing Mal

---

81. Keener, *Gospel of John*, 1136–37.
82. *CCC*, §1366.

1:11 as prophetic support.[83] Protestants counter that this interpretation imposes a later framework on a text that originally critiqued Israel's corrupt sacrifices and foresaw a future global reverence for God's name—not a literal, repeated offering. Thus, while Rome views the Mass as a sacramental re-presentation of Calvary, Protestants contend that such language of "offering" and "making present" risks obscuring the once-for-all nature of the cross and undermines the sufficiency of Christ's atonement (Heb 10:10–14).[84] Hebrews drives this point home: "He offered one sacrifice for sins forever" (10:12); "by one offering He has perfected forever those who are being sanctified" (10:14). The biblical witness leaves no room for repetition, mystical or otherwise. *Tetelestai* means finished.[85]

Just as the veneration of saints shifts trust from Christ's sole intercession to human mediators, so too the Roman Catholic Mass shifts the focus of salvation from Christ's finished work to an ongoing ritual. Both practices, though different in form, share the same underlying problem: they obscure the sufficiency of Christ by introducing substitutes— whether in intercessors or in repeated offerings. Different tactics, same objective: reroute allegiance from the King to the system.

The doctrine of transubstantiation—defined earlier as the claim that the bread and wine become Christ's body and blood in essence, though not in appearance—places the priest in a mediatorial role that Scripture reserves for Christ alone. It also implies that grace is dispensed through ritual rather than received by faith. That's authority centralization: make access dependent on a human operator, and you control the line of supply.

Such a view undermines the absolute sufficiency of Christ's atonement and it contradicts the biblical teaching that Christ will

---

83. Calvin, *Zechariah and Malachi*, 438–42; see also *Institutes* 4.18.17. Calvin argues that Malachi's "pure offering" is fulfilled not in a renewed sacrificial system but in the new covenant's spiritual sacrifices of praise and prayer (see Heb 13:15).

84. Deuteronomy 12:5–14 makes clear that sacrifices were restricted to the place God chose—namely, Jerusalem. This context renders the idea of a universal sacrificial system implausible.

85. The phrase *hocus pocus* is often thought to derive from the Latin words of Eucharistic consecration, *hoc est corpus meum*—"This is my body" (see Skeat, *Etymological Dictionary of the English Language*, 259; Weekley, *Etymological Dictionary of Modern English*, 721). Misheard or mocked, the phrase came to connote deception and illusion, underscoring concerns about the Eucharist's ritual transformation in Roman Catholic doctrine. Early critics such as John Tillotson and Thomas Ady suggested it was a parody of the Mass, though the link remains debated (see Tillotson, *Works*, 1:480–81; Ady, *Candle in the Dark*, 39–40).

return only once, at the end of time—not repeatedly through ritual. Jesus himself declared, "Then the sign of the Son of Man will appear in heaven, and then all the tribes of the earth will mourn, and they will see the Son of Man coming on the clouds of heaven with power and great glory" (Matt 24:30).

Similarly, Heb 9:28 states, "So Christ was offered once to bear the sins of many. To those who eagerly wait for Him He will appear a second time, apart from sin, for salvation."

The Mass, by claiming to make Christ present again and again, risks diminishing the uniqueness of his second coming and the once-for-all nature of his sacrifice. It replaces the finality of "It is finished" with the uncertainty of "It is ongoing."

Scripture consistently affirms that Christ's return will be a future, visible, and final event—not a recurring presence at each Mass. The claim that a priest can call down Christ repeatedly through the Eucharist reduces his second coming from a climactic fulfillment of God's redemptive plan to a ritualistic reenactment, distorting the profound significance of his promised return.

Just as the pageantry of a papal funeral captivates millions with its display of power and tradition, the ritual of the Mass reinforces doctrines that elevate human institutions above biblical truth. Incense burns, Latin chants rise, and ornate vestments create an air of sacred authority—but beneath these outward forms lies a critical theological distortion. While Scripture declares Christ's sacrifice *finished*, Roman Catholic tradition reframes it as a continually offered mystery, mediated through priestly consecration. Camouflage can be beautiful and still be camouflage.

This outward ritual is then defended by appeal to Scripture, most notably Jesus' words in John 6:53–58. The Roman Catholic Church teaches that this passage, where he commands his followers to eat his flesh and drink his blood, should be understood literally, forming the basis for the doctrine of transubstantiation. The catechism teaches that "in the most blessed sacrament of the Eucharist 'the body and blood, together with the soul and divinity, of our Lord Jesus Christ . . . is truly, really, and substantially contained.'"[86] Building on this, Catholic theologians argue that Jesus did not correct his disciples when they reacted with shock to his statement, implying that he truly meant his words as a literal command. They also cite early church fathers, such as Ignatius

---

86. CCC, §1374.

of Antioch and Justin Martyr, who affirmed belief in the real presence of Christ in the Eucharist.[87]

However, this interpretation fails to account for the broader context of Jesus' teaching and the literary style he often employed. Jesus frequently used metaphor to convey spiritual truths—he called himself the door (John 10:9), the vine (John 15:5), and the bread of life (John 6:35). These were not literal claims but symbolic illustrations of his role in salvation.

When this interpretive lens is applied to John 6, it becomes clear that Jesus is again speaking metaphorically. In John 6:35, he declares, "I am the bread of life. He who comes to Me shall never hunger, and he who believes in Me shall never thirst." This suggests that eating and drinking symbolize coming to Christ and believing in him, rather than a physical act.

Further evidence of this interpretation arises when considering the context in which Jesus made these statements. At this point in his ministry, the Eucharist had not yet been instituted, and his followers had no concept of the Last Supper or transubstantiation. When Jesus spoke of eating his flesh and drinking his blood, his audience responded with confusion, struggling to understand his meaning. However, rather than clarifying that he was speaking of a future sacrament, Jesus equated eating his flesh and drinking his blood with believing in him and coming to him.

This is reinforced by John 6:63, where Jesus says, "It is the Spirit who gives life; the flesh profits nothing. The words that I speak to you are spirit, and they are life." The point is unmistakable: the focus is spiritual, not physical.

Roman Catholic interpreters sometimes appeal either to John 6 or to the rare Greek word *epiousios* (ἐπιούσιος) in the Lord's Prayer as support for the Eucharist. Yet John 6 itself clarifies that "eating" means believing in Christ (See John 6:35 quoted earlier; see also 6:63). Moreover, when

---

87. Reformers such as Martin Luther (1483-1546) and John Calvin (1509-1564) rejected the Catholic view. Calvin, in particular, emphasized that Christ is spiritually present in the Supper, not physically localized. Huldrych Zwingli (1484-1531) went further, asserting the Eucharist is purely symbolic—a memorial of Christ's death. Other Reformers, including Martin Bucer (1491-1551), Peter Martyr Vermigli (1499-1562), William Tyndale (c. 1494-1536), among many others, likewise rejected transubstantiation, defending either a spiritual presence or memorial view. This rejection was not entirely new: earlier critics such as Berengarius of Tours (c. 999-1088), John Wycliffe (c. 1320-1384), and Jan Hus (c. 1369-1415) had already denied the Catholic doctrine of transubstantiation, paving the way for Reformation critiques.

WHAT ARE TRUTH AND FALSEHOOD?

Jesus first spoke these words, the Eucharist had not yet been instituted, so his hearers would not have understood them sacramentally.

Likewise, the word *epiousios* occurs only in Mat 6:11 and Luke 11:3 and is virtually unattested elsewhere in Greek literature, which explains why Jerome called it a "new word." Standard lexical authorities—BDAG ("daily, for the coming day"), LSJ ("for the coming day, necessary for existence"), and *TDNT* ("sufficient for the day")[88]—consistently render it as referring to ordinary bread needed for each day. Jerome's Latin Vulgate introduced the rendering *supersubstantialis* ("super-substantial bread") in Matthew (though he used *quotidianum*, meaning 'daily' or 'for the day,' in Luke), which later became the basis for Eucharistic interpretation. Yet this reflects later theological development rather than the plain sense of Jesus' model prayer.[89]

Such an interpretation does not fit the context. The Lord's Prayer consists of straightforward petitions—God's name honored, his kingdom come, forgiveness granted, deliverance from evil, and provision for each day. To suddenly inject a mystical Eucharistic meaning into the middle of this prayer is anachronistic. The natural reading of *epiousios* is "bread for the coming day" or "bread necessary for life."[90] It reflects the same dependence God taught Israel in the wilderness when he provided manna daily (Exod 16:4).

Appeals to the early church fathers must also be read carefully. Ignatius of Antioch and Justin Martyr spoke of Christ's presence in vivid terms, but their language reflects sacramental realism, not the scholastic construct of transubstantiation later defined at the Fourth Lateran Council (1215) and entrenched at Trent (1545–1563). The doctrine emerged not from apostolic command but from medieval development.[91]

This raises a deeper concern: Can the infinite God be localized in a physical object? The claim that bread and wine become Christ's literal body and blood—objects to be adored and reserved in tabernacles—finds no support in Scripture. The God who spans galaxies and speaks stars into being cannot be reduced to a wafer without diminishing his majesty.

---

88. BDAG, s.v. "ἐπιούσιος," 378–79; LSJ, s.v. "ἐπιούσιος," 660; Schlier, "ἐπιούσιος."

89. Jerome, *Commentary on Matthew* 1.6.11. Ott, *Fundamentals of Catholic Dogma*; Schillebeeckx, *Eucharist*; Cavanaugh, *Torture and Eucharist*; Power, *Eucharistic Mystery*; Pitre, *Jesus and the Jewish Roots*.

90. BDAG, s.v. "ἐπιούσιος," 378–79.

91. Ignatius, *Smyrnaeans* 7.1; Justin Martyr, *First Apology* 66. For historical development, see Pelikan, *Growth of Medieval Theology*, 190–96; Schaff, *Nicene and Post-Nicene Christianity*, 492–95.

The practice extends further in the form of Eucharistic processions, where the consecrated host is placed in a golden vessel called a *monstrance* and carried through the streets to be worshiped by onlookers. The faithful kneel as the host is paraded, hymns are sung, incense rises, and prayers are directed toward what is, in essence, a piece of bread believed to contain God himself. However sincere, such displays come dangerously close to the very thing Scripture forbids: the veneration of created objects as though they contained the divine presence. This is object fixation—tactical focus on the wrong target.

Such practices stand in stark contrast to the biblical witness. Scripture consistently affirms that the infinite God cannot be confined within created things. As the Lord declares, "'Heaven is My throne, and earth is My footstool. Where is the house that you will build Me? And where is the place of My rest? For all those things My hand has made, and all those things exist,' says the LORD. 'But on this one will I look: On him who is poor and of a contrite spirit, and who trembles at My word'" (Isa 66:1–2). Paul echoes this in Athens, proclaiming, "God, who made the world and everything in it, since He is Lord of heaven and earth, does not dwell in temples made with hands. Nor is He worshiped with men's hands, as though He needed anything, since He gives to all life, breath, and all things" (Acts 17:24–25).

Jesus likewise corrected the Samaritan woman's view of localized worship: "The hour is coming, and now is, when the true worshipers will worship the Father in spirit and truth; for the Father is seeking such to worship Him. God is Spirit, and those who worship Him must worship in spirit and truth" (John 4:23–24).

Far from descending repeatedly into earthly elements, Christ's presence is heavenly and exalted. "For Christ has not entered the holy places made with hands, which are copies of the true, but into heaven itself, now to appear in the presence of God for us" (Heb 9:24). Paul likewise directs believers upward: "If then you were raised with Christ, seek those things which are above, where Christ is, sitting at the right hand of God" (Col 3:1).

The testimony of Scripture is clear: God cannot be contained in ritual objects, nor is Christ's saving presence mediated through bread and wine. To claim otherwise is to exchange the majesty of the infinite God for the limitations of human ceremony, obscuring the sufficiency of Christ's once-for-all sacrifice and the glory of his heavenly reign.

WHAT ARE TRUTH AND FALSEHOOD?

If the King sits enthroned, do not mistake the parade ground for the throne room.

John Calvin captured this danger well when he wrote, "To bind Christ, or to include Him under the bread, or to attach Him to the bread, is contrary to the nature of heaven."[92] The infinite Christ, now reigning in glory at the Father's right hand, cannot be shut up in perishable elements.

But this is not merely a question of metaphysics—it is a question of worship. The second commandment forbids the making of graven images (Exod 20:4–5, Deut 5:8–9), not because art is evil but because any attempt to represent the invisible God risks misrepresenting him. God is spirit (John 4:24), and he has revealed himself through his word, not through objects to be venerated. To claim that the Creator of the cosmos is physically present in a consecrated host is to risk collapsing the infinite into the finite, the transcendent into the tangible.

The question echoes through the ages: What altar, what vessel, what ceremony could ever contain the One who fills all in all? No reliquary can hold the Commander of heaven's armies.

To be clear, the incarnation is the glorious mystery of God entering time and space in the person of Jesus Christ. But the incarnation was not a sacramental abstraction—it was a historical reality. Christ's body was broken once for all (Heb 10:10), and his resurrection body is now glorified, seated at the right hand of the Father. The Roman Catholic notion that the Mass "makes present" his one sacrifice—re-presented sacramentally—diminishes the finality of the cross and risks obscuring the heavenly reality of Christ's ascended body. Worse still, it borders on violating the very commandment that guards God's holiness from human distortion (Exod 20:4–5 and Deut 5:8–9, as noted above).

The heavens declare his glory—not a tabernacle (Ps 19:1). The stars proclaim his handiwork—not a monstrance (Ps 19:1). Let us worship the God who cannot be contained, who dwells not in temples made by hands (Acts 7:48–49, Isa. 66:1–2) but in the hearts of those who fear him (Isa 57:15, John 14:23, 1 Cor 3:16) and in the vastness of a universe that still cannot hold him (1 Kgs 8:27). Worship is not a supply chain to be managed; it is allegiance to a finished victory (John 19:30, Heb 10:12–14).

This is more than a theological debate—it is a matter of profound spiritual consequence. If transubstantiation is not biblically supported, then what is truly at stake? The answer is far-reaching: the church's grip

---

92. Calvin, *Institutes* 4.17.19.

on salvation itself. By declaring that the Eucharist is the literal body and blood of Christ, the Roman Catholic Church ensures that divine grace is not freely given but distributed through the hands of ordained clergy. In shifting the focus from Christ's completed work to a structure of religious obligation, this approach does more than mislead—it creates a system that binds the soul in a cycle of institutional authority rather than liberating it through faith in Christ alone. That is dependency by design—the hallmark of enduring influence operations.

At the heart of this dependency is the role of the priest. By defining the Eucharist as the literal body and blood of Christ, Roman Catholic doctrine elevates the clergy, who alone possess authority to consecrate the elements. This makes the church the necessary mediator of grace rather than Christ himself. If the Eucharist were understood as purely symbolic, priestly mediation would lose its necessity, and the church's exclusive control over the means of grace would collapse. Control the chokepoint, control the movement. Historically, this doctrine also reinforced church power against the Protestant Reformation, which emphasized salvation by faith alone (Eph 2:8–9) and rejected the idea that priests control access to grace.[93]

Yet if Rome is right, Scripture should clearly support it. But when we turn to Jesus' words in John 6, the opposite emerges. If, according to Jesus, eating his flesh and drinking his blood means coming to him and believing in him, then did those who believed in him that day spiritually partake of his flesh and blood? The answer, according to Jesus' own words, is yes. Faith in him was the key to eternal life, independent of any later sacramental practice. This suggests that his teaching in John 6 was focused on belief rather than a future ritual.

Additionally, in Roman times, the phrase "eat my flesh" was often used figuratively to signify hostility or destruction. Psalm 27:2 provides an example: "When the wicked came against me to eat up my flesh, my enemies and foes, they stumbled and fell." This historical and linguistic context further supports a symbolic interpretation of John 6. Context is your IFF—identify friend or foe—in interpretation.

This distinction is central to understanding how the Roman Catholic Church's view of grace contradicts Scripture. Rather than recognizing justification as the result of faith alone, the Roman Catholic Church

---

93. Scholars such as White, *Roman Catholic Controversy*, and Webster, *Church of Rome*, argue that the Catholic reading of John 6 misinterprets metaphorical language and overlays later doctrinal developments.

teaches that grace is *infused* into the believer through the sacraments, particularly baptism and the Eucharist. It is as though grace were delivered by IV drip—slowly poured into the soul over time—requiring constant replenishment through the sacramental system. In Roman Catholic theology, the sacraments are outward rites believed to convey inward grace, functioning as necessary channels of divine life to the faithful. Traditionally numbered as seven—baptism, confirmation, Eucharist, penance, anointing of the sick, marriage, and holy orders—each sacrament is administered by the church as a means of imparting grace. Their cumulative role is not simply symbolic but instrumental, forming the backbone of Catholic spirituality and ecclesial authority.

This claim is not abstract—it undergirds the church's broader assertion, expressed in the dogma *extra ecclesiam nulla salus*—"outside the church there is no salvation."[94] This teaching conditions believers to equate salvation not with Christ's finished work but with institutional membership and submission. By framing eternal destiny as dependent on loyalty to Rome, the church transforms the simplicity of the gospel into a mechanism of leverage, where access to grace is mediated through sacraments, indulgences, and priestly authority. This is deception at its most strategic: instead of outright denying Christ, it redefines him in institutional terms, convincing souls that freedom can only be found under the church's covering. In PSYOP terms, this is controlling the chokepoint—dictating that every line of supply runs through Rome. Scripture, by contrast, declares that salvation is found in Christ alone (Acts 4:12, John 14:6), apart from any earthly institution.

This means that righteousness is not merely credited to the believer externally, as the Bible teaches, but rather poured into the soul, requiring continual participation in the sacramental system for spiritual progress. Roman Catholic theology holds that this infused grace enables believers to cooperate with God in their sanctification, making salvation a process dependent on human effort.

In contrast, Scripture clearly asserts that righteousness is imputed—legally declared—by God, meaning that believers are justified by faith alone, without an intrinsic change in their nature at the moment of justification. It is not dripped in over time like an IV, but credited instantly like a wire transfer that clears in full the moment faith is exercised.

---

94. *CCC*, §§846–48. See also Boniface VIII, *Unam Sanctam* (1302), in Denzinger, *Sources*, §468; Council of Florence, *Cantate Domino* (1442), in Denzinger, *Sources*, §714; Council of Trent, *Decree on the Sacraments* (1547), in Denzinger, *Sources*, §§844–54.

Rather, sanctification—the process of growing in holiness—follows as a separate work of God in the believer's life.

This distinction between justification and sanctification is not a minor theological nuance—it is the heart of the gospel. To confuse the two is to confuse the gift of salvation with the fruit of salvation. Confusing ROE with the mission objective leads to friendly fire; confusing sanctification with justification leads to bondage.

This fundamental difference underscores how Roman Catholic sacramental theology distorts the biblical message of grace. By redefining Jesus' teaching to preserve hierarchical authority rather than biblical truth, it shifts the focus from Christ's completed work to institutional control over salvation.[95]

Furthermore, Scripture itself clarifies what Jesus meant. The New Testament presents the metaphorical sense of bread: "I am the bread of life; he who comes to Me shall never hunger, and he who believes in Me shall never thirst" (John 6:35). Faith in Christ—not the literal consumption of consecrated elements—is what truly satisfies the soul. Early Christian interpreters like Chrysostom recognized the Lord's Prayer as a petition for God's provision, both physical and spiritual, not a sacramental formula.[96]

The implications of such distortions reach beyond theology; they strike at the heart of the gospel itself. Either the cross finished the mission, or the mission remains open. Scripture leaves no ambiguity: *Tetelestai*.

A Gospel Distorted—Satan's Subtle Strategy

If the gospel is the power of God unto salvation, then any distortion of it is not merely error—it is spiritual sabotage. Having examined how Roman Catholic sacramental theology departs from the biblical model of grace through faith, we must now ask, What lies beneath such persistent deviation? Why would a system so rigorously defend practices that obscure the simplicity of the cross?

The answer is not merely institutional inertia or historical tradition. It is spiritual warfare. Paul warned that "Satan disguises himself as an angel of light" (2 Cor 11:14), and his servants as ministers of righteousness. Satan's most effective strategy is not open rebellion but religious

---

95. McGrath, *Iustitia Dei*, 273–98.
96. John Chrysostom, *Homilies on Matthew* 19.5.

imitation. He does not always oppose Christ with horns and hatred—he often mimics him with robes and ritual. By embedding false assurance within sacred language, he can inoculate souls against the true gospel. The sacraments, when elevated above Scripture and made prerequisites for grace, become tools not of redemption but of control. This is deception doctrine: don't tell people the truth; feed them a near-truth that steers them off course. In military PSYOP terms, this is not a frontal assault but a perception operation, embedding a false map so the enemy walks willingly into the wrong objective.

Consider the implications:

- When baptism is no longer a public declaration of faith but a mechanical rite that regenerates apart from belief, the gospel is muted.
- When the Eucharist is no longer a remembrance of Christ's finished work but treated as a repeated offering, the sufficiency of Calvary is denied.
- When confession is no longer a cry to God but a transaction with a priest, the veil torn at Christ's death is stitched back together.

In each case, the sacrament becomes a substitute for the Savior. False assurance is perhaps Satan's most dangerous gift: a person convinced that ritual secures salvation, rather than repentance and faith, may never seek the Savior. This is not merely theological error—it is spiritual misdirection. A little leaven leavens the whole lump (Gal 5:9). Satan thrives where grace is confused, where access to God is mediated by men, and where salvation is tied to obedience to a system rather than surrender to a Savior. He does not need to destroy the gospel outright; he only needs to distort it enough that it loses its power. This is the same principle that underlies classic military deception operations—from feigned retreats to dummy tanks in World War II. Victory doesn't require eliminating the enemy; it requires confusing him so thoroughly that he fights the wrong battle.

And what better way to thwart the Great Commission than to convince the world it has already fulfilled it? If the church becomes a dispenser of ritual rather than a herald of redemption, then the urgency of evangelism fades. Evangelism gives way to maintenance, discipleship to duty, and mission to mere membership. The nations are not called to repentance—they are invited to ceremony. It's the difference between an army on the march and an army standing at parade rest—still impressive to look at but no longer advancing the cause.

This is how Satan wages war: not with chaos but with counterfeit. Not with denial but with distortion. And the church, if it is to be faithful to Christ, must not only proclaim the gospel; it must protect it from every subtle imitation. Every distortion shares one common effect: it shifts the gaze away from the cross. Instead of resting in Christ's finished work, souls are tethered to an ongoing cycle of rites and mediators. Like a PSYOP broadcast that repeats half-truths until they sound like reality, these distortions create a fog of war in which clarity is lost and obedience to Christ is replaced with submission to a system.

These distortions are not confined to Rome. Across cultures and centuries, the enemy has used the same tactic of turning ordinary practices into supposed channels of salvation. Other religions also attach salvific meaning to eating. In Hindu practice, food offered to idols (*prasad*) is believed to absorb divine essence, while in Sikhism, the communal langar meal symbolizes blessing and equality.[97] Both systems, like Catholic transubstantiation, invest ordinary food with supernatural significance. Yet Scripture teaches that Christ's once-for-all sacrifice is sufficient; salvation is not mediated through ritual consumption but secured by faith in him (Heb 10:10–14). The strategy is the same: bind assurance to the senses, and faith is redirected from Christ's finished work to repeating ceremonies.

A striking cultural parallel is the Cardiff Giant hoax of 1869. Farmers in upstate New York "discovered" a ten-foot petrified man, which many hailed as proof of biblical giants.[98] Crowds flocked to see it, convinced by the tangible "evidence" before their eyes. Though later exposed as a carved fraud, the spectacle had already deceived thousands. Eucharistic miracles work in the same way: material signs presented as confirmation, drawing attention to the object rather than to Christ himself.

Purgatory extends the same strategy into the afterlife. It replaces the assurance of Christ's finished work with the uncertainty of postmortem purification, offering another form of false assurance that binds souls to the church rather than to Christ. It is, in essence, a psychological warfare campaign against assurance—convincing believers that victory at Calvary was only partial, that the battle still rages in the grave, and that the institution, not the Savior, controls the outcome.

---

97. Klostermaier, *Survey of Hinduism*, 302–5; Mann, *Sikhism*, 67–72.
98. Wallace, *Great Giant Hoax*, 14–29.

After-Action Fog: Purgatory and the Psychology of Control

Just as the Roman Catholic doctrine of the Eucharist distorts Christ's promised return, the belief in purgatory similarly contradicts Scripture's clear teaching on the afterlife. Purgatory, according to Catholic teaching, is a state of postmortem purification where the faithful must undergo suffering until they are made ready for heaven.[99] Because the church also teaches that indulgences, Masses, and prayers for the dead can shorten this time, the doctrine inevitably fosters fear and dependency—keeping Catholics tied to sacramental performance and priestly mediation as the supposed means of relief.[100] This very dynamic was exposed at the dawn of the Reformation, when Martin Luther denounced indulgence preaching for turning purgatory into a fear-based revenue stream. He warned that promises of release from suffering in exchange for indulgence letters not only corrupted the gospel but ensnared consciences in perpetual uncertainty.[101]

Both doctrines shift the focus from Christ's finished work to an ongoing system of human mediation. Baptism is sometimes drawn into this same framework, for Roman Catholic theology often interprets Jesus' words in John 3:5 ("No one can enter the kingdom of God unless they are born of water and the Spirit") as a basis for baptismal regeneration—treating water baptism as a sacramental necessity that infuses grace and even shortens purgatory. Yet in context, Jesus is calling Nicodemus to spiritual rebirth, drawing on Ezek 36:25–27, where "water and Spirit" signify cleansing and new life, not a church ordinance.

Scripture itself provides exceptions, most notably the thief on the cross (Luke 23:42–43), who entered paradise without baptism. Salvation is grounded in repentant faith, not ritual. At the same time, those who come to saving faith are commanded to be baptized as a public sign of union with Christ. Baptism thus washes away the past, marks new life in him, and testifies to grace, but it is not a meritorious work or prerequisite for eternal life.

In PSYOP terms, purgatory and baptismal regeneration both create a dependency loop—shifting trust from the decisive victory (the cross) to perpetual "resupply" through institutional channels. By contrast,

---

99. *CCC*, §§1030–32.

100. *CCC*, §§1471–79.

101. Luther, *Disputation*, theses 27–32, 36, 62. See also Heb 9:26, 10:14, Luke 23:43, 2 Cor 5:8.

Scripture affirms the finality of Christ's work: he "has appeared once for all... to put away sin by the sacrifice of himself" (Heb 9:26), and "by one offering He has perfected forever those who are being sanctified" (Heb 10:14). To be "absent from the body" is to be "at home with the Lord" (2 Cor 5:8). No delay, no holding pattern—Christ's finished mission secures direct and immediate fellowship with him.

The Roman Catholic Church defines purgatory as a state of purification for souls who die in God's grace and friendship but are not yet fully purified. According to Roman Catholic teaching, these souls undergo a final cleansing to achieve the holiness necessary to enter heaven. This doctrine is based on the idea that nothing unclean can enter God's presence (Rev 21:27) and that some sins require purification after death. This reframes assurance as "pending clearance," like keeping units stuck at a staging area rather than allowing them to redeploy home. To substantiate the doctrine of purgatory, the Roman Catholic Church maintains the Apocrypha (discussed in chapter 2). One of the key passages used is 2 Macc 12:45 (RSVCE), which describes prayers for the dead: "Therefore he made atonement for the dead, that they might be delivered from their sin."[102] Yet this book is not part of the inspired Hebrew Scriptures and was never cited by Jesus or the apostles as canonical. Its use as a doctrinal foundation reflects a reliance on extra-biblical tradition rather than the authoritative canon of Scripture. That's a shift of the map reference—from the issued grid (canon) to a nonstandard overlay—guaranteeing navigational drift.

Beyond scriptural interpretations, the doctrine of purgatory is tied to the treasury of merit, the belief that the church holds a reservoir of spiritual merits from Christ's sacrifice, the virtues of the Virgin Mary, and the deeds of saints. Catholic teaching holds that these merits can be applied to souls in purgatory, helping their purification process. This has led to centuries of prayers for the dead, with the expectation that intercession can hasten their release. The idea that prayers and indulgences—including Mass cards and monetary contributions—can accelerate a soul's journey through purgatory builds upon this unbiblical framework. Though indulgences were a major catalyst for the Reformation—challenged by Luther in his *Ninety-Five Theses*—they never disappeared. While their outright sale was abolished, indulgences persist in acts such as Mass

---

102. See also Hayes, "Catholic View of Purgatory," 103–5.

offerings, devotional practices, and charitable contributions for the dead, all of which imply that human actions can lessen postmortem suffering.[103]

Central to this doctrine is the concept of *satispassio*, the Latin term referring to the suffering endured as satisfaction for sins. Purgatory functions as the place where souls undergo this purification process, enduring suffering to satisfy the remaining consequences of their sins before entering God's presence.[104] Yet this concept risks undermining the gospel itself. Scripture teaches that Christ alone is the exclusive mediator between God and mankind (1 Tim 2:5). By suggesting that human suffering contributes to what Christ has already accomplished, the sufficiency of his atonement is obscured. As Scripture affirms, Christ "has appeared once for all . . . to put away sin by the sacrifice of himself" (Heb 9:26).[105] It's like being told to keep taking treatments after the doctor has declared you fully healed.

One of the clearest refutations of purgatory comes from Christ's words to the thief on the cross. A condemned man—guilty and without the opportunity for restitution—turned to Jesus in his final moments, pleading, "Lord, remember me when You come into Your kingdom" (Luke 23:42). Without hesitation, Jesus replied, "Assuredly, I say to you, today you will be with Me in Paradise" (Luke 23:43). This exchange is profoundly significant. Jesus did not place the man in a holding pattern of purification or assign him further suffering. "Paradise" was promised that very day, not at the end of an intermediate process. The thief did not undergo *satispassio*, nor did he require additional merits from saints or the church's treasury. By faith alone, he was granted immediate fellowship with Christ—no delay, no purgatory, no priestly mediation. Paul echoes the same truth: "to be absent from the body" is "to be at home with the Lord" (2 Cor 5:8).[106] Scripture is consistent: faith secures direct insertion into Christ's presence. Any "intermediate staging area" is an overlay not found on the inspired grid map.

The practice of purgatorial suffering introduces an unbiblical reliance on works. Scripture is explicit: salvation is "by grace . . . through faith . . . not of works, lest anyone should boast" (Eph 2:8–9). Paul, recognizing the inadequacy of personal righteousness, declared that he

---

103. *CCC*, §§1471–79.

104. Ott, *Fundamentals of Catholic Dogma*, 483–85.

105. *CCC*, §§1476–77.

106. No intermediary process is described—Paul presents assurance, not a purgatorial sequence. Faith in Christ secures eternal life without delay.

wanted to be found "not having my own righteousness . . . but that which is through faith in Christ" (Phil 3:9). This is why Scripture consistently locates assurance in Christ's finished work, not in human contribution. If Christ's righteousness is imputed to believers through faith alone, then purification after death is unnecessary.

By revisiting these foundational truths, it becomes clear that purgatory and the treasury of merit contradict biblical teachings. Salvation is found in Christ alone—without intermediaries, without postmortem purification, and without human contributions. Indulgence practices, both medieval and modern, only reinforce this distortion. Anything added becomes ballast; it doesn't help the ship—it sinks it. Some Catholic interpreters point to Phil 1:23, where Paul expresses his desire "to depart and be with Christ," as well as his broader teaching in 2 Cor 5 about longing for the heavenly dwelling. Far from implying an intermediate state of purgation, these texts reinforce the immediacy of hope: to leave this life is to be with the Lord.[107] The teaching of purgatory undermines Christ's completed work on the cross. When Jesus declared, "It is finished" (John 19:30), he meant that the debt of sin had been paid in full—leaving no further atonement required after death. The Commander's "mission complete" cannot be downgraded to "mission pending."

Just as purgatory contradicts the sufficiency of Christ's sacrifice, the Roman Catholic concept of priesthood similarly undermines his exclusive role as our high priest. The New Testament teaches that Christ alone serves as the eternal priest, eliminating the need for a human priesthood to mediate between God and man. Heb 7:23–27 affirms,

> Also there were many priests, because they were prevented by death from continuing. But He, because He continues forever, has an unchangeable priesthood. Therefore He is also able to save to the uttermost those who come to God through Him, since He always lives to make intercession for them. For such a High Priest was fitting for us, who is holy, harmless, undefiled, separate from sinners, and has become higher than the heavens; who does not need daily, as those high priests, to offer up sacrifices, first for His own sins and then for the people's, for this He did once for all when He offered up Himself.

That's the end of the old rotation schedule—no more mortal priests cycling through. One high priest, forever on station.

---

107. Beckwith, *Old Testament Canon*.

Christ established no priesthood other than the priesthood of all believers for the New Testament church, as seen in 1 Pet 2:5, 9:

> You also, as living stones, are being built up a spiritual house, a holy priesthood, to offer up spiritual sacrifices acceptable to God through Jesus Christ.... But you are a chosen generation, a royal priesthood, a holy nation, His own special people, that you may proclaim the praises of Him who called you out of darkness into His marvelous light.

This priesthood is not hierarchical or sacrificial—it is spiritual and communal. Every believer, through Christ, has direct access to God. No gatekeepers on this net; every believer has secure comms to the throne through Christ.

The New Testament provides criteria for pastors and deacons, but nowhere does it establish a separate priesthood resembling the one seen in the Roman Catholic Church. There is no mention of a priest being ordained and set apart, nor of a priestly role practicing the type of sacrificial ministry that Roman Catholicism teaches. Creating that office is like inventing a rank that does not exist, then demanding people salute it.

Additionally, Paul admonishes believers to hold fast to apostolic traditions, ensuring faithfulness to Christ's teachings:

> Therefore, brethren, stand fast and hold the traditions which you were taught, whether by word or our epistle. (2 Thess 2:15)

> But we command you, brethren, in the name of our Lord Jesus Christ, that you withdraw from every brother who walks disorderly and not according to the tradition which he received from us. (2 Thess 3:6)

These verses refer to the teachings of the apostles—not evolving ecclesiastical customs. Apostolic tradition is preserved in Scripture, not in a clerical hierarchy. The only standing orders binding the conscience are those issued by the apostles and preserved in Scripture. Any later additions are not orders but counterfeits.

A comparative analysis between Roman Catholic tradition and the teachings of the apostles demonstrates clear contradictions. The apostles did not establish a special priesthood within the community of believers, nor did they advocate for the creation of papal authority.

The same logic appears in Islam. The Qur'an describes a final judgment in which each person's deeds are weighed on a scale: those whose good outweighs their bad will succeed, while those whose scales are light will face eternal loss.[108] Like purgatory, this system withholds assurance, leaving followers bound to uncertainty and striving. Both operate as spiritual PSYOPs: keep salvation always just out of reach, and the soul remains captive to fear rather than anchored in grace.

History offers a striking financial counterpart. In 1720, the South Sea Company promised investors untold wealth through vague overseas ventures. The speculation ballooned until it collapsed, ruining thousands and shaking the British economy.[109] The scheme thrived because people kept pouring in resources, convinced the payoff was just beyond reach. Works-based salvation functions the same way: an endless investment of effort with no true return, until the collapse is revealed at judgment.

Where Does Authority Lie?

The central question is one of authority: Who has the right to define doctrine—Christ through his word, or the church through its traditions?

At the heart of every uniquely Roman Catholic doctrine—purgatory, the priesthood, the Mass, indulgences, Marian dogmas—lies a single, towering claim: that the church has the authority to define them. And that authority, in turn, rests entirely on one foundational belief: that Peter was the first pope. If Peter was not the pope, then his successors could not inherit an office that never existed—and the entire structure of papal authority collapses. This is not a peripheral issue; it is the linchpin. Without Peter as pope, there is no papacy. And without the papacy, the Roman Catholic Church loses its claim to exclusive doctrinal authority—not just in part but in principle. The entire edifice of Roman tradition, with all its accumulated dogmas and rituals, stands or falls on this one assertion. If the foundation is false, then everything built upon it is exposed—not as divine revelation but as human invention.

This claim of papal infallibility illustrates the problem. According to Rome, when the Pope speaks *ex cathedra*—that is, "from the chair" of Peter—his declarations on faith and morals are considered infallible. Yet here lies a serious dilemma: if papal statements are only accepted when they align with established Roman Catholic doctrine, then it is the doctrine—not the pope—that functions as the true authority. This creates a

---

108. Al-Mu'minun 23:102-3.
109. Carswell, *South Sea Bubble*, 45-67.

WHAT ARE TRUTH AND FALSEHOOD?

circular system: the pope is infallible because the church says so, and the church is authoritative because the pope affirms it. This kind of closed loop is indistinguishable from information warfare techniques—where the source validates itself by its own broadcast, immune to external verification.

History itself exposes the danger of such unchecked authority. During World War II, when the Nazi regime carried out the Holocaust, the institutional church—most notably the Vatican under Pope Pius XII—did not issue a clear and forceful public denunciation of the genocide. Historians continue to debate the reasons for this silence, but the absence of a decisive moral stand remains undeniable. While many individual Catholics displayed remarkable courage in protecting Jewish lives, the lack of an official, unambiguous condemnation from Rome revealed the weakness of a system that claims infallibility yet falters when confronted with evil. Infallibility in theory promised certainty, but in practice it produced institutional paralysis—a refusal to speak truth when it mattered most, undermining the very moral authority Rome claimed to possess.[110] Historians continue to debate Pius XII's wartime actions, but the absence of a public, unequivocal condemnation remains undisputed. Nor was Rome alone; many Protestant pulpits across Europe also remained silent during the Holocaust, a sobering reminder of how institutional fear and compromise can dull prophetic witness. Yet here is the critical distinction: Protestant churches never claimed universal, infallible authority over all Christians. The pope did—and that makes his silence far more consequential.

This is where the question of truth becomes unavoidable. If the Roman Catholic Church has built its authority on a historical fiction—retroactively assigning divine weight to human constructs—then its teachings are not merely mistaken; they are deceptive. Here deception operates like a PSYOP: the authority structure is framed as immovable and inevitable, when in reality it rests on a contested premise. The "center of gravity" (papal succession) is treated as untouchable, so the entire population is conditioned to accept the system without questioning its origin. The issue is not just doctrinal error but theological misdirection.

---

110. Historians continue to debate the role of Pope Pius XII during the Holocaust. Critics argue that his silence amounted to moral failure (see Cornwell, *Hitler's Pope*), while others contend he worked quietly behind the scenes to aid Jews, cautioning against overly harsh judgments (Dalin, *Myth of Hitler's Pope*). For a balanced overview of recent scholarship, see Kertzer, *Pope at War*.

What is presented as eternal truth is, in fact, a carefully curated illusion. And when human tradition is elevated above Scripture, the result is not clarity but confusion—not light but shadow.

Roman Catholic apologists frequently appeal to the early church fathers to defend doctrines such as transubstantiation, purgatory, and apostolic succession. Yet this approach is deeply problematic. The church fathers were not a monolithic voice—they often disagreed with one another and held views that contradict both Scripture and each other. Roman Catholic tradition tends to highlight those statements that appear to support its theology while minimizing or ignoring others that do not, resulting in a curated and often misleading picture of early Christian belief.[111] This is the classic "selective dissemination" tactic in PSYOP—flooding the field with carefully chosen voices to create the illusion of unanimity.

Moreover, the fathers were fallible men—not inspired apostles. Like all humans, they were shaped by their time, culture, and philosophical influences, and they were capable of theological error. While their writings can offer valuable historical insight, they must never be elevated above or placed alongside the authority of Scripture. The church fathers should be respected but never revered, and their teachings must always be tested against the unchanging word of God.

This selective use of the fathers feeds directly into Rome's larger claim of "doctrinal development." When Scripture does not support uniquely Roman Catholic doctrines—such as papal infallibility, purgatory, or Marian dogmas—the church turns to the early church fathers as a secondary source of authority. While many Catholic doctrines (like the Trinity or the deity of Christ) are firmly rooted in Scripture, others are not. In these cases, Roman Catholic theologians appeal to tradition and claim that these teachings were always present, even if not explicitly taught in the Bible. They argue that doctrines such as the Assumption of Mary, transubstantiation, or papal infallibility were not invented later but rather were always present—implicitly—in the deposit of faith. Latin phrases like *semper existit* or *semper fuit* ("it has always existed") are used to assert that these teachings were true from the beginning, even if they were not formally defined until centuries later.[112] As we saw with Rome's appeal to Luke 22:32, such claims often rest on retroactive readings that

---

111. Webster, "Patristic Exegesis."

112. Newman, *Development of Christian Doctrine*, 29–31; Geisler and MacKenzie, *Roman Catholics and Evangelicals*, 156–61.

the early church itself never recognized. But this is not biblical theology—it is theological retrofitting.

Indeed, if a person were to read the Bible from Genesis to Revelation without the filter of church tradition, councils, or magisterial decrees, they would never construct Roman Catholicism as it exists today. Nor would they invent Mormonism, Jehovah's Witnesses, or any other system that requires supplemental revelation. Each emerges not from the plain sense of the text but from external authorities claiming equal or greater weight than Scripture itself. The contrast underscores the Reformers' cry: *sola scriptura*. Scripture alone is sufficient.[113]

This method often involves selectively quoting the church fathers to support later doctrines, while ignoring the broader context or contradictory statements. This selective approach constructs a curated narrative—one that mimics continuity while concealing theological dissonance. Doctrinal development, when untethered from Scripture, becomes a license for innovation. And when those innovations are declared infallible, they are no longer subject to correction—even by the word of God. This is not fidelity to the faith once delivered to the saints (Jude 1:3); it is a distortion of it. In military terms, the operation has shifted from defending ground already secured (Scripture) to constructing artificial terrain—manufacturing new doctrinal ground through information dominance. But new terrain built on illusion cannot hold against the fire of God's truth. Even more dangerously, such "development" gives the Catholic Church a license to retroactively justify virtually any practice or belief, cloaking novelty in the language of continuity. This is not preservation of the gospel but a strategic deception—an illusion of legitimacy that undermines the sufficiency of God's word.

And this is precisely where the deeper problem emerges: doctrinal development gives Rome a way to retroactively validate any teaching by claiming it was always present in seed form, even when absent from Scripture and apostolic witness. This is not development; it is doctrinal inflation. From a PSYOP perspective, it is the equivalent of planting "after-action reports" into the historical record, making it appear that

---

113. William Whitaker, an English Reformer, argued that Scripture is "the certain and infallible rule by which all controversies of religion are to be tried," rejecting any appeal to unwritten traditions (Whitaker, *Disputation on Holy Scripture*, 362–64). Benjamin Warfield likewise affirmed that "inspiration is that extraordinary, supernatural influence exerted by the Holy Ghost on the writers of our sacred books, by which their words were rendered also the words of God, and, therefore, perfectly infallible" (Warfield, *Revelation and Inspiration*, 65–67).

operations were always intended that way, even when they were not. In effect, it becomes a theological sleight of hand, where the absence of early evidence is reframed as hidden presence.

In addition to citing the fathers, Roman Catholic apologists sometimes appeal to Heb 13:17—"Obey your leaders and submit to them"—to argue that Protestants are in rebellion against church authority. But this text cannot be stretched to mean blind submission to any institution that claims authority. In context, the author of Hebrews is exhorting believers to respect local shepherds who faithfully guard their souls and teach God's word. Biblical submission is always conditioned on faithfulness to Christ. The same Scriptures that call us to honor leaders also warn us to test all teaching by the word of God (Acts 17:11, 1 Thess 5:21).

The Reformers were not guilty of rebellion against God but of fidelity to him—resisting leaders who had abandoned the gospel. Peter himself taught that when human authority contradicts divine command, "We must obey God rather than human beings!" (Acts 5:29 NIV). Far from being an act of sin, the break with Rome led by the early Reformers—figures like Luther, Calvin, and Zwingli—was an act of fidelity to Christ, the true Head of the church (Col 1:18). United by their conviction that Scripture alone is the final authority, they rejected ecclesiastical traditions that obscured the gospel and restored the centrality of Christ's atoning work and lordship over his church.

Clarifying the Target: Individuals vs. the Institution

At this point, it's important to clarify: the concern here is not to attack individuals within Roman Catholicism nor to question the sincerity of their faith. Many Catholics genuinely love Jesus and earnestly seek to honor God with their lives. The critique is directed at the system itself, which risks leading people away from the sufficiency of Christ and the authority of Scripture. Roman Catholicism offers a textbook example of how spiritual deception can be both subtle and systemic. It wraps error in the language of tradition, cloaks human authority in divine terminology, and quietly redefines the gospel of grace through ritual and hierarchy. Like a well-executed PSYOP, the system's power lies in its plausibility—it looks familiar, it feels sacred, and it appeals to deep human instincts for order and belonging.

You are not being asked to abandon faith—but to examine it. To test every teaching, every tradition, and every authority against the word of God. Truth is not afraid of scrutiny. And Christ is not hidden behind ceremony—he is revealed in his word.

This is not to say that every Roman Catholic knowingly embraces falsehood. But the system itself illustrates how deception can flourish when it mimics truth just closely enough to go unquestioned. The danger is not in the blatantly false but in the "almost true"—the counterfeit bill that passes because it resembles the genuine currency.

While these concerns must be examined carefully, it's also important to acknowledge where Catholic and Protestant traditions stand together. Despite deep theological differences, the Roman Catholic Church and Protestantism affirm a number of foundational truths rooted in Scripture and historic Christian orthodoxy. Each holds to the inspiration of the Bible, the triune nature of God, and the belief in the historical death and bodily resurrection of Jesus Christ. Both defend the sanctity of human life, affirm marriage as the union of one man and one woman, and promote the importance of nuclear families grounded in biblical morality. They reject atheism, relativism, and paganism, and generally affirm that Jesus is the exclusive path to salvation—even if they differ on how that salvation is received.

These shared convictions reflect a commitment to moral clarity, reverence for Scripture (despite differing views on its authority), and a belief in the centrality of Christ. While doctrinal divergence must be addressed honestly, recognizing common ground between Protestantism and the Roman Catholic Church opens the door for respectful dialogue and clarifies that the concern is not with every teaching or moral stance, but with those doctrines that distort or displace the gospel.

Many trust what they've been taught, often assuming it aligns with Scripture—unaware of where tradition diverges from God's word. The deception lies not in the hearts of the people but in the institution that claims divine authority while contradicting the word of God. This complexity—spanning councils, catechisms, and centuries of theological layers—makes it unsurprising that many Roman Catholics, despite sincere devotion, remain unaware of where tradition diverges from Scripture. Its teachings have developed over two millennia, shaped through twenty-one ecumenical councils—some lasting years or even decades—along with thousands of papal statements, theological treatises, and doctrinal refinements. The Council of Trent alone spanned eighteen years, involved three popes, and issued sweeping declarations on justification, sacraments, and ecclesiastical authority. Today, the *Catechism of the Catholic Church* stretches across more than nine hundred pages, and even the Vatican's website still loads in Latin—reinforcing a legacy of tradition that is often inaccessible to lay believers.[114] Latin itself is a language no longer spoken in daily life, preserved almost exclusively for religious observances, which only deepens the sense of distance between the hierarchy and the average follower. This layering of authority functions much like camouflage in warfare: complexity itself becomes a form of concealment, hiding distortions beneath centuries of accumulated ritual and language.

In light of this complexity, many Catholics may unknowingly diverge from official doctrine yet possess genuine saving faith grounded in Christ alone. Their trust may not rest in ritual but in the simplicity and clarity of Rom 10:9: "If you confess with your mouth the Lord Jesus and believe in your heart that God raised Him from the dead, you will be saved."

In the end, the danger of deception lies not only in what is blatantly false—but in what is almost true. When religious systems elevate tradition above Scripture, they risk leading sincere believers away from the sufficiency of Christ. The call of the gospel is not to ritual, hierarchy, or human mediation—but to Christ alone, by grace alone, through faith alone.

This pattern is not confined to the past. Today, the language may be different, but the strategy remains the same. When churches redefine sin to align with culture, or when leaders claim new revelations that contradict Scripture, they are not advancing truth—they are repackaging deception. The playbook remains unchanged: infiltrate, confuse, and redirect allegiance away from Christ's sufficiency. The enemy's tactics have not changed; only the packaging has.

Throughout Scripture, God makes one truth abundantly clear—he desires a relationship, not a religion built on rituals and hierarchy. "Behold, I stand at the door and knock. If anyone hears My voice and opens the door, I will come in to him and dine with him, and he with Me" (Rev 3:20). Salvation is not a system of works-based approval but a divine invitation into personal communion with Christ, as seen in Jas 4:8: "Draw near to God and He will draw near to you."

---

114. McBrien, *Catholicism*, 45–52.

It is not earned through effort but received by grace—a divine invitation into communion with Christ, not a reward for performance. Yet human nature gravitates toward structure, tradition, and the belief that effort earns favor—an inclination the Roman Catholic Church has woven into its doctrine.

Roman Catholic tradition introduces several doctrines absent from the apostolic era, including its views on the priesthood, the Eucharist, and Marian dogmas. The apostles did not espouse the notion that the Lord's Supper should be seen as a sacrificial offering, nor did they establish beliefs regarding Mary's sinlessness, perpetual virginity, bodily assumption, or intercessory role. Instead, their teachings focused solely on Christ as the mediator between God and humanity, affirming that salvation and divine communion occur directly through him (1 Tim 2:5).[115]

Likewise, the apostles never suggested that their position would be passed down after their deaths, nor did they establish apostolic succession as an ongoing church institution.

The Roman Catholic Church claims that authority is transmitted from generation to generation, like a relay race where a baton is handed off to the next leader. But Scripture places authority solely in God's word, not in an unbroken human chain. The true "relay baton" of spiritual leadership remains firmly within God's grasp, never delegated to institutional succession.

Additionally, the apostles did not establish sacraments as formal rituals, nor did they endorse intercessory prayer directed toward specific saints. Instead, their writings emphasize direct communion with God through Christ, reinforcing the biblical foundation that bypasses intermediaries.

This distinction is particularly significant in cultures where work ethic shapes identity. In nations like the United States, where people are conditioned to believe hard work leads to achievement, figures like Daniel Eugene "Rudy" Ruettiger, who defied the odds to play football at Notre Dame, as portrayed in the Heartland International Film Festival–winning movie *Rudy*; Audie Murphy, who rose from poverty to become

---

115. For the development of these doctrines within post-apostolic Catholic tradition, see *CCC*, §§964–75, 1367, and 1548–51; see also Pelikan, *Emergence of the Catholic Tradition*, 127–31, 245–49. For the modern Roman Catholic position on Marian mediation, see Francis, *Homily*, in which he rejects the title "Co-Redemptrix" while affirming Mary's role as disciple and mother. See also Dicastery for the Doctrine of the Faith, *Mater Populi Fidelis*, which reiterates that the title "Co-Redemptrix" is "always inappropriate," though Mary remains central to salvation history.

one of the most decorated soldiers in US history, as depicted in the box-office success *To Hell and Back*; and Chris Gardner, who overcame homelessness to become a successful stockbroker and entrepreneur, as shown in the Academy Award–nominated film *The Pursuit of Happyness*,[116] embody this deeply ingrained belief.

These stories reinforce the cultural notion that persistence, discipline, and relentless effort unlock opportunity and earn reward. In this way, the Roman Catholic emphasis on rituals, indulgences, and priestly mediation can feel like a spiritual extension of that mindset—the idea that religious effort secures divine favor.

By tying divine acceptance to works rather than faith, this tradition capitalizes on humanity's natural inclination to earn approval by meeting expectations, echoing the same deception Satan uses to distort the simplicity of grace through faith. Here again, the parallel to PSYOP is striking: the adversary doesn't need to deny Christ outright—he only needs to reframe him through a lens of endless striving, convincing people that they are close to freedom when they are still under control.

A modern Roman Catholic teacher recently explained discipleship this way: "The only thing lacking in Jesus's work is our participation in it—our being absorbed into the work of Jesus. This is what Paul describes in Romans 8:13, putting to death the deeds of the body."[117]

At first glance, this sounds biblical. After all, Paul does command believers to put sin to death. Yet here lies the deception: the Bible never presents mortification of sin as the *cause* of salvation, but as its *fruit*. Romans 8:13 is not a formula for earning eternal life—it is evidence of the Spirit's presence in those already made alive by Christ (Rom 8:9–11).

Scripture declares that justification is a once-for-all act of God's grace, not a process we complete (John 19:30, Eph 2:8–9). To suggest that something is still "lacking" until we contribute is to shift the foundation of salvation from Christ's finished work to human effort.

The Bible consistently warns against this distortion: "If it is by grace, it is no longer of works; otherwise grace is no longer grace" (Rom 11:6). Works of obedience are essential as evidence of new life (Jas 2:17), but

---

116. The title *The Pursuit of Happyness* intentionally uses "Happyness" with a "y," reflecting Chris Gardner's real experience of seeing the word misspelled outside his son's daycare—a detail he later embraced as a symbolic marker in his journey toward success.

117. Hahn, *First Comes Love*, 100.

WHAT ARE TRUTH AND FALSEHOOD?

they do not secure it. Discipleship flows from salvation—it never completes it.

This is how deception operates. It cloaks error in biblical language, presenting half-truths that sound pious but undermine the sufficiency of Christ. A modern example of this dynamic is Dan Brown's bestselling novel *The Da Vinci Code*. Though marketed as fiction, Brown frames his story as if it reveals suppressed truths about Jesus, the church, and Christian history. Millions of readers walked away questioning the reliability of Scripture, not realizing they had absorbed a blasphemous narrative woven from distortion. Its reach only expanded when the story was showcased in theaters through a major film adaptation starring Tom Hanks, further blurring the line between entertainment and supposed history.

Brown's method illustrates deception's power: he sprinkles fact into fiction—real names, locations, and events—so that his fabrications feel plausible. He even stumbles over basic chronology, repeatedly conflating centuries with years—for instance, treating the "third century" as if it referred to the 300s, when in fact the third century encompasses AD 201–300. Such errors may appear minor, yet they reveal how carelessly truth is handled when the aim is provocation rather than accuracy. Like all spiritual PSYOP, *The Da Vinci Code* captivates precisely because it wraps falsehood in the clothing of truth.

Such modern distortions remind us that deception is never neutral—it always aims to undermine Christ's sufficiency. To say that Jesus' work is "lacking" apart from our participation is not merely a mistake—it is a direct contradiction of the gospel, which proclaims that Christ alone is sufficient to save. Our obedience, empowered by the Spirit, is not the missing ingredient in redemption—it is the overflow of a salvation that has already been accomplished.

When evaluating Roman Catholic traditions through the lens of Scripture, it becomes evident that many doctrines developed outside apostolic teaching. The apostles entrusted ultimate authority to God's word alone—a timeless standard that transcends human additions and traditions.

Regrettably, the Roman Catholic traditions discussed here represent only a small portion of practices that diverge from the teachings of the apostles as recorded in the New Testament Scriptures. It is essential to recognize that many other instances of such deviations exist.[118]

---

118. See Gendron, *Preparing for Eternity*.

Numerous additional doctrines stem from human desires for structure, authority, and achievement rather than the personal relationship with Christ that God himself freely offers.

Each person stands at a crossroads, faced with a profound decision: Will they trust the Bible as God's authoritative and complete word, or place their faith in human traditions, institutions, or individuals?

This is no mere academic debate—it is a matter of eternal consequence. The two cannot both be correct, for their teachings often stand in direct contradiction to one another.

THE URGENCY OF DISCERNMENT

In 1986, NASA launched the *Challenger* shuttle into space. Engineers had warned of a small flaw in the O-ring seals, but their concerns were dismissed. The launch proceeded—and seventy-three seconds later, the shuttle exploded, killing all seven crew members. The tragedy was not caused by a massive failure but by a small, overlooked detail.[119] In the same way, spiritual deception rarely begins with blatant heresy; it often slips in through a minor compromise—a doctrine accepted without testing, a tradition embraced without question. Yet the consequences can be eternal.

Deception is not always loud. Sometimes, it whispers. Sometimes, it wears robes. Sometimes, it quotes Scripture. But in every case, it mimics legitimacy closely enough to bypass suspicion—just as a counterfeit signal in warfare diverts the enemy's defenses. Its strategy is always the same: to lead hearts away from Christ while appearing safe, even holy.

This is why the word of God is essential. The Bible does not merely claim to be divinely inspired—it proves it. Its words pulse with life, backed by fulfilled prophecy, remarkable harmony across sixty-six books, and a unified story penned by more than forty authors over centuries.

It is not just literature—it is power. It transforms hearts, restores souls, and illuminates truth. Its universal appeal stretches across cultures and generations, testifying to the authority of Jesus Christ and his apostles. Only Scripture has the clarity to unmask deception and the strength to guard the believer from it.

It is in this context that we must heed a solemn warning—one that reverberates throughout the New Testament: "Do not be deceived." This phrase is not a casual suggestion but a divine alarm, cautioning believers

---

119. Rogers et al., "Cause of the Accident."

WHAT ARE TRUTH AND FALSEHOOD?

against the subtle distortions that seek to corrupt truth, erode faith, and lead hearts astray.

This warning is not isolated to a single passage—it appears repeatedly, underscoring its urgency. Paul, James, and other apostles echo this command, emphasizing the danger of deception:

> Do you not know that the unrighteous will not inherit the kingdom of God? Do not be deceived. (1 Cor 6:9–10)

> Let no one say when he is tempted, "I am tempted by God"; for God cannot be tempted by evil, nor does He Himself tempt anyone. But each one is tempted when he is drawn away by his own desires and enticed. Then, when desire has conceived, it gives birth to sin; and sin, when it is full-grown, brings forth death. Do not be deceived, my beloved brethren. Every good gift and every perfect gift is from above, and comes down from the Father of lights, with whom there is no variation or shadow of turning. Of His own will He brought us forth by the word of truth, that we might be a kind of firstfruits of His creatures. (Jas 1:13–18)

> Do not be deceived, God is not mocked; for whatever a man sows, that he will also reap. (Gal 6:7)

The New Testament warns against deception, false doctrine, and false prophets over forty times, underscoring the gravity of this spiritual battle. These warnings are not theoretical—they are urgent because deception is not always obvious. It often comes cloaked in religious language, institutional authority, or emotional appeal. This is spiritual irregular warfare: the enemy does not always charge head-on but infiltrates quietly, using disguise, diversion, and delay until the damage is irreversible.

Though the world may appear dominated by material and technological advantages, Scripture reminds us that the true struggle is not merely physical. It is deeply spiritual: "We wrestle not against flesh and blood, but against principalities, against powers, against the rulers of the darkness of this world, against spiritual wickedness in high places" (Eph 6:12).

Truth often battles falsehood that hides behind the subtle art of manipulation, much like camouflage in warfare. This struggle underscores the importance of discernment, a quality that Charles Spurgeon (1834–1892), a renowned English Baptist preacher often called the "Prince of

Preachers," is commonly believed to have described: "Discernment is not a matter of simply telling the difference between right and wrong; rather it is telling the difference between right and almost right."

Spurgeon's words resonate profoundly in the context of spiritual deception, particularly when examining the chilling case of the *People's Temple* led by Jim Jones. Jones masterfully blended Christian teachings with socialist ideologies, twisting Scripture to justify his control over followers. This manipulation culminated in the tragic Jonestown massacre of 1978. In the jungles of Guyana, deception masqueraded as faith. Over nine hundred followers perished in a harrowing culmination of spiritual manipulation—a chilling reminder of the stakes in failing to discern truth from error.[120]

Jim Jones preyed on the vulnerabilities of his followers, many of whom were searching for hope, belonging, and purpose. His charismatic personality and promises of utopia allowed him to exploit their emotional needs. Under the guise of a spiritual leader, Jones selectively used Scripture to assert his authority, blending elements of Christianity with socialist rhetoric to create a distorted yet compelling narrative. This false spiritual foundation fostered unwavering loyalty among his followers while suppressing their ability to question his actions.

A particularly haunting example of this manipulation can be seen in the story of Christine Miller, one of the Jonestown members who courageously voiced dissent against Jim Jones's call for mass suicide. Christine's plea for reason amid the chaos highlights the tragic loss of critical discernment among the group. Despite her bravery, Jones's oppressive control and the overwhelming atmosphere of fear ultimately silenced dissent.

Christine's story serves as a poignant reminder that discernment is not merely intellectual—it is spiritual courage. Her voice, though silenced, echoes a warning to every generation: deception thrives where truth is untested.[121]

Jones's techniques of deception extended beyond theological manipulation; he employed practical methods to entrench his control. Followers were isolated both physically, in the remote jungles of Guyana, and emotionally, through intense indoctrination. Dependency was fostered as Jones portrayed himself as the sole provider of spiritual guidance and

---

120. Moore, *Understanding Jonestown*, 45–47.
121. Reiterman, *Raven*.

material needs. Fear became a weapon, suppressing dissent and ensuring compliance.

This combination mirrors military PSYOP doctrine: isolate the target, control the narrative, induce dependency, and eliminate competing voices. It is not only a cult tactic—it is the devil's oldest tactic.

These strategies reveal how deception often thrives under the guise of benevolence and divine authority, making it all the more insidious. The most dangerous lies are not the ones shouted from pulpits of rebellion but the ones whispered from altars of tradition.

The tragic case of Jonestown underscores the necessity of discernment in recognizing subtle distortions of truth. Just as military strategies aim to counter enemy deception by uncovering false signals, spiritual vigilance equips individuals to identify manipulative practices hidden within seemingly noble intentions.

The call to discernment is not optional—it is essential. In an age of religious confusion and doctrinal compromise, believers must test every teaching, every tradition, and every authority against the unchanging standard of Scripture.

Chapter 4 delves further into Satan's strategies, examining their parallels to military tactics of deception and exploring practical approaches to safeguard against the dangers of falsehood.

But for now, the question remains: Will you recognize deception when it comes cloaked in reverence? Will you test every voice against the voice of the Shepherd? Will you stand on the word of God, even when tradition, culture, or emotion urge you to compromise?

The battle for truth is not passive—it demands vigilance. The time for passive belief has ended; the call to discernment is urgent.

Will you test every tradition by Scripture? Will you follow the Shepherd's voice—even when it leads away from the familiar?

The truth is not hidden—but it must be sought. And when it is found, it must be followed—no matter the cost.

And here is the good news: that truth is not scattered or hidden in rituals, traditions, or human authority. It is fully revealed in the word of God. Scripture alone provides everything the believer needs for salvation and for faithful Christian living. As Paul declared, "All Scripture is given by inspiration of God, and is profitable for doctrine, for reproof, for correction, for instruction in righteousness, that the man of God may be complete, thoroughly equipped for every good work" (2 Tim. 3:16–17). No sacrament, hierarchy, or additional revelation is necessary to make us right with God. The gospel is clear: Christ has accomplished our salvation once for all, and his word is sufficient to bring us to faith, sustain us in life, and prepare us for eternity.

This is why discernment is not only about avoiding deception—it is about embracing truth. For centuries, believers have sealed this truth with their lives.

In 1555, Hugh Latimer and Nicholas Ridley were tied to the stake in Oxford for refusing to deny the gospel of justification by faith alone. As the flames rose beneath them, Latimer turned to Ridley and cried out, "Be of good comfort, Master Ridley, and play the man; we shall this day light such a candle, by God's grace, in England, as I trust shall never be put out."[122]

Their courage did not earn them heaven. Their martyrdom did not purchase their salvation. They are in heaven for one reason only: because their Savior sacrificed himself for them.

And here lies the same choice before every reader. The afterlife offers only two outcomes: justice or grace. Justice means bearing your own punishment before an infinitely holy God. Grace means trusting the innocent Substitute who bore that punishment in your place.

I don't want justice. I want grace. What about you?

Latimer and Ridley fixed their eyes on eternity. They knew life was not about prestige, comfort, or survival. It was about knowing Christ and making him known—even if it cost everything.

So where are your eyes fixed? If you stood before God today, would you ask for justice—or for grace? What will you do with the truth you have just encountered?

PERSONAL APPLICATION: DISCERNING TRUTH FROM FALSEHOOD

The battle between truth and deception is not fought only in theological debates—it is waged in everyday decisions, in the whispers of doubt, in the subtle compromises that shift convictions. Scripture warns that Satan's most effective strategy is not an obvious falsehood but a distortion of truth, making spiritual discernment an essential skill for every believer.

Here are five transformative steps to sharpen your ability to discern truth and stand firm in faith:

---

122. Foxe, *Book of Martyrs*, 123.

WHAT ARE TRUTH AND FALSEHOOD?

1. *Anchor Yourself in God's Word*—True discernment begins with Scripture as the immovable foundation. Roman Catholic teaching often places tradition and magisterial authority alongside—or even above—the Bible. But Jesus declared that his word is truth (John 17:17). Immerse yourself in Scripture, committing to study, memorize, and meditate on passages like John 8:31–32 and 2 Tim 3:16–17, which affirm its sufficiency. When confronted with competing voices, Scripture becomes the decisive test.

2. *Examine the Sources of Authority in Your Life*—Ask yourself, Am I relying on God's word as the highest authority, or allowing tradition, cultural opinion, or institutional voices to carry more weight? Rome claims authority through the papacy; modern culture claims it through relativism. Both distract from Christ's supremacy. By holding fast to the Bible alone, you remain anchored in God's unchanging truth rather than shifting sands.

3. *Develop Spiritual Discernment*—False teachings rarely come as blatant lies. They mimic the real thing—robes, rituals, even Scripture quotes—yet subtly divert allegiance away from Christ. Paul warns that Satan "disguises himself as an angel of light" (2 Cor 11:14). Pray for discernment (Jas 1:5), asking God to sharpen your ability to detect when truth is being diluted by tradition or misdirection. Like a soldier navigating a minefield, discernment helps you step safely while others stumble.

4. *Guard Your Heart and Mind*—Deception thrives not just in false systems like indulgences or purgatory, but also in the cultural pressure to blur absolutes. Be intentional about the teachings you accept and the influences you allow. Test everything against Scripture, as the Bereans did (Acts 17:11). This vigilance fortifies your spiritual defenses and equips you to recognize when something is being added to—or taken away from—the finished work of Christ.

5. *Pray for Insight and Protection*—Spiritual deception is not merely intellectual; it is warfare. Ask God daily to guard your heart from misplaced trust, to expose counterfeit authority, and to anchor your confidence in Christ alone. Like a compass cutting through battlefield fog, God's Spirit will direct you into truth and away from snares.

Personal Reflection

1. How would you define "truth" in your own words, and how does that compare with the biblical definitions of *aletheia* (Greek, meaning unconcealed, genuine, in accord with reality) and *'emeth* (Hebrew, meaning firmness, faithfulness, reliability, moral integrity)?[123]
2. Where do you feel the pull of competing authorities—tradition, culture, or human voices—tempting you to compromise?
3. In what areas of life do you find it most difficult to stand for absolute truth when pressured by authority figures or cultural norms?
4. Reflect on a time when something that sounded "close to the gospel" turned out to be misleading. How did Scripture bring clarity?

Group Discussion

1. How does the chapter's analysis of Roman Catholic authority claims highlight the danger of placing tradition above Scripture?
2. Why is it dangerous to blur the lines between truth and falsehood, even when done with "good intentions"?
3. How can believers encourage younger generations to resist cultural relativism and stand firm on biblical truth?
4. What are some practical ways your group or church can guard against spiritual deception and remain Christ-centered?

Scripture Connection

- Read Rom 1:18–25 and John 17:17. What do these passages teach us about truth, falsehood, and the consequences of rejecting God's truth?
- In light of Matt 7:24–27, what does it mean to build your life on the "rock" of truth? How can we help one another stay grounded?

Spiritual deception is rarely loud—it is often quiet, creeping in unnoticed until convictions gradually shift. Like a battlefield shrouded in

---

123. *Strong's* (1996), s.v. "ἀλήθεια (aletheia)," G225, and s.v. "אֱמֶת (emeth)," H571.

fog, deception obscures truth, making discernment essential for every believer.

The battle for truth is not passive—it demands vigilance. Make the choice today to stand firm, test every voice against Scripture, and anchor your hope in Christ alone.

Just as a soldier depends on an unerring compass to navigate hostile terrain, believers must turn to God's unshakable word as their ultimate guide. By committing to these practices, you will confidently distinguish light from darkness, truth from error, and stand fortified against the enemy's schemes.

4

Strategic Deception Buries Lies in Truths

Two dummy planes placed near an airfield in Kadena, Okinawa, on April 2, 1945. These decoys were designed to draw Allied fire away from real aircraft and the airfield itself. Like all effective deception, they worked by appearing credible— illustrating that lies survive only when they are cloaked in truth.[1]

1. Image: Signal Corps Archive, SC 205559, Apr. 2, 1945. Public Domain.

> Propaganda more than ever is an instrument of aggression, a new means for rendering a country defenseless in the face of an invading army.
>
> —Alfred McClung Lee and Elizabeth Briant Lee, *Fine Art of Propaganda*

Propaganda, in its broadest sense, is the deliberate shaping of perception through selective messaging, imagery, and repetition. Yet propaganda is not an isolated phenomenon; it operates as a subset of PSYOP. In military doctrine, PSYOP is the overarching campaign designed to influence beliefs and behavior, while propaganda is one of its most visible tools—the broadcast of carefully crafted narratives. If PSYOP is the strategy, propaganda is the delivery system.

This distinction matters. Nations employ propaganda to mobilize populations, justify wars, and suppress dissent. In the same way, Satan conducts his own spiritual PSYOP—weaponizing distorted narratives to bend allegiance, manipulate perception, and redirect trust away from God's truth. Just as military commanders bury lies within believable truths to mislead their enemies, Satan cloaks poison in familiar language so that deception tastes like wisdom.

In this chapter, I use examples of distortion not to target one tradition but to highlight how all distortions stand in contrast to the clarity of the biblical gospel. Recognizing the critical importance of resisting deception—and Satan's relentless desire to mislead humanity—we now move from defining truth and falsehood to examining how deception actually operates. As emphasized throughout this book, deception is rarely a naked lie. It is most dangerous when interwoven with truth, appearing credible enough to pass inspection. That is why it is vital to remember this: propaganda is never the whole campaign. It is only one weapon in the larger arsenal of PSYOP, and understanding that connection equips us to recognize not just the message but the strategy behind it. This chapter advances the purpose of volume 1 by showing how Satan's method of burying lies within truths obscures the path to salvation and weakens discernment, both in history and in our lives today.

HOW LIES HIDE IN TRUTH

Deception, at its core, thrives on subtlety—crafting lies that are intertwined with truth. This approach is evident not only in historical examples but also in everyday tactics. Consider how modern scams and counterfeit currency illuminate the dangers of mixing falsehood with truth. While deception adapts with technology, its fundamental mechanics remain unchanged—just as phishing scams exploit digital trust, historical propaganda weaponized mass communication to manipulate entire populations. In World War II, Operation Copperhead (1944) provides a chilling example: the British trained an actor, M. E. Clifton James, to impersonate General Bernard Montgomery and sent him to Gibraltar and North Africa in the weeks before D-Day. German intelligence tracked "Monty's" movements, convinced the real commander was nowhere near England.[2] The genius of the ruse was not in elaborate theatrics but in burying a simple counterfeit within believable truths. Satan's strategy mirrors this: he cloaks spiritual poison in familiar language so that falsehood appears like truth. The evolution of deception demonstrates its adaptability. The strategy remains eerily consistent: distort reality just enough to make the falsehood indistinguishable from truth.

The same counterfeiting principle corrupts doctrine: when truth is trimmed or genre ignored, error feels orthodox.

Counterfeit currency offers a striking analogy. It mimics authenticity so convincingly that, without close scrutiny, it can pass as genuine. This deception disrupts economic stability and erodes trust. Spiritually, Satan employs similar tactics—constructing doctrines or ideologies that feel credible yet are fundamentally false. Phishing scams exploit digital trust with the same finesse, preying on our instinctive confidence in reputable institutions. During the Cold War, the Soviets launched Operation INFEKTION, a global disinformation campaign that spread the lie that the AIDS virus had been engineered by the US military. The claim was woven into forged documents, "leaked" through friendly newspapers, and repeated until it took on the appearance of credibility. The genius of the ruse was not the boldness of the lie but its careful packaging within believable half-truths. This is precisely how Satan wages war: by normalizing distortion until the counterfeit feels like the standard. As deception adapts to each era's vulnerabilities, its aim remains unchanged: to undermine trust and lead astray.[3]

---

2. Montagu, *Beyond Top Secret Ultra*, 228–32.
3. Boghardt, *Operation INFEKTION*, 29–33.

SCRIPTURE TWISTED AND MISUSED

Such distortion is not confined to secular systems; it also infiltrates religious frameworks, even within traditions that invoke the name of Christ. A common Roman Catholic apologetic asserts that the church possesses the "fullness of the truth." At first hearing, this sounds charitable and ecumenical. Indeed, Roman Catholic theology reflects centuries of doctrinal development and genuine devotion to Christ, and many Catholics earnestly pursue biblical truth. Yet beneath this language lies an implicit assumption: that other Christian expressions are deficient unless completed by Roman tradition. In doing so, the claim subtly challenges the doctrine of *sola scriptura* (discussed in chapter 2) by elevating human tradition alongside the word of God.

One meme captures this tactic with deceptive wit: a Protestant affirms a literal reading of Gen 1; a Roman Catholic priest responds, "And John 6 should be taken literally as well." At first glance, it's clever—suggesting interpretive consistency. Yet it conflates genres, equating a historical narrative with a symbolic discourse. In John 6, Jesus speaks metaphorically about eating his flesh and drinking his blood. The meme distorts interpretation by disregarding context, genre, and authorial intent. It's more than rhetoric—it's strategic misdirection, designed to provoke doubt about the clarity of Scripture. This is doctrinal PSYOP—truths embedded in distortions to destabilize confidence in God's word, much like a forged battlefield signal sows chaos in enemy ranks.

Examples like this are not confined to Roman Catholicism. They reflect a broader interpretive challenge—where any tradition or viewpoint risks obscuring meaning if context and authorial intent are overlooked. Hermeneutics protects against this across denominational lines. This is why sound hermeneutics—the disciplined approach to biblical interpretation—is indispensable. Without it, believers become vulnerable to persuasive arguments that twist Scripture to support flawed teachings. Hermeneutics demands an understanding of literary form, historical backdrop, and theological purpose. It protects truth from distortion and enables us to rightly divide the word of God, as Paul exhorts in 2 Tim 2:15.

The same principle operates today in the digital age. Cybercriminals exploit trust through phishing emails, masquerading as banks or government entities. These schemes bypass skepticism by blending credibility with falsehood—mirroring Satan's strategy of embedding lies in truth to deceive even the discerning. Just as Schwarzkopf's "left hook" in Desert

Unveiling Deception

Storm succeeded by feinting along Kuwait's coast while the main thrust swept wide through the desert, Satan feints with familiar Scripture, then strikes with twisted interpretation.

What we botch in interpretation, tyrants weaponize in public: the very mechanics of deception—omission, repetition, spectacle—scaled to a nation.

PROPAGANDA ON A NATIONAL SCALE

Scaled from inbox to empire, the same tactics—omission, repetition, spectacle—capture not just individuals but peoples.

Yet deception is not merely digital—it is historical, ideological, and spiritual. Just as modern scams prey on misplaced trust, history reveals deception as a timeless weapon, shaping world events and shifting ideologies. Mass propaganda efforts, such as those orchestrated by the Nazi regime during World War II, exemplify this strategy. Lies were meticulously wrapped in fragments of truth, distorting public perception and manipulating entire nations.[4] This was weaponized psychological warfare on an industrial scale—what military analysts would later classify as strategic PSYOP, designed to saturate every channel of perception. This is precisely how Satan works—he has no creative power of his own, but he twists what God has said, camouflaging error with fragments of truth.

By blending truth with falsehood, Nazi propaganda shaped both public sentiment and the minds of its leaders. William L. Shirer, a journalist stationed in Berlin, observed the regime's deceit firsthand. His warning—"It can happen again"—remains sobering.[5]

Shirer's insight is more than a historical caution—it is a spiritual one. Propaganda does not need banners and rallies to be effective; it only needs unchallenged repetition. The believer's defense, then, is not passive awareness but active discernment—testing every message, every claim, every "truth" against God's word.

What numbed an entire nation can just as easily numb a soul. When truth is left untested, we are discipled more by headlines, slogans, and social feeds than by Scripture. Deception rarely storms the gates with banners flying; more often, it seeps under the door, normalizing distortions until a population forgets what truth even sounds like. Totalitarianism

---

4. Krebs, *Spam Nation*, 67.
5. Shirer, *Rise and Fall of the Third Reich*, 5–7; Shirer, *Berlin Diary*, 12–15.

doesn't arrive with fanfare; it creeps in through distortion and erosion. Nazi propaganda didn't merely mislead—it rewrote reality, entwining lies so tightly into public perception that millions embraced illusion as truth. For beneath every human tyrant's deception is the greater deceiver, who has been orchestrating falsehood since Eden.

Berlin only echoed Eden; propaganda perfected what the serpent pioneered. Propaganda didn't just enslave a nation—it mapped the architecture of control. And that blueprint is still in circulation. From Goebbels's Berlin to Stalin's Moscow, from ISIS recruitment videos to state-run disinformation campaigns today, the fingerprints of the ancient deceiver are visible. Indeed, it is Satan's blueprint—tested in Eden, perfected through empires, and still deployed in every age.

As Shirer later chronicled in *Berlin Diary* (1941) and *The Rise and Fall of the Third Reich* (1960), Nazi propaganda revealed how authoritarian regimes manipulate truth to consolidate power. His analysis underscores that tyranny is never a relic of the past but a recurring threat—one that resurfaces whenever vigilance fades and societies grow numb to lies repeated as truth.

Yet deception of this scale is not confined to political tyranny; it mirrors the strategies of an even more insidious adversary. Satan—the master deceiver—wields similar tactics in his spiritual warfare against humanity. Jesus himself warned of his deceptive nature, calling him the "father of lies" (John 8:44). Like the architects of propaganda, Satan does not simply fabricate falsehoods—he distorts truth, embedding half-truths within his lies to make them irresistibly plausible. His goal is not just manipulation but spiritual enslavement, luring people into ideologies, temptations, and worldviews that subtly detach them from the truth of God's word.

The parallels are sobering. Just as the Nazi machine orchestrated mass indoctrination to shape public perception, Satan infiltrates thought, emotion, and belief—whispering false assurances, sowing doubt, and camouflaging deception as wisdom. Nazi Germany revealed how an entire nation could be swept into moral blindness through repetition and suggestion. Likewise, Satan weaponizes the same principles, blinding minds and numbing consciences until deception takes hold before resistance can begin.

Shirer's warning demands vigilance—not just against political tyranny but against the deception that pervades every aspect of life. The lessons of history are not simply academic; they are spiritual. If we forget

Unveiling Deception

that what happened once can happen again, we leave ourselves vulnerable to the same spiritual traps that ensnared generations before us. If entire nations can fall victim to propaganda, how much more must believers guard their hearts and minds against the enemy's relentless distortions? Vigilance today requires more than historical awareness—it requires spiritual discernment. In a world increasingly flooded with misinformation and ideological manipulation, believers must actively seek truth, test narratives against Scripture, and stand firm against deception in all its forms. Recognizing Satan's schemes is no less urgent than recognizing the early signs of authoritarian control. Both rely on the same chilling principle—convincing people that lies are truth and that truth is the lie.

Deception's endgame is not merely assent but a seared conscience—error repeated until truth no longer registers (see 2 Cor 4:4). Repetition is not filler—it is formation. Nazi rallies, chants, and slogans worked the same way that false doctrine repeated week after week reshapes the moral compass.

This manipulation did not merely sway the German people—it infiltrated Nazi leadership itself, as was starkly revealed in the Nuremberg trials. Held between 1945 and 1946 in Nuremberg, Germany, these military tribunals prosecuted high-ranking Nazi officials for war crimes, crimes against humanity, and crimes against peace. Among the most heinous atrocities judged was the Holocaust—the systematic extermination of six million Jews, along with millions of others deemed "undesirable" by the Nazi regime.[6]

The evidence was overwhelming—survivor testimonies, Nazi documents detailing extermination plans, and footage of liberated concentration camps—but despite undeniable proof, many Nazi leaders showed no remorse. When faced with judgment, not a single one expressed genuine sorrow or acknowledged responsibility for attempting to destroy millions of lives. Their unwavering indifference was a chilling testament to the power of deception—so deeply ingrained that even in the face of undeniable horror, they refused to accept guilt.[7] This hardness of heart mirrors Satan's goal: to so enslave minds in lies that truth itself no longer registers.

This manipulation didn't just shape ideology—it crafted illusions of hope, using deception as a psychological weapon. Among the most

---

6. Taylor, *Anatomy of the Nuremberg Trials*.
7. Shirer, *Rise and Fall of Adolf Hitler*, 180.

insidious examples was the iron gate inscription at Nazi concentration camps: *Arbeit macht frei*, "Work sets you free." A calculated false hope, it misled prisoners into believing their labor might secure their release. Instead, they faced starvation, forced labor, and ultimately a brutal demise orchestrated with industrial precision. The inscription wasn't just a lie—it was a weapon designed to manipulate, demoralize, and crush the spirits of those who passed beneath it.[8] This is Satan's signature: offering counterfeit freedom that leads only to bondage and ultimately, spiritual death. Every *Arbeit macht frei* is a theological echo of "You shall not surely die" (Gen 3:4). Both promise liberty; both deliver slavery.

So too in Eden: a promise of freedom that delivered only bondage (see John 8:44).

In much the same way, spiritual deception operates under similar principles; Satan's greatest weapon is not merely lying but making the lie indistinguishable from truth, leading people to embrace falsehood without realizing they have been deceived. Deception thrives on misplaced trust, false promises, and the distortion of reality. Satan's strategy mirrors Nazi propaganda, embedding half-truths within falsehoods to subtly mislead. Recognizing these mechanics is essential for resisting deception, ensuring that truth—rather than illusion—guides our hearts, minds, and faith.

From Berlin back to the garden, the blueprint is stable: embed lies within plausibility until perception bends.

Both phishing scams and historical propaganda reveal a critical reality: deception thrives when falsehood is embedded within plausibility. Military deception doctrine has long taught that the most convincing ruse is 80–90 percent true; Satan uses the same ratio to bait the soul. Just as these tactics manipulate perception to achieve their aims, spiritual deception operates in the same way—relying on half-truths to erode faith and distort biblical doctrine.

Like a master weaver, Satan spins lies so tightly into the fabric of truth that they become nearly indistinguishable. John MacArthur explains this strategy succinctly: "Satan's most effective weapon is to mix a little truth with a great lie, making the lie more palatable and the truth less discernible."[9]

---

8. Kallis, *Nazi Propaganda*, 301.
9. MacArthur, *Truth War*, 45.

Unveiling Deception

From the serpent's temptation of Eve to modern ideologies that subtly challenge Scripture, deception remains one of the enemy's most powerful tools. R. C. Sproul warns, "The greatest danger in deception is not the lie itself, but the willingness of the deceived to believe it."[10]

By anchoring themselves in Scripture, believers gain the discernment needed to expose falsehood and stand firm in the light of God's unchanging truth. In an age where deception grows more sophisticated, vigilance is not optional—it is essential.

Satan's agenda remains the same: to distort truth. Understanding his tactics through the lens of psychological warfare helps Christians recognize how spiritual deception works. PSYOP, after all, are strategies crafted to shape beliefs, emotions, and decisions—often through carefully framed communication, persuasive imagery, and controlled narratives. The US military has used such techniques to influence attitudes in wartime; in spiritual warfare, Satan adapts the same playbook to manipulate perception and obscure truth. Just as military commanders use deception to fix enemy forces in the wrong place, Satan fixes hearts in the wrong trust—on works, on tradition, on self—so they miss the rescue of Christ. His goal is not merely to deceive but to blur the line until deception feels indistinguishable from reality.

Satan and his demon army wage war against God and humanity, orchestrating an elaborate campaign of deception that began in the garden of Eden. When he deceived Eve, a cascade of falsehoods was set in motion, continuing to influence humankind today.

Christians stand at the front lines of this battle, called to recognize and resist deception. Understanding Satan's tactics is not merely intellectual—it is spiritual armor, equipping believers to stand firm against his schemes and remain anchored in faith.

Deception thrives by exploiting uncertainty, whether in matters of faith or public discourse. A striking modern parallel is the COVID-19 pandemic, where misinformation about vaccines preyed on fear and doubt, leading to widespread hesitancy, avoidable deaths, and strained public health systems.[11] Just as misinformation thrives on vulnerabilities, spiritual deception preys on humanity's weaknesses, distorting truth to

---

10. Sproul, *Consequences of Ideas*, 78.

11. This reference to COVID-19 vaccine misinformation is not intended as an argument against vaccination. It illustrates how misinformation fosters uncertainty, influences decision-making, and serves as a modern example of deception's impact on public perception.

lead people astray. This pattern is not new; it is simply a modern expression of an ancient reality. Beneath both Eden and Berlin lies the same engine: fallen human nature.

Yet deception is not merely an external force; it thrives within human nature itself. At the core of human vulnerability to falsehood lies the sin nature—the inherent inclination to rebel against God. When faced with the choice between God's will and our own, humanity instinctively chooses self-will.

No one needs to teach a child to lie or be selfish; rather, we invest great effort in teaching honesty and selflessness. This instinct toward sin is not learned—it is inherent, woven into human nature from birth. The world's brokenness offers abundant evidence—conflict permeates society, and tragedy fills the news, all reinforcing the biblical truth that humanity is sinful by nature.

Scripture repeatedly affirms the reality of this sinful condition. Jeremiah 17:9 declares, "The heart is deceitful above all things, and desperately wicked; who can know it?" Romans 6:6 speaks of "the body ruled by sin," while Rom 8:3 describes "sinful flesh." Colossians 3:5 further exposes the depths of this earthly nature, listing sins rooted in human corruption: "fornication, uncleanness, passion, evil desire, and covetousness, which is idolatry."

Our sinful and corrupt essence shapes our earthly existence, permeating every aspect of our being. The sin nature is innate to humanity. While Satan cannot force us to sin, he skillfully leverages deception—his most potent weapon—to distort truth and entice us into rebellion against God. Scripture affirms that humans sin by their own choice: "Each one is tempted when he is drawn away by his own desires and enticed" (Jas 1:14). Yet even in temptation, God provides hope, for "no temptation has overtaken you except such as is common to man; but God is faithful, who will not allow you to be tempted beyond what you are able, but with the temptation will also make the way of escape, that you may be able to bear it" (1 Cor 10:13).

Throughout history, deception has been a constant in the human struggle with sin, manifesting globally and individually. Its roots trace back to the garden of Eden, where humanity first fell victim to subtle distortions of truth. A striking modern example occurred almost a century ago, as the Nazi regime cast a devastatingly potent spell over the German people, transforming a nation into a mass of individuals enthralled by myths and intoxicated by iconography.

Unveiling Deception

Germany's susceptibility to deception stemmed from a convergence of economic, political, and social factors. The Treaty of Versailles (1919), which formally ended World War I, imposed harsh penalties on Germany—including territorial losses, military restrictions, and the infamous "War Guilt Clause" that held Germany solely responsible for the war. These terms fueled economic turmoil, hyperinflation, and unemployment—all worsened by the Great Depression. Politically, the Weimar Republic—the fragile democratic government established in Germany after World War I—faced constant instability as extremist groups gained traction and engaged in violent power struggles. Socially, national humiliation and despair created fertile ground for radical ideologies, allowing the Nazi Party to manipulate public sentiment through propaganda and promises of renewal. Hitler's charismatic leadership added further appeal, drawing in countless followers seeking hope and restoration.[12]

Germany's post-war desperation provided the perfect landscape for exploitation. Satan, ever the opportunist, exploited this wounded landscape just as he has in every age—weaponizing fear, despair, and national humiliation to make deception appear like deliverance. The Nazi regime skillfully channeled public grievances, weaving deception into national rhetoric to reshape history, command loyalty, and justify extreme actions. Here the serpent's Edenic whisper—"Has God indeed said?"—was nationalized, turning wounded pride into a weaponized lie.

Adolf Hitler, a failed landscape artist, rose to power as a charismatic dictator, assuming the title of *Führer und Reichskanzler* (Leader and Chancellor of the Reich). Popularly known as *der Führer* (the Leader), he has long been regarded as a master of strategic deception and propaganda. His ability to blend lies with truth exemplifies how propaganda shapes perception, influencing not just individuals but entire societies. Even the iconic Nazi salute, often assumed to have ancient Roman origins, was built on myth. Contrary to popular belief, there is no historical evidence that the salute was used in ancient Rome or Greece. Instead, its roots lie in misinterpretations of eighteenth-century neoclassical art and its deliberate adoption by twentieth-century fascist movements. The Nazi regime, like many totalitarian systems, understood the power of symbols and gestures in reinforcing ideological control. By presenting the salute as a timeless tradition, they further entrenched their myth-making,

---

12. Evans, *Coming of the Third Reich*.

ensuring that even their most recognizable imagery was steeped in deception.[13]

Just as Nazi symbols cloaked manipulation in the guise of tradition, modern regimes use even more sophisticated tools to achieve the same end. One of the most striking examples is Communist China, where the state has constructed a vast system of surveillance—millions of cameras with facial recognition, algorithms that monitor online activity, and digital trackers that follow citizens' finances, movements, and associations. This is not merely about preventing crime; it is about enforcing loyalty. The party watches not only what people do but how they think.[14]

From this surveillance emerges what is known as the social credit system, a national PSYOP designed to engineer obedience. Every citizen is evaluated, their behavior scored, and their loyalty rewarded or punished depending on whether it aligns with party expectations.[15] Those who comply—who praise the party, work cheerfully, pay debts, and avoid "unapproved" beliefs—enjoy privileges such as easier travel, better jobs, and access to education. Those who resist—who criticize the party, worship in unregistered churches, or spread unwelcome ideas—are blacklisted, denied opportunities, slowed, shamed, and sometimes cut off from society altogether.[16]

The genius of the system is its subtlety. Open coercion is less effective than conditioning the population to police itself. By attaching comfort and privilege to compliance, and hardship to dissent, the party manipulates hearts and minds until self-censorship becomes instinct. It is a digital prison without walls, where fear of punishment and desire for reward do the work of chains and guards.

Rome once used similar tactics through its imperial (loyalty) cults. Citizens of the empire were required to burn incense before the emperor's image, not so much as a theological demand but as a political one.[17] Those who complied were rewarded with safety and recognition as good Romans; those who refused, especially Christians who confessed "Jesus is Lord," faced exclusion, imprisonment, or death. What Rome accomplished through incense and sacrifice, China now enforces through

---

13. Lundmark, *Tales of Hi and Bye*, 18–25.
14. Hoffman, *Programming China*, 54–60.
15. Creemers, "China's Social Credit System," 2–8.
16. Economy, *Third Revolution*, 137–42.
17. Ferguson, *Backgrounds of Early Christianity*, 222–26; Pliny the Younger, *Letters* 10.96.

cameras, data, and digital scoring. In both cases, allegiance to the state is made the measure of loyalty, and refusal is treated as treason.

From a military perspective, this is classic PSYOP at scale: shaping behavior not primarily through weapons but through perception, incentives, and fear. It demonstrates how deception thrives when truth is redefined by the state and freedom is bartered for the illusion of safety. Scripture warns of such systems of control: "The fear of man brings a snare, but whoever trusts in the LORD shall be safe" (Prov 29:25). Communist China has institutionalized the fear of man, ensnaring its people in a web of surveillance and rewards. But God's word reminds us that true security is never found in the approval of rulers or the dictates of a party. It rests only in Christ, who alone sets us free. This strategy of control—whether through Rome's incense, China's cameras, or modern propaganda—always points back to the same principle: regimes manufacture loyalty by redefining truth and shaping perception.

This myth-making extended beyond gestures to the very foundation of Nazi ideology. The concept of the Third Reich was deliberately framed as the successor to two previous German empires: the Holy Roman Empire (962–1806), a loose confederation of territories in Central Europe that claimed to carry on the legacy of the ancient Roman Empire under Christian authority, and the German Empire (1871–1918), the unified nation-state established under Otto von Bismarck and Kaiser Wilhelm I. By invoking the Holy Roman Empire, the Nazis sought to present themselves as heirs of a thousand-year-old tradition, projecting legitimacy, continuity, and even divine sanction for their regime. By positioning themselves as the rightful heirs to these historical legacies, the Nazis sought to legitimize their rule and reinforce their claim to a grand, uninterrupted lineage of German dominance. The appropriation of Roman imagery and rhetoric further substantiated this myth, as the Nazis drew parallels between their regime and the imperial grandeur of ancient Rome. This strategic manipulation of history allowed them to present their movement as both a restoration of past glory and an inevitable continuation of Germany's supposed destiny.[18]

This brings us to a pivotal concept central to understanding truth and deception: propaganda. It is often misunderstood as simple political rhetoric, but it is far more insidious—an intentional weapon of deception designed to manipulate and control.

---

18. Whaley, *Maximilian I*, 18–25.

Throughout history, truth has been obscured by calculated rhetoric, proving that propaganda is not just persuasive speech but a powerful tool for reshaping reality.

Through purposeful distortion and calculated presentation, propaganda is a tool used to influence how people think and feel, often by stirring strong emotions and twisting the truth to fit an agenda. Recognizing its mechanics is crucial in unraveling the complexities of deception and understanding the pivotal role truth plays in resisting its grasp.

According to the Federal Research Division at the US Library of Congress,

> "Propaganda" is a broad term that means management of collective attitudes through communications and symbols, for the purpose of promoting or damaging a cause. Among its non-PSYOP applications are commercial advertising, political campaigning, and religious exhortation. (The term was invented by the Roman Catholic Church in its seventeenth-century campaigns against Protestantism.) But in the contemporary public understanding, those aspects have been overshadowed by the widespread political uses of propaganda in the twentieth century. Although the term had become associated with untruth, propaganda in the PSYOP context must contain large amounts of true information, because of the primary requirement that the audience believe the message.[19]

Satan operates the same way—his lies are most effective when dressed in enough truth to be convincing.

In the US, propaganda is most often seen as political propaganda, especially as we have regarded the Nazis and the Soviets. Nazi propaganda, which was often based on the preexisting traditional German values, culture, religion, and mindset, was used to distract the people from the brutal, anti-Semitic actions being taken to reinstitute those values and to explain previous and present world events by focusing on emotional manipulation and national political support for restoring ideological German culture.[20]

Modern techniques of opinion formation employed by the Nazis created what has been described as a "truly religio-psychological phenomenon,"[21] amplifying the potency of their propaganda. Propaganda

---

19. Curtis, *Overview of Psychological Operations*.
20. Kallis, *Nazi Propaganda*, 301.
21. Bracher, *German Dictatorship*, 48.

was not merely a tool of the Third Reich—it was its operational backbone, systematically deployed to promote Nazi ideology and entrench its control. Albert Speer, the chief architect of Hitler's regime, underscored this during his testimony at the Nuremberg Tribunal: "What distinguished the Third Reich from all previous dictatorships was its use of all the means of communication to sustain itself and to deprive its objects of the power of independent thought."[22] This strategic exploitation of mass communication demonstrates how the Nazis used propaganda not only to disseminate their ideology but also to stifle dissent and suppress critical thinking among the populace. The devil's goal is the same: not merely to lie but to remove your capacity to question the lie.

Cultural historian Piers Brendon, a respected authority on the psychological dynamics of totalitarian regimes, characterized Nazi propaganda as the "gospel" of the Third Reich—a doctrine of deception so insidious that it twisted reality into a grotesque parody of truth. At its dark heart stood Dr. Joseph Goebbels, the *Reichsminister of Public Enlightenment and Propaganda*, a man whose power lay not in brute force but in the terrifying ability to manipulate minds.

His ascent was meteoric. In 1926, he caught Hitler's eye and was appointed *Gauleiter of Berlin*, a title that made him the Nazi Party's undisputed ruler of the German capital.[23] In this position, Goebbels operated as both a political enforcer and a master propagandist, wielding absolute control over party activities in the city. His authority extended beyond mere administration—he shaped the very way Berliners thought, flooding the metropolis with Nazi ideology through speeches, rallies, and relentless media campaigns. Gauleiters like Goebbels were often ruthless, ensuring ideological purity and silencing dissent with brutal efficiency.

By 1933, at the mere age of thirty-five, Goebbels became the youngest minister in German history, cementing his role as the regime's supreme manipulator.[24] Intoxicated by ambition, he wielded his authority with a fanatical devotion to the Nazi cause. He was not merely a propagandist—he was an architect of illusion, a master of manipulation who understood that fear, repetition, and spectacle could turn lies into absolute truths.

Goebbels reveled in his dominion over perception, crafting narratives that blurred truth and fiction until they became indistinguishable in

---

22. Rutherford, *Hitler's Propaganda Machine*, 32.
23. Evans, *Coming of the Third Reich*, 182–83.
24. Evans, *Third Reich in Power*, 97.

the minds of the people. It is deeply ironic that propaganda was explicitly embedded in his official title—yet millions surrendered to his distortions without question, swallowed up by the tide of manufactured loyalty and ideological fervor. He frequently echoed Hitler, proclaiming that "Jesus Christ [was] a master of propaganda and that the propagandist must be the man with the greatest knowledge of souls."[25] With chilling precision, he ensured that Nazi messaging seeped into every aspect of life, shaping thoughts, warping reality, and suffocating dissent. These same methods resurface in our own lives. Satan rarely invents new tactics; he recycles old ones. Just as Goebbels conditioned a population through repetition until lies felt like truth, so too does the enemy whisper distortions until we barely notice them. When a culture repeats that sin is "identity," or that truth is "relative," it isn't just rhetoric—it is propaganda at work, training hearts to accept bondage as freedom.

His work was not merely a campaign—it was a calculated, ruthless effort to imprison an entire nation within the suffocating embrace of a fabricated truth. The consequences would be devastating, as his relentless myth-making solidified the Reich's grip on the German people, plunging the world into one of its darkest chapters.

Historian Neil Gregor, an expert on the social and cultural history of Nazi Germany, offers additional insight into the objectives of Nazi propaganda. Gregor asserts that its primary aim was "to absorb the individual into a mass of like-minded people, and the purpose of the 'suggestion' was not to deceive but to articulate that which the crowd already believed."[26] Thus, a fundamental component of the Nazi grand strategy was the overthrow of reason and the exaltation of emotion.

As Nazism appealed to emotions rather than the intellect, its propaganda appealed to feelings rather than thought. The orchestration of sentiments formed the foundation of all Nazi actions; it was the operational formula of their propaganda. For Goebbels, the role of the propagandist was to verbalize the emotions that his audience felt in their hearts.[27] Therefore, propaganda had to be primitive, appealing to what Hitler described as man's inner *Schweinehund* (pig dog).[28] The propaganda typically demonstrated a cruel either/or perspective which appeals to our primitive desire for simplification, as in, "There are . . . only two

---

25. Hitler, *Mein Kampf*, 51; Taylor, *Goebbels*, 155.
26. Gregor, *How to Read Hitler*, 54.
27. Paxton, *Anatomy of Fascism*, 78–82.
28. Newcourt-Nowodworski, *Black Propaganda*, 154.

possibilities: either the victory of the Aryan side or its annihilation and the victory of the Jews."[29] The Nazis believed that a formulaic propaganda methodology had to be applied even at the cost of alienating sophisticated members of its audience.

The essence of the Nazi propaganda method, as with so many others, was repetition. The Nazis' ideological message saturated the barriers of inattention through its overwhelming insistence on its replication. Goebbels advocated for the "repeated exposure effect."[30] Ideas had to be continually reseeded to germinate as Hitler's Nazis believed the collective mind was dull and sluggish, thus, repetition could facilitate the phases of the cognitive process that comprise the mass mind: recognition, comprehension, retention, and conviction. Hence, it is critical to remember that Nazi propaganda additionally provided the dubious advantage of sensory exhaustion. The citizen was not so much an object to be convinced as a victim to be subdued and even devoured.

The takeaway is clear—propaganda, whether political or spiritual, relies on repetition, emotional manipulation, and the blending of truth and falsehood. It is Satan's strategy repackaged through human systems, aiming always to obscure Christ, enslave the mind, and corrupt the heart. Modern technologies exemplify this same dynamic. Social media and smartphone platforms, under the guise of connection and entertainment, subtly shape perception, distort affections, and addict the mind to an endless stream of distraction. We will return to these in more detail later, for they are among the clearest modern demonstrations of deception's power. Recognizing these methods equips believers to remain steadfast against both historical and spiritual attempts to distort truth, "that we should no longer be children, tossed to and fro and carried about with every wind of doctrine, by the trickery of men, in the cunning craftiness of deceitful plotting" (Eph 4:14).

While repetition was the foundation of Nazi propaganda, its ultimate goal extended beyond external compliance—it sought to cultivate internal commitment. Goebbels asserted that the Nazis were distinguished by "the ability to see into the soul of the people and to speak the language of the man in the street."[31] The propagandist was an artist who "sensed the secret vibrations of the people."[32]

29. Bracher, *German Dictatorship*, 85.
30. Pierre, "Illusory Truth."
31. Spotts, *Hitler*, 98–101.
32. Rutherford, *Hitler's Propaganda Machine*, 64.

European fascism was further distinguished by its embrace of mass media and marketing. Fascists understood the culture of consumerism and the pervasive influence of media on public life. They mastered this new language, including its styles, forms, and assumptions, and used it as both a method of communication and a novel cultural framework. By mastering the language of mass media, fascists redefined propaganda as a tool not just for political gain, but for reshaping societal values and assumptions—a legacy that continues to influence modern strategies of persuasion.

Nazism did not ask for belief but for surrender, which was primarily accomplished through an assault on consciousness rather than through coercion. The fundamental objective was to eradicate independent thought through the use of images that would think for people. Yet the seeming ease with which Germans went along with, or apparently ignored, the true frauds continues to astonish.[33]

While this deception and propaganda focused on restoring Germany to a state of supremacy and traditional values, Hitler's plan included the control and annexation of many countries and cultures. Nazi Germany's annexation of the Sudetenland in the prelude to World War II is an example of well-executed deception and showcases the extent to which deception can be used to wield significant influence. This is more than a political maneuver; it reflects the deeper spiritual pattern by which Satan advances his purposes (Eph 6:11–12)—using false grievances (Gen 3:1–5), manufactured crises (John 8:44), and counterfeit promises to justify aggression (2 Cor 11:14; Rev 12:9). The annexation of the Sudetenland, which was then a part of Czechoslovakia and was inhabited primarily by Sudeten Germans, involved clever propaganda and strategic deception aimed at many groups to further the Nazi cause, including residents of the Sudetenland as well as the German people.[34]

Czechoslovakia was strategically located, and its subjugation was central to Hitler's plans for European conquest as it had one of the strongest armies in Europe and an ample arms industry. Additionally, it included the Sudeten Mountains, a militarized, fortified barrier deterring Hitler's plans to sweep across Europe. As an outright military campaign to seize this land seemed impossible, given Czech military strength in the area and the guarantee by Western powers to resist aggressive attack

---

33. O'Shaughnessy, *Selling Hitler*, 32–87.
34. Shirer, *Rise and Fall of the Third Reich*, 448.

via the Treaty of Versailles, Hitler instigated an unparalleled crusade to politically coerce the Czechs to surrender their land. He was able to do this by pushing the narrative that the Sudetenland's inhabitants were predominantly of German origin and deserved the right of self-determination. This was despite the fact that Sudeten Germans already enjoyed full civil rights and economic prosperity under the democratic government of Czechoslovakia. To give his lies the appearance of legitimacy, Hitler orchestrated the creation of the *Sudetendeutsches Freikorps* (Sudeten German Free Corps), a puppet liberation movement drenched in orchestrated violence. The uprisings they incited surged through Czechoslovakia like a wildfire, forcing Czech forces to quell the chaos as Hitler watched with calculated satisfaction. Additionally, Hitler commissioned Goebbels to orchestrate a disinformation crusade about "Czech terror" and Sudeten German oppression.[35]

Hitler asserted that the Czech government's refusal to return the Sudeten territories to their "rightful" German owners was an impediment to regional peace. Moreover, the Czechs were trying to hasten a European crisis in order to prevent the breakup of their state. The choice between war and peace in Europe rested in Czech hands. Hitler graciously offered a simple solution: the Western powers could force Czechoslovakia to relinquish these "rightfully" German territories.[36]

On September 18, 1938, under the pressure of a September 28 deadline set by Hitler, a consensus was reached between the British and French that Czechoslovakia must accede to Hitler's demands. Despite the Versailles agreement that the West would go to war to defend the Czech borders, it agreed that the Sudetenland must be relinquished to maintain peace and protect its vital interests. In exchange, Britain and France would provide an additional international guarantee to defend the new borders against unprovoked foreign aggression.[37] If the Czechs chose not to accept this plan, they would be left to face Germany alone. However, British Prime Minister Neville Chamberlain knew, as the world closely watched, that if the Czechs chose to fight, France and Britain would very likely be forced to fight also.[38] Chamberlain became progressively more desperate to deter war by buying off Hitler and, moments before the looming September 28 deadline, pleaded with Hitler to participate in an

---

35. Shirer, *Rise and Fall of the Third Reich*, 524–26.
36. Shirer, *Rise and Fall of the Third Reich*, 490, 519, 538.
37. Shirer, *Rise and Fall of the Third Reich*, 489.
38. Shirer, *Rise and Fall of the Third Reich*, 535.

international peace conference starting the following day, to which Hitler eventually agreed.

At the Munich peace conference, after eleven hours of pleading, Britain and France convinced Hitler to compromise and take the Sudetenland peacefully. The Sudetenland was duly annexed to Germany without a single shot fired. At this moment, Hitler was at the apogee of his power—his ability to manipulate Western leaders and bend international politics to his will had reached its peak. He had succeeded in elevating propaganda over reality. The speed and readiness with which this transparent ruse was received, digested, and adopted by the West are astonishing. As the Western leaders returned home in supposed victory, Chamberlain declared, "I believe it is peace for our time," a statement that would soon prove to be tragically misplaced.[39] Just as nations were lulled into complacency, so too Satan lulls souls into false assurance, promising peace while plotting destruction.

This example just scratches the surface of propaganda-driven dictatorship deception. There are many examples of truth-manipulating tyrants that institutionalized propaganda to sway the public to their agenda—Idi Amin of Uganda, Muammar Gaddafi of Libya, Fidel Castro of Cuba, Joseph Stalin of the Soviet Union, Saddam Hussein of Iraq, among many others, all of whom employed propaganda from the same playbook. These examples of state-level deception illustrate the diverse techniques employed in propaganda. Unsurprisingly, this same playbook is in use today in spiritual warfare waged by Satan and his demon army.

As demonstrated in this example, well-executed deception can have a tremendous effect: advantageous to the entity inflicting the deception and deleterious to the recipient. Similarly, Satan's well-executed deception can have a profound consequence: advantageous to his campaign to deter people from God and to bolster his pride and deleterious to those that fall for his deceptions, which distort their understanding of God and the truth of Scripture, thus affecting salvation and eternal life.

Propaganda in this and many other forms has the capacity to incorporate any information, ranging from unadulterated truth to flagrant deceit. To assist in classifying it, in order to appropriately counter it, propaganda is categorized into three distinct domains on the basis of the veracity of the information disseminated and the recognition of its source: white, gray, and black.

---

39. As quoted in Evans, *Third Reich in Power*, 703.

White propaganda comes from a clear and credible source and shares mostly accurate information. Think of it like the "Voice of America," a platform often trusted by its audience for its generally truthful messaging, though it leans toward democratic values. It's the kind of information you might encounter and feel you can trust without a second thought. The source may or may not be accurately identified in gray propaganda, rendering the information's veracity uncertain. An instance of this category of propaganda was a Russian television documentary concerning the Afghanistan War, which posited that the conflict had been instigated by external forces. Additionally, an individual identified as a Turkish national testified that he had been sent to carry out a mission for the CIA—a fabricated detail added to bolster the credibility of the narrative. Black propaganda provides a fabricated source and intentionally disseminates falsehoods, fabrications, and deceptions. A more precise term for this form of propaganda, as modernly redefined, is disinformation.[40]

Interestingly, the use of propaganda by the US military dates back to the American Revolution, regarded as the first people's war. Before the war began, it was a struggle for the hearts and minds of the people, according to John Adams.[41] America's architects might not have been able to accomplish their objectives without the assistance of the press and an effective propaganda campaign that embellished successes and softened setbacks. Benjamin Franklin may have been the first American to employ black propaganda; he composed a number of letters and documents under aliases in an attempt to incite other nations to oppose the British government.[42] George Washington employed the press as a tool of disinformation to maintain public morale by disseminating fabricated accounts of enemy casualties. In 1777 he wrote, "It is in our interest, however much our characters may suffer by it, to make small numbers appear large."[43] The inference that can be drawn from this earliest example of the use of propaganda employed during wartime is that our forefathers, who

---

40. Crumm, *Information Warfare*, 15.

41. Adams, "To Hezekiah Niles."

42. Benjamin Franklin's forged letters and fabricated newspaper pieces are often cited as among the earliest American uses of black propaganda. See Pratkanis and Aronson, *Age of Propaganda*, 240; see also Paddock, "U.S. Military Psychological Operations."

43. Crumm, *Information Warfare*, 17.

established the foundations of our democratic system, used every variety of propaganda.[44]

Deception, whether political or spiritual, thrives on manipulation and calculated persuasion. Just as Nazi propaganda weaponized half-truths in the Sudetenland annexation—shaping perception through omission, repetition, and spectacle—the serpent's deception in the garden of Eden exemplifies the same timeless strategy: mixing falsehood with truth to achieve a devastating effect. History's propaganda and Scripture's warnings converge on one conclusion: discernment is not optional—it is survival. The tragedy of Nazi Germany is not just that propaganda swayed a nation but that it numbed consciences until evil looked ordinary, even respectable. The same danger faces us today. What we laugh at in entertainment, tolerate in politics, or excuse in daily choices may shape what we accept tomorrow. Propaganda always aims at the conscience, and if the conscience is dulled, discernment disappears. And it is worth remembering this: propaganda is never the whole campaign. It is one weapon in Satan's larger PSYOP. To dismiss it as mere rhetoric is to underestimate the scale of the deception—and to lower our guard when vigilance is most needed.

Another striking example of deception comes from modern naval warfare. During the Cold War, US Navy ships practiced deceptive lighting and emissions control (EMCON) to mislead enemy sensors. A carrier group might run "darkened ship," eliminating nearly all visible light to vanish into the night, or use staged lighting patterns to appear smaller, slower, or like an entirely different class of vessel. Radio traffic was equally controlled—sometimes silenced entirely, other times mimicked or spoofed to suggest a false location.

The brilliance of this tactic was that it weaponized absence as much as presence. Darkness became a mask; silence became its own broadcast. Intelligence analysts trained to read signals were instead fed confusion. In PSYOP terms, this was "controlling the electromagnetic spectrum"— dictating not only what the enemy saw but what they failed to see.

Spiritually, the same principle applies. The enemy manipulates perception not only through lies spoken but also through truths withheld. Just as the Navy shaped conclusions by managing light and silence, Satan often works by omission—hiding what God has said, suppressing clarity,

---

44. Crumm, *Information Warfare*, 16–17.

or distracting with half-truths until reality is misread. What is absent can be as deceptive as what is present.

FROM EDEN TO TODAY'S BATTLEFIELDS

Genesis 3 sketches the pattern: omission ("Has God indeed said . . . ?"), repetition (sustained doubt), and spectacle ("pleasant to the eyes," Gen 3:6).

Genesis 3:1–6 illustrates how deception operates with precision:

> Now the serpent was more cunning than any beast of the field which the LORD God had made. And he said to the woman, "Has God indeed said, 'You shall not eat of every tree of the garden'?"
> And the woman said to the serpent, "We may eat the fruit of the trees of the garden; but of the fruit of the tree which is in the midst of the garden, God has said, 'You shall not eat it, nor shall you touch it, lest you die.'"
> Then the serpent said to the woman, "You will not surely die. For God knows that in the day you eat of it your eyes will be opened, and you will be like God, knowing good and evil."
> So when the woman saw that the tree was good for food, that it was pleasant to the eyes, and a tree desirable to make one wise, she took of its fruit and ate. She also gave to her husband with her, and he ate.

This isn't abstract philosophy—it's the story that explains every struggle we face today.

The story is rich in detail for a good reason: this is where everything goes wrong for God's creation as a result of human sin. From this point forward, creation is subject to futility and decay—its consequences reverberate throughout history, altering the human condition itself. Here Scripture intentionally slows the narrative, underscoring that deception is not accidental but systemic—a pattern Satan has repeated across the centuries. Romans 8:20–23 speaks to this tragic reality:

> For the creation was subjected to futility, not willingly, but because of Him who subjected it in hope; because the creation itself also will be delivered from the bondage of corruption into the glorious liberty of the children of God. . . . Not only that, but we also who have the firstfruits of the Spirit, even we ourselves groan within ourselves, eagerly waiting for the adoption, the redemption of our body.

Romans 5:12–18 further expounds on sin's lasting effect:

> Therefore, just as through one man sin entered the world, and death through sin, and thus death spread to all men, because all sinned ... (Death reigned from Adam to Moses, even over those who had not sinned according to the likeness of the transgression of Adam, who is a type of Him who was to come. But the free gift is not like the offense. For if by the one man's offense many died, much more the grace of God and the gift by the grace of the one Man, Jesus Christ, abounded to many. And the gift is not like that which came through the one who sinned. For the judgment which came from one offense resulted in condemnation, but the free gift which came from many offenses resulted in justification. For if by the one man's offense death reigned through the one, much more those who receive abundance of grace and of the gift of righteousness will reign in life through the One, Jesus Christ.) Therefore, as through one man's offense judgment came to all men, resulting in condemnation, even so through one Man's righteous act the free gift came to all men, resulting in justification of life.

Genesis places considerable emphasis on the serpent's conversation with Eve—because deception, in its most subtle form, sets a precedent for human frailty. Later biblical passages reinforce this truth, with Rev 12:9 identifying Satan as the serpent and John 8:44 confirming his nature as the "father of lies" and declaring that he has no truth in him.

In this passage of Genesis, Satan wields deception with chilling precision, blending 80 percent of God's words into a weapon of white propaganda, feigning credibility while corrupting truth with a single subversive word—a lie cloaked in black propaganda, calculated to distort Eve's perception of divine truth. This dual-layer tactic—truth mixed with lies—demonstrates how partial accuracy can be more dangerous than outright falsehood. This is the same technique Goebbels later refined—burying lies in a flood of familiarity until perception itself was reshaped, the repeated exposure effect where plausibility accrues not from proof but from repetition.

This calculated distortion makes the serpent's words appear true at first glance. Genesis 3:5 states that God knows Adam and Eve will gain knowledge of good and evil upon eating the fruit—a statement that on the surface seems factual (see Gen 3:22, where God says, "The man has become like one of Us, to know good and evil").

However, according to Jesus, Satan has nothing to do with the truth and is the father of lies. How is this possible?

Satan's deception in Gen 3:5 is not through outright falsehood but through omission. By withholding key details, he employs gray propaganda, allowing Eve to infer meaning from what remains unsaid, ultimately distorting her perception of divine truth. Here, Scripture is cited—but subtly, and dangerously, misrepresented. Omission thus becomes as deadly as fabrication.

By exploiting omission, Satan masterfully manipulates Eve's understanding of God's intentions, preying on the frailties of the human spirit. His temptation is designed to shake Eve's faith in God's goodness, casting doubt on his nature and intentions toward creation. Eve begins to wonder—why would God withhold knowledge of good and evil? Could it be that he fears his creation becoming too powerful, too much like him? It all appeals to human vanity—the hunger for knowledge, the desire for independence. Yet even in this first moment of deception, God's mercy was not absent. He immediately promised redemption (Gen 3:15), foreshadowing the One who would crush the serpent's head. From the very beginning, God signaled that he would not leave his people blind to lies, but would provide truth and deliverance through Christ. What Nazi propaganda achieved through half-told truths, the serpent achieved through a single insinuation. In the same way Hitler's narrative of "Czech terror" omitted critical realities to justify aggression, the serpent left out the full truth of God's goodness, letting Eve draw her own poisoned conclusions.

Selective silence weaponizes hearsay; the listener supplies the lie's missing logic.

The serpent does not say much; he is more subtle than that. With a voice as smooth as silk and eyes gleaming with guile, he wields his words like a craftsman, chipping away at Eve's confidence in God's goodness. His cunning tone, neither confrontational nor overtly persuasive, cloaks his malice beneath a facade of curiosity and wisdom. He simply leaves Eve to her own devices, knowing she will derive the conclusions he desires.

In that moment, Eve's trust in God falters—her doubt itself becomes the first act of rebellion. The sin is committed before she ever takes a bite.

Eve's plunge into sin is the first recorded example of spiritual deception in action—her doubt led her to distort God's command and ultimately defy him. In Gen 3:1–3, the serpent asks, "Has God indeed said . . . ?" Eve recites God's command but adds an extra restriction—that they must not even touch the tree. Such a detail is significant because it shows how the enemy works: not by immediate rebellion, but by creating just enough confusion to make obedience seem unreasonable. This subtle shift reveals how deception distorts understanding, making her vulnerable to doubt. Error always enters first in interpretation, then in action. In the same way, Nazi Germany did not initially force its citizens into submission; rather, like Eve, the people were slowly persuaded into complicity through suggestion, doubt, and subtle distortion.

Persuasion births complicity; only later does coercion harvest it.

According to 2 Cor 11:3, Eve was undoubtedly deceived, and the serpent was crafty, but ultimately she chose to disobey God, pursuing gratification and advancement beyond what God had desired for her. When God confronted her regarding her sin, she deflected, "The serpent deceived me, and I ate" (Gen 3:13). Instead of acknowledging her own choice, Eve shifts blame onto the serpent, continuing the cycle of deception.[45]

Satan's deception continues today, exploiting human desires to lead us away from God. He disguises sin as alluring, making false teachings appear enlightening—offering what seems better than God's truth but is ultimately destructive. Because Satan masquerades as an angel of light (2 Cor 11:14), his deception is subtle, appealing, and dangerously effective.

Another vivid picture of deception comes from the Cold War. In May 1960, U-2 pilot Francis Gary Powers was shot down on a reconnaissance mission over the Soviet Union. His sleek spy plane—believed to be beyond Soviet reach—was crippled by a surface-to-air missile. Powers parachuted into enemy territory and was captured. Soon he found himself in Moscow's infamous Lubyanka prison—the KGB's fortress of interrogations, where fear itself seemed to seep from the walls.

It was there that he met his "cellmate." The man seemed ordinary enough—another prisoner suffering under the same iron fist. He offered companionship, conversation, even sympathy. Isolated and vulnerable, Powers welcomed the human contact. But the "fellow captive" was a KGB operative, placed there to earn his confidence and extract intelligence. The friendship was an act. The comfort was calculated. Every word Powers shared, every sigh of despair or flicker of hope, was weighed, reported, and used against him.[46]

---

45. Storms, *Understanding Spiritual Warfare*, 139.
46. Powers, *Operation Overflight*. See also Tenet, "U-2 Program."

Unveiling Deception

This is the brilliance—and the cruelty—of deception. The most effective lies do not march in under banners of hostility; they slip in wearing the uniform of friendship. What Powers mistook for solidarity was actually surveillance. What seemed like a companion was in fact a handler. In military terms, this was infiltration—a false-flag operative behind the wire. Spiritually, the same pattern plays out. The enemy does not always confront us with open hostility; he often comes cloaked in empathy, counsel, or even piety. Paul warned that "Satan himself transforms himself into an angel of light," and his servants into "ministers of righteousness" (2 Cor 11:14–15).

The lesson is clear: discernment is not optional. Powers learned that not every voice in his cell was a friend; believers must learn that not every voice in their life is from God. The enemy's most dangerous tactic is not brute force but counterfeit fellowship. The garden's whisper and the prison's whisper are the same tactic—comfort that conceals capture.

Despite his cunning, Satan knew the truth—God cared for his creation. Yet his deception sought to distort this reality, leading Eve to question God's goodness. Eve had every reason to trust God—he created her, sustained her, and provided abundantly. Yet under the serpent's influence, doubt crept in.

Before deception entered the picture, Gen 2:16–22 offers a glimpse into God's perfect design for humanity:

> And the LORD God commanded [Adam], saying, "Of every tree of the garden you may freely eat; but of the tree of the knowledge of good and evil you shall not eat, for in the day that you eat of it you shall surely die."
> And the LORD God said, "It is not good that man should be alone; I will make him a helper comparable to him." Out of the ground the LORD God formed every beast of the field and every bird of the air, and brought them to Adam to see what he would call them. And whatever Adam called each living creature, that was its name. . . . But for Adam there was not found a helper comparable to him.
> And the LORD God caused a deep sleep to fall on Adam, and he slept; and He took one of his ribs, and closed up the flesh in its place. Then the rib which the LORD God had taken from man He made into a woman, and He brought her to the man.

But in contrast to God's abundant generosity, Satan twisted the narrative, making it all about power and the vanity of being like God—he wanted God's creation to mirror his own fallen nature.

Like Eve, we all face the same temptation—to question God's goodness and seek fulfillment apart from him. Sin is rebellion against God, an outright rejection of his ways and a denial of his trustworthiness.

Sin creates a devastating rift between humanity and God, cutting off his presence and favor. Isaiah 59:1–2 speaks to this separation:

> Behold, the LORD's hand is not shortened,
> That it cannot save;
> Nor His ear heavy,
> That it cannot hear.
> But your iniquities have separated you from your God;
> And your sins have hidden His face from you,
> So that He will not hear.

Yet despite sin's consequences, God offers redemption. Romans 6:16–23 reveals the transformative power of his grace:

> But God be thanked that though you were slaves of sin, yet you obeyed from the heart that form of doctrine to which you were delivered. And having been set free from sin, you became slaves of righteousness. I speak in human terms because of the weakness of your flesh. . . . For when you were slaves of sin, you were free in regard to righteousness. What fruit did you have then in the things of which you are now ashamed? For the end of those things is death. But now having been set free from sin, and having become slaves of God, you have your fruit to holiness, and the end, everlasting life. For the wages of sin is death, but the gift of God is eternal life in Christ Jesus our Lord.

Here's a brief takeaway—spiritual deception thrives on distorting truth and manipulating trust, reminding us why Scripture repeatedly warns believers to remain vigilant and anchored in God's word. Recognizing deception equips believers to stand firm in faith, rooting their trust in the true nature of God—a sovereign Creator who desires to bless his people in Christ.

The Bible affirms his sovereignty and generosity, declaring, "God, who made the world and everything in it, since He is Lord of heaven and earth, does not dwell in temples made with hands" (Acts 17:24). It also proclaims, "Blessed be the God and Father of our Lord Jesus Christ, who has blessed us with every spiritual blessing in the heavenly places in Christ" (Eph 1:3).

God's sovereignty extends to his moral standards, which are holy, profitable, and designed for our good. Yet Scripture reveals the tension between the desires of the flesh and the leading of the Spirit:

> For the flesh lusts against the Spirit, and the Spirit against the flesh; and these are contrary to one another, so that you do not do the things that you wish. But if you are led by the Spirit, you are not under the law. . . . The fruit of the Spirit is love, joy, peace, longsuffering, kindness, goodness, faithfulness, gentleness, self-control. Against such there is no law. (Gal 5:17–24)

Despite the Spirit's guidance, humanity has always struggled with doubt and deception. Eve's temptation in the garden of Eden exemplifies this timeless challenge.

God never gives us a reason to doubt his goodness and affection, yet, like Eve, we are easily deceived. We frequently find his standards burdensome, if not in words, then in practice. We wrestle with life's difficult questions, wondering why God allows hardship, why he permits suffering, and why things unfold as they do.

These temptations erode our faith, and in the moments we stop trusting God and place our faith in something else, sin has already taken root—even before we act on the impulse.

Scripture consistently highlights the deep connection between sin and deception, revealing that spiritual blindness is not merely a lack of understanding but a refusal to embrace truth. Warren Wiersbe captured this tension well: "Truth without love is brutality, and love without truth is hypocrisy."[47] When separated, both become distortions that Satan exploits—either to bludgeon or to seduce. But joined together, truth and love guard the believer and strengthen the church against his schemes.

Salvation is not dependent on human wisdom or status; rather, it is freely given to all. The Bible affirms this truth:

> There is neither Jew nor Greek, there is neither slave nor free, there is neither male nor female; for you are all one in Christ Jesus. (Gal 3:28)

> Where is the wise? Where is the scribe? Where is the disputer of this age? Has not God made foolish the wisdom of this world?

---

47. Wiersbe, *On Being a Leader*, 39.

STRATEGIC DECEPTION BURIES LIES IN TRUTHS

... For you see your calling, brethren, that not many wise according to the flesh, not many mighty, not many noble, are called. (1 Cor 1:20, 26)

Yet, spiritual deception thrives when people embrace what they wish were true rather than the undeniable truth of Scripture—even when evidence is clear. Jesus warned of this hardened resistance: "But he said to him, 'If they do not hear Moses and the prophets, neither will they be persuaded though one who rises from the dead'" (Luke 16:31). John 12:37 reinforces this reality: "But although he had done so many signs before them, they did not believe in him." Despite witnessing Christ's miracles firsthand, many deliberately chose to reject him, proving that deception is often a matter of the heart rather than the mind.

Few biblical stories illustrate deception's devastating consequences more vividly than Jacob and Esau. Desperate and famished, Esau carelessly surrendered his birthright for a simple meal—a bowl of lentil stew and bread—trading away his inheritance for immediate gratification (Gen 25:29–34). Jacob, calculating and opportunistic, seized the moment, binding his brother with an oath that could not be undone. But that deception was only the beginning. Years later, urged on by his mother, Rebekah, Jacob cloaked himself in Esau's identity. He covered his arms and neck with goat skins to mimic Esau's hair, dressed in his brother's clothes, and carried in his father's favorite meal. With lies on his lips, he convinced the aged, blind Isaac that he was Esau and stole the blessing intended for the firstborn (Gen 27).

The fallout was immediate and brutal: Esau wept bitterly, begging for some leftover blessing, while Jacob was forced to flee for his life as his brother's murderous anger boiled over. What had once been a family bound by covenant promise was now torn by betrayal, estrangement, and years of bitter division—a solemn warning of deception's destructive power.

Jacob's actions echo the infamous Trojan Horse deception—a strategy that capitalized on misplaced trust. The Greeks, unable to conquer Troy by brute force, devised a masterful ruse: they built a massive wooden horse, hid warriors inside, and presented it as a peace offering. Believing they had won, the Trojans welcomed the gift into their city—only to be ambushed from within, leading to their downfall.[48] Like the Trojans, Esau failed to recognize deception before it was too late, embracing a

---

48. Virgil, *Aeneid*, bk. 2 (Fagles, 45).

decision that would cost him greatly. Whether in warfare or personal choices, deception always carries unintended consequences.

Though Jacob and Esau eventually reconciled, the scars of deceit ran deep. Their story is a timeless cautionary tale—a reminder that deception doesn't just damage trust; it reshapes destinies. Spiritually, it warns against the allure of dishonest shortcuts, showing how deceit entices with promises of gain but always demands a costly price. In contrast, Scripture calls believers to uphold integrity, rejecting deceit in favor of God's unwavering truth.

Propaganda's bitter fruit is always the same: a costly trade that looks like gain—until the trap springs.

This theme reverberates throughout biblical history. Consider Eve's encounter with the serpent, where deception shattered her trust in God and severed humanity's perfect communion with him. Like Esau, Eve was convinced she was gaining something, only to realize too late that she had lost far more. This is propaganda's bitter fruit—whether in Eden's garden or in Europe's heartland, deception persuades us that loss is gain until the trap is already sprung. If she had fully grasped the weight of her decision—the ripple effect of sin—would she have acted differently?

This drives home what the opening chapters have already made clear: deception does not exist on its own. A lie has no power in isolation—it must borrow the credibility of truth to gain traction. Deception always clings to what is real, twisting what God has spoken until the counterfeit feels indistinguishable from the genuine. Satan has never created anything new; he only corrupts what God has established—language, morality, worship, even authority. The closer the imitation lies to the truth, the more dangerous the deception becomes. Without truth to parasitize, deception would collapse under its own weight. Its very existence testifies to the reality of objective truth, and its danger lies in how skillfully it camouflages the lie within what God has made plain.

Likewise, if we truly understood the depth of sin's consequences, wouldn't we reconsider the compromises we so easily make? Scripture is unflinching: "The wages of sin is death" (Rom 6:23). Sin is not a minor misstep but a rupture of fellowship with a holy God. It corrodes the soul, poisons relationships, and spreads its corruption through families, nations, and generations. It blinds, enslaves, and ultimately destroys. Every deception, however small it seems in the moment, carries seeds of death—seeds that, if left to grow, bear fruit in eternal separation from God himself.

The serpent's prototype scales seamlessly to modern PSYOP: shape beliefs with omission, cement them with repetition, sell them with spectacle. Today, Satan's deception still prowls, working tirelessly to obscure truth and ensnare both believers and nonbelievers alike. His tactics—subtle yet lethal—mirror the psychological warfare of a seasoned strategist. Understanding his PSYOP strategy is essential for believers to stand guard, recognizing his manipulations and equipping themselves with the armor of God. Deception doesn't always come in an obvious form—it often masquerades as wisdom, progress, or even faithfulness, making vigilance all the more necessary.

While deception is most often a tool of destruction, its use throughout history—including in biblical narratives—reveals complexities that test our understanding. The story of King David offers a striking example of deception used for survival. Fleeing Saul, David found himself in enemy territory, in the land of the Philistines. Recognized as the warrior who had slain "tens of thousands" (1 Sam 21:11), he quickly realized the danger he faced among those who once saw him as their greatest enemy. In a moment of desperation, David resorted to deception—feigning madness before King Achish of Gath, scratching at doors and letting saliva run down his beard (1 Sam 21:13). His ploy worked, and Achish dismissed him as harmless, allowing David to escape unharmed.

Yet this act of deception invites deep reflection. Was David's decision justified by the need for survival, or did it reflect a lapse of trust in God's protection? Scripture consistently warns against deceit, emphasizing that truth and integrity should define a believer's character (Prov 12:22). At the same time, David himself would later write, "The LORD is my light and my salvation; whom shall I fear? The LORD is the strength of my life; of whom shall I be afraid?" (Ps 27:1). The tension raises a sobering question: Did his actions align with the faith he professed? His story challenges believers to weigh the ethical weight of their own decisions, especially when circumstances press them toward compromise.

David's story also points us to a deeper reality: deception is never merely human cunning. From Eden onward, it has been the adversary's chosen weapon, sharpened to obscure God's glory and derail his people. To grasp the full scope of deception, we must now consider the deceiver himself—his fall, his ambitions, and his relentless campaign against truth. Even in desperate situations, navigating deception requires wisdom, vigilance, and unwavering trust in God's principles. As believers, we must remain steadfast, ensuring our choices align with God's truth rather than the temptations of expedience.

At its core, deception remains a weapon of spiritual warfare, a tool Satan expertly crafts to distort God's truth and entangle souls in falsehoods that feel dangerously plausible. But believers are not defenseless. Anchored in Scripture, they sharpen their discernment and stand firm against the enemy's schemes with vigilance and faith.

Chapter 4 has exposed deception's layered complexities—the art of weaving lies into truth, disguising falsehood as something palatable and convincing. These examples are not merely historical curiosities; they reveal the recurring patterns by which deception gains power and spreads. By tracing these patterns across time, we learn to recognize the same tactics when they surface in our own day. But deception is no accident; it is designed, strategized, and perfected. To resist Satan's schemes effectively, believers must first understand his origins, ambitions, and the scope of his power. Whether in Eden's garden or Europe's heartland, the defense is discernment trained by Scripture and fitted with armor (Eph 6:11–12).

The takeaway is clear: propaganda, whether political or spiritual, relies on repetition, emotional manipulation, and the blending of truth and falsehood. It is one of the enemy's classic PSYOP tactics, repackaged through human systems, aiming always to obscure Christ, enslave the mind, and corrupt the heart. Recognizing these methods equips believers to remain steadfast against both historical and spiritual attempts to distort truth, "that we should no longer be children, tossed to and fro and carried about with every wind of doctrine, by the trickery of men, in the cunning craftiness of deceitful plotting" (Eph 4:14).

Accordingly, chapter 5 turns from the patterns of deception to the deceiver himself—his beginnings, aims, and boundaries under God's sovereignty—so we may stand firm.

PERSONAL APPLICATION: GUARDING AGAINST STRATEGIC DECEPTION

Deception isn't always blatant; it's often subtle, woven into truths that seem credible. Whether it's misleading headlines, cleverly disguised propaganda, or spiritual half-truths, deception thrives where discernment is weak. Chapter 4 explores how deception works—how it hides in counterfeits, historical manipulation, and spiritual distortions. These lessons aren't just theoretical; they are essential for recognizing and resisting deception in our own lives.

Here's how you can actively guard against deception:

1. *Train Your Spiritual Instincts to Detect Deception*—Just as counterfeit currency requires close examination to detect, spiritual deception demands careful discernment. Regularly study Scripture, pray for wisdom, and ask the Holy Spirit to help you uncover half-truths disguised as credibility.

2. *Analyze What You Consume—Does It Align with Truth or Manipulate Emotions?*—Whether it's media, teachings, or ideologies, assess the sources of influence in your life. Ask yourself, Does this align with God's word, or is it appealing to my emotions or biases rather than the truth?

3. *Identify Previous Blind Spots—Learn from Them So Deception Doesn't Strike Twice*—Take time to consider where you may have been misled in the past. What warning signs did you overlook? What patterns led to deception? Use these experiences as learning opportunities to strengthen your spiritual awareness.

4. *Pray for Wisdom to Guard Against Manipulation*—Just as Nazi propaganda appealed to emotions to weaken reasoning, Satan uses similar tactics to distort truth. Pray for wisdom to guard against these manipulations and for the protection of your heart and mind (Phil 4:7).

5. *Suit Up with the Armor of God—Your Best Defense Against Deception*—Apply Eph 6:10–18 by putting on the spiritual armor daily. The belt of truth and the sword of the Spirit (God's word) are especially critical in resisting deception.

Recognizing the subtle workings of deception reveals the critical importance of small acts of vigilance. Just as counterfeit currency erodes trust in financial systems, spiritual deception undermines the very foundation of our faith.

Imagine walking through a dense fog—so thick you can barely see the path ahead. Without discernment, every step becomes risky, every choice uncertain. But when the light of God's truth pierces through, deception loses its power. Each act of discernment—whether questioning a misleading claim, resisting a disguised temptation, or examining a spiritual teaching—shines a light that dispels the shadows of deception, guiding you safely toward truth.

This vigilant awareness is more than just a defense; it is an active participation in the spiritual warfare we face every day. Yet, as a child of God, you are not left to fight this battle alone. You have been given powerful tools: God's word, prayer, and the Holy Spirit as your guide. By leaning on these divine resources, you can withstand the enemy's ploys and remain firmly anchored in God's unchanging truth.

Personal Reflection

1. Have you ever believed something that turned out to be false because it was wrapped in a partial truth? How did you come to realize it?
2. What helps you personally discern between truth and deception when they're closely intertwined?
3. Are there "harmless" cultural beliefs or messages you've accepted that may actually conflict with biblical truth?
4. How often do you examine spiritual messages—books, sermons, media—against the Bible? What challenges or helps you in doing this?

Group Discussion

1. The chapter describes how Satan embeds lies in plausible truths. Why is this strategy so effective, and how do we guard against it?
2. What role does spiritual discernment play in resisting deception? How can a believer grow in discernment?
3. Discuss how the enemy might use even "Christian-sounding" language to twist truth. Can you identify examples?
4. How do you respond when someone you care about has embraced a belief that is part truth but ultimately deceptive?

Scripture Connection

- Read 2 Cor 11:13–15 and 1 John 4:1. What do these verses reveal about the need for discernment in spiritual matters?
- Reflect on Eph 6:11–17. How does the "armor of God" equip us to identify and resist lies hidden in truths?

The enemy thrives on confusion, preying on those who lack spiritual vigilance. But deception holds no power against truth that is actively lived and defended. You are not called to passively avoid deception—you are called to expose it, counter it, and stand firm against it. By staying rooted in God's word, equipped in prayer, and discerning in spirit, you can resist Satan's ploys and live in the clarity of divine truth.

5

Satan's Fall, His Ambitions, and His Power

Moritz Retzsch's *The Chess Players*, painted in the nineteenth century and once displayed in the Louvre, illustrates the deceptive finality of defeat—where the devil thinks he has won, but in reality, God always holds the last move, offering redemption and victory through Christ.[1]

---

1. Image: Friedrich August Moritz Retzsch, *Die Schachspieler* [The chess players], 1831. Public Domain.

SATAN'S FALL, HIS AMBITIONS, AND HIS POWER

> It is your attitude, and the suspicion that you are maturing the boldest designs against him, that imposes on your enemy.
>
> —FREDERICK THE GREAT, *INSTRUCTIONS FOR HIS GENERALS*

In the early hours of September 2, 1666, a small fire broke out in a London bakery. At first, it seemed contained—just another mishap in the bustling city. But within hours, flames raged through wooden structures, igniting an inferno that would consume thousands of buildings and leave much of London in ruins. The panic was immediate, yet misinformation spread even faster. Instead of focusing on containment, rumors swept through the city, blaming foreign conspirators, Roman Catholic plots, or even supernatural forces. Wrongful accusations led to arrests, fear drowned out reason, and the true cause—the unchecked spread of fire—continued its devastation.[2]

In the same way, misidentifying the source of danger leads to greater destruction.

This chapter serves as the turning point in volume 1: having traced deception's patterns and strategies in the previous chapters, we now focus on the deceiver himself. Just as Londoners misidentified the fire's cause, humanity often misidentifies the true source of spiritual destruction. To understand deception fully, we must look beyond symptoms to the adversary who fuels them—Satan, his fall, his ambitions, and his power under God's sovereignty.

The flames may look like cultural drift, technological distraction, or generational decline—but behind the smoke stands a greater adversary. Satan's ambition is not simply to tempt in the shadows but to exploit every instrument available to ensnare perception and enslave hearts. Few modern tools illustrate this more vividly than the smartphone. What began as a neutral piece of technology—capable of enormous good when used wisely—has arguably become one of the most potent delivery systems for deception in history.

A generation ago, cultural corruption required effort. If you wanted to watch an R-rated movie, you had to show ID at the box office. If you wanted to hear explicit lyrics, you had to buy a CD with a parental-advisory sticker on the cover. And if you wanted to view pornography, you had to search for a hidden magazine stand or subscribe to a mail-order service that arrived in a plain brown envelope. Sin required pursuit, and

2. Pepys, *Diary*.

shame acted as a deterrent. Today those barriers are gone. What once had to be sought out in hidden corners of society now arrives uninvited, delivered instantly to a device in every pocket.

The trends in youth mental health over the past decade are deeply concerning. Since the rise of smartphones and social media in the US, for example, the two-week prevalence of depressive symptoms among individuals aged twelve and older rose from about 8.2 percent in 2013–2014 to 13.1 percent in 2021–2023.[3] Among adolescents, other studies report even steeper rises—depression rates increasing by about 60 percent from 2017 to 2021 in some cohorts, and anxiety (excluding comorbid depression) rising about 31 percent.[4] While these shifts cannot be attributed to smartphones and/or social media alone, the timing and scale suggest that digital technology has been a major contributing factor.[5] These increases are likely influenced by multiple factors: social, economic, environmental, and biological—not just digital technology use.[6]

Suicide rates among young people have also climbed (e.g., from 2007 to 2021 the suicide rate of youth from ten to twenty-four years old rose about 62 percent).[7] The burden is especially heavy on adolescent girls, who consistently report higher rates of depressive symptoms, suicidal ideation, and self-harm thoughts than boys in many national surveys—for example, in the 2023 Youth Risk Behavior Survey, about

3. Brody and Hughes, "Depression Prevalence," 2.

4. Mayne et al., "COVID-19."

5. See Haidt, *Anxious Generation* and Twenge et al., "Age, Period, and Cohort Trends." As Jonathan Haidt has argued in *The Anxious Generation*, the smartphone era has created an environment uniquely corrosive to adolescent mental health, accelerating anxiety, depression, and social withdrawal.

6. There are many studies showing associations between heavy social media use and worse mental health outcomes (depression, anxiety, suicidal ideation). There are very few studies that demonstrate causation (i.e., social media directly causes mental illness or suicide). Most research is observational, and the causal chain is complicated. Additionally, for many disorders (e.g., ADHD, bipolar disorder, anorexia, schizophrenia, substance use), the evidence for dramatic multipliers is less consistent, and trends often reflect a mixture of better detection, evolving diagnostic criteria, and changing help-seeking behavior rather than straightforward surges in prevalence. Scholars also note that other social, cultural, and environmental factors have coincided with the rise in youth mental health challenges, including heightened academic pressures, economic uncertainty, pandemic-related isolation, cultural and identity stressors, and widespread sleep disruption. Thus, while digital technology is a major contributor, it is best understood as part of a larger ecosystem of stressors. See Anderson et al., "Contributing Factors"; Davico et al., "COVID-19 Pandemic School Disruptions"; Kirkbride et al., "Social Determinants"; and Collins et al., "Making Cities."

7. Curtin and Garnett, "Suicide and Homicide."

30 percent of female students but about 14 percent of male students reported seriously considering suicide.[8]

If these numbers were attached to any other product—food, drug, or vehicle—it would be pulled from the shelves immediately. Yet society tolerates what is plainly toxic, shrugging it off as the unavoidable cost of modern life. This is no accident. The irony is that many of the very executives who design these platforms impose strict limits on their own children's use of them. Steve Jobs reportedly restricted iPad use for his children when it was first released, and Bill Gates delayed giving his children phones until they were teenagers.[9] Other Silicon Valley leaders have chosen low-tech schools such as the Waldorf School of the Peninsula, where screens are discouraged. These choices underscore a striking irony: those who design the platforms often limit their own families' exposure to them.

Social media platforms are not neutral tools. They are engineered to addict, employing methods drawn from behavioral psychology. This is sometimes called the *hook model* (or *habit loop* or *compulsion cycle*): notifications serve as external triggers; the action follows (open the app); then comes the variable reward (a like, a comment, a video), though not every time. The more users invest in building profiles and connections, the more tightly they become bound to the cycle. That unpredictability fuels compulsive checking. Finally, the investment of building a profile, curating images, and gaining followers ties personal identity to the platform itself. This cycle mirrors reinforcement schedules used to condition animals in laboratories. A rat pressing a lever for food pellets surges with dopamine not at the reward itself but in the anticipation of it.[10] The same dynamic now governs human behavior online. Bottomless feeds and endless scrolls ensure there is no natural stopping point, keeping minds tethered to glowing screens for hours at a time. In other words, what begins as a clever design trick quickly becomes a neurochemical trap, turning simple actions into ingrained compulsions.

Dopamine is not merely a "pleasure chemical" but the brain's primary messenger of motivation. It spikes in anticipation of reward, pushing us to repeat behaviors again and again. What once drove human beings toward noble pursuits—building, creating, discovering—has been hijacked by the false promises of novelty. Social media delivers

---

8. Verlenden et al., "Mental Health"; Twenge et al., "Increases in Depression."
9. Bilton, "Steve Jobs"; Weller, "How Bill Gates Limits Tech."
10. Eyal, *Hooked*, 37–56; Lembke, *Dopamine Nation*, 46–52.

these dopamine hits in rapid-fire sequence: a new post, a new notification, a new video on autoplay. Each surge reinforces the habit, wiring the brain to crave more.[11] Over time, the reward pathways adapt, demanding greater stimulation while dulling the ability to enjoy ordinary life. This is why so many who spend hours scrolling feel restless, anxious, and unable to focus when the phone is finally set aside. It is not just distraction; it is dependency.

Researchers studying attention disorders note that the digital environment is uniquely toxic. Edward Hallowell and John Ratey, in *ADHD 2.0*, describe modern life as an "assault on attention"[12] where constant pings, alerts, and fragmented tasks make sustained focus nearly impossible.[13] What was once an occasional challenge for some has become a universal condition: an environment engineered to fracture concentration and keep minds addicted to novelty. The effect is especially devastating on those already prone to ADHD, but in truth it has turned much of society into a culture of distracted minds.

Neuroscience makes clear why this is so powerful. Addiction is not simply about liking something too much; it is about the way the brain's pathways become rewired. With repeated dopamine hits, the reward system grows tolerant, requiring more stimulation to achieve the same effect. When the stimulation is withheld, a kind of behavioral withdrawal sets in—not seizures or tremors, but restlessness, irritability, and a gnawing urge to check the phone again. Over time, the prefrontal cortex—the very part of the brain responsible for self-control and long-term planning—loses its grip.[14] In other words, the very circuitry God designed to help us say *no* is weakened, leaving the heart wide open to deception.

Therefore Scripture's call is urgent: "Do not be conformed to this world, but be transformed by the renewing of your mind" (Rom 12:2). Where addiction erodes the brain's ability to resist compulsion, the Spirit restores clarity, renewing thought and reshaping desire so that we may discern the will of God. Satan exploits dopamine to enslave; Christ renews the mind to set free.

Add to this the unique cruelty of social comparison. A generation ago, you might not know if friends were gathering without you. Today,

---

11. Lembke, *Dopamine Nation*, 54–65; Schultz, "Dopamine Reward Prediction."
12. Hallowell and Ratey, *ADHD 2.0*, 10.
13. See Hallowell and Ratey, *ADHD 2.0*, 77–84.
14. Berridge and Robinson, "Parsing Reward," 507–8; Volkow et al., "Brain Disease Model of Addiction," 365.

group texts, Instagram stories, and Snapchat posts make exclusions visible in real time. A teenager scrolling through her feed sees classmates at a party she wasn't invited to, or friends laughing together at lunch while she eats alone. Mixed in are highlight reels of peers dressed in the latest brands, showing off vacations, and posting achievements—college acceptances, athletic scholarships, music recitals, or perfect report cards—all on public display. The result is anxiety, depression, and withdrawal, compounded by the gnawing sense that real life and ordinary effort can never measure up to the curated life she sees online.

Technology, of course, is not in itself evil. There is real utility in the devices we hold: the ability to call loved ones, navigate unknown cities, share information quickly, even spread the gospel with unprecedented reach. Used wisely, these are powerful tools. But like money, power, or music, technology can be twisted into a weapon. Its misuse is not the root cause but a symptom of the deeper disease—the sin that bends every good gift into idolatry. The true issue lies in the human heart, which takes what is good and bends it toward envy, distraction, and despair.

Scripture offers a sobering reminder of our responsibility in the face of this deception: "Above all else, guard your heart, for everything you do flows from it" (Prov 4:23). The question presses in: Who or what is guarding our hearts today? Is it the word of God shaping our perception, or the algorithms of Silicon Valley? In many ways, technology companies have read Deuteronomy's playbook for discipleship and inverted it. Where God commanded his people to bind his words to their hands, to write them on doorframes, and to impress them on their children, tech companies bind devices to our hands, etch their icons into our doorways, and impress their narratives on our minds. Their goal is nothing less than a lifelong catechism—a phone-based liturgy that shapes attention, affection, and identity.

This is not theoretical. It is a generational PSYOP—an all-out assault on perception, attention, and identity. Unless we recognize the adversary behind the algorithm, we will continue to treat symptoms while missing the disease. Technology can be used for good, but apart from discernment and devotion to God's word, it becomes one of the enemy's most effective instruments. The task before us is to redeem the tool without succumbing to the trap—to see technology not as savior or scapegoat but as a battleground where the deeper war for our hearts is already underway.

And this is only one front of a much larger campaign. Just as Londoners misread the source of the Great Fire, we too risk misreading the source of today's spiritual destruction. Behind the smoke stands a strategist who crafts deceptive narratives, manipulates perception, and shifts the battle onto false fronts.

FROM FIRE TO PSYOP: KNOWING THE ENEMY

C. S. Lewis observed this phenomenon in *Mere Christianity*: "One of the things that surprised me when I first read the New Testament seriously was that it talked so much about a Dark Power in the universe—a mighty evil spirit who was held to be the Power behind death and disease, and sin."[15] His tactics are rarely direct; instead, he employs PSYOP-like strategies—distracting, misleading, and distorting truth—ensuring that many remain unaware of the real spiritual war unfolding behind the scenes.

To fully grasp Satan's strategy in relation to PSYOP—the focus of this book series—we must first understand his nature and motivation. John MacArthur emphasizes the importance of knowing the enemy, likening spiritual warfare to military strategy: "Every military leader devours intelligence reports on the enemy before he enters battle. The intelligence report on Satan is in the Bible. Therefore, ignorance of the enemy will never be a valid excuse for defeat. God has given Christians a decided edge in the contest with advance information on the enemy."[16] Without understanding Satan's tactics, believers risk entering battle blind.

Sun Tzu (544–496 BC), the renowned Chinese military strategist and philosopher, authored *The Art of War*, a timeless work that has shaped both Western and Eastern military thought. He advises, "If you know the enemy and know yourself, you need not fear the result of a hundred battles."[17]

Understanding Satan's background—his relationship with God, his fall, and his ultimate motivations—is crucial for grasping the deceptive PSYOP strategy he employs. His rebellion provides the blueprint for every false narrative since Eden.

---

15. Lewis, *Mere Christianity*, 45.
16. MacArthur and Mayhue, *Biblical Doctrine*, 685–86.
17. Tzu, *Art of War*, 84.

SATAN'S FALL, HIS AMBITIONS, AND HIS POWER

THE BLUEPRINT: PRIDE AND THE FALL

To fully comprehend the depth of Satan's strategic deception, we must first examine the pivotal event that shaped his identity—the moment of his fall from heaven. His descent from a position of glory into rebellion laid the foundation for his ambitions and influence. This chapter explores Satan's fall, his aspirations, and his power in order to truly "know the enemy."

Across the pages of Scripture, the enigmatic fall of Satan stands as one of the most dramatic and symbolically charged events in biblical history. A high-ranking celestial being—possibly a cherub, a powerful angelic order associated with God's presence—once radiant in glory, transformed into the greatest enemy of God, cast down from heaven in an act of divine judgment. Unlike Michael, the warrior archangel who defends God's people (Dan 10:13, Rev 12:7), and Gabriel, the messenger of divine revelation (Luke 1:19, 26), Satan abandoned his exalted role in defiance. His fall was not a mere demotion or act of exile—it was a cataclysmic rebellion, marking the beginning of his relentless war against God and shaping spiritual warfare for eternity.

While accounts of Satan's fall appear throughout the Old and New Testaments, they often depict it as an event shrouded in mystery, occurring at an unspecified time in the past. Isaiah 14:12 echoes through time with its haunting declaration, "How you are fallen from heaven, O Lucifer, son of the morning! How you are cut down to the ground." This passage has long been interpreted as describing a moment of cosmic upheaval, an irreversible descent from honor into corruption.[18]

Satan's descent was not simply a fall—it was a willful plunge, a rebellion driven by pride so consuming that reason and reality became secondary. His ambition to "be like the Most High" (Isa 14:14) blinded him to the inevitable consequence of his defiance: absolute ruin.

History repeatedly confirms this PSYOP dynamic—self-deception born of pride, blinding leaders and nations to reality.

Case Studies in Hubris: Custer and the Third Reich

Few examples illustrate this better than the tragic final moments of George Armstrong Custer. A brilliant yet reckless cavalry officer, Custer graduated last in his class at West Point but rose to prominence through his

---

18. Gathercole, "Jesus' Eschatological Vision," 145.

audacity on the battlefield. By the age of twenty-three, he had become the youngest general in the Union Army, earning fame for his fearless leadership in the Civil War. At Gettysburg, his bold cavalry charge turned the tide of battle, repelling J. E. B. Stuart's Confederate forces and solidifying his reputation as a daring warrior. His long, flowing blond hair became a symbol of defiant confidence—an image of a man who believed himself invincible.[19]

But invincibility is an illusion, and on June 25, 1876, Custer's pride led him to his final stand. Ignoring warnings, dismissing intelligence reports, and underestimating his enemy, he divided his forces and pressed forward, convinced of his superiority. As the Lakota, Cheyenne, and Arapaho warriors encircled his men, the reality of his miscalculation became undeniable. The battlefield, once a place of glory, became a death trap. His soldiers, loyal yet doomed, fought desperately, but they were overwhelmed. Custer himself, standing amid the chaos, must have realized in those final moments that his arrogance had sealed their fate.[20]

Like Satan's rebellion, Custer's downfall was not a mere accident—it was the consequence of his own hubris. He refused reinforcements, dismissed caution, and pressed forward, blinded by his belief in his own legend.

And just as Hitler, Goering, Himmler, and Goebbels clung to their delusions in the face of inevitable defeat, Custer clung to his belief in his own superiority until the bitter end. His pride ensured not only his own destruction but the annihilation of his command. His story, like those of fallen tyrants and deceived leaders, echoes the ancient warning: pride leads not to glory but to ruin.

As Hitler's empire collapsed around him, he refused to accept responsibility. His rhetoric, once filled with grand visions of conquest, turned to bitter condemnation of his own people. In his final days, he issued the infamous Nero Decree—an order demanding the destruction of Germany's infrastructure rather than allowing it to fall into enemy hands.[21] It was a final act of vengeance, born of pride, fueled by his inability to face defeat. Like Satan, he would rather watch everything burn than admit he had lost.

Hermann Goering, *Reichsmarschall* and Hitler's designated successor, sank into delusion. As the Third Reich crumbled, he focused not

19. Barnard, *George Armstrong Custer*, 30–80.
20. Truman, *Downfall of Pride*, 90–130.
21. Kershaw, *Hitler*, 932–34.

on survival, not on repentance, but on his personal hoard of stolen artwork—thousands of pieces meant for Carinhall, his envisioned postwar estate.[22] As the Reich collapsed, he commanded Carinhall be destroyed—a final act of pride that mirrored the ruins of his own delusion. Even as the world rejected the Nazi regime, Goering held onto the illusion that he would be named chancellor, that his power would endure beyond the rubble of Berlin. His pride mirrors Satan's own—clutching onto false hope, refusing to acknowledge the inevitability of his fall.

Heinrich Himmler, head of the SS (*Schutzstaffel*, "Protection Squadron") and chief architect of the Holocaust, played the role of a calculating pragmatist. Originally formed as Hitler's elite bodyguard unit, the SS grew under Himmler's leadership into one of the most powerful and feared organizations of the Third Reich—responsible for enforcing Nazi racial policy, running the concentration camp system, and orchestrating mass murder on an industrial scale. With concentration camps in chaos at the war's end, Himmler orchestrated the release of Jewish prisoners—not out of remorse but as a last-ditch effort to secure leniency from the Allies. He imagined himself not as a condemned war criminal but as a viable leader of postwar Germany, believing—against all reason—that he could negotiate his way to survival.[23] His arrogance echoes Satan's deception—the refusal to accept consequence, the belief that one can rewrite fate.

While Himmler sought survival through pragmatism, Joseph Goebbels, minister of propaganda, remained bound to his ideology until the bitter end. As the Third Reich crumbled, Goebbels chose to die beside his leader in the *Führerbunker*—the underground command shelter in Berlin where Adolf Hitler spent his final days directing a war already lost. Built beneath the Reich Chancellery, the bunker became the claustrophobic stage for the regime's collapse, a tomb-like fortress where delusion clung to power as reality closed in. As Goebbels sent staff out of the bunker, he dismissed them with the chilling words, "The game is over," urging some to take their own lives rather than witness defeat. Goebbels's decision to follow Hitler into death proved that the ideological spell of National Socialism was more than political—it was spiritual in its possession of those who embraced it. His wife, Magda, chillingly declared, "I couldn't imagine a world without National Socialism."[24] Her words, spoken on

---

22. Edsel, *Monuments Men*, 148–55; Overy, *Dictators*, 561–62.
23. Paehler, *Third Reich's Intelligence Services*.
24. Fest, *Inside Hitler's Bunker*, 117.

the brink of oblivion, expose the ultimate deception—the inability to see beyond the lie that had defined their lives.

The grip of National Socialism did not loosen simply because its leaders perished; its influence had woven itself into the very identity of its followers. This moment of absolute ideological possession did not die with Hitler's inner circle. The challenge of denazification in postwar Germany revealed how deeply embedded National Socialism had become, particularly within the troops and the Hitler Youth. These were not just soldiers and citizens but individuals shaped from childhood to see Nazism as truth—indoctrinated through propaganda, education, and forced loyalty to the Führer.

For many, surrender did not mean abandoning belief—it meant redefining reality itself. Allied forces quickly recognized that denazification was not merely about removing symbols or leaders—it was about dismantling the spiritual and psychological grip of an ideology that had rewritten history in the minds of millions.

The Hitler Youth, trained from their earliest years to revere Hitler as nearly messianic, were among the hardest to rehabilitate. The war had ended, but many refused to believe in Germany's defeat, clinging to conspiracies, disillusionment, and resentment. The ideological indoctrination had functioned like a false gospel, creating generations willing to fight to the bitter end rather than accept the collapse of their worldview. From early childhood, they memorized Hitler's speeches as scripture, chanted slogans of supremacy, and absorbed his ideology through schoolbooks, youth rallies, and military-style drills. Allegiance to Hitler was not taught as politics—it was instilled as an unshakable spiritual conviction.[25]

This warped devotion parallels the spiritual deception Satan weaves—not just leading people astray but embedding a lie so deeply that rejecting it feels like rejecting one's identity.

In one of the most horrifying displays of absolute devotion, Magda insisted that if National Socialism could not survive, neither could her children. She orchestrated their deaths, ensuring that they would not grow up in a world free from the ideology that had consumed her. With cold determination, she poisoned all six of her children, extinguishing their lives before taking her own. Joseph followed suit, committing suicide beside her.[26]

---

25. Taylor, *Exorcising Hitler*, 215.
26. Peter Longerich, *Goebbels*, 663–68.

Their final moments were not acts of defiance but of desperation—pride, deception, and delusion driving them to their tragic end.

Pride brings absolute ruin—not just in fleeting moments of arrogance but in the choices that shape destinies. As Lucifer refused submission, so too did these men, their blind devotion sealing their destruction.

Hitler, Goering, Himmler, and Goebbels clung to a doomed ideology, refusing to abandon their pride even as destruction loomed. Likewise, Satan wages war against God, knowing his fate is sealed yet still rejecting surrender. This descent into self-delusion and ruin did not end with them—it is a pattern echoed throughout history, from despots to fallen angels.

These historical moments of prideful defiance serve as a sobering reflection of Satan's own refusal to yield before God. He would rather reign in chaos than bow in humility. He would rather deceive than accept truth. He would rather lead others to destruction than face his own downfall alone. Just as Hitler's regime required forceful intervention to shatter its illusions, Satan's deception must be confronted with unyielding truth—because falsehood, left unchecked, does not merely mislead, it enslaves.

Chapter 4 exposed the mechanics of Nazi deception—how illusions were crafted and sustained. Chapter 5 now reveals their inevitable cost: ruin. Pride ensured their collapse, just as it secured Satan's condemnation. The connection is clear: deception and pride lead not to glory but to destruction. The pattern repeats across history—whether in the spiritual rebellion of Satan or the earthly arrogance of tyrants, pride always ends in downfall.

Even linguistic interpretations reflect this battle over identity, for the name *Lucifer* carries layers of meaning shaped by translation and tradition. The King James Version (KJV) and New King James Version (NKJV) use "Lucifer," while the New International Version (NIV) renders it "morning star," the English Standard Version (ESV) calls him "Day Star," and the New English Translation (NET) translates it as "shining one." These variances have fueled centuries of debate: Does Isaiah's passage refer directly to Satan, or is it a metaphor for a Babylonian ruler whose arrogance led to his fall—mirroring Satan's rebellion? Further complicating this identity discussion is the fact that Scripture assigns him numerous titles throughout the canon: among his names are "Abaddon" and "Apollyon," meaning "destroyer" (Rev 9:11); Peter describes him as a roaring lion seeking someone to devour (1 Pet 5:8); Jesus calls him a murderer and "the father of lies" (John 8:44), "the wicked one" (Matt 13:19), and "the ruler of this world" (John 12:31); and Paul identifies him as "the god of this age" (2 Cor 4:4), "the prince of the power of the air" (Eph 2:2), and the leader of the cosmic forces of evil (Eph 6:10–12). These titles collectively portray not only his character but the destructive scope of his influence.

Regardless of translation differences, the essence of Satan's fall remains undeniable—a catastrophic shift from divine presence to defiant rebellion.

Biblical accounts often connect Satan's exile from heaven with his transformation into the ultimate adversary. His fall was not merely a banishment—it was the beginning of his relentless war against God, manifesting most clearly in his role as an accuser, deceiver, and master of spiritual warfare. From a throne of light to an empire of darkness, Satan's ambitions did not die with his fall—they intensified.

Like a star torn from the heavens, Satan plunged into darkness, consumed by his own pride and thirst for dominion. No longer the bearer of divine light, he prowls like a roaring lion, stalking his prey and searching for souls to ensnare in his web of lies (1 Pet 5:8). His rebellion turned him into the architect of deception, weaving falsehoods with the precision of a master manipulator—his whispers of doubt, temptation, and distortion echoing through the ages.

Yet Satan's downfall was not an isolated event; it was the beginning of a relentless campaign to distort truth and manipulate perception, infiltrating human institutions, ideologies, and everyday life. His influence has shaped generations, blurring the lines between authenticity and deception.

Appearance vs. Reality: Branding, Social Media, and the Accuser

One striking example of this manipulation is corporate greenwashing, where companies deceive consumers by falsely marketing their products as environmentally friendly. These corporations craft emotionally compelling narratives—invoking imagery of lush forests, pristine oceans, and sustainable communities—to appeal to consumers' deep-seated desire to make ethical choices. Time and again, major corporations have been exposed for exaggerating sustainability efforts, projecting an illusion of ethical responsibility while continuing harmful practices. By tapping into people's guilt, hope, and sense of social responsibility, they mask deception with feel-good branding, leading consumers to unknowingly support businesses that contradict the very ideals they promote.[27]

Just as corporations use branding to disguise harmful practices, deception operates on a much larger scale, infiltrating institutions, ideologies, and even personal beliefs. This strategy of misdirection is not exclusive to corporate marketing—it's a universal tactic, echoed in surprising ways, including in pop culture. Take *Armageddon* (1998), a late-nineties blockbuster directed by Michael Bay and starring Bruce Willis, Ben Affleck, Liv Tyler, and the ever-charismatic Steve Buscemi, where a ragtag group of drillers attempts to save Earth from a doomsday asteroid.

One of the film's many memorable moments comes from Russian cosmonaut Lev Andropov (played by Peter Stormare) and NASA pilot Watts (Jessica Steen), who struggle with a malfunctioning component aboard the spacecraft. Amid the chaos, Lev delivers a brilliantly absurd but strangely insightful observation about global manufacturing:

> LEV ANDROPOV: "It's stuck, yes?"
> WATTS: "Back off! You don't know the components!"
> LEV ANDROPOV: (annoyed) "Components? American components, Russian components, ALL MADE IN TAIWAN!"[28]

Lev's frustration, shouted amid the tension of repairing the shuttle, is the kind of blunt truth that hits harder than expected. His point? No matter where the label says a component was made, the underlying reality is that mass production and hidden flaws are universal. The humor lies in how he dismisses national pride, stripping away the illusion of technological superiority with a single exasperated line.

Now, applying this idea to spiritual deception: Satan operates much like faulty components in a global supply chain—his lies aren't bound by geography, ideology, or tradition. Whether the deception comes wrapped in corporate slogans, political movements, or religious distortions, its origin remains the same. Every falsehood, every misleading doctrine, and every manipulation is ultimately "manufactured" from the same source—Satan himself.

Just as Lev Andropov unveils the inconvenient truth about manufactured parts, believers must unveil the deeper reality behind deception. It doesn't matter whether misinformation is packaged in sophisticated

---

27. Poiriazi et al., "Analyzing the Interconnection."
28. Bay, *Armageddon*, 02:15:47.

language or ancient traditions—the core issue remains unchanged. The source of all spiritual falsehood is Satan, and his tactics, much like those flawed components, are carefully designed to malfunction when tested. His goal is simple: to distort truth, obscure reality, and lure people away from the light of God's word.

This method of deception—relying on appearances rather than substance—is not exclusive to corporations. It mirrors an even greater strategy of falsehood, one designed to lead souls astray.

Just as Goebbels repackaged lies in the form of "truth," corporations repackage exploitation in the form of "sustainability." In both cases, the deception operates as PSYOP—strategically shaping perception by appealing to emotions, values, and trust.

In the same way, Satan's deception thrives on appearances, twisting lies into alluring disguises and luring people into spiritual confusion. His distortions are subtle yet corrosive, planting seeds of doubt, distorting truth, and leading souls astray. Just as consumers must sharpen their awareness to identify deceptive branding, believers must cultivate spiritual discernment to separate illusion from truth—rejecting Satan's manipulations and standing firm in God's word.

Similarly, in the realm of social media, false accusations and smear campaigns have become a modern battlefield for deception. Political actors and organizations weaponize misinformation, using it to discredit opponents, twist narratives, and manipulate public perception. A striking example of this occurred during the 2020 US presidential election, where social media platforms became flooded with fabricated claims, doctored images, and misleading headlines, influencing public trust and deepening societal divisions.

This is classic psychological warfare: perception management. In military PSYOP manuals, such tactics are described as "denial and deception" operations—flooding the environment with enough distortion that the truth becomes impossible to discern. Satan wields the same method in spiritual warfare, ensuring the signal of truth is drowned in the noise of accusation.

This mirrors Satan's role as the accuser in Rev 12:10, where he seeks to sow doubt, fracture unity, and weaken faith among believers. Just as misinformation corrodes trust in society, Satan's accusations erode spiritual stability, leaving individuals questioning their standing with God. His deception thrives on distortion and manipulation, making vigilance and discernment crucial in both the spiritual realm and everyday life.

Throughout Scripture, Satan's accusations serve as tools of spiritual warfare, targeting believers in moments of vulnerability to sow doubt, discord, and pride. His strategy often exploits human weakness, using pride as a foothold to unravel faith and foster rebellion. Paul's warning in 1 Tim 3:6 (NIV) highlights this very danger, cautioning against placing new converts into leadership roles too quickly: "He must not be a recent convert, or he may become conceited and fall under the same judgment as the devil."

Here, Paul draws a direct parallel between Satan's downfall and the risks of unchecked pride. Just as Satan's arrogance led him to rebel against God, a new convert elevated prematurely to leadership may become entangled in the same cycle of conceit and rebellion. Pride, when left unchecked, can distort judgment, erode humility, and ultimately lead to spiritual ruin. Paul's warning is not merely about leadership—it's a reminder of how Satan's tactics thrive on exploiting pride, making vigilance and humility essential for all believers.

Satan's fall from grace was not a single misstep; it marked the beginning of his complete transformation into a force of rebellion, a tragic distortion of his former glory. His insatiable pride fueled his defiance, and its consequences continue to ripple through history. As biblical authors repeatedly warn, unchecked ambition can ensnare even the faithful, mirroring Satan's tragic descent.

Scholars have long examined the New Testament's portrayal of Satan, illustrating how Old Testament themes carry over into the Gospels and other writings. William G. Bellshaw, a scholar of New Testament theology, explores these themes—particularly Satan's role as an accuser. According to Bellshaw, John's description in Rev 12:10, where Satan is called "the accuser of the brethren," reflects a deep-rooted Jewish tradition portraying him as the adversary—one who relentlessly charges righteous individuals with hidden sins.[29]

Satan hurls accusations like flaming arrows, aiming to fracture faith and sow doubt among believers. His voice echoes through the corridors of fear and insecurity, whispering deceit that erodes confidence in God's promises. Every believer who wrestles with guilt and condemnation feels the sharp sting of his relentless assault—yet Scripture stands as a shield against his deception.

---

29. Bellshaw, "Doctrine of Satan," 25.

A similar motif unfolds in Job 1, where Satan prowls the throne room of heaven, hurling accusations like weapons, determined to dismantle Job's integrity and provoke his downfall. His presence is not passive—it's calculated, confrontational, relentless. He challenges Job's devotion, seeking to prove that faith crumbles under pressure.

Here again the parallel to PSYOP is striking: discredit the target, isolate him, and erode confidence until collapse occurs. Yet Job resisted, showing that spiritual resilience can withstand even the most aggressive campaigns of deception.

Just as Job endured a spiritual trial rooted in deception, believers today must remain vigilant against Satan's tactics, recognizing that his lies are designed to erode trust, unravel faith, and replace assurance with fear. His strategy hasn't changed—he still whispers doubt, distorts truth, and exploits weakness. But like Job, those who stand firm in unshaken faith will expose his deception for what it truly is—a desperate attempt to destroy what cannot be broken.

PRIDE BEFORE THE FALL

A striking reference to Satan's fall appears in Luke 10:18, where Jesus declares, "I saw Satan fall like lightning from heaven." His words come just as his followers celebrate their power over demonic forces, rejoicing in their newfound authority. Yet beneath this moment of triumph lies a subtle warning—a caution against pride.[30]

Satan, once exalted in heaven, fell because of his arrogance, blinded by his ambition to surpass God. He sought to elevate himself beyond his rightful place, refusing to submit to divine authority. His pride led to rebellion, and the consequences of that rebellion continue to ripple through history.

Just as Satan's thirst for self-glory ended in destruction, followers of Christ must remain vigilant, ensuring they never fall into the same trap of self-exaltation. This temptation manifests in countless ways—leaders who seek personal recognition over humble service, individuals who measure their worth by success and status, and even those who place their own desires above God's will. Scripture warns against such arrogance, reminding believers that power without humility breeds downfall.

---

30. Löfstedt, "Satan's Fall," 98.

A powerful biblical example of this danger appears in the life of King Nebuchadnezzar, ruler of Babylon, who arrogantly declared, "Is not this great Babylon, that I have built for a royal dwelling by my mighty power and for the honor of my majesty?" (Dan 4:30). His unchecked pride led to a humbling judgment as he was stripped of his throne and made to wander like a beast until he acknowledged God's sovereignty.

Nebuchadnezzar's downfall is more than ancient history—it is a timeless warning. The same spirit of arrogance that brought kings low in Scripture has reemerged throughout the centuries, toppling rulers who exalted themselves above God. One of the most chilling examples is Adolf Hitler, whose delusional self-glorification followed the same destructive pattern. Convinced of his own superiority and blinded by ideology, he plunged nations into war and brought death to millions.

By April 1945, the cost of pride could no longer be denied. Allied forces had encircled Berlin, and the Red Army pressed in with relentless fury. Artillery thundered day and night, shaking the city to its foundations and reducing streets to smoldering ruins. Hitler, now a hollow remnant of the dictator who once dominated Europe, withdrew into the *Führerbunker* beneath the Reich Chancellery. In that subterranean refuge, paranoia deepened and despair took hold, even as his empire disintegrated above him.

The bunker itself was a claustrophobic maze, filled with dim lighting, stale air, and the weight of inevitable defeat. Hitler's once-commanding presence had vanished—his body frail, his hands trembling uncontrollably from disease and addiction. As the Soviets closed in, he penned his last will and testament, obsessed with his own legacy rather than the destruction he had wrought.

On April 30, 1945, with artillery rounds shaking the bunker and the Soviets mere blocks away, Hitler made his final decision. He and his wife of one day, Eva Braun, retreated to his private study. There, Hitler shot himself, while Eva took cyanide. Their bodies were carried to the Chancellery Garden, doused in petrol, and set ablaze by loyal aides.[31]

From commanding armies to hiding underground, trembling in fear, Hitler's story mirrors Satan's own tragic descent—from exaltation to ruin, from power to isolation. Both relied on psychological dominance and grand illusions, but when the lies collapsed, so did their kingdoms. These vivid historical parallels underscore the timeless warnings found

---

31. Fest, *Inside Hitler's Bunker*, 98.

in Scripture, where prophetic imagery reveals the dangers of pride and rebellion.

This theme extends beyond Luke 10:18, woven throughout key Scriptures, including Ezek 28 and the incendiary pronouncement of Isa 14:12–21:

> How you are fallen from heaven,
> O Lucifer, son of the morning!
> How you are cut down to the ground,
> You who weakened the nations!
> For you have said in your heart:
> "I will ascend into heaven,
> I will exalt my throne above the stars of God;
> I will also sit on the mount of the congregation
> On the farthest sides of the north;
> I will ascend above the heights of the clouds,
> I will be like the Most High."
> Yet you shall be brought down to Sheol,
> To the lowest depths of the Pit.
> (Isa 14:12–15)

Throughout Scripture, Israel's prophets deliver searing judgments against foreign rulers who mock God's laws and threaten Israel's existence through conquest and subjugation. These passages address the kings of Babylon and Tyre, blending political critique with deeper theological insights about rebellion and divine justice.

But these warnings aren't confined to history. The forces that led to Satan's downfall—pride, unchecked ambition, and defiance—are just as dangerous today as they were in the courts of heaven. They remain a persistent threat, lurking not just in the corridors of power but within the hearts of men. Every era has its propaganda—whether royal decrees, Nazi broadcasts, or social media campaigns—that disguises rebellion as progress and pride as liberation.

The fall of Satan stands as a powerful biblical motif, interwoven with prophetic rebukes against earthly rulers who seek to elevate themselves beyond their rightful place. Harold Willmington, a respected theologian and scholar, provides valuable insight into this connection, particularly in his analysis of Ezek 28. He explains that this passage condemns the king of Tyre for his cruelty, pride, and rebellion against God's laws, while indirectly attributing similar crimes to Satan.[32] This thematic parallel

---

32. Willmington, *Doctrine of Satan*, 4.

underscores a broader truth: rebellion, spiritual usurpation, and divine judgment are cyclical patterns throughout Scripture, serving as perpetual warnings against arrogance and defiance.[33]

This passage isn't just an ancient tale—it's a cautionary narrative with enduring relevance, reminding us that the battle between pride and humility, rebellion and obedience, is one every generation must face. Here again we see the anatomy of deception: inflate the ego, mask the consequences, and erode trust in God until pride makes rebellion seem rational.

This theme finds a vivid expression in Ezek 28:13–19, where the prophet describes a figure once adorned in splendor, only to descend into corruption:

> You were in Eden, the garden of God;
> Every precious stone was your covering:
> The sardius, topaz, and diamond,
> Beryl, onyx, and jasper,
> Sapphire, turquoise, and emerald with gold.
> The workmanship of your timbrels and pipes
> Was prepared for you on the day you were created.
> ....
> You were perfect in your ways from the day you were created,
> Till iniquity was found in you.
> ....
> Your heart was lifted up because of your beauty;
> You corrupted your wisdom for the sake of your splendor;
> ....
> You defiled your sanctuaries
> By the multitude of your iniquities,
> ....
> And I turned you to ashes upon the earth
> In the sight of all who saw you.
> All who knew you among the peoples are astonished at you;
> You have become a horror,
> And shall be no more forever.
> (Ezek 28:13, 15, 17–19)

The description of Satan's pre-fallen state—his beauty, adornment with jewels, and musical abilities—reflects a heavenly grandeur that ultimately leads to pride and ruin. Here, the prophet attributes Satan's downfall to his arrogance and self-exaltation, a theme mirrored in the

---

33. Henry, "Commentary on Ezekiel 28," 719–23.

indictment against the king of Tyre, who likewise allows his own power and vanity to blind him to divine authority.

This pattern of arrogance and downfall is not confined to one ruler. As Isa 14 previously illustrated, the fall of Babylon's ruler serves as a direct parallel to Satan's own rebellion, reinforcing the recurring theme of pride leading to destruction.[34]

Isaiah's prophecy presents a dual layer of judgment—one addressing the earthly ruler of Babylon and another pointing toward Satan himself. His pride, ambition, and desire for divine status find echoes in human leaders who seek to elevate themselves beyond their rightful place. These prophetic warnings illustrate a recurring pattern: just as Satan fell from glory, so too will those who follow his path—whether heavenly beings or earthly rulers.

This discussion underscores an important interpretive challenge: while a number of scholars contend that Ezek 28 and Isa 14 refer strictly to historical rulers, the descriptions reach far beyond human attributes. For this reason, many interpreters in the Christian tradition have understood these prophecies not only as near fulfillments in earthly kings but also as pointing to a deeper reality in Satan's original rebellion—a cosmic insubordination that set the pattern for pride and judgment throughout history.[35]

In the end, whether applied to Babylon's ruler, Tyre's king, or Satan himself, the message is clear: pride leads to destruction, whether for kings on earth or angels in heaven.

The key insight remains clear: Satan's fall from grace is a powerful testament to the destructive nature of pride and rebellion against God. John MacArthur emphasizes this truth, stating, "Satan's power lies not in his strength but in his ability to deceive; he is the master of lies, twisting truth to ensnare the unwary."[36] His ambitions—born from his desire to usurp God's authority—continue to shape his strategies of deception and spiritual warfare.

The biblical account of Lucifer's fall from heaven stands as the foundational example of how pride corrupts. Once a beautiful and

---

34. Henry, "Commentary on Ezekiel 28," 719–23.

35. For interpreters who see Isa 14 and Ezek 28 as describing Satan's fall, see MacArthur, *Study Bible*, notes on Isa 14:12–15 and Ezek 28:12–19; Grudem, *Systematic Theology*, 414–16. For scholars who restrict the passages to human kings, see Oswalt, *Chapters 1–39*, 315–19; Eichrodt, *Ezekiel*, 380–85.

36. MacArthur, *Standing Strong*, 87.

exalted angel, Lucifer's ambition to "be like the Most High" (Isa 14:14) drove him to rebel against God, leading to his expulsion from heaven and transformation into Satan, the adversary. His story illustrates how pride not only corrupts the soul but also separates individuals from God, serving as a stark warning for believers to guard against arrogance and self-exaltation.[37]

Isaiah 14 highlights pride as the driving force behind Satan's downfall—an enduring temptation that still lures humanity today. Even now, he operates with the same relentless ambition, using deception to draw people away from God and fuel his pursuit of dominance.

FROM WAR TO VICTORY: PROTOEVANGELIUM, THE CROSS, AND COUNTER-PSYOP

Historical and scriptural parallels reinforce these themes. One striking example comes from World War II: following the Japanese bombing of Pearl Harbor on December 7, 1941, that "day of infamy,"[38] the United States declared war, cementing a pivotal moment in history. The Joint Resolution, signed by Congress, declared, "That the state of war between the United States and the Imperial Government of Japan which has thus been thrust upon the United States is hereby formally declared."[39] This was not just a military declaration but a recognition of reality—a refusal to allow deception and surprise attack to dictate the course of history.

In a similar way, Gen 3:15 records God's declaration of war against Satan after the temptation and fall of humanity: "I will put enmity between you and the woman, and between your seed and her seed; He shall bruise your head and you shall bruise His heel."

This verse, known as the *protoevangelium*, originates from two Greek words: *protos*, meaning "first," and *evangelion*, meaning "good news" or "gospel." It marks the first mention in Scripture of the promise

---

37. Grudem, *Systematic Theology*, 413.

38. The "Day of Infamy" speech was delivered by Franklin D. Roosevelt, the thirty-second president of the United States, to a joint session of Congress on December 8, 1941. The speech is known for its first line: "Yesterday, December 7, 1941—a date which will live in infamy." The first draft, Roosevelt originally dictated the phrase "a date which will live in world history" before revising it by hand to the far more searing "a date which will live in infamy." With that single edit, he didn't just describe the moment—he inscribed it into history. See Miller, "FDR's 'Day of Infamy.'"

39. Office of the Historian, "State of War."

of salvation, signaling God's plan to redeem humanity even as sin entered the world.

Though the term may sound complex, its meaning is simple: "first gospel." Found in Gen 3:15, the protoevangelium is God's initial promise of victory over sin and Satan. Think of it as the opening act in the grand narrative of salvation, where God declares that evil will not have the final say. Scholars recognize this passage as a foundational verse pointing to Christ, setting the stage for his ultimate triumph over darkness.

The passage introduces two crucial themes unknown in Eden before the fall: the curse upon humanity due to Adam's sin and God's provision of a Savior who would bear that curse. While Gen 3:14 addresses the serpent—condemning it to "eat dust" for the rest of its days—verse 15 shifts focus to Satan himself, the true power behind the deception. God curses Satan to an eternal conflict with humanity, embodied in the struggle between the woman's offspring and the forces of darkness.

The hostility between humans and demons originates here, continuing throughout history. Evil angels and wicked men are often termed serpents—even a "brood of vipers" (Matt 3:7)—and they have waged war against God's people since the fall. The "offspring" of the woman refers specifically to Jesus Christ, born of a woman, who would confront and defeat Satan's schemes.

This cosmic war reached its climax at Christ's crucifixion, when malevolent men and demonic forces struck at the heel of the Messiah, believing they had secured their triumph. Like the bulls of Bashan encircling their prey, they surrounded him, their mouths open wide, ready to devour (Ps 22:12).[40] This prophetic imagery captures the fierce opposition Christ faced—not only from human rulers but from unseen spiritual forces determined to destroy him. In that moment, we glimpse something beyond comprehension: the unfathomable cost of sin, borne not just in human cruelty but in the concentrated fury of hell itself.

Yet what Satan intended as his ultimate victory proved to be his greatest defeat. The resurrection of Christ shattered the dominion of darkness,

---

40. The bulls of Bashan symbolize powerful, oppressive enemies—both human and spiritual—who seek to crush the righteous. Bashan, a fertile region known for its strong, well-fed cattle, became a biblical metaphor for arrogant rulers and fierce adversaries. In prophetic literature, these bulls represent those who mock, persecute, and attempt to destroy God's chosen servant. Additionally, Caesarea Philippi, located at the base of Mount Hermon within the ancient region of Bashan, was known as the "gates of hell" for its associations with pagan worship and the underworld, and it was there that Jesus proclaimed His church's triumph over the forces of darkness (Matt 16:18).

securing victory not only for Jesus but for all who follow him. The suffering Servant, once crushed and afflicted, rose in triumph, proving that no force—human or demonic—could thwart God's redemptive plan.

This wound was not the final blow, for on the third day, Christ rose, claiming victory for every believer. In the ultimate triumph, he crushed Satan's head, marking the end of Satan's dominion over humanity forever and sealing his fate under the weight of divine justice. Christ's resurrection doesn't just win back souls; it detonates the enemy's information architecture. At Calvary, the centerpiece of Satan's PSYOP—fear of death—was neutralized (Heb 2:14–15), collapsing the narrative that he still holds ultimate leverage.

Through the power of the cross, Christ dismantled Satan's empire, stripped him of authority, and ended his reign of oppression over mankind. As Heb 2:14–15 declares, Christ's suffering and sacrifice destroyed Satan's hold on death, ensuring that his defeat was final and irreversible.

The protoevangelium affirms that God always had a plan for humanity's salvation—and he announced it the moment sin entered the world: "For this purpose the Son of God was manifested, that He might destroy the works of the devil" (1 John 3:8).[41]

In short, Satan's ultimate goal is to distort, deceive, and destroy. He seeks to undermine God's kingdom by targeting human hearts and minds through manipulation, temptation, and lies—always positioning himself as an alternative to divine truth.

But the cross sealed his fate. Christ reigns victorious, and Satan's power—however real—remains temporary and broken beneath the weight of divine redemption.

Since sin first entered creation, spiritual warfare has raged—a relentless battle between truth and deception. If this sounds like a cosmic tug-of-war, you wouldn't be wrong. But there is one crucial difference: the war's outcome has already been decided.

The fall of man introduced sin into the world, giving Satan an avenue to deceive and disrupt, but Christ's victory on the cross sealed the enemy's fate. Believers aren't fighting for victory—they're fighting from victory. Understanding this flips the perspective: instead of fearing Satan's influence, we walk in the confidence that his rule is crumbling under the weight of Christ's triumph.

---

41. Pettus, "Reading a Protoevangelium."

Unveiling Deception

R. C. Sproul poignantly observes, "The Christian life is not a playground but a battlefield, and vigilance is the price of victory."[42] This truth comes to life in Jesus' temptation in the wilderness (Matt 4:1–11), where Satan twisted Scripture in an attempt to lure Jesus with physical sustenance, worldly power, and divine protection. Yet each time, Jesus countered deception with the unshakable truth of God's word, demonstrating that scriptural understanding is the key to resisting lies. This account underscores the necessity of knowing and relying on Scripture—not just as knowledge but as active vigilance against deception.[43] Notice the pattern: Satan's offers sound plausible, feel urgent, and quote Scripture. This is classic influence ops: authority appeal, scarcity, and selective citation. Jesus counters each with context and the whole counsel of God. That's doctrinal counterintelligence in action.

Just as soldiers study enemy strategies before battle, believers must train their minds to recognize the enemy's deceit. Ephesians 5:11 instructs believers to "have no fellowship with the unfruitful works of darkness, but rather expose them." Exposure is the antidote to indoctrination. In PSYOP terms, bringing lies into the light degrades the adversary's credibility, interrupts his repetition cycle, and restores decision-making to truth.

Spiritual deception, like counterfeit money, mimics the truth convincingly—yet a trained eye quickly uncovers its flaws. Bank workers don't memorize every type of counterfeit bill; instead, they master the details of real currency so they can easily detect a fake. In the same way, believers sharpen their discernment by immersing themselves in the truth of Scripture—knowing God's word so well that deception becomes unmistakable. So the training objective is clear: master the authentic—sound doctrine, tested exegesis, historic orthodoxy—so anomalies in tone, text, or theology trigger immediate suspicion.

Christianity stands or falls on the reality of Satan and demons, for Jesus dedicated his ministry to exposing their influence and equipping his followers with divine truth. Recognizing deception isn't just about avoiding falsehood—it's about actively identifying and confronting the lies that seek to distort faith.

Now, picture yourself on the front lines of a battlefield. The enemy is relentless, strategic, and determined to claim victory. Wars are never won

---

42. Sproul, *Holiness of God*, 89.
43. Carson, "Spiritual Warfare," 253.

by chance—they are fought with precision, cunning, and ruthless determination. Tactics matter. Strategies evolve. Every move is calculated.

The spiritual realm mirrors this reality, as Satan has launched an unceasing campaign against God's kingdom, striking at its very foundations with methodical precision. His war is not a chaotic struggle—it is a targeted offensive, executed through five primary objectives aimed at undermining God's plan for humanity.

This war began at the dawn of time, and its battles continue to shape the course of human history. The conflict is not merely philosophical—it is real, intentional, and deeply personal, targeting the very heart of God's creation. Yet while Satan's strategies are ruthless, God's sovereignty remains absolute—ensuring that no scheme of darkness will ultimately prevail.

THE ENEMY'S CAMPAIGN PLAN: FIVE STRATEGIC OBJECTIVES

Every successful commander fights with a plan, and the enemy of our souls is no exception. Satan wages war with precision, leveraging misinformation, misdirection, and manipulation like a general deploying his forces. His objective is nothing less than the total sabotage of God's purposes in history.

In military language a campaign plan is a coordinated sequence of objectives and actions designed to achieve a commander's strategic end state—not a single battle but the whole series of moves, feints, and follow-throughs that win a war. A campaign plan defines the targets, assigns priorities, times the operations, and anticipates countermoves; it turns scattered skirmishes into a cohesive strategy.[44]

Read this way, the enemy's pattern of deception is not random mischief but a coherent campaign aimed at specific vulnerabilities. What follows is his campaign plan—five strategic objectives that reveal both his methods and his malice. Each objective targets a vital node in God's design: humanity's identity, Israel's covenant witness, the messianic line, the Messiah's mission, and the church's witness. If any of these were compromised, the enemy's cause would advance. Beneath each objective lies the *commander's intent*—a clear and concise expression of the purpose of an operation and the desired end state, the mission statement that

---

44. Joint Chiefs of Staff, *Joint Planning*, II-1.

clarifies what Satan aims to accomplish and therefore what God's people must guard.[45] By studying these objectives, we expose his tactics and learn how to resist them; for every move of deception, God has already prepared a countermeasure rooted in truth.

Objective One: Corrupt the Image of God in Humanity

- *Commander's Intent:* Undermine human identity by erasing the *imago Dei*—replace God-given dignity with empty substitutes.
- *PSYOP Angle:* Attack identity. Redefine humanity's origin and purpose so lesser labels feel normal and corruption becomes culture.

From humanity's first moments on earth, Satan has worked to sabotage God's plan, beginning with his attack on the human race. God created mankind in his own image and likeness, bestowing upon them an identity that reflects his nature and purpose. Ephesians 2:10 (NIV) affirms, "For we are God's handiwork, created in Christ Jesus to do good works, which God prepared in advance for us to do." The *imago Dei* (discussed in chapter 1) distinguishes humans from animals, grants them dominion over the earth (Gen 1:28), and enables communication with their Creator. This moral, social, and intellectual likeness bears God's personal touch. Adam was formed from the dust, and God breathed life into him (Gen 2:7), making humanity distinct in its possession of both material bodies and immaterial souls.

Yet one of Satan's modern strategies is to erode this very foundation through the framework of naturalistic evolution. If humans are explained as products of chance, shaped by blind processes over eons, then their role as image bearers of God is recast as an illusion. As noted in chapter 1, evolution does more than deny a Creator—it reframes existence itself as accidental, stripping humanity of inherent dignity and purpose. In PSYOP terms, this is "reframing the environment": alter the origin story, and every conclusion downstream—about morality, meaning, and accountability—collapses.

Adam and Eve were created "very good" and placed in a world God himself declared "good." Throughout Gen 1, God saw that his creation was good, and on the sixth day, "God saw everything that He had made, and indeed it was very good" (Gen 1:31). Yet Satan tempted them to sin,

---

45. Joint Chiefs of Staff, *Joint Operations*, I-15.

and they yielded, introducing corruption into God's flawless design. From that moment, sin spread like a contagion through their descendants, twisting human desires and distorting God's image in man. The tragic trajectory is clear: what began with disobedience in the garden escalated into a world consumed by violence and rebellion. Genesis 6:5–6 records, "Then the LORD saw that the wickedness of man was great in the earth, and that every intent of the thoughts of his heart was only evil continually. And the LORD was sorry that He had made man on the earth, and He was grieved in His heart." In response, God sent the flood to judge the world's wickedness, sparing only eight individuals. This divine intervention not only displayed God's justice but also thwarted Satan's attempt to corrupt humanity beyond recovery.[46]

Objective Two: Eradicate Israel and Nullify the Covenant

- *Commander's Intent:* Eliminate or discredit Abraham's line to make the covenant look void and Scripture unreliable.
- *PSYOP Angle:* Decapitate the covenant line—attack the community that preserves God's promises so the covenant's credibility is eroded (though providence repeatedly frustrates this aim).

The second objective concerns the nation of Israel. Four thousand years ago, God made a covenant with Abraham, promising him a lasting legacy.

> Now the LORD had said to Abram:
> "Get out of your country,
> From your family
> And from your father's house,
> To a land that I will show you.
> I will make you a great nation;

---

46. A local or symbolic flood fails on multiple levels. Logically, the Genesis narrative emphasizes the destruction of "all flesh" (Gen 6:13) and the covering of "all the high hills under the whole heaven" (Gen 7:19), which a regional flood could not accomplish. Theologically, God's covenant with Noah (Gen 9:11, 15) promises never again to destroy the earth with a flood; if the event were local, God has broken his word countless times since, as regional floods still devastate communities. Scientifically, widespread flood geology—from marine fossils on mountain ranges to massive sedimentary layers extending across continents—points to a catastrophic global deluge, not isolated flooding. The reality of a worldwide flood best explains the biblical text, preserves the integrity of God's covenant, and coheres with observable geological evidence. See Whitcomb and Morris, *Genesis Flood*, 33–54; Snelling, *Earth's Catastrophic Past*, 1:493–522.

> I will bless you
> And make your name great;
> And you shall be a blessing.
> I will bless those who bless you,
> And I will curse him who curses you;
> And in you all the families of the earth shall be blessed."
> (Gen 12:1–3)

If Israel were ever destroyed, God's word would be rendered false, which is precisely why Satan has continually targeted Abraham's descendants. One of the most striking examples appears in the book of Esther, where Haman orchestrates an attempt to eradicate the Jewish people: "To destroy, to kill, and to annihilate all the Jews, both young and old, little children and women, in one day" (Esth 3:12–14). Had Satan succeeded in this plot, the promises God made to Abraham would have been nullified. Yet once again, God intervened, preserving his chosen nation.[47]

The New Testament genealogies underscore this truth. Matthew traces Christ's lineage from Abraham to David to the Messiah (Matt 1:1–17), highlighting God's faithfulness to the covenant line, while Luke carries the genealogy back even further, ultimately to Adam (Luke 3:23–38). These records are not incidental details but living reminders that God's promises to Abraham remained intact across centuries of opposition. Every name preserved in the line is evidence that providence overrules Satan's schemes.

Objective Three: Sever the Messianic Line

- *Commander's Intent:* Disrupt, disqualify, or sever the ancestral line to the Messiah, making prophecy seem unreliable.
- *PSYOP Angle:* Use "gotcha" texts, selective readings, and genealogical confusion to erode confidence in the messianic promise.

Note: God's providence preserves the line—biblical history shows how the promise is vindicated despite every attempt to derail it.

The third objective concerns the messianic lineage, the divinely appointed ancestral line through which the Messiah—Jesus Christ—would come. Since the beginning, Satan has sought to obstruct the arrival of the

---

47. Wishart, "Preservation," 19.

Messiah, knowing that God had declared his plan to judge Satan through Christ (Gen 3:15). The Bible records numerous instances where Satan attempted to sever the messianic line. One of the earliest examples is Cain's murder of Abel, a crime driven by envy and rage. First John 3:12 warns, "Do not be like Cain, who belonged to the evil one and murdered his brother." Yet despite Abel's death, Adam and Eve bore another son, Seth, through whom the messianic lineage continued. Throughout history, Satan's attacks on the promised line failed to halt its progress, as God sovereignly preserved the path leading to Christ.[48]

Another striking example of Satan's interference is the curse of Jeconiah (also called Jehoiachin or Coniah) found in Jer 22. In this passage, God pronounces judgment on the wicked kings of Judah, including Jeconiah—a king whose short reign was marked by rebellion against God and covenant unfaithfulness:

> Thus says the LORD:
> "Write this man down as childless,
> A man who shall not prosper in his days;
> For none of his descendants shall prosper,
> Sitting on the throne of David,
> And ruling anymore in Judah."
> (Jer 22:30)

This curse appears to invalidate Jesus' rightful claim to the Davidic throne—a throne eternally guaranteed by the Davidic covenant. First Chronicles 17:11 and 14 affirms, "I will establish his throne forever. . . . I will establish him in My house and in My kingdom forever; and his throne shall be established forever."

Had Jesus been a descendant of Jeconiah, the curse would have cast a shadow over his rightful place as Messiah, seemingly disqualifying him from the throne of David. Yet in the face of what appeared to be an insurmountable obstacle, God's divine providence provided the solution—a miraculous virgin birth.

Mary, his only human parent, carried the royal bloodline of David, untainted by Jeconiah's judgment (Luke 3:31). Though Joseph held the title of legal father, he was not Jesus' biological parent, ensuring that the curse did not pass to him. In this moment, heaven's design overturned earthly limitation—Satan's scheme to sever the messianic line was once again foiled by God's sovereign hand.

---

48. Wishart, "Preservation," 18.

Through perfect orchestration, Christ fulfilled both legal and bloodline requirements for kingship, untouched by Jeconiah's curse. This was not mere chance—it was divine intervention, a declaration that no opposition, no scheme of darkness, could override God's ultimate will.

Objective Four: Stop the Messiah at the Cross

- *Commander's Intent:* Prevent Christ from accomplishing his mission of redemption—kill, detain, or discredit him before the work is finished.
- *PSYOP Angle:* Declare a false victory early. Hell celebrated the heel-strike as headlines; heaven published the head-crush as history. The cross is the ultimate narrative reversal.

Satan's fourth objective was to prevent Jesus Christ from fulfilling his destiny—to offer himself as the ultimate sacrifice for the salvation of the world. Throughout history, Satan worked to obstruct God's plan, from the massacre of innocent children in Bethlehem (Matt 2:16–18) to the temptation of Jesus in the wilderness. Behind Herod's violent decree to slaughter infants lay Satan's attempt to eliminate the Messiah before his mission even began. Later, in the wilderness, Satan confronted Jesus directly, seeking to divert him from his divine purpose by offering power and dominion in exchange for worship: "And he said to Him, 'All these things I will give You if You will fall down and worship me'" (Matt 4:9). Jesus, unwavering, refused.

In one final, desperate attempt to halt God's redemptive plan, Satan entered Judas Iscariot, ensuring the betrayal that would send Jesus to the cross. The weight of deception, greed, and darkness pressed upon Judas as he turned against the very One who had called him friend. "Then Satan entered Judas, surnamed Iscariot, who was numbered among the twelve" (Luke 22:3). "Now after the piece of bread, Satan entered him. Then Jesus said to him, 'What you do, do quickly'" (John 13:27).

With silver in his grasp and guilt tightening around his throat, Judas set the plan in motion, and the forces of darkness rejoiced, believing they had finally secured their triumph. But they could not comprehend the greater plan unfolding before them.

They saw only the suffering—the blood-stained cross, the broken body—blind to the coming triumph.

As Jesus endured the agony of crucifixion, every lash, every insult, every nail fulfilled what had been foretold. And in his final breath, he did not whisper defeat—he declared victory.

"It is finished!" (John 19:30)—a cry not of surrender but of completion. The debt had been paid in full, sin was conquered, and redemption was sealed.

In that moment, all of Satan's efforts unraveled, his schemes collapsing beneath the weight of divine justice. What he had intended as the final blow against God's plan became his greatest defeat.[49]

Objective Five: Destroy the Church and Corrupt Its Mission

- *Commander's Intent:* If the mission cannot be killed, corrupt the message—seed false teachers, incite division, infiltrate from within, and persecute from without.
- *PSYOP Angle:* Target morale and truth through infiltration, impersonation, and coercion.

The fifth objective concerns the church, the living body of believers whom Jesus established to carry his light into the world. It is more than an institution—it is a movement, a people bound together by faith, shaped by grace, and entrusted with his mission.

In Matt 16:18, Jesus makes a bold, unshakable promise: "And I also say to you that you are Peter, and on this rock I will build My church, and the gates of Hades shall not prevail against it."

These words resound through history, an unbreakable declaration that no force of darkness—no persecution, no deception, no spiritual attack—will ever destroy what he has built.

From the first gathering in the upper room to the present day, the church has stood against waves of opposition—martyrs gave their lives, missionaries ventured into the unknown, and countless believers clung to truth amid oppression. And yet, through every trial, it endured, sustained by the power of Christ himself.

Though Satan wages war against it, though generations rise and fall, the mission continues—faithful followers standing firm, advancing the gospel, ensuring that his message reaches every nation and generation, just as he ordained.

---

49. Wishart, "Preservation," 14.

The church is more than a congregation—it is a testament to Christ's victory, a living reminder that no scheme of the enemy will ever silence God's truth.

Despite Satan's relentless attempts to thwart God's purposes, the mission of Christ prevails. His past efforts to obstruct God's plans have failed, yet his focus remains fixed on the church—the body of believers entrusted with advancing the kingdom of God. This ongoing battle demands unwavering vigilance, as the church stands at the forefront of spiritual warfare.

Every believer steps onto a battlefield unseen yet deeply felt—a relentless clash where truth and deception collide like swords in combat. The forces of darkness advance, whispering half-truths and counterfeit promises, seeking to dismantle faith piece by piece. Yet those clothed in the armor of God stand resolute, wielding the sword of the Spirit to cut through deception with the unyielding edge of divine truth.

Victory is not achieved through passive belief but through unwavering resolve, anchored in Scripture and prayer. The battle rages on, but Christ has already secured the triumph, calling his followers to walk boldly in his truth, unwavering against the enemy's schemes.

At the heart of this mission lies the Great Commission—Christ's direct call for believers to advance God's kingdom and spread his truth to all nations. In Matt 28:19-20, Jesus commands his followers, "Go therefore and make disciples of all the nations, baptizing them in the name of the Father and of the Son and of the Holy Spirit, teaching them to observe all things that I have commanded you; and lo, I am with you always, even to the end of the age."

Through his words, Jesus entrusts the church with a divine mission, reinforcing the urgency of spreading the gospel. We have been given a priceless gift—"the faith which was once for all delivered to the saints" (Jude 1:3). This faith is rooted in God's desire for salvation, as expressed in 1 Tim 2:4: "Who desires all men to be saved and to come to the knowledge of the truth."

The Great Commission compels believers to share this message until it reaches all people. Like the faithful servants in Jesus' parable of the talents (Matt 25:14-30), who wisely invested what their master entrusted to them, the church is called to actively engage in the work of the kingdom. In that parable, Jesus teaches about stewardship, responsibility, and readiness for his return, showing that God expects his people to multiply what he has given rather than bury it. In the same way, the church must

SATAN'S FALL, HIS AMBITIONS, AND HIS POWER

not stand passively by, but make disciples of all nations, carrying forward Christ's mission and ensuring that God's truth is proclaimed across the world.

As stated in Luke 19:13, the church is called to "occupy till I come" (KJV)—a charge not of passive waiting but of active engagement in the spiritual battle. From the very first mention of the church by Jesus, a warning was given—it would face fierce opposition, as Satan would seek to tear it down, corrupt its message, and weaken its foundation.

The attacks have been relentless. Satan has attempted to destroy the church from within, infiltrating its ranks with false teachings: "Now the Spirit expressly says that in latter times some will depart from the faith, giving heed to deceiving spirits and doctrines of demons" (1 Tim 4:1).

He has disguised his own workers, masquerading them as righteous messengers to lead believers astray: "Therefore it is no great thing if his ministers also transform themselves into ministers of righteousness, whose end will be according to their works" (2 Cor 11:15).

He has used persecution, seeking to crush faith through suffering and fear: "Indeed, the devil is about to throw some of you into prison, that you may be tested" (Rev 2:10).

And he has succeeded in tempting believers to sin, using deception to turn hearts away: "But Peter said, 'Ananias, why has Satan filled your heart to lie to the Holy Spirit and keep back part of the price of the land for yourself?'" (Acts 5:3).

Yet despite Satan's unceasing war against the church, history proves that he cannot prevail. The book of Acts and two thousand years of perseverance stand as a testament that, though battered and tested, the mission of Christ endures. Faith is not easily broken, and truth cannot be silenced. What these centuries of struggle reveal is that Satan's tactics are not random—they mirror classic PSYOP techniques: insider threats through false teachers, impersonation through masquerading ministers of righteousness, and coercion through persecution. Each of these attacks runs in parallel, aimed at breaking morale and distorting truth. But just as military forces resist deception by holding fast to reality, the church resists by clinging to Scripture and the Spirit of truth.

For as Revelation proclaims, the battle is far from over:[50]

> And the dragon was enraged with the woman, and he went to make war with the rest of her offspring, who keep the

---

50. Ressa, *Satanic Influences*, 116–38.

commandments of God and have the testimony of Jesus Christ. (Rev 12:17)

This is the enduring battlespace: doctrine, worship, and witness. The church prevails not by better slogans but by Scripture, Spirit-empowered holiness, and stubborn, joyful endurance. Yet even in this war, the church stands firm, unshaken by the enemy's schemes—because its foundation is built on the unshakable rock of Christ.

While Satan's time to target the first four objectives has passed, his war against the church rages on. He knows that the body of believers is Christ's instrument for spreading truth, advancing the gospel, and fulfilling God's kingdom on earth. If he cannot undo the past, he will corrupt the present—striking at the heart of the church with deception, division, and relentless opposition.

Yet despite his efforts, Satan has failed and continues to fail. His schemes crumble against God's sovereign plan, and his ultimate defeat is inevitable. But in his desperate attempt to fight a losing war, he still claims casualties—luring people away from Christ, sowing confusion, and distorting truth. Every deception, every moment of doubt, every believer led astray is a reminder that this battle is far from over.

The remainder of this book series is dedicated to equipping Christians—arming them with spiritual discernment, biblical knowledge, and unwavering conviction to resist Satan's attempts to infiltrate and sway the church.

Throughout history, the Christian church has faced many challenges, often encountering groups that sought to reshape its teachings. One of the earliest and most significant threats was Gnosticism—a movement that mixed Christian beliefs with secretive, mystical philosophies. Gnostics claimed to have hidden spiritual knowledge, often contradicting the message of the Bible and distorting the true gospel.

In response, strong leaders emerged to defend Christian doctrine, ensuring that biblical truth remained intact. One of the most important figures in this battle was Irenaeus of Lyons (c. AD 130–202), a bishop and theologian. He played a crucial role in refuting Gnostic teachings and reinforcing the authority of Scripture. His work, especially his famous text *Against Heresies*, systematically dismantled Gnostic claims and upheld the original teachings passed down from the apostles. By firmly standing against deception, Irenaeus helped preserve the foundational truths of Christianity, ensuring they would be passed on to future generations.[51]

This historical struggle underscores the church's divine calling—not just as a gathering of believers but as a fortified bulwark against spiritual corruption. The war continues, but so does the mission of Christ, unwavering and victorious.[52]

Throughout history, remarkable individuals have stood unwavering in their faith against deception, refusing to compromise truth in the face of adversity. Their courage serves as a beacon for believers today, illuminating the path of discernment and resilience. Recognizing how deception operates—both on a grand scale and in personal faith journeys—strengthens our ability to stand firm.

One such figure is Martin Luther, whose bold defiance of doctrinal falsehood reshaped Christianity. His unwavering commitment to biblical truth and refusal to submit to corrupted teachings offer timeless inspiration in the ongoing spiritual battle for truth.

Luther remains a towering figure in the history of Christianity, celebrated for his bold defiance of doctrinal deception and his unwavering commitment to biblical truth. In 1517, Luther famously nailed his *Ninety-Five Theses* to the door of the Castle Church in Wittenberg, Germany—a symbolic act that ignited the Protestant Reformation. His theses, or set of propositions, challenged the sale of indulgences, a practice whereby the church claimed to offer forgiveness of sins in exchange for monetary payment. Luther viewed this as a grave distortion of Scripture, exploiting the faithful and undermining the foundational Christian principle of salvation by grace through faith alone.

Luther's doctrine of *sola scriptura* (discussed in chapter 1) became the cornerstone of his theological stance. He argued that the Bible, as God's inspired word, was the sole authority for Christian faith and practice, rejecting the notion that human traditions or ecclesiastical decrees could supersede Scripture. This conviction led him to confront the powerful institution of the Roman Catholic Church, risking excommunication—a formal expulsion from the church, severing him from its sacraments and community.

His defiance culminated at the Diet of Worms in 1521, an imperial assembly where he was summoned to defend his teachings before the

---

51. See Irenaeus, *Against Heresies*.
52. Schaff, *Ante-Nicene Christianity*, 566.

Holy Roman Emperor Charles V. When pressured to recant, Luther famously declared, "Here I stand, I can do no other. God help me. Amen."[53]

This moment epitomized his courage and steadfastness in the face of overwhelming opposition, solidifying his role as a leader in the Protestant Reformation.

Luther's actions not only exposed the spiritual deception of his time but also paved the way for profound theological and societal transformation. By translating the Bible into German, he made Scripture accessible to ordinary people, empowering them to read and interpret God's word for themselves. His work inspired generations of believers to seek truth and resist falsehood, demonstrating that faith rooted in Scripture can overcome even the most entrenched systems of deception.[54]

Luther's example proves that truth prevails, but it also serves as a reminder that the spiritual battle is never over. Just as deception threatened the early church, it continues today—reshaping itself to fit the cultural and ideological challenges of the modern world. While Christianity remains a powerful force globally, its influence is waning in key regions, particularly in the US and Europe, where secularism is rising at an alarming rate.

Pew Research predicts that if the current trend continues, less than half of Americans will identify as Christian within the next fifty years.[55] The situation in the UK is even more dire, with only 28 percent of respondents affirming belief in God or a higher power.[56] UK church membership has plummeted from 10.6 million in 1930 to just 5.5 million in 2010, dropping from about 30 percent of the population to 11.2 percent. By 2013, this number fell further to 5.4 million (10.3 percent), and if trends persist, church membership is expected to decline to 8.4 percent by 2025.[57] These numbers are not merely statistics; they are indicators of a spiritual landscape where the enemy's strategy appears to be gaining ground. Decline in affiliation translates to decline in discipleship, worship, and witness—making the urgency of discernment and faithful perseverance all the more pressing.

This erosion of faith is not accidental; it reflects the same age-old schemes of Satan, who continues to claim casualties by luring people

---

53. Bainton, *Here I Stand*, 55–57.
54. Wiersbe, *On Being a Leader*, 39.
55. Kramer et al., "Modeling the Future."
56. Field, "Counting Religion in Britain."
57. Brierley, *UK Church Statistics*, 1–7.

away from Christ and working tirelessly to thwart God's plan. However, just as in Luther's time, the call remains the same—to stand firm, vigilant, and unyielding in the face of deception, ensuring that the truth of the gospel endures despite opposition.

Limited but Lethal: The Scope of Satan's Power

While they are not as powerful as God, Satan and his demon army are real, active forces in the spiritual realm, working to obstruct and deceive. Scripture repeatedly warns of their influence. Paul describes Satan as "the prince of the power of the air" (Eph 2:2) and "the god of this world" (2 Cor 4:4). Jesus himself acknowledges Satan's dominion, calling him "the ruler of this world" (John 12:31, 14:30) and condemning him as "a murderer, a liar, and the father of lies" (John 8:44). Revelation 12:9-10 further exposes his schemes, describing him as the one who "deceives the whole world" and "accuses the brethren before God day and night."

When theologians speak of "Satan's dominion," they do not mean that he holds ultimate power but rather that he influences the fallen world, shaping its values and culture through deception. Think of it like a corrupt ruler controlling a broken system—he does not govern everything, but his influence distorts truth and leads people astray. That's why Paul calls him "the god of this world"—his deception blinds many from seeing the light of Christ.

Yet his power is temporary and limited. Christ's victory has already sealed his fate, ensuring that Satan's dominion will ultimately crumble under the weight of divine justice.

Even Satan's names reveal his nature. The title *Satan* means "adversary," while *Devil* translates to "accuser" or "slanderer."[58] From the very beginning, deception has been his primary weapon. In Gen 3, he appears as the serpent who deceives Eve, leading humanity into sin. Paul reminds believers in Eph 6:12 that our real battle is not against flesh and blood but against unseen spiritual forces in heavenly places—forces that, though immaterial, actively influence the physical world. As evidenced throughout Scripture, demons can interact with humans, sometimes through possession, illness, or unusual behavior, seeking to manipulate and destroy. Here are just a few examples:

---

58. Storms, *Understanding Spiritual Warfare*, 108.

> Now there was a man in their synagogue with an unclean spirit. And he cried out, saying, "Let us alone! What have we to do with You, Jesus of Nazareth? Did You come to destroy us? I know who You are—the Holy One of God!" But Jesus rebuked him, saying, "Be quiet, and come out of him!" And when the unclean spirit had convulsed him and cried out with a loud voice, he came out of him. (Mark 1:23-26)

> And when He had come out of the boat, immediately there met Him out of the tombs a man with an unclean spirit, who had his dwelling among the tombs; and no one could bind him, not even with chains, because he had often been bound with shackles and chains. And the chains had been pulled apart by him, and the shackles broken in pieces; neither could anyone tame him. And always, night and day, he was in the mountains and in the tombs, crying out and cutting himself with stones. (Mark 5:2-5)

> Now when He rose early on the first day of the week, He appeared first to Mary Magdalene, out of whom He had cast seven demons. (Mark 16:9)

Satan and his demonic followers certainly have direct ways of influencing individuals, but their most insidious and far-reaching strategy is deception. Rather than always working in obvious manifestations, they weave their influence through non-Christian belief systems, cultural movements, political structures, and media platforms—all carefully orchestrated to oppose God's truth and derail his mission. Through these avenues, they subtly distort morality, undermine faith, and promote ideologies that lead people further from God, creating a world that unknowingly advances Satan's rebellion against divine authority.[59]

Humans do not fully understand the complexities of the spiritual world or how Satan and his demons interact with humankind, but Scripture provides insight into their nature and power. Psalm 103:20 declares that angels "excel in strength," while 2 Pet 2:11 affirms that angels are "greater in power and might" than humans. Since Satan and his demons are fallen angels, we can infer that they possess significant strength. However, their power remains subject to God's sovereign authority, as he states in Isa 45:7: "I form the light and create darkness, I make peace and create calamity."

Contrary to common misconceptions, Satan is neither omniscient nor omnipresent—he does not know everything, nor can he

---

59. Carson, "Spiritual Warfare," 253-54.

SATAN'S FALL, HIS AMBITIONS, AND HIS POWER

be everywhere at once. If he were omniscient, he would be God. First Corinthians 2:6–8 provides a relevant perspective: "However, we speak wisdom among those who are mature, yet not the wisdom of this age, nor of the rulers of this age, who are coming to nothing. But we speak the wisdom of God in a mystery . . . which none of the rulers of this age knew; for had they known, they would not have crucified the Lord of glory." This passage indicates that Satan and the spiritual forces opposed to Christ lacked full knowledge of God's redemptive plan—proof that their understanding is limited. Furthermore, nowhere in Scripture does it suggest that Satan possesses omnipresence. While his influence is widespread, he cannot be in all places at once.

A key takeaway is that while Satan wields significant power in the spiritual realm, his authority is ultimately restricted by God. Through Christ, believers are equipped to resist his schemes and stand firm against his attacks. Nevertheless, Satan does not act alone. His army of demons actively supports his deceptive initiatives, ensuring that his influence reaches across nations and generations. This is why humans must never attempt to oppose Satan using their own strength alone—our power is insufficient against such forces without the protection and authority of God.[60]

This battle between deception and divine wisdom is beautifully illustrated in Moritz Retzsch's *The Chess Players*, a powerful painting depicting a young man locked in a chess match with the devil, seemingly on the brink of defeat. The devil, confident in his victory, leans forward with a sinister grin, believing he has secured the soul of his opponent. The young man, overwhelmed by despair, appears to have no way out.

Yet, the story behind the painting reveals a profound truth—one that echoes throughout Scripture. While *The Chess Players* was displayed in the Louvre, a chess master closely examined the board and discovered that the young man was not actually defeated. The king still had one more move.[61]

This revelation serves as a powerful metaphor for the Christian life. Satan may believe he has won, that he has ensnared us in deception, fear, or hopelessness. But God, the true King, always has another move. No matter how dire our circumstances may seem, no matter how trapped we feel, God's sovereignty remains unshaken. He is in control, and his plan for redemption cannot be thwarted.

---

60. Grudem, *Systematic Theology*, 412–15.
61. Harrison, "Statement."

This truth aligns perfectly with the message of 1 Cor 2:6–8—Satan and the rulers of this age lacked full knowledge of God's redemptive plan. Had they understood, they would not have crucified Christ. But their blindness to God's wisdom only served to fulfill his greater purpose. Just as the young man in *The Chess Players* was not truly defeated, neither are we. Through Christ, we have victory over deception, sin, and spiritual oppression.

Strategically, that "one more move" is the enemy's blind spot: God's sovereignty. It breaks every predictive model built on pride and partial data (1 Cor 2:6–8).

The spiritual influence of this satanic force is strikingly revealed in Dan 10. After praying and fasting for three weeks, Daniel encounters an angel, who explains that he was dispatched in response to Daniel's prayer but was delayed due to opposition from "the prince of the kingdom of Persia" (Dan 10:13). Only with the assistance of Michael, one of God's archangels, was the angel able to break through the spiritual obstruction to deliver God's message.[62] This passage offers a rare glimpse into the hidden battle between angelic and demonic forces, highlighting the strength and breadth of the adversary's power.[63]

Up to this point, we've mapped the adversary's doctrine of deception—the why and the what. What remains is tradecraft: how to spot, test, and neutralize it at speed.

The second and third books in this series further expand on the foundations laid here. Volume 2 examines the techniques used to mislead believers into accepting distorted versions of Christian salvation. Volume 3 outlines tested methods for remaining on the correct path and recognizing the dangers of false prophets, doctrines, and teachers.

Ultimately, Satan's fall, ambitions, and power reveal the complexities of spiritual warfare. His tactics are calculated—woven with deception, exploiting trust, and leading countless souls into ruin.

But deception operates not just in the spiritual realm but in everyday life, preying on human vulnerability and misplaced trust. Consider the collapse of Enron, once hailed as one of America's most innovative companies. Behind glowing reports and soaring stock prices lay a web of accounting fraud that eventually wiped out billions in savings and pensions. What appeared prosperous was, in reality, hollow—a façade of

---

62. See 2 Kgs 6:17 for the reality of the unseen spiritual world.
63. Longman, "Daniel," 178–83.

success built on lies. This mirrors Satan's modus operandi—offering false promises, disguising destruction as prosperity, and leading people away from God's truth under the guise of security.

But deception doesn't just affect financial trust—it affects spiritual faith. Just as corporate fraud lures investors into a false sense of gain, spiritual deception subtly persuades people to abandon what is real for what merely looks appealing.

Recognizing deception is only the first step. Believers must actively resist it, standing firm against every scheme designed to separate them from God. This is not a battle of passive awareness but of deliberate resistance, ensuring victory in the ongoing war for truth.

To discern and expose Satan's strategies is to reclaim ground—to stand firm, unwavering in the truth of Scripture and strengthened by the power of Christ. As this volume concludes, the battle does not. Satan's schemes have been unveiled, but awareness alone is not enough. The next step is action—applying biblical wisdom to recognize and counter his psychological operations.

Volume 1 has mapped the terrain of deception: identifying truth as the ultimate target, tracing Satan's reframing tactics through history, culture, philosophy, and even the denial of our design in God's image. From battlefield misdirection to digital algorithms, from prosperity preaching to evolutionary ideology, the strategy is the same: obscure the Creator by distorting his truth. With Satan's fall and ambitions exposed, the first phase of this series concludes. The war for truth, however, is not finished.

Volume 2 shifts from reconnaissance to analysis of the enemy's playbook—tracing deceptive PSYOP across biblical history and revealing how Scripture exposes the adversary's tactics. In other words, it functions as a biblical intelligence manual: identify the pattern of deception, observe how biblical figures responded, extract God-given principles of discernment, and watch how truth consistently dismantles the lie.

Though the war continues, so does our victory in Christ—for God's truth remains unshaken, illuminating the path forward for all who seek it. The battlefield is real, but so is the victory of Christ. What lies ahead is not merely defense but confidence—walking in truth that cannot be shaken.

Unveiling Deception

PERSONAL APPLICATION: UNDERSTANDING AND RESISTING THE ENEMY

Chapter 5 provides a vital foundation for understanding Satan's nature, ambitions, and tactics in spiritual warfare. Recognizing his strategies is only the first step—true victory comes through active resistance, standing firm against deception, and living in alignment with God's truth. Here's how to apply these insights:

1. *Know Your Enemy*—A skilled warrior understands the mind of his opponent. Military leaders like Sun Tzu emphasized that knowing one's adversary sharpens defenses. Likewise, believers must discern Satan's schemes, recognizing that this battle is spiritual, not physical (Eph 6:12). Awareness of the enemy's tactics, temptations, and deception strengthens our ability to stand firm.

2. *Stand Firm in the Victory of Christ*—While Satan wields power, Scripture affirms that his authority is limited and his defeat was sealed by Christ's work on the cross (Col 2:15). In moments of spiritual attack, believers must cling to the truth—Christ has already overcome, and no force of darkness can undo his victory.

3. *Guard Against Pride*—Pride led to Satan's downfall, and he now uses the same temptation to lead people astray (Isa 14:13–14). Reflect on areas in your life where pride may be a subtle distraction, distorting humility and reliance on God. Ask him for wisdom and guidance to keep your heart aligned with his will.

4. *Equip Yourself Daily*—No soldier enters battle unarmed. Ephesians 6:10–18 outlines the armor of God, essential for confronting spiritual warfare. The shield of faith deflects lies, the helmet of salvation guards the mind, and the sword of the Spirit—God's word—is the ultimate weapon against darkness.

5. *Pray for Spiritual Discernment*—Deception thrives in subtlety. Satan rarely presents obvious lies—he twists the truth just enough to make falsehoods seem reasonable. Pray for divine wisdom to expose deceit, both in personal struggles and in the world around you. James 1:5 promises that God grants wisdom to those who seek it.

6. *Stay Rooted in Scripture*—Satan seeks to distract, distort, and weaken devotion to God's word. Yet Scripture is the believer's unshakable foundation. Make a habit of memorizing verses that affirm God's

power, truth, and victory, such as 1 John 4:4 and Rom 8:37. When deception arises, the word becomes your defense.

Spiritual warfare is never passive—it requires constant vigilance, like a soldier navigating hostile terrain. Believers must be equipped and alert, discerning truth from deception, standing firm against every scheme of the enemy.

Every decision carries weight—what news you trust, the voices you listen to, how you distinguish truth from distortion. Just as misinformation manipulates thoughts and actions, spiritual deception subtly influences faith. Without an anchor in Scripture and prayer, confusion can overtake clarity, and doubt can erode conviction.

In our culture, prayer is often referenced in vague or generalized ways. Popular culture sometimes echoes biblical-sounding phrases without grounding them in Christ. For example, actor Mark Wahlberg often uses the tagline "Stay prayed up." While it encourages prayer in general, it does not specify who that prayer is directed to—leaving the door open to vague spirituality, saints, Mary, or rituals like the rosary. Scripture, however, makes clear that prayer is powerful only when rooted in the name of Jesus Christ, the sole Mediator between God and man (1 Tim 2:5). To be "prayed up" is not about a generic posture of religiosity but about continual dependence on Christ, in whose authority alone our prayers are heard.

This distinction matters: prayer that is detached from Christ is merely religious sentiment, but prayer in Christ's name is spiritual warfare grounded in truth.

The battle is relentless, but so is God's power. Every believer must wear the full armor of God, ensuring they remain steadfast against deception. Spiritual warfare is not just knowing the enemy exists—it is actively resisting him, armed with faith, truth, and discernment.

Just as a soldier must discern between ally and adversary, believers must cultivate spiritual awareness, navigating a world of false narratives and deceptive influences. Through Scripture, prayer, and wisdom, they sharpen their ability to stand against Satan's lies.

Though the battle rages on, victory is already secured through Christ. By standing resolute, equipped with divine truth, you are prepared to face opposition and walk steadfastly in the light of God's word.

Personal Reflection

1. How has your understanding of Satan's origin and role changed after reading this chapter?
2. In what ways do you see Satan's ambition—"to be like God"—reflected in the attitudes or systems of today's world?
3. Have you ever underestimated the enemy's power or influence in your own life? How did that affect your spiritual walk?
4. What steps are you taking to remain spiritually vigilant against the enemy's schemes?

Group Discussion

1. What are some common misconceptions people have about Satan's nature, power, and limits? How can we correct these using Scripture?
2. How does knowing Satan's downfall and limited power shape your confidence in spiritual warfare?
3. The chapter emphasizes that Satan operates through deception. What are some deceptive narratives you've encountered in culture, education, or media?
4. How can your group develop a stronger sense of spiritual preparedness and unity in resisting the enemy?

Scripture Connection

- Read Isa 14:12–15 and Ezek 28:12–17. What do these passages teach about Satan's fall and motivations?
- Reflect on Jas 4:7 and Rom 16:20. What hope and instruction do these verses offer for resisting spiritual attack?

The battle between truth and deception is ongoing, but it is not one we face alone. Scripture equips us with wisdom, prayer strengthens our resolve, and Christ himself has already secured victory. As believers, we are called to stand firm, not just in knowledge but in active resistance—rejecting falsehood, confronting deception, and clinging to the unchanging truth of God's word.

Spiritual warfare demands awareness, discernment, and courage, but above all, it requires unshakable trust in God's promises. No attack from the enemy can override his sovereignty, and no darkness can extinguish the light of Christ's redemption.

As you move forward, reflect on the lessons of this chapter, apply them to your daily life, and walk boldly in faith, knowing that God has already overcome. The call to vigilance remains, but so does the assurance of victory—for those who remain steadfast in him. For deception may grow louder, but it cannot undo what Christ has secured. His Spirit guides believers into all truth (John 16:13), his hand protects them from the enemy's grasp (John 10:28), and sanctification builds a wisdom that no lie can withstand (Heb 5:14). In Christ, victory is not just promised—it is already won.

About the Author

JONATHAN K. CORRADO is a Bible scholar whose extensive background in the military and defense industry gives him a unique perspective. He connects Satan's deceptive strategies with military psychological operations (PSYOP), developing counter-PSYOP methods that help Christians recognize and resist deception, engaging in spiritual battle and living the life God intends. As Scripture says, "For we wrestle not against flesh and blood, but against principalities, against powers, against the rulers of the darkness of this world, against spiritual wickedness in high places" (Eph 6:12).

Corrado served over two decades in the US Navy, active and reserve, attaining the rank of captain (O-6). His assignments spanned shipboard operations, aircraft carrier nuclear plant management, amphibious warfare, military intelligence, and joint operations. He holds qualifications as a surface warfare officer, nuclear engineering officer, and Seabee combat warfare officer, and completed five deployments at sea and in ground combat theaters.

Beyond the Navy, he worked in the defense industry and at a Department of Defense laboratory, overseeing sensitive programs in cyber warfare, covert communications, and clandestine electronics. His direct involvement in military deception and PSYOP further deepened his expertise.

His academic credentials include a BS in mechanical engineering from the Virginia Military Institute, an MEM from Old Dominion University, and a PhD in systems engineering from Colorado State University. He also holds theological degrees from Nations University and Liberty University (MTS, MDiv, ThM). He is a graduate of the Navy Nuclear Power Program, Naval Postgraduate School, Joint Forces Staff College, US Air Force Command and Staff College, and US Air Force War College, and is licensed as a professional engineer in Ohio. An adjunct professor

ABOUT THE AUTHOR

of engineering at Liberty University, he invests in the next generation of leaders by integrating faith, scholarship, and real-world application.

Corrado's research interests include theology, apologetics, creation science, nuclear and systems engineering, human performance, and military affairs. He has authored numerous refereed journal articles and books and contributes regularly to *Creation Magazine* and the Institute for Creation Research's Creation Science Update. A passionate defender of the faith, he has a heart for apologetics and longs to help believers love God with both heart and mind, standing confident in the truth of Scripture.

While his résumé reflects years of rigorous training and worldly accomplishments, Corrado's deepest passion is not in titles or degrees but in pointing people to Christ. He views every chapter of his life as part of God's classroom for shaping a servant of the kingdom. Each trial and triumph has been used by the Lord to deepen his faith and sharpen his mission. As the apostle Paul wrote, "But whatever gain I had, I counted as loss for the sake of Christ. Indeed, I count everything as loss because of the surpassing worth of knowing Christ Jesus my Lord" (Phil 3:7–8).

Corrado lives with an urgency to help believers see through the fog of deception that clouds today's world. He longs for Christians to stand firm on the unshakable truth of God's word, to develop the discernment needed to resist the enemy's schemes, and to live courageously for the gospel in a culture bent on compromise. His calling is not merely to teach ideas but to rally the church to active, Spirit-empowered faith.

For Corrado, fulfilling his kingdom purpose means equipping others to wage spiritual warfare with confidence, clarity, and hope. His zeal is contagious: he speaks and writes with the conviction that victory is already secured in Christ and that every believer is called to live boldly as a light in the darkness.

Corrado resides in Cincinnati, Ohio, with his wife, Erin, and their four children—Vince, Bentley, Naomi, and Scarlett—where they cherish family, faith, and service to their local church.

Bibliography

Abagnale, Frank W. *The Art of the Steal: How to Protect Yourself and Your Business from Fraud*. New York: Broadway, 2001.
Abagnale, Frank W., and Stan Redding. *Catch Me If You Can: The True Story of a Real Fake*. New York: Broadway, 2000.
Abanes, Richard. *One Nation Under Gods: A History of the Mormon Church*. New York: Four Walls Eight Windows, 2002.
Abdel Haleem, M. A. S., trans. *The Qur'an*. Oxford: Oxford University Press, 2004.
Adams, John. "From John Adams to Hezekiah Niles, 13 February 1818." Founders Online, National Archives. https://founders.archives.gov/documents/Adams/99-02-02-6854.
Ady, Thomas. *A Candle in the Dark*. London, 1656.
Akin, Jimmy. "The Limits of Scripture Interpretation." Catholic Answers, Jan. 1, 2001. https://www.catholic.com/magazine/print-edition/the-limits-of-scripture-interpretation.
Allen, James Peter. *Middle Egyptian: An Introduction to the Language and Culture of Hieroglyphs*. 3rd ed. Cambridge: Cambridge University Press, 2014.
Allison, Gregg R. *Roman Catholic Theology and Practice: An Evangelical Assessment*. Wheaton, IL: Crossway, 2014.
Anderson, Thea L., et al. "Contributing Factors to the Rise in Adolescent Anxiety and Depression." *Journal of Child and Adolescent Psychiatric Nursing* 38 (2024): e70009. https://pmc.ncbi.nlm.nih.gov/articles/PMC11683866/.
Anselm of Canterbury. *Proslogion*. Translated by Thomas Williams. Indianapolis: Hackett, 2001.
Aquinas, Thomas. *Summa Theologica*. Translated by the Fathers of the English Dominican Province. New York: Benziger, 1947.
Augustine. *The Retractations*. Translated by Mary Inez Bogan. Fathers of the Church 60. Washington, DC: Catholic University of America Press, 1968.
———. *Tractates on the Gospel of John: 112–24*. Translated by John W. Rettig. Fathers of the Church 92. Washington, DC: Catholic University of America Press, 1995.
Bainton, Roland H. *Here I Stand: A Life of Martin Luther*. New York: Abingdon, 1950.
Baker, R. A. *How the New Testament Canon Was Formed*. Church History 101, 2008. https://www.churchhistory101.com/docs/New-Testament-Canon.pdf.
Balestrieri, Annalisa. "How Music Lyrics Shape Our Behaviour and Psychology." Psychreg, Nov. 6, 2023. https://www.psychreg.org/how-music-behaviour-shape-psychology/.

Barna, George. *American Worldview Inventory 2024: Release #1—Biblical Worldview Trends Among Christian Believers*. Glendale, AZ: Cultural Research Center at Arizona Christian University, 2024.

Barnard, Sandy. *George Armstrong Custer: A Military Life*. Pierre, SD: South Dakota Historical Society, 2021.

Barnett, John. "Sober Minded—Choosing Restrained Living in an Unrestrained Culture." DTBM, Aug. 1, 2018. https://dtbm.org/sober-minded-choosing-restrained-living-in-an-un-restrained-culture/.

Barradas, Gonçalo T., and Laura S. Sakka. "When Words Matter: A Cross-Cultural Perspective on Lyrics and Musical Emotion." *Psychology of Music* 50 (2022) 650–69. https://doi.org/10.1177/03057356211013390.

Barrick, William D. "Ancient Manuscripts and Biblical Exposition." *Master's Seminary Journal* 9 (1998) 25–38. https://tms.edu/wp-content/uploads/2021/09/tmsj9b.pdf.

Bateson, Patrick, et al. "New Trends in Evolutionary Biology: Biological, Philosophical and Social Science Perspectives." *Interface Focus* 7 (2017) e20170051. https://doi.org/10.1098/rsfs.2017.0051.

Baucham, Voddie. "Why I Believe the Bible." Posted Jan. 27, 2014 by Chris J. YouTube video, 31:38. https://www.youtube.com/watch?v=15E0R6O-rUA.

Bauckham, Richard. *Jesus and the Eyewitnesses: The Gospels as Eyewitness Testimony*. Grand Rapids: Eerdmans, 2006.

Bauer, Joseph. "Biblical Preservation: Examining the Historical Preservation of the Biblical Text Through the Providence of God." *Diligence: Journal of the Liberty University Online Religion Capstone in Research and Scholarship* 1 (2016) article 18. https://digitalcommons.liberty.edu/djrc/vol1/iss1/18.

Bauer, Walter, et al. *A Greek-English Lexicon of the New Testament and Other Early Christian Literature*. 3rd ed. Chicago: University of Chicago Press, 2000.

Bay, Michael, dir. *Armageddon*. Burbank, CA: Buena Vista, 1998.

Beck, Julie. "The Church of CrossFit." *Atlantic*, June 24, 2017. https://www.theatlantic.com/health/archive/2017/06/the-church-of-crossfit/531501/.

Beckwith, Roger T. *The Old Testament Canon of the New Testament Church and Its Background in Early Judaism*. Grand Rapids: Eerdmans, 1985.

Begg, Alistair. "The Power and Message of the Cross." Truth for Life, June 28, 2022. Sermon excerpt from Baylor University National Preaching Conference, 2019. https://blog.truthforlife.org/the-man-on-the-middle-cross-said-i-can-come.

Bellshaw, William G. "The New Testament Doctrine of Satan." *Grace Theological Journal* 9.3 (1968) 24–39.

Bergsma, John. *Bible Basics for Catholics*. Notre Dame, IN: Ave Maria, 2012.

Bergsma, John, and Brant Pitre. *A Catholic Introduction to the Bible: Old Testament*. San Francisco: Ignatius, 2018.

Berman, Karen, and Joe Knight. "What Did Bernard Madoff Do?" *Harvard Business Review*, June 30, 2009. https://hbr.org/2009/06/what-did-bernard-madoff-do.

Berridge, Kent C., and Terry E. Robinson. "Parsing Reward." *Trends in Neurosciences* 26 (2003) 507–13. https://doi.org/10.1016/S0166-2236(03)00233-9.

Bilton, Nick. "Steve Jobs Was a Low-Tech Parent." *New York Times*, Sept. 10, 2014. https://www.nytimes.com/2014/09/11/fashion/steve-jobs-apple-was-a-low-tech-parent.html.

Biran, Avraham. *Biblical Dan*. Washington, DC: Biblical Archaeology Society, 1994.

Bist, Dinesh, et al. "Music and Spirituality: An Auto-Ethnographic Study of How Five Individuals Used Music to Enrich Their Soul." *Religions* 15 (2024) 858. https://doi.org/10.3390/rel15070858.

Blomberg, Craig L. *The Historical Reliability of the Gospels*. 2nd ed. Downers Grove, IL: InterVarsity, 2007.

Boghardt, Thomas. *Operation INFEKTION: Soviet Bloc Intelligence and Its AIDS Disinformation Campaign*. Washington, DC: Center for the Study of Intelligence, 2009.

Bowler, Kate. *Blessed: A History of the American Prosperity Gospel*. Oxford: Oxford University Press, 2013.

Boylan, Anne M. *Sunday School: The Formation of an American Institution, 1790–1880*. New Haven: Yale University Press, 1988.

Boyle, Robert. *The Christian Virtuoso*. London: J. Taylor, 1690.

Bracher, Karl. *The German Dictatorship*. New York: Holt, Rinehart & Winston, 1970.

Brecht, Martin. *Martin Luther: The Preservation of the Church*. Minneapolis: Fortress, 1993.

Brierley, Peter. *Introduction: UK Church Statistics 2; 2010–2020*. Tonbridge: ADBC, 2014. https://faithsurvey.co.uk/download/csintro2.pdf.

Brodie, Fawn M. *No Man Knows My History: The Life of Joseph Smith*. New York: Knopf, 1945.

Brody, Debra J., and Jeffery P. Hughes. "Depression Prevalence in Adolescents and Adults: United States, August 2021–August 2023." NCHS Data Brief no. 527 (2025) 1–11. https://www.cdc.gov/nchs/data/databriefs/db527.pdf.

Brooke, John Hedley. "Darwin and God: Then and Now." *Harvard Divinity Bulletin*, 2006. https://bulletin.hds.harvard.edu/darwin-and-god-then-and-now/.

Brown, Dan. *The Da Vinci Code*. New York: Doubleday, 2003.

Browning, Christopher R. *The Origins of the Final Solution: The Evolution of Nazi Jewish Policy, September 1939–March 1942*. Lincoln: University of Nebraska Press, 2004.

Bruce, F. F. *The Canon of Scripture*. Downers Grove, IL: InterVarsity, 1988.

———. *The New Testament Documents: Are They Reliable?* Grand Rapids: Eerdmans, 2003.

Buckley, Theodore Alois, trans. *Canons and Decrees of the Council of Trent*. London: George Routledge and Co., 1851.

Bullinger, E. W. *Figures of Speech Used in the Bible: Explained and Illustrated*. New York: E. & J. B. Young, 1898.

Butterfield, Rosaria. *The Secret Thoughts of an Unlikely Convert: An English Professor's Journey into Christian Faith*. Pittsburgh: Crown & Covenant, 2012.

Caldwell, Simon. "Dr. Michael Nazir-Ali, Former Anglican Bishop of Rochester, Joins the Catholic Church." *Catholic Herald*, Oct. 14, 2021. https://thecatholicherald.com/article/dr-michael-nazir-ali-former-anglican-bishop-of-rochester-joins-the-catholic-church.

Callender, Gae. *Egyptian Temples*. London: Routledge, 2000.

Calvin, John. *Institutes of the Christian Religion*. Translated by Henry Beveridge. Peabody, MA: Hendrickson, 2008.

———. *Zechariah and Malachi*. Vol. 5 of *Commentaries on the Twelve Minor Prophets*. Translated by John Owen. Grand Rapids: Eerdmans, 1950.

Carson, D. A. *Exegetical Fallacies*. 2nd ed. Grand Rapids: Baker Academic, 1996.

———. "God, the Bible and Spiritual Warfare: A Review Article." *Journal of the Evangelical Theological Society* 42 (1999) 251–69.

———. *The Gospel According to John*. Pillar New Testament Commentary. Grand Rapids: Eerdmans, 1991.

———. "Matthew." In *Expositor's Bible Commentary*, rev. ed., edited by Tremper Longman III and David E. Garland, 9:23–670. Grand Rapids: Zondervan, 2010.

Carswell, John. *The South Sea Bubble*. London: Cresset, 1960.

Carter, Joe. "The State of Theology: What Evangelicals Believe in 2022." The Gospel Coalition, Sept. 22, 2022. https://www.thegospelcoalition.org/article/state-theology-2022/.

Catechism of the Catholic Church. 2nd ed. Washington, DC: United States Conference of Catholic Bishops, 1997.

Catholic Answers. "Has the Magisterium Only Definitively Interpreted Five or Six Passages of Scripture?" https://www.catholic.com/qa/has-the-magisterium-only-definitively-interpreted-five-or-six-passages-of-scripture.

———. "Relics." Last modified Jan. 4, 2016. https://www.catholic.com/tract/relics.

Chadwick, Henry. "Diocletian and the Great Persecution; Rise of Constantine." In *The Church in Ancient Society: From Galilee to Gregory the Great*, 176–89. Oxford: Oxford University Press, 2001.

———. *The Early Church*. Rev. ed. London: Penguin, 1993.

Chadwick, Samuel. *The Way to Pentecost*. London: Hodder & Stoughton, 1932.

Chesterton, G. K. *The Everlasting Man*. New York: Macmillan, 1925.

Chryssides, George D. *The Advent of Sun Myung Moon: The Origins, Beliefs and Practices of the Unification Church*. New York: St. Martin's, 1991.

The Church of Jesus Christ of Latter-day Saints. *Doctrine and Covenants*. Salt Lake City, UT: The Church of Jesus Christ of Latter-day Saints, 1979.

———. *Gospel Principles*. Salt Lake City, UT: The Church of Jesus Christ of Latter-day Saints, 2011.

The Church Will Sing. "Make Room." Track 2 on The Church Will Sing, *Volume 2*. Featuring Elyssa Smith and Community Music. Community Music, 2020.

Cohn, Norman. *Warrant for Genocide: The Myth of the Jewish World-Conspiracy and the Protocols of the Elders of Zion*. London: Eyre & Spottiswoode, 1967.

Collins, Pamela Y., et al. "Making Cities Mental Health Friendly for Adolescents and Young Adults." *Nature* 627 (2024) 137–48. https://doi.org/10.1038/s41586-023-07005-4.

Copernicus, Nicolaus. *On the Revolutions of the Celestial Spheres*. Translated by Charles Glenn Wallis. Amherst, NY: Prometheus, 1995.

Cornwell, John. *Hitler's Pope: The Secret History of Pius XII*. New York: Viking, 1999.

Corrado, Jonathan K. *Defying Deception: A Field Guide to Understanding and Countering Satan's Strategy of Deception*. Eugene, OR: Wipf and Stock, 2024.

———. "God Perfectly Keeps His Promises." *Baptist Bulletin*, 2023. https://baptistbulletin.org/the-baptist-bulletin-magazine/god-perfectly-keeps-his-promises/.

———. "Imago Dei: Man's Designed Role as Image-Bearer." Institute for Creation Research, Apr. 25, 2022. https://www.icr.org/article/mans-designed-role.

———. "The Importance of Context in Sound Biblical Interpretation." Institute for Creation Research, Jan. 9, 2023. https://www.icr.org/article/importance-of-context-in-sound/.

———. "Is There Evidence for a Creator?" Institute for Creation Research, Feb. 26, 2024. https://www.icr.org/article/evidence-for-creator.
———. "The Role and Realm of Science." Institute for Creation Research, Jan. 17, 2022. https://www.icr.org/article/role-and-realm-of-science.
Costigan, Richard F. *The Consensus of the Church and Papal Infallibility: A Study in the Background of Vatican I*. Washington, DC: Catholic University of America, 2005.
Creemers, Rogier. "China's Social Credit System: An Evolving Practice of Control." *SSRN Electronic Journal* (2018). https://doi.org/10.2139/ssrn.3175792.
Crumm, Robin K. *Information Warfare: An Air Force Policy for the Role of Public Affairs*. Master's thesis, Air University, 1996.
Cruz, Nicky. *Run Baby Run*. Old Tappan, NJ: Chosen, 1968.
Cullmann, Oscar. *Peter: Disciple, Apostle, Martyr*. London: SCM, 1962.
Curtin, Sally C., and Matthew F. Garnett. "Suicide and Homicide Death Rates Among Youth and Young Adults Aged 10–24: United States, 2001–2021." NCHS Data Brief no. 471 (2023). https://www.cdc.gov/nchs/products/databriefs/db471.htm.
Curtis, Glenn. *An Overview of Psychological Operations (PSYOP)*. Washington, DC: Library of Congress Federal Research Division, 1989. https://apps.dtic.mil/sti/pdfs/ADA302389.pdf.
Dalin, David G. *The Myth of Hitler's Pope: How Pope Pius XII Rescued Jews from the Nazis*. Washington, DC: Regnery, 2005.
Darwin, Charles. *On the Origin of Species by Means of Natural Selection, or the Preservation of Favoured Races in the Struggle for Life*. 1st ed. London: John Murray, 1859.
Davico, Chiara, et al. "COVID-19 Pandemic School Disruptions and Acute Mental Health in Children and Adolescents." *JAMA Network Open* 7 (2024): e2425829. https://pubmed.ncbi.nlm.nih.gov/39102265/.
Davies, Paul. *The Goldilocks Enigma: Why Is the Universe Just Right for Life?* London: Penguin, 2006.
Dembski, William A. *Intelligent Design: The Bridge Between Science and Theology*. Downers Grove, IL: InterVarsity, 1999.
Denzinger, Henry. *The Sources of Catholic Dogma*. 30th ed. Translated by Roy J. Deferrari. St. Louis: B. Herder, 1957.
Déroche, François. *The Abbasid Tradition: Qur'ans of the 8th to the 10th Centuries AD*. London: Nour Foundation, 1992.
———. *The Qur'an Manuscripts: A Paleographical Study*. Turnhout: Brepols, 2009.
DiAngelo, Robin. *White Fragility: Why It's So Hard for White People to Talk About Racism*. Boston, MA: Beacon, 2018.
Dicastery for the Doctrine of the Faith. *Mater Populi Fidelis*. Holy See, Nov. 4, 2025. https://www.vatican.va/roman_curia/congregations/cfaith/documents/rc_ddf_doc_20251104_mater-populi-fidelis_en.html.
Dubos, René. *Louis Pasteur: Free Lance of Science*. New York: Da Capo, 1986.
The Eagles. "Hotel California." Track 1 on *Hotel California*. Written by Don Felder et al. Asylum, 1976.
Economy, Elizabeth C. *The Third Revolution: Xi Jinping and the New Chinese State*. Oxford: Oxford University Press, 2018.
Eddy, Mary Baker. *Science and Health with Key to the Scriptures*. Boston, MA: Christian Science Publishing Society, 1875.
Edsel, Robert M. *The Monuments Men: Allied Heroes, Nazi Thieves, and the Greatest Treasure Hunt in History*. New York: Center Street, 2009.

Ehrman, Bart D. *Did Jesus Exist? The Historical Argument for Jesus of Nazareth.* New York: HarperOne, 2012.

———. *The New Testament: A Historical Introduction to the Early Christian Writings.* 6th ed. New York: Oxford University Press, 2016.

Eichrodt, Walther. *Ezekiel: A Commentary.* Old Testament Library. Philadelphia: Westminster, 1970.

Ekman, Ulf, and Birgitta Ekman. *The Great Discovery: Our Journey to the Catholic Church.* San Francisco: Ignatius, 2018.

Eliot, Marc. *To the Limit: The Untold Story of the Eagles.* New York: Little, Brown, 1998.

Englebert, Omer. *The Hero of Molokai: Father Damien, Apostle of the Lepers.* New York: Sheed & Ward, 1955.

Evans, Richard J. *The Coming of the Third Reich.* New York: Penguin, 2004.

———. *The Third Reich in Power.* New York: Penguin, 2005.

Eyal, Nir. *Hooked: How to Build Habit-Forming Products.* New York: Portfolio, 2014.

Faraday, Michael. *The Life and Letters of Faraday.* Edited by Bence Jones. 2 vols. London: Longmans, Green, and Co., 1870.

Fee, Gordon D. *God's Empowering Presence: The Holy Spirit in the Letters of Paul.* Peabody, MA: Hendrickson, 1994.

Ferguson, Everett. *Backgrounds of Early Christianity.* 3rd ed. Grand Rapids: Eerdmans, 2003.

Fest, Joachim. *Inside Hitler's Bunker: The Last Days of the Third Reich.* Translated by Margot Dembo. New York: Farrar, Straus & Giroux, 2004.

Field, Clive. "Counting Religion in Britain, December 2016." *Counting Religion in Britain* 15 (2016). http://www.brin.ac.uk/counting-religion-in-britain-december-2016/.

Finocchiaro, Maurice A. *Retrying Galileo, 1633–1992.* Berkeley: University of California Press, 2005.

Fisher, Alec. *The Logic of Real Arguments.* 2nd ed. Cambridge: Cambridge University Press, 2004.

Flood, Gavin D. *An Introduction to Hinduism.* Cambridge: Cambridge University Press, 1996.

Foxe, John. *Foxe's Book of Martyrs.* Edited by William Byron Forbush. Grand Rapids: Baker, 1967.

Francis. *Homily of His Holiness Pope Francis: Feast of Our Lady of Guadalupe.* Holy See, Dec. 12, 2019. https://www.vatican.va/content/francesco/en/homilies/2019/documents/papa-francesco_20191212_omelia-guadalupe.html.

———. *Misericordiae Vultus: Bull of Indiction of the Extraordinary Jubilee of Mercy.* Papal Bull. Holy See, Apr. 11, 2015. https://www.vatican.va/content/francesco/en/bulls/documents/papa-francesco_bolla_20150411_misericordiae-vultus.html.

Frankel, Tamar. *The Ponzi Scheme Puzzle: A History and Analysis of Con Artists and Victims.* Oxford: Oxford University Press, 2012.

Freeman, Charles. *AD 381: Heretics, Pagans, and the Dawn of the Monotheistic State.* New York: Overlook, 2009.

Fudge, Thomas A. *Jan Hus: Religious Reform and Social Revolution in Bohemia.* London: Tauris, 2010.

Gabriel, Richard A. *The Culture of Conquest: Ancient Israel and the Military and Public Health.* Westport, CT: Greenwood, 1991.

Galilei, Galileo. *Letter to the Grand Duchess Christina.* Translated by Maurice A. Finocchiaro. Berkeley: University of California Press, 1989.

Garcia, L. Jared. *Mariology in the First Five Centuries: An Introduction to the Development of Mariology in the Early Church*. Greenville, SC: Bob Jones University, 2016.

Gathercole, Simon. "Jesus' Eschatological Vision of the Fall of Satan: Luke 10:18 Reconsidered." *New Testament Studies* 49 (2003) 145–65.

Geisler, Norman L. *Baker Encyclopedia of Christian Apologetics*. Grand Rapids: Baker, 1999.

———. *The Big Book of Christian Apologetics*. Grand Rapids: Baker, 2012.

Geisler, Norman L., and Ralph E. MacKenzie. *Roman Catholics and Evangelicals: Agreements and Differences*. Grand Rapids: Baker, 1995.

Gendron, Mike. *Preparing for Eternity: Should We Trust God's Word or Religious Traditions?* Southlake, TX: PTG, 2011.

Gervais, Ricky. "Why I'm an Atheist." *Wall Street Journal*, Dec. 19, 2010. https://www.wsj.com/articles/BL-SEB-56643?msockid=14fbb233e8716d4b100ba767e9106c8e.

Gibbon, Edward. *The Decline and Fall of the Roman Empire*. Vol. 3. New York: Modern Library, 1932.

Gibson, Keith E. *Virginia Military Institute: 150 Years of Tradition*. Charlottesville, VA: Howell, 1989.

Gillespie, Neal C. *Charles Darwin and the Problem of Creation*. Chicago: University of Chicago Press, 1979.

Glantz, David M. *Soviet Military Deception in the Second World War*. London: Cass, 1989.

Goodman, Matthew. *The Sun and the Moon: The Remarkable True Account of Hoaxers, Showmen, Dueling Journalists, and Lunar Man-Bats in Nineteenth-Century New York*. New York: Basic, 2008.

Grady, John. *Matthew Fontaine Maury, Father of Oceanography: A Biography, 1806–1873*. Jefferson, NC: McFarland, 2015.

Gregor, Neil. *How to Read Hitler*. London: Granta, 2005.

Griffith, Frances Llewellyn. *Catalogue of the Egyptian Antiquities in the Museum of Isma'ilya*. Cairo: Government Press, 1898.

Grimes, Donald Joseph. *The Papacy and the Petrine Texts: A Study in the History of Biblical Exegesis (A.D. 800–1300)*. PhD diss., Fordham University, 1981.

Groothuis, Douglas. *Confronting the New Age*. Downers Grove, IL: InterVarsity, 1988.

Grudem, Wayne. *Systematic Theology: An Introduction to Biblical Doctrine*. Grand Rapids: Zondervan, 1994.

Habermas, Gary R. "Near-Death Experiences and the Evidence for an Afterlife." *Journal of the Evangelical Theological Society* 49 (2006) 287–303.

———. *The Risen Jesus and Future Hope*. Lanham, MD: Rowman & Littlefield, 2003.

Habermas, Gary R., and J. P. Moreland. *Beyond Death: Exploring the Evidence for Immortality*. Wheaton, IL: Crossway, 1998.

Habermas, Gary R., and Michael R. Licona. *The Case for the Resurrection of Jesus*. Grand Rapids: Kregel, 2004.

Hahn, Scott. *First Comes Love: Finding Your Family in the Church and the Trinity*. New York: Doubleday, 2002.

Haidt, Jonathan. *The Anxious Generation: How the Great Rewiring of Childhood Is Causing an Epidemic of Mental Illness*. New York: Penguin, 2024.

Hall, William J., et al. "Sexual Orientation Identity Development Milestones Among Lesbian, Gay, Bisexual, and Queer People: A Systematic Review and

Meta-Analysis." *Frontiers in Psychology* 12 (2021). https://doi.org/10.3389/fpsyg.2021.753954.

Hallowell, Edward M., and John J. Ratey. *ADHD 2.0: New Science and Essential Strategies for Thriving with Distraction—From Childhood Through Adulthood.* New York: Ballantine, 2021.

Ham, Ken. "The Big Picture." *Creation* 23, Mar. 2001, 16–18. https://creation.com/en/articles/the-big-picture.

———. *Divided Nation: Cultures in Chaos and a Conflicted Church.* Green Forest, AR: Master, 2021.

Hayes, Zachary. "A Catholic View of Purgatory." In *Four Views on Hell*, edited by William Crockett, 101–20. Grand Rapids: Zondervan, 1996.

Harrison, R. R. "Statement of Rev. R. R. Harrison." *Columbia Chess Chronicle* 9 (1889) 4–5. https://books.google.com/books/about/Columbia_Chess_Chronicle.html?id=Fv42AAAAYAAJ.

Henry, Matthew. "Commentary on Ezekiel 28." In *Isaiah to Malachi*, 767–72. Vol. 4 of *Matthew Henry's Commentary on the Whole Bible.* Peabody, MA: Hendrickson, 2018.

Hentz, John. *History of the Lutheran Version.* Columbus, OH: Heer, 1910.

Hilary of Poitiers. *The Trinity.* Translated by Stephen McKenna. Fathers of the Church 25. Washington, DC: Catholic University of America Press, 1954.

Hippolytus. *Against the Heresy of One Noetus.* In *The Ante-Nicene Fathers*, vol. 5, edited by Alexander Roberts and James Donaldson. 1886. Repr., Grand Rapids: Eerdmans, 2000. https://biblehub.com/library/hippolytus/the_extant_works_and_fragments_of_hippolytus/against_the_heresy_of_one.htm.

Hitler, Adolf. *Mein Kampf.* Translated by Ralph Manheim. Boston, MA: Houghton Mifflin, 1999.

Hodges, Donald A., and David C. Sebald. *Music in the Human Experience: An Introduction to Music Psychology.* 3rd ed. New York: Routledge, 2017.

Hoffman, Samantha. *Programming China: The Communist Party's Autonomous Approach to Managing State Security.* Oxford: Oxford University Press, 2019.

Hoffmeier, James K. *Israel in Egypt: The Evidence for the Authenticity of the Exodus Tradition.* Oxford: Oxford University Press, 1997.

Holtz, Peter. "Does Postmodernism Really Entail a Disregard for the Truth? Similarities and Differences in Postmodern and Critical Rationalist Conceptualizations of Truth, Progress, and Empirical Research Methods." *Frontiers in Psychology* 11 (2020). https://doi.org/10.3389/fpsyg.2020.545959.

Horton, Michael S. *Christless Christianity: The Alternative Gospel of the American Church.* Grand Rapids: Baker, 2008.

———. "Evangelicals and Catholics Together: A Critical Review." *Modern Reformation* 3, Mar./Apr. 1994, 5–11.

Hoyle, Fred. *Religion and the Scientists.* London: SCM, 1959.

Hubbard, L. Ron. *Dianetics: The Modern Science of Mental Health.* New York: Hermitage House, 1950.

IDEA Center. "Primer: Summary of Problems with Biological and Chemical Evolution." http://www.ideacenter.org/contentmgr/showdetails.php/id/1510.

Ihm, Claudia Carlen, ed. *The Papal Encyclicals 1878–1903.* Raleigh, NC: Pierian, 1981.

International Council on Biblical Inerrancy. "Chicago Statement on Biblical Hermeneutics." Nov. 1982. https://library.dts.edu/Pages/TL/Special/ICBI_2.pdf.

Jerome. *Commentary on Matthew*. Translated by Thomas P. Scheck. Fathers of the Church 117. Washington, DC: Catholic University of America Press, 2008.

———. *Preface to Proverbs, Ecclesiastes, and the Song of Songs*. Translated by W. H. Fremantle. In *Nicene and Post-Nicene Fathers*, 2nd ser., edited by Philip Schaff and Henry Wace 6:492–93. 1893. Repr., Grand Rapids: Eerdmans, 1983.

Jeyaretnam, Miranda. "All the Times Trump Has Talked About the Afterlife." *Time*, last updated Sept. 2, 2025. https://time.com/7311354/donald-trump-heaven-hell-afterlife-quotes/.

Johnson, James J. S. "Genesis Is History, Not Poetry: Exposing Hidden Assumptions About What Hebrew Poetry Is and Is Not." *Acts and Facts* 40.6 (2011) 8–9.

———. "Matthew Maury's Paths of the Sea." *Acts and Facts* 49 (2020). https://www.icr.org/article/matthew-maury-paths-of-the-sea//1000.

John Chrysostom. *Homilies on the Gospel of Matthew*. Translated by George Prevost. In *Nicene and Post-Nicene Fathers*, 1st ser., vol. 10, edited by Philip Schaff. 1888. Repr., Peabody, MA: Hendrickson, 1994.

Joint Chiefs of Staff. *Joint Operations*. Joint Publication 3-0. Washington, DC: Joint Chiefs of Staff, 2018.

———. *Joint Planning*. Joint Publication 5-0. Washington, DC: Joint Chiefs of Staff, 2020.

———. *Joint Publication 3-13.2: Military Information Support Operations*. Washington, DC: Joint Chiefs of Staff, 2014. https://www.esd.whs.mil/Portals/54/Documents/FOID/Reading%20Room/Joint_Staff/Military_Information_Support_Operations.pdf.

Jones, Alex. *No Price Too High: A Pentecostal Preacher Becomes Catholic*. San Francisco: Ignatius, 2006.

Jones, Jeffrey M. "LGBT Identification in U.S. Ticks Up to 7.1%." Gallup, Feb. 17, 2022. https://news.gallup.com/poll/389792/lgbt-identification-ticks-up.aspx.

Josephus, Flavius. *The Works of Josephus: Complete and Unabridged*. Translated by William Whiston. Peabody, MA: Hendrickson, 1987.

Kaczor, Christopher. "Thomas Aquinas on the Development of Doctrine." *Theological Studies* 62 (2001) 283–302.

Kallis, Aristotle A. *Nazi Propaganda and the Second World War*. New York: Palgrave Macmillan, 2008.

Kampourakis, Kostas. *Understanding Evolution*. Cambridge: Cambridge University Press, 2020.

Katsidou, Osia. "Ricky Gervais: 'The Truth Is More Devastating Than a Lie.'" Interview with Ricky Gervais. The Talks. https://the-talks.com/interview/ricky-gervais/.

Keener, Craig S. *The Gospel of John: A Commentary*. 2 vols. Peabody, MA: Hendrickson, 2003.

———. *The Gospel of Matthew: A Socio-Rhetorical Commentary*. Grand Rapids: Eerdmans, 2009.

Keller, Timothy. *Counterfeit Gods: The Empty Promises of Money, Sex, and Power, and the Only Hope That Matters*. New York: Dutton, 2009.

Kelly, John N. D. *Early Christian Doctrines*. San Francisco: Harper & Row, 1978.

———. *Oxford Dictionary of Popes*. Oxford: Oxford University Press, 1986.

———. "Papacy." In *New Catholic Encyclopedia*, by The Catholic University of America, 2nd ed., 11:861–75. Detroit: Gale, 2003.

Kennedy, D. James. *Why I Believe*. Nashville: Word, 1999.

Kepler, Johannes. *Harmonices Mundi* [The harmony of the world]. Translated with commentary by E. J. Aiton et al. Philadelphia: American Philosophical Society, 1997.

Kerr, Fergus. "Vatican I and the Papacy 6: The Question of Infallibility." *Journal of Ecclesiastical History* 28 (1977) 283–302.

Kershaw, Ian. *Hitler: A Biography*. New York: Norton, 2008.

Kertzer, David I. *The Pope at War: The Secret History of Pius XII, Mussolini, and Hitler*. New York: Random House, 2022.

King, David T. *A Biblical Defense of the Reformation Principle of Sola Scriptura*. Vol. 1 of *Holy Scripture: The Ground and Pillar of Our Faith*. Battle Ground, WA: Christian Resources, 2001.

Kirk, Charlie. *The Christian Response to the Cult of Progressive Ideology*. Washington, DC: Salem, 2023.

Kirkbride, James B., et al. "The Social Determinants of Mental Health and Disorder: Evidence, Prevention and Recommendations." *World Psychiatry* 23 (2024) 58–90. https://pubmed.ncbi.nlm.nih.gov/38214615/.

Kitchen, Kenneth A. *On the Reliability of the Old Testament*. Grand Rapids: Eerdmans, 2003.

Klostermaier, Klaus K. *A Survey of Hinduism*. 3rd ed. Albany: State University of New York Press, 2007.

Koelsch, Stefan. "Towards a Neural Basis of Music-Evoked Emotions." *Trends in Cognitive Sciences* 14.3 (2010) 131–37. https://doi.org/10.1016/j.tics.2010.01.002.

Kohm, Joseph A. "What the Bird Said Early in the Year." *Knowing and Doing*, June 1, 2015. https://www.cslewisinstitute.org/resources/what-the-bird-said-early-in-the-year/.

Kolyadyuk, Yelena. "The Patristic Interpretation of the 'Rock' in Mt 16:18 Through the Prism of Polemics Between Lev Krevza and Zachariya Kopystensky." *Analecta of the UCU: Theology* 6 (2019) 207–20.

Kramer, Stephanie, et al. "Modeling the Future of Religion in America." Pew Research Center, Sept. 13, 2022. https://www.pewresearch.org/religion/2022/09/13/modeling-the-future-of-religion-in-america.

Krebs, Brian. *Spam Nation: The Inside Story of Organized Cybercrime*. Naperville, IL: Sourcebooks, 2014.

Kruger, Michael J. "Early Christian Manuscripts and the Text of the New Testament." *Journal of Theological Studies* 63 (2012) 1–25.

Lapine, Matthew A. *The Logic of the Body: Retrieving Theological Psychology*. Bellingham, WA: Lexham, 2020.

Leith, John H., ed. *Creeds of the Church: A Reader in Christian Doctrine from the Bible to the Present*. Louisville: Westminster John Knox, 1982.

Lembke, Anna. *Dopamine Nation: Finding Balance in the Age of Indulgence*. New York: Dutton, 2021.

Lemonick, Michael. "'Intelligent Design' on Trial." *Time*, Sept. 29, 2005. https://time.com/archive/6919048/intelligent-design-on-trial/.

Lewis, C. S. *The Abolition of Man*. In *The Complete C. S. Lewis Signature Classics*, 689–730. San Francisco: HarperOne, 2002.

———. *The Great Divorce*. In *The Complete C. S. Lewis Signature Classics*, 463–542. San Francisco: HarperOne, 2002.

———. *Mere Christianity*. In *The Complete C. S. Lewis Signature Classics*, 1–178. San Francisco: HarperOne, 2002.

———. *Miracles: A Preliminary Study*. In *The Complete C. S. Lewis Signature Classics*, 297–462. San Francisco: HarperOne, 2002.

———. *The Problem of Pain*. New York: HarperOne, 2009.

———. *They Stand Together: The Letters of C. S. Lewis to Arthur Greeves (1914–1963)*. Edited by Walter Hooper. New York: Macmillan, 1979.

Lewis, Charles L. *Matthew Fontaine Maury: The Pathfinder of the Seas*. New York: AMS, 1927. Repr., Annapolis, MD: United States Naval Institute, 1969.

Liddell, Henry George, et al. *A Greek-English Lexicon*. 9th ed. Oxford: Clarendon, 1996.

Locke, John. *An Essay Concerning Human Understanding*. London: Basset, 1690.

Loewe, Raphael. "The Medieval History of the Latin Vulgate." In *The West from the Fathers to the Reformation*, edited by G. W. H. Lampe, 102–54. Vol. 2 of *The Cambridge History of the Bible*. Cambridge: Cambridge University Press, 1969.

Löfstedt, Torsten. "Satan's Fall and the Mission of the Seventy-Two." *Scandinavian Evangelical Review* 76 (2011) 95–114.

Longerich, Peter. *Goebbels: A Biography*. New York: Random House, 2015.

———. *The Wannsee Conference and the Final Solution: A Reconsideration*. Translated by Lesley Sharpe. Oxford: Oxford University Press, 2016.

Longman, Tremper, III. "Daniel." In *The Expositor's Bible Commentary*, edited by Tremper Longman III and David E. Garland, 7:21–212. Grand Rapids: Zondervan, 2008.

Lüdemann, Gerd. *The Resurrection of Christ: A Historical Inquiry*. Amherst, NY: Prometheus, 2004.

Lumpkin, Joseph B. *The Encyclopedia of the Lost and Rejected Scriptures: The Pseudepigrapha and the Apocrypha*. Blountsville, AL: Fifth Estate, 2010.

Lundmark, Torbjörn. *Tales of Hi and Bye: Greeting and Parting Rituals Around the World*. Cambridge: Cambridge University Press, 2009.

Luther, Martin. *The Bondage of the Will*. Translated by J. I. Packer and O. R. Johnston. Grand Rapids: Revell, 1957.

———. *Disputation on the Power and Efficacy of Indulgences (95 Theses)* (1517). In *Career of the Reformer 1*, edited by Harold J. Grimm, 17–33. Vol. 31 of *Luther's Works*. Philadelphia: Fortress, 1957.

———. *Lectures on Galatians, 1535*. Vol. 26 of *Luther's Works*, edited by Jaroslav Pelikan. St. Louis, MO: Concordia, 1963.

MacArthur, John. *The Gospel According to Jesus: What Is Authentic Faith?* Grand Rapids: Zondervan, 1988.

———. *The MacArthur Study Bible*. Rev. and updated ed. Nashville: Nelson, 2010.

———. *Standing Strong: How to Resist the Enemy of Your Soul*. Colorado Springs, CO: Cook, 2006.

———. *Strange Fire: The Danger of Offending the Holy Spirit with Counterfeit Worship*. Nashville: Nelson, 2013.

———. *The Truth War: Fighting for Certainty in an Age of Deception*. Nashville: Nelson, 2007.

MacArthur, John F., and Richard Mayhue, eds. *Biblical Doctrine: A Systematic Summary of Bible Truth*. Wheaton, IL: Crossway, 2017.

Macintyre, Ben. *Operation Mincemeat: How a Dead Man and a Bizarre Plan Fooled the Nazis and Assured Allied Victory*. New York: Crown, 2010.

Major, Trevor. "Honor to Whom Honor: Matthew Fontaine Maury (1806–1873)." *Creation Research Society Quarterly* 32 (1995) 82–87.

Mann, Gurinder Singh. *Sikhism*. Upper Saddle River, NJ: Prentice Hall, 2004.

Marsden, George M. *Fundamentalism and American Culture*. New York: Oxford University Press, 1980.

Marshall, George C. "The Marshall Plan Speech." Delivered June 5, 1947. George C. Marshall Foundation. https://www.marshallfoundation.org/the-marshall-plan/speech/.

Martines, Lauro. *Fire in the City: Savonarola and the Struggle for the Soul of Renaissance Florence*. Oxford: Oxford University Press, 2006.

Marturano, Antonio. "Non-Cognitivism in Ethics." *Internet Encyclopedia of Philosophy*. https://iep.utm.edu/non-cogn/.

Mathison, Keith A. *The Shape of Sola Scriptura*. Moscow, ID: Canon, 2001.

Maury, Matthew Fontaine. *The Physical Geography of the Sea*. 6th ed. New York: Harper & Brothers, 1959.

Maxwell, James Clerk. *The Life of James Clerk Maxwell*. Edited by Lewis Campbell and William Garnett. London: Macmillan, 1882.

Mayne, Sally L., et al. "COVID-19 and Adolescent Depression and Suicide Risk Screening Outcomes." *Pediatrics* 148 (2021) e2021051507. https://doi.org/10.1542/peds.2021-051507.

McBrien, Richard P. *Catholicism*. Rev. ed. San Francisco: HarperSanFrancisco, 1994.

McDonald, Lee Martin. *The Biblical Canon: Its Origin, Transmission, and Authority*. 3rd ed. Grand Rapids: Baker Academic, 2007.

McDowell, Sean. "The Debate over Evolution and Intelligent Design Heats Up (w/ Doug Axe)." *Sean McDowell Show*, posted Mar. 11, 2025. YouTube video, 44:25. https://youtu.be/YGggxHBqPRc.

McGrath, Alister E. *Iustitia Dei: A History of the Christian Doctrine of Justification*. Cambridge: Cambridge University Press, 2005.

McMillen, S. I., and David E. Stern. *None of These Diseases*. Grand Rapids: Revell, 2000.

Meier, John P. *The Roots of the Problem and the Person*. Vol. 1 of *A Marginal Jew: Rethinking the Historical Jesus*. New York: Doubleday, 1991.

Metzger, Bruce M. *The Canon of the New Testament: Its Origin, Development, and Significance*. Oxford: Clarendon, 1987.

———. *The Early Versions of the New Testament: Their Origin, Transmission, and Limitations*. Oxford: Oxford University Press, 1977.

Metzger, Bruce M., and Bart D. Ehrman. *The Text of the New Testament: Its Transmission, Corruption, and Restoration*. 4th ed. New York: Oxford University Press, 2005.

Meyer, Stephen C. *Darwin's Doubt: The Explosive Origin of Animal Life and the Case for Intelligent Design*. New York: HarperOne, 2013.

———. *Signature in the Cell: DNA and the Evidence for Intelligent Design*. New York: HarperOne, 2009.

Mihalache, Robert-Marius. "The Institution of the Papal Legation (12th–14th Centuries): Historical and Historiographical Benchmarks." *Transylvanian Review* 28 (2019) 45–60.

Miller, Harold L. "FDR's 'Day of Infamy' Speech." *Prologue Magazine*, 2001. National Archives. https://www.archives.gov/publications/prologue/2001/winter/crafting-day-of-infamy-speech.

Miller, Herbert. *General Biblical Introduction*. Houghton, NY: Word-Bearer, 1960.

Montagu, Ewen. *Beyond Top Secret Ultra*. New York: Coward, McCann & Geoghegan, 1978.

———. *The Man Who Never Was*. Philadelphia: J. B. Lippincott & Co., 1954.

Moore, Rebecca. *Understanding Jonestown and Peoples Temple*. Westport, CT: Praeger, 2009.

Moreland, J. P., et al., eds. *Theistic Evolution: A Scientific, Philosophical, and Theological Critique*. Wheaton, IL: Crossway, 2017.

Morris, Henry M. *The Long War Against God: The History and Impact of the Creation/Evolution Conflict*. Grand Rapids: Baker, 1989.

———. *Scientific Creationism*. San Diego: Creation-Life, 1974.

Morris, John D. *The Young Earth*. Colorado Springs, CO: Master Books, 2007.

Müller, Gerd B. "The Explanatory Deficits of the Modern Synthesis." Paper presented at New Trends in Evolutionary Biology: Biological, Philosophical and Social Science Perspectives, Royal Society, London, Nov. 7–9, 2016.

Newcourt-Nowodworski, Stanley. *Black Propaganda in the Second World War*. Stroud, UK: Sutton, 2005.

Newman, John Henry. *An Essay on the Development of Christian Doctrine*. Notre Dame: University of Notre Dame Press, 1989.

Newport, Kenneth. *The Branch Davidians of Waco: The History and Beliefs of an Apocalyptic Sect*. Oxford: Oxford University Press, 2006.

Newton, Isaac. *Newton's Religion of Nature and Prophecy*. Edited by Frank E. Manuel. London: Cambridge University Press, 1974.

———. *The Principia: Mathematical Principles of Natural Philosophy*. Translated by I. Bernard Cohen and Anne Whitman. Berkeley: University of California Press, 1999.

New World Bible Translation Committee. *New World Translation of the Holy Scriptures*. Wallkill, NY: Watch Tower and Bible Tract Society, 2013. https://www.jw.org/en/library/bible/nwt/books/.

Nongbri, Brent. "The Date of Codex Sinaiticus." *Journal of Theological Studies* 73 (2022) 516–34. https://doi.org/10.1093/jts/flac083.

Nutton, Vivian. *Ancient Medicine*. London: Routledge, 2013.

Office of the Historian. "Declaration by the United States of America of a State of War with Japan, December 8, 1941." https://history.state.gov/historicaldocuments/frus1931-41v02/d423.

Olson, Roger E. *The Journey of Modern Theology: From Reconstruction to Deconstruction*. Downers Grove, IL: InterVarsity, 2013.

O'Shaughnessy, Nicholas. *Selling Hitler: Propaganda and the Nazi Brand*. London: Hurst, 2016.

Oswalt, John N. *The Book of Isaiah: Chapters 1–39*. New International Commentary on the Old Testament. Grand Rapids: Eerdmans, 1986.

———. *The Book of Isaiah: Chapters 40–66*. Grand Rapids: Eerdmans, 1998.

Ott, Ludwig. *Fundamentals of Catholic Dogma*. Translated by Patrick Lynch. Rockford, IL: TAN, 1974.

Overy, Richard. *The Dictators: Hitler's Germany and Stalin's Russia*. New York: Norton, 2004.

Packer, J. I. "The Doctrine of Justification in Development and Decline." In *Honouring the People of God: Collected Shorter Writings of J. I. Packer on the Church, the Bible, and the Christian Life*, edited by Ian Hugh Clary, 4:145–64. Bellingham, WA: Lexham, 2021.

———. *God Has Spoken: Revelation and the Bible*. Grand Rapids: Baker, 1979.

Paddock, Alfred H., Jr. "U.S. Military Psychological Operations, 1917–1953." *Public Opinion Quarterly* 29 (1965) 93–107.

Paehler, Katrin. *The Third Reich's Intelligence Services: The Career of Walter Schellenberg*. Cambridge: Cambridge University Press, 2017.

Parkinson, Richard. *The Rosetta Stone*. London: British Museum Press, 2005.

Pascal, Blaise. *Pensées*. Edited and translated by Roger Ariew. Indianapolis: Hackett, 2005.

Pasquini, Giancarlo, et al. "Why Some Americans Do Not See Urgency on Climate Change." Pew Research Center, Aug. 9, 2023. https://www.pewresearch.org/science/2023/08/09/why-some-americans-do-not-see-urgency-on-climate-change/.

Paxton, Robert O. *The Anatomy of Fascism*. London: Allen Lane, 2004.

Payne, J. Barton. *Encyclopedia of Biblical Prophecy: The Complete Guide to Scriptural Predictions and Their Fulfillment*. New York: Harper & Row, 1973.

Pelikan, Jaroslav. *The Emergence of the Catholic Tradition (100–600)*. Vol. 1 of *The Christian Tradition: A History of the Development of Doctrine*. Chicago: University of Chicago Press, 1971.

———. *The Growth of Medieval Theology (600–1300)*. Vol. 3 of *The Christian Tradition: A History of the Development of Doctrine*. Chicago: University of Chicago Press, 1978.

———. *The Spirit of Eastern Christendom (600–1700)*. Vol. 2 of *The Christian Tradition: A History of the Development of Doctrine*. Chicago: University of Chicago Press, 1974.

Penrose, Roger. *The Road to Reality: A Complete Guide to the Laws of the Universe*. New York: Knopf, 2005.

Pettus, David. "Reading a Protoevangelium in the Context of Genesis." *Eruditio Ardescens* 1.2 (2014): 1–18. https://digitalcommons.liberty.edu/jlbts/vol1/iss2/8/.

Pierre, Joe. "Illusory Truth, Lies, and Political Propaganda." *Psychology Today*, Mar. 21, 2024. https://www.psychologytoday.com/us/blog/psych-unseen/202001/illusory-truth-lies-and-political-propaganda.

Pinch, Geraldine. *Egyptian Myth: A Guide to the Gods, Goddesses, and Traditions of Ancient Egypt*. Oxford: Oxford University Press, 2002.

Plimer, Ian. *Heaven and Earth: Global Warming—The Missing Science*. Ballan, VIC: Connor Court, 2009.

Pliny the Younger. *Letters*. Translated by Betty Radice. Loeb Classical Library. Cambridge, MA: Harvard University Press, 1969.

Poiriazi, Eleni, et al. "Analyzing the Interconnection Between Environmental, Social, and Governance (ESG) Criteria and Corporate Corruption: Revealing the Significant Impact of Greenwashing." *Administrative Sciences* 15 (2025) 100. https://doi.org/10.3390/admsci15030100.

Postman, Neil. *Amusing Ourselves to Death: Public Discourse in the Age of Show Business*. New York: Viking, 1985.

Powers, Francis Gary. *Operation Overflight: The U-2 Spy Pilot Tells His Story for the First Time*. With Curt Gentry. New York: Holt, Rinehart & Winston, 1970.

Pratkanis, Anthony R., and Elliot Aronson. *Age of Propaganda: The Everyday Use and Abuse of Persuasion*. Rev. ed. New York: Freeman, 2001.

Pratte, David E. "Bible Preservation: Scripture Transmission, Ancestry, Canon, Criticism." GospelWay. https://gospelway.com/bible/bible_preservation.php.

Rahula, Walpola. *What the Buddha Taught*. Rev. ed. New York: Grove, 1974.

Ramsey, William M., and Mark Wilson, eds. *St. Paul: The Traveler and Roman Citizen*. Grand Rapids: Kregel, 2001.

Ratliff, Ben. "Keith Emerson, '70s Rock Showman with a Taste for Spectacle, Dies at 71." *New York Times*, Mar. 11, 2016. https://www.nytimes.com/2016/03/12/arts/music/keith-emerson-70s-rock-showman-with-a-taste-for-spectacle-dies-at-71.html.

Reiterman, Tim. *Raven: The Untold Story of the Rev. Jim Jones and His People*. New York: Penguin, 2008.

Ressa, Jerry F. *Satanic Influences in the American Christian Church in a Postmodern Consumer Society*. PhD diss., George Fox University, 2018.

Retzsch, Friedrich August Moritz. *Die Schachspieler* [The chess players]. 1831. Oil on panel. 32.3 × 39 cm. Private collection. Wikimedia Commons. https://commons.wikimedia.org/wiki/File:Frederick_August_Moritz_Retzsch.jpg.

Robertson, James I., Jr. *Stonewall Jackson: The Man, the Soldier, the Legend*. New York: Macmillan, 1997.

Rockwell, Theodore. *The Rickover Effect: How One Man Made a Difference*. Annapolis: Naval Institute, 1992.

Rogers, Alan R. "Evolution: Evidence and Acceptance." *BioScience* 62 (2012) 845–47.

Rogers, William P., et al. "The Cause of the Accident." In *Report of the Presidential Commission on the Space Shuttle Challenger Accident*. Published 1986. https://www.nasa.gov/history/rogersrep/v1ch4.htm.

Rufito. "William Martin Burial." Photograph, Aug. 15, 2013. Wikimedia Commons. Licensed under CC BY-SA 4.0. https://commons.wikimedia.org/wiki/File%3AWiliam_Martin_burial.jpg.

Rutherford, Ward. *Hitler's Propaganda Machine*. London: Bison, 1978.

Sakr, Johnny. "Peter, the Rock and Matthew 16:18: A Grammatical Analysis." *Biblical Linguistics Review* 32 (2020) 67–89.

Salvesen, Alison G., and Timothy Michael Law, eds. *The Oxford Handbook of the Septuagint*. Oxford: Oxford University Press, 2021.

Sanford, John C. *Genetic Entropy and the Mystery of the Genome*. 4th ed. Waterloo, NY: FMS, 2014.

Sarna, Nahum M. *Genesis: The Traditional Hebrew Text with New JPS Translation*. Philadelphia: Jewish Publication Society, 1989.

Signal Corps Archive. SC 205559. Apr. 2, 1945. Photograph. US National Archives. Accessed on Wikimedia Commons. https://commons.wikimedia.org/wiki/File:SC_205559_-_These_dummy_planes_are_two_of_many_decoys_placed_near_airfield_in_Kadena,_Okinawa,_to_lure_machine_gun_fire_from_Allied_pilots._2_April,_1945._(51360531411).jpg.

Schaff, Philip. *Ante-Nicene Christianity, AD 100–325*. Vol. 2 of *History of the Christian Church*. Grand Rapids: Eerdmans, 1910.

———. *Apostolic Christianity, AD 1–100*. Vol. 1 of *History of the Christian Church*. Peabody, MA: Hendrickson, 2006.

———. *Nicene and Post-Nicene Christianity, AD 311–600*. Vol. 3 of *History of the Christian Church*. Grand Rapids: Eerdmans, 1910.

Schiffman, Lawrence H. *From Text to Tradition: A History of Second Temple and Rabbinic Judaism*. Hoboken, NJ: Ktav, 1991.

Schlier, Heinrich. "ἐπιούσιος." In *Theological Dictionary of the New Testament*, edited by Gerhard Kittel and Gerhard Friedrich, translated by Geoffrey W. Bromiley, 2:590–99. Grand Rapids: Eerdmans, 1964.

Schroeder, Henry J., trans. *The Canons and Decrees of the Council of Trent*. Rockford, IL: TAN, 1978.

Schultz, Wolfram. "Dopamine Reward Prediction Error Coding." *Dialogues in Clinical Neuroscience* 20 (2018) 393–402.

Scurlock, JoAnn. *Sourcebook for Ancient Mesopotamian Medicine*. Atlanta: SBL, 2014.

Sears, Stephen W. *The Battle of Chancellorsville*. Boston: Houghton Mifflin, 1996.

Shanks, Hershel. *The Mystery and Meaning of the Dead Sea Scrolls*. New York: Random House, 1998.

Shirer, William L. *Berlin Diary: The Journal of a Foreign Correspondent, 1934–1941*. New York: Knopf, 1941.

———. *The Rise and Fall of Adolf Hitler*. New York: Random House, 1961.

———. *The Rise and Fall of the Third Reich: A History of Nazi Germany*. New York: Simon & Schuster, 1950.

Siecienski, Edward. *The Papacy and the Orthodox: Sources and History of a Debate*. Oxford: Oxford University Press, 2017.

Sire, James W. *The Universe Next Door: A Basic Worldview Catalog*. 5th ed. Downers Grove, IL: InterVarsity, 2009.

Skeat, Walter W. *An Etymological Dictionary of the English Language*. Oxford: Clarendon, 1910.

Skousen, Royal. *1 Nephi–2 Nephi*. Part 1 of *Analysis of Textual Variants of the Book of Mormon*. Book of Mormon Critical Text Project 4. Provo, UT: Foundation for Ancient Research and Mormon Studies, 2004.

Smith, Joseph. *The Book of Mormon*. Nauvoo, IL: Robinson and Smith, 1840.

———. *History of the Church of Jesus Christ of Latter-day Saints*. Edited by B. H. Roberts. 7 vols. Salt Lake City, UT: Deseret, 1978.

———. *Teachings of the Prophet Joseph Smith*. Salt Lake City: Deseret, 1976.

Snelling, Andrew A. *Earth's Catastrophic Past: Geology, Creation and the Flood*. 2 vols. Dallas: Institute for Creation Research, 2009.

Spotts, Frederic. *Hitler and the Power of Aesthetics*. New York: Overlook, 2004.

Sproul, R. C. *The Consequences of Ideas*. Wheaton, IL: Crossway, 2000.

———. *Faith Alone: The Evangelical Doctrine of Justification*. Grand Rapids: Baker, 1995.

———. *The Holiness of God*. Wheaton, IL: Tyndale House, 1985.

———. *Scripture Alone: The Evangelical Doctrine*. Phillipsburg, NJ: P&R, 2005.

———. *The Truth of the Cross*. Orlando: Reformation Trust, 2007.

Spurgeon, Charles. "Exposition of the Doctrines of Grace." In *The Metropolitan Tabernacle Pulpit Sermons*, vol. 7, sermons 385–88. London: Passmore & Alabaster, 1861.

———. *The Treasury of David*. London: Passmore & Alabaster, 1869.

Stoner, Peter. *Science Speaks*. Chicago: Moody, 1963.

Storms, Sam. *Understanding Spiritual Warfare: A Comprehensive Guide*. Grand Rapids: Zondervan Reflective, 2021.

Stott, John. *Understanding the Bible*. Grand Rapids: Zondervan, 1972.

Strobel, Lee. *The Case for Christ: A Journalist's Personal Investigation of the Evidence for Jesus*. Grand Rapids: Zondervan, 1998.

———. *A Case for the Creator: A Journalist Investigates Scientific Evidence That Points Toward God*. Grand Rapids: Zondervan, 2004.

Strong, James. *The New Strong's Expanded Exhaustive Concordance of the Bible*. With contributions by John R. Kohlenberger III. Nashville: Nelson, 1996.

———. *The New Strong's Expanded Exhaustive Concordance of the Bible: Every Word of the Bible Indexed, Red Letter Edition*. Nashville: Nelson, 2010.

Tacitus. *The Annals of Imperial Rome*. Translated by Michael Grant. New York: Penguin Classics, 1996.

Tanner, Jerald, and Sandra Tanner. *3,913 Changes in the Book of Mormon*. Sandy, UT: Utah Lighthouse Ministry, 1996.

Tanner, Norman P., ed. *Nicaea I to Lateran V*. Vol. 1 of *Decrees of the Ecumenical Councils*. Washington, DC: Georgetown University Press, 1990.

Taylor, Charles. *A Secular Age*. Cambridge: Harvard University Press, 2007.

Taylor, Frederick. *Exorcising Hitler: The Occupation and Denazification of Germany*. New York: Bloomsbury, 2011.

———. *Goebbels: Mastermind of the Third Reich*. New York: Holt, 2010.

Taylor, Telford. *The Anatomy of the Nuremberg Trials: A Personal Memoir*. New York: Knopf, 1992.

Tenet, George L. "The U-2 Program: The DCI's Perspective." *Studies in Intelligence* 42 (1998–1999). https://www.cia.gov/resources/csi/static/U2-Program-DCI-Perspective-2.pdf.

Tillotson, John. *Works*. Vol. 1. London, 1678.

Tolkien, J. R. R. *The Letters of J. R. R. Tolkien*. Edited by Humphrey Carpenter, with the assistance of Christopher Tolkien. Boston: Houghton Mifflin, 1981.

Trueman, Carl. *The Rise and Triumph of the Modern Self: Cultural Amnesia, Expressive Individualism, and the Road to Sexual Revolution*. Wheaton, IL: Crossway, 2020.

Truman, Davis. *The Downfall of Pride: Custer's Catastrophic Decisions at Little Bighorn*. N.p.: Vincenzo Nappi, 2024.

Turner, Eric G. *Greek Manuscripts of the Ancient World*. Princeton: Princeton University Press, 1971.

Twenge, Jean M., et al. "Age, Period, and Cohort Trends in Mood Disorder Indicators and Suicide-Related Outcomes in a Nationally Representative Dataset, 2005–2017." *Journal of Abnormal Psychology* 128 (2019) 185–99.

Twenge, Jean M., et al. "Decreases in Psychological Well-Being Among American Adolescents After 2012 and Links to Screen Time During the Rise of Smartphone Technology." *Emotion* 18 (2018) 765–80. https://doi.org/10.1037/emo0000403.

Twenge, Jean M., et al. "Increases in Depression, Self-Harm, and Suicide Among Adolescents After 2012, Especially Among Girls and Young Women: Time Trend Study." *Journal of Adolescent Health* 65 (2019) 917–20. https://pmc.ncbi.nlm.nih.gov/articles/PMC9176070/.

Tzu, Sun. *The Art of War*. Translated by Lionel Giles. New York: Race Point, 2017.

Ullmann, Walter. *The Growth of Papal Government in the Middle Ages*. London: Methuen, 1962.

US Commission on Civil Rights. *Public Hearing on Creationism and Intelligent Design*. Transcript. Washington, DC: Government Printing Office, 2005.

BIBLIOGRAPHY

US Military. "Your future al-Zarqawi." US PSYOP leaflet. Accessed on Wikimedia Commons, uploaded by Psywar, 2005. https://commons.wikimedia.org/wiki/File:Your_future_al-Zarqawi.jpg.

VanderKam, James, and Peter Flint. *The Meaning of the Dead Sea Scrolls: Their Significance for Understanding the Bible, Judaism, Jesus, and Christianity*. New York: HarperCollins, 2002.

Vatican II. "Decree on Ecumenism: *Unitatis Redintegratio.*" In *Vatican Council II: The Conciliar and Post Conciliar Documents*, edited by Austin Flannery, 452–64. Northport, NY: Costello, 1996.

———. *Dei Verbum: Dogmatic Constitution on Divine Revelation*. Promulgated Nov. 18, 1965, by Paul VI. https://www.vatican.va/archive/hist_councils/ii_vatican_council/documents/vat-ii_const_19651118_dei-verbum_en.html.

Veniamin, Christopher. *The Orthodox Understanding of Salvation: "Theosis" in Scripture and Tradition*. Dalton, PA: Mount Thabor, 2013.

Verlenden, Jorge V., et al. "Mental Health and Suicide Risk Among High School Students and Protective Factors—Youth Risk Behavior Survey, United States, 2023." *Morbidity and Mortality Weekly Report Supplements* 73.4 (2023) S79–86. https://www.cdc.gov/mmwr/volumes/73/su/su7304a9.htm.

Vermes, Geza. *The Complete Dead Sea Scrolls in English*. London: Penguin, 2011.

Virgil. *The Aeneid*. Translated by Robert Fagles. New York: Penguin, 2006.

Mukhranov, Alexey. "VMI Battery." Photograph, Apr. 20, 2015. Wikimedia Commons. Licensed under CC BY-SA 4.0. https://commons.wikimedia.org/wiki/File:VMI_battery.jpg.

Volkow, Nora D., et al. "Neurobiologic Advances from the Brain Disease Model of Addiction." *New England Journal of Medicine* 374 (2016) 363–71. https://doi.org/10.1056/NEJMra1511480.

Walcott, Escher. "'God's Influencer' Carlo Acutis Becomes First Millennial Saint 20 Years Later." *People*, Sept. 7, 2025. https://people.com/gods-influencer-carlo-acutis-becomes-first-millennial-saint-20-years-later-11805002.

Wallace, Daniel B. "The Reliability of the New Testament Manuscripts." *Bibliotheca Sacra* 165.658 (2008) 179–200.

———. *Revisiting the Corruption of the New Testament: Manuscript, Patristic, and Apocryphal Evidence*. Grand Rapids: Kregel Academic, 2011.

Wallace, Michael. *The Great Giant Hoax: The Cardiff Giant and American Imagination*. Ithaca: Cornell University Press, 1972.

Warfield, Benjamin B. *Revelation and Inspiration*. Vol. 1 of *The Works of Benjamin B. Warfield*. Grand Rapids: Baker, 1981.

Washington, George. "Farewell Address, September 17, 1796." In *A Compilation of the Messages and Papers of the Presidents, 1789–1897*, 11 vols., edited by James D. Richardson, 1:213–14. Washington, DC: Government Printing Office, 1896.

Watch Tower Bible and Tract Society of New York. *The Truth That Leads to Eternal Life*. Brooklyn, NY: Watch Tower Bible and Tract Society of New York, 1968.

Webster, William. *The Church of Rome at the Bar of History*. Carlisle, PA: Banner of Truth, 1995.

———. "The Patristic Exegesis of the Rock of Matthew 16:18." *Reformation and Revival Journal* 11 (2002) 89–120.

Weekley, Ernest. *An Etymological Dictionary of Modern English*. London: John Murray, 1921.

Weiner, J. S. *The Piltdown Forgery*. Oxford: Oxford University Press, 1955.
Weller, Chris. "How Bill Gates Limits Tech Use for His Kids." Business Insider, Jan. 22, 2018. https://www.businessinsider.com/how-bill-gates-limits-tech-use-for-his-kids-2018-1.
Wells, Jonathan. *The Myth of Junk DNA*. Seattle: Discovery Institute, 2011.
Wellum, Stephen. *God the Son Incarnate: The Doctrine of Christ*. Wheaton, IL: Crossway, 2016.
Whaley, Joachim. *Maximilian I to the Peace of Westphalia, 1493–1648*. Vol. 1 of *Germany and the Holy Roman Empire*. Oxford: Oxford University Press, 2012.
Whitaker, William. *A Disputation on Holy Scripture: Against the Papists, Especially Bellarmine and Stapleton*. Cambridge: Cambridge University Press, 1849.
Whitcomb, John C., and Henry M. Morris. *The Genesis Flood: The Biblical Record and Its Scientific Implications*. Phillipsburg, NJ: P&R, 1961.
White, James R. *The Roman Catholic Controversy: Catholics and Protestants—Do the Differences Still Matter?* Minneapolis: Bethany House, 1996.
———. *Scripture Alone: Exploring the Bible's Accuracy, Authority and Authenticity*. Minneapolis: Bethany House, 2004.
The Who. *Tommy*. Produced by Kit Lambert. Decca, Kensington, UK, 1969.
Whyte, George R. *The Dreyfus Affair: A Chronological History*. London: Palgrave Macmillan, 2008.
Wiersbe, Warren W. *On Being a Leader for God*. Grand Rapids: Baker, 2011.
Wilkinson, Richard H. *The Complete Gods and Goddesses of Ancient Egypt*. New York: Thames & Hudson, 2017.
Willmington, Harold. *The Doctrine of Satan*. Lynchburg, VA: Liberty University, 2018.
———. "Old Testament Passages Quoted by Jesus Christ." *The Second Person File* 71 (2017). https://digitalcommons.liberty.edu/second_person/71.
Wishart, Mervyn. "The Preservation of the Messianic Line—Part 1." *Precious Seed* 76.3 (2021) 18–19.
Wycliffe, John. *On the Truth of Holy Scripture*. Translated by Ian Christopher Levy. Kalamazoo, MI: Medieval Institute, 2001.
Yellowhorn, Eldon, and Kathy Lowinger. *Turtle Island: The Story of North America's First People*. Toronto: Annick, 2017.
Zhang, Weixia, et al. "Effects of Lyrics on the Processing of Musical Emotion: Behavioural and ERP Study." *Acta Psychologica Sinica* 50 (2018) 1346–55. https://journal.psych.ac.cn/acps/EN/10.3724/SP.J.1041.2018.01346.
Zielinski, Sarah. "The Great Moon Hoax Was Simply a Sign of Its Time." *Smithsonian Magazine*, July 2, 2015. https://www.smithsonianmag.com/smithsonian-institution/great-moon-hoax-was-simply-sign-its-time-180955761/.

Subject Index

Note: n indicates footnotes, and italicized page numbers indicate illustrations.

Aaron [biblical], 130
Abaddon, 281
Abagnale, Frank Jr., 162
Abel [biblical], 106, 299
Abraham (Abram) [biblical], 14, 105–6, 110, 127–30, 195, 297–98
Abrahamic Covenant, 127–29, 145, 297–98
absolute truth. *See* truth, absolute (universal)
Academy Awards, 224
Achish, King, 265
Acts, Book of, 74, 90, 92, 303
Acutis, Carlo, 26
Adam [biblical]
    deception's roots as being in Scripture, xiv
    defending truth in a postmodern age, 36, 47–48
    from Eden to today's battlefields, 257, 260
    imago Dei as truth written into human design, 77
    preservation and historical confirmation of Scripture, 105
    protoevangelium, the Cross, and counter-PSYOP, 292
    strategic objectives of the enemy, 296, 298–99
Adams, John, 254

Addison's Walk, Magdalen College, 120
ADHD, 272n6, 274
ADHD 2.0 (Hallowell and Ratey), 274
Adventism, 156
Ady, Thomas, 200n85
Affleck, Ben, 283
Afghanistan War, 254
Africa, 236
Against Heresies (Irenaeus of Lyons), 304
Agatho, Pope, 185
agnosticism, 44, 52–53, 58, 65
AI (artificial intelligence), 5–6, 85
AIDS/HIV, 10, 236
Airola, Paavo, 100
Allah, 9, 125–26, 158
Allies, 140–41, 153, 234, 279–80, 287
al-Qaeda, 148
Ambrosian Library, 177
American Revolution, 254
American Worldview Inventory, 87
Amin, Idi, 253
Amorites, 128
Ananias [biblical], 303
Andropov, Lev [character], 283
Anglicanism, 12, 90, 102
Annals (Tacitus), 107
Antioch [historical], 74–75
Antiquities of the Jews (Josephus), 107
anti-Semitism, 191, 247
The Anxious Generation (Haidt), 272n5
Apocrypha, 112–14, 135n97, 212
Apollyon, 281
Apostles' Creed, 180n47
Aquinas, Thomas, 44, 57n94
Arapaho tribe, 278

SUBJECT INDEX

Arbeit macht frei ("work sets you free"), 241
ARCINT (architectural intelligence), 102
Arianism, 13, 15, 96, 167
Aristotelian philosophy, 26
Aristotle, 71, 137–38
Arizona Christian University, 87
Armageddon [movie], 283
Arminianism, 77n128
Army, Union, 278
Army of Northern Virginia, 2
The Art of War (Sun Tzu), 276
artificial intelligence (AI), 5–6, 85
Aryans, 250
Asia Minor, 74–75
Assumption of Mary, 197n80, 218
Assyria [historical], 113
The A-Team [TV show], 54
ATF (Bureau of Alcohol, Tobacco, Firearms and Explosives), 6
Athanasius of Alexandria, 90, 96, 116, 177
atheism
    defending truth in a postmodern age, 21, 28, 38, 43–45, 52–56
    distortions in practice, 221
    the nature of deception, 153
    preservation and historical confirmation of Scripture, 111, 118
    prophecy, science, and the Bible's enduring accuracy, 65
    Scripture as our final and sufficient authority, 173
    trusting the Bible, 136
Athens [historical], 204
Augustine of Hippo, Saint, 118, 183, 186
Augustus, Emperor, 189
authority
    of God's word, 86–87
    question of, 165–72
    Scripture alone as final, 87–102
    Scripture as our final and sufficient, 172–81
    who has, 216–20
Axe, Douglas, 56

Babylon [historical], 23, 113, 287–88, 290
Babylonian Talmud, 107, 114
Babylonians, 68, 281
Baptism, 167n21, 227
Barna, George, 88
Barnabas [biblical], 75
Bashan [historical], 63, 292
Battle of Chancellorsville, *1*, 1–5, 7–9, 17, 79–81
Battle of Gettysburg, 278
Battle of Kursk, 155
Baucham, Voddie, 122
Bauckham, Richard, 110
Bay, Michael, 283
Bedouins, 133
Begg, Alistair, 161
Bellshaw, William G., 285
Ben-Gurion, David, 129
Benjamin, King [biblical], 135
Bereans, 93, 167–68, 171–72, 186, 231
Berechiah [biblical], 106
Berengarius of Tours, 202n87
Bergsma, John, 90–91
Berlin, Germany, 238–39, 241, 243, 279, 287
Berlin Diary (Shirer), 239
Bethlehem [historical], 300
Bhagavad Gita, 63
biblical truth. *See* truth, biblical
Big Bang, 57, 59
Biola University, 56
Blomberg, Craig L., 108
Bohemia, 117
Boyle, Robert, 44, 51
Branch Davidians, 6–7
Braun, Eva, 287
Brendon, Piers, 248
Brown, Dan, 225
Bruce, F. F., 140
Bryan, William Jennings, 50
Bucer, Martin, 202n87
Buddhism, 9, 63
Bureau of Alcohol, Tobacco, Firearms and Explosives (ATF), 6
Buscemi, Steve, 283
Butterfield, Rosaria, 118
Byzantine Empire, 118

Caesar, Julius, 137–38

Caesarea Philippi [historical], 292n40
Cain [biblical], 299
Cairo, Egypt, 103
Calais, France, 85
Caleb [biblical], 104
Callistus I, Bishop, 189
Calvary [historical], 26, 200, 209–10, 293
Calvin, John, 169, 193, 200n83, 202n87, 205, 220
Calvinism, 77n128
Cambrian period, 61
Canaanites, 128
Cardiff Giant hoax of 1869, 210
Carinhall, 279
Carthage [historical], 177
The Case for Christ (Strobel), 173
Castle Church, 305
Castro, Fidel, 253
Catch Me If You Can [movie], 162
Catechetical School of Alexandria, 177
Catechism of the Catholic Church, 222
Catherine of Bologna, Saint, 25
Catholicism. *See also* Roman Catholicism
    the biblical case against merit-based salvation, 168, 171
    defending truth in a postmodern age, 26n40
    distortions in practice, 182n49, 184, 194–96, 199, 201, 202n87, 206n93, 207, 210–12, 214, 217–22
    Gospel compromisers and man-pleasers, 11–12
    preservation and historical confirmation of Scripture, 117–18
    Scripture alone as final authority, 95
    Scripture as twisted and misused, 237
Center for Science and Culture, Discovery Institute, 60
Central Intelligence Agency (CIA), 254
Cephas (Simon) [biblical], 186. *See also* Peter [biblical]
Chadwick, Samuel, 163
Challenger disaster, 88, 226
Chamberlain, Neville, 252–53

Chancellery Garden, 287
Charles V, Holy Roman Emperor, 306
The Chess Players [painting], 270, 270, 309–10
Chesterton, G. K., 62
Cheyenne tribe, 278
Chief Shepherd, 191
China, 132, 245–46
Christ. *See* Jesus Christ [biblical]
Christ myth theory, 107
Christian Science, 192
Christianity
    the biblical case against merit-based salvation, 155, 158–61, 163, 164n18, 167
    deception as the art of misdirection, 3, 5
    deception's roots as being in Scripture, xi–xiii, xv
    defending truth in a postmodern age, 17–18, 21, 24n34, 30, 32–33, 38, 42–46, 50, 52–53, 59, 62
    distortions in practice, 189–90, 193, 195, 197, 208, 217–18, 221, 225
    God's covenant promises and enduring word, 131–32
    Gospel compromisers and man-pleasers, 11, 13–15
    guarding against strategic deception in your own life, 268
    knowing the enemy, 276
    modern manifestations of spiritual deception, 10–11
    the nature of deception, 153
    preservation and historical confirmation of Scripture, 107–8, 110–11, 114–18
    propaganda as on a national scale, 242, 245–46
    prophecy, science, and the Bible's enduring accuracy, 65, 69–72, 75
    protoevangelium, the Cross, and counter-PSYOP, 294
    Satan's pride and fall, 290
    Scripture alone as final authority, 87, 90, 92–95, 99
    Scripture as our final and sufficient authority, 172–74, 176–77, 179

SUBJECT INDEX

Christianity (continued)
   Scripture as twisted and misused, 237
   strategic objectives of the enemy, 304–6, 308–10
   the transformative power of Scripture, 119–22, 124
   trusting the Bible, 134n93, 136–38, 141
   the urgency of discernment, 228–29
Christianity Today [magazine], 69
Christology, 110n47, 127, 167, 197n80
Christus, 65
Chrysostom, John, 183, 186, 208
Church of Jesus Christ of Latter-day Saints. *See* Mormonism
Church of Rome (Webster), 206n93
Churchill, Winston, 149
CIA (Central Intelligence Agency), 254
Civil War, US, 2, 278
Clement of Alexandria, 176, 177n40
Clement of Rome, 115
Cliff College, 163
Codex Sinaiticus, 118–19, 139
Codex Vaticanus, 139
Cold War, 152, 236, 255, 259
College of Pontiffs, 188–89
Commission on Civil Rights, US, 51
Communism, 53, 245–46
Confederate States of America, 1, 3–4, 278
Congress, US, 5, 291
Coniah (Jeconiah, Jehoiachin) [biblical], 299–300
Constitution, US, 169
Copernicus, Nicolaus, 45, 71
Corinth [historical], 194
Corinthians, 115, 181
Cornelius [biblical], 196
Cornell University, 45, 56
Council of Carthage, 90, 177
Council of Constance, 117
Council of Ephesus, 197
Council of Hippo, 90, 177
Council of Jamnia, 114, 134n93
Council of Nicaea, 13, 96
Council of Rome, 90
Council of Trent

the biblical case against merit-based salvation, 154, 167–68, 171
defending truth in a postmodern age, 26
distortions in practice, 203, 221
preservation and historical confirmation of Scripture, 112, 114
COVID-19, 242
creation
   defending truth in a postmodern age, 28, 34–35, 37–38, 40, 43–50, 52, 54–55, 59
   from Eden to today's battlefields, 256, 258
   Gospel compromisers and man-pleasers, 14n22
   imago Dei as truth written into human design, 76, 79
   preservation and historical confirmation of Scripture, 109–10, 113
   prophecy, science, and the Bible's enduring accuracy, 62, 70–73
   strategic objectives of the enemy, 296
   the transformative power of Scripture, 120
   trusting the Bible, 142
creationism, 35, 47, 51, 54–55
CrossFit, 99
Cruz, Nicky, 121–22
Cuba, 253
cultural relativism, 16–22, 43, 232
Cultural Research Center, Arizona Christian University, 87
Custer, George Armstrong, 277–82
Czechoslovakia, 251–52

The Da Vinci Code (Brown), 225
Damasus I, Pope, 112, 189
Damien, Father, 100
Daniel [biblical], 66, 106, 111, 310
Dark Power, 276
Darrow, Clarence, 50
Darwin, Charles, 48, 51–53, 60–61
Darwinism, 45, 47–48, 56–57, 61–62
Das Kapital (Marx), 53
David, King [biblical]

SUBJECT INDEX

the biblical case against merit-based salvation, 159n13
defending truth in a postmodern age, 29
distortions in practice, 197
from Eden to today's battlefields, 265
modern manifestations of spiritual deception, 6n8
preservation and historical confirmation of Scripture, 102–3, 106
strategic objectives of the enemy, 298–99
Davidic Covenant, 299
Dawkins, Richard, 53
Day of Atonement, 199
"Day of Infamy" speech, 291
D-Day, 85, 153, 236
Dead Sea Scrolls, 125, 133–35
deception
as the art of misdirection, 3–5
as beginning with truth, 1–82
guarding against the strategy of in your own life, 266–69
military. *see* military deception (MILDEC)
modern manifestations of spiritual, 5–11
the nature of, 151–53
recognizing in everyday life, 80–82
and the reliability of Scripture, 84–85
roots of as being in Scripture, xi–xv
spiritual. *see* spiritual deception
strategy of as burying lies in truths, 234–69
decisionism, 169
deepfakes, 85
Denver Seminary, 108
depression, 272, 275
Derbe [historical], 74–75
Deuteronomy, Book of, 275
Devil
the biblical case against merit-based salvation, 163, 170
propaganda as on a national scale, 248
protoevangelium, the Cross, and counter-PSYOP, 293
Satan's ambitions, power, and fall, 270
Satan's pride and fall, 285
strategic objectives of the enemy, 303, 307, 309
truth vs. falsehood, definitions of, 150
the urgency of discernment, 229
Devil's Island, 151
DiAngelo, Robin, 98
DiCaprio, Leonardo, 162
Diet of Worms, 305
Diocletian, Emperor, 131–32
discernment between truth and deception
the biblical case against merit-based salvation, 154, 161–63, 165, 168, 171
biblical trust as your own foundation, 145, 147
deception as the art of misdirection, 4
deception's roots as being in Scripture, xi, xiii–xv
defending truth in a postmodern age, 16–19, 20n29, 22, 32, 43, 46, 50, 52, 56, 62
distortions in practice, 182, 185–86, 192
from Eden to today's battlefields, 260, 266
Gospel compromisers and man-pleasers, 11
guarding against strategic deception in your own life, 266–69
imago Dei as truth written into human design, 77
inspiration and authority of God's word, 87
modern manifestations of spiritual deception, 6, 8–9
preservation and historical confirmation of Scripture, 116n57
propaganda as on a national scale, 238, 240–42, 255
prophecy, science, and the Bible's enduring accuracy, 75

343

SUBJECT INDEX

discernment between truth and deception (continued)
protoevangelium, the Cross, and counter-PSYOP, 294
recognizing deception in everyday life, 80–82
Satan's ambitions, power, and fall, 274–75
Satan's pride and fall, 284
Scripture alone as final authority, 91–93
Scripture as our final and sufficient authority, 173, 175, 177–78
Scripture as twisted and misused, 237
strategic deception as burying lies in truths, 235
strategic objectives of the enemy, 304–6, 311
trusting the Bible, 141, 143–44
truth vs. falsehood, definitions of, 149–50
understanding and resisting the enemy in your own life, 312–13, 315
urgency of the, 226–30
in your own life, 230–33
Discovery Institute, 60
disinformation as deception
the biblical case against merit-based salvation, 155
deception and the reliability of Scripture, 85
defending truth in a postmodern age, 38
distortions in practice, 182
how lies hide in truth, 236
the nature of deception, 152
preservation and historical confirmation of Scripture, 107
propaganda as on a national scale, 239, 252, 254
distortion as deception
the biblical case against merit-based salvation, 154–55, 157–59, 161–66, 168, 170, 172
deception and the reliability of Scripture, 85

deception as the art of misdirection, 4–5
deception's roots as being in Scripture, xi
defending truth in a postmodern age, 16, 18–19, 29–30, 52
discerning truth from falsehood in your own life, 230
from Eden to today's battlefields, 257–62, 266
God's covenant promises and enduring word, 128
Gospel compromisers and man-pleasers, 11, 13–15
guarding against strategic deception in your own life, 266–67
how lies hide in truth, 236
imago Dei as truth written into human design, 76, 78
inspiration and authority of God's word, 86–87
knowing the enemy, 276
modern manifestations of spiritual deception, 5, 7–9
the nature of deception, 152
in practice, 181–226
propaganda as on a national scale, 238–43, 247, 249–50, 253
protoevangelium, the Cross, and counter-PSYOP, 293–94
Satan's pride and fall, 282–86
Scripture alone as final authority, 88–89, 94, 96, 101
Scripture as our final and sufficient authority, 175, 178, 180
Scripture as twisted and misused, 237
strategic deception as burying lies in truths, 235
strategic objectives of the enemy, 297, 303–5, 307–8, 310–11
trusting the Bible, 133, 141, 143–44
truth vs. falsehood, definitions of, 150–51
understanding and resisting the enemy in your own life, 312–13
the urgency of discernment, 227–29
why God's word is true, 84
DNA, 48–49, 51, 60, 149

344

SUBJECT INDEX

DOCEX (document exploitation), 107
Don't Have Enough Faith to Be an Atheist (Turek), 141
Dreyfus, Alfred, 151–52
Dreyfus Affair, 151–52
Dyson, Hugo, 120

Eagles, the, 30
Eastern Orthodoxy, 92–93, 94n15, 164, 168, 170
Ecclesiasticus (Sirach), Book of, 112
Eddy, Mary Baker, 192
Egypt, 84, 103–4, 110, 118, 128–29
Ehrman, Bart, 65
Einstein, Albert, 84
Ekman, Ulf, 12
El Arish, Egypt, 103
El Arish Stone, 103–4
Elijah [biblical], 106
EMCON (emissions control), 255
Emerson, Keith, 10
Emerson, Lake & Palmer, 10
E-meter, 25
emotivism, 20
Encyclopedia of Biblical Prophecy (Payne), 64
England, 39, 72, 117, 192, 236, 271
English Standard Version (ESV), 281
Enlightenment, 41
Enoch, Book of, 112
Enron, 310
Ephesians, 185
epiousios (bread for the coming day), 203
Esau [biblical], 263–64
eschatology, 34, 134
Esterhazy, Maj. Ferdinand, 151
Esther, Book of, 134, 298
ESV (English Standard Version), 281
Eucharist
    the biblical case against merit-based salvation, 159
    defending truth in a postmodern age, 26–27
    distortions in practice, 200n85, 201–4, 206–7, 209–11, 223
    Gospel compromisers and man-pleasers, 11–12

    Scripture as our final and sufficient authority, 174
Euphrates River, 128
Europe
    defending truth in a postmodern age, 39
    distortions in practice, 187, 217
    from Eden to today's battlefields, 264, 266
    propaganda as on a national scale, 246, 251–52
    Satan's pride and fall, 287
    strategic objectives of the enemy, 306
Evangelicalism
    the biblical case against merit-based salvation, 164, 169–70
    defending truth in a postmodern age, 33, 38
    Gospel compromisers and man-pleasers, 11–13, 15
    preservation and historical confirmation of Scripture, 102
    prophecy, science, and the Bible's enduring accuracy, 69
"Evangelicals and Catholics Together" statement, 12
evangelism
    the biblical case against merit-based salvation, 164
    distortions in practice, 190, 209
    Gospel compromisers and man-pleasers, 13n21, 14
    prophecy, science, and the Bible's enduring accuracy, 69n119
    Scripture alone as final authority, 100
    the transformative power of Scripture, 121–22
Eve [biblical]
    deception's roots as being in Scripture, xiv
    defending truth in a postmodern age, 47
    from Eden to today's battlefields, 257–62, 264
    imago Dei as truth written into human design, 77
    preservation and historical confirmation of Scripture, 105

propaganda as on a national scale, 242
strategic objectives of the enemy, 296, 299, 307
evolution and evolutionism
defending truth in a postmodern age, 28
distortions in practice, 192
and the foundation of relativism, 34–62
imago Dei as truth written into human design, 76
naturalistic, 34, 38, 53, 296
strategic objectives of the enemy, 296, 311
theistic, 35–36, 46–49
expressivism, 20
Ezekiel [biblical], 131

Faraday, Michael, 45
Farewell Address, 41
Federal Bureau of Investigation (FBI), 7
Federal Research Division, US Library of Congress, 247
Filioque clause, 168
Final Solution, 39
Fine Art of Propaganda (Lee and Lee), 235
First and the Last, 125–26
First Cause, 57
First Vatican Council, 185
Fixx, Jim, 100
Founders, 41
Fourth Lateran Council, 26, 203
France, 39, 85, 151–53, 252–53
Francis, Pope, 187–88
Franklin, Benjamin, 254
Frederick the Great, 271
Frey, Glenn, 30n47

Gabriel [angel], 125, 277
Gaddafi, Muammar, 253
Galatians, 98, 156
Galileo Galilei, 45, 71, 151
Gallic Wars (Caesar), 137, 138n105
Gallup polls, 28
Garden of Eden
knowing the enemy, 276

propaganda as on a national scale, 239, 241–44, 255
protoevangelium, the Cross, and counter-PSYOP, 292
Satan's pride and fall, 289
strategic objectives of the enemy, 297
to today's battlefields, from the, 256–66
Gardner, Chris, 224
Gates, Bill, 29n43, 273
Gath [historical], 265
Geisler, Norman L., 63n107
Gemara (Talmud), 107, 114
General Government, 39
General Scholium, 51
Generation Z, 28
Genesis, Book of
biblical trust as your own foundation, 145
defending truth in a postmodern age, 34–38, 47, 49–50
distortions in practice, 219
from Eden to today's battlefields, 256–57
God's covenant promises and enduring word, 127
strategic objectives of the enemy, 297n46
the transformative power of Scripture, 123
GEOINT (geospatial intelligence), 102
German Empire, 246
Germany
defending truth in a postmodern age, 39
from Eden to today's battlefields, 259
the nature of deception, 151
propaganda as on a national scale, 238–41, 243–44, 246, 249, 251–53, 255
Satan's pride and fall, 278–80, 287
strategic objectives of the enemy, 305
Gervais, Ricky, 21, 136
Gibraltar, 236
Girgashites, 128
Gnosticism, 304

God
- the biblical case against merit-based salvation, 154, 156–60, 162–72
- biblical trust as your own foundation, 144–47
- covenant promises and enduring word of, 127–33
- deception and the reliability of Scripture, 85
- deception as beginning with truth, 2
- deception as the art of misdirection, 3
- deception's roots as being in Scripture, xii–xv
- defending truth in a postmodern age, 17, 21–25, 27–34, 36–38, 40, 42–54, 56–59, 62
- discerning truth from falsehood in your own life, 231–33
- distortions in practice, 182–83, 185–87, 190–91, 193–98, 200–201, 203–5, 207–9, 211–15, 218–26
- from Eden to today's battlefields, 256–62, 264–66
- Gospel compromisers and man-pleasers, 11, 13–15
- guarding against strategic deception in your own life, 267–69
- *imago Dei* as truth written into human design, 76–80
- inspiration and authority of the word of, 86–87
- knowing the enemy, 276
- modern manifestations of spiritual deception, 6n8, 8–10
- the nature of deception, 153
- preservation and historical confirmation of Scripture, 102–12, 114–16, 118–19
- propaganda as on a national scale, 238–39, 242–46, 253, 255
- prophecy, science, and the Bible's enduring accuracy, 62–67, 70, 72–75
- protoevangelium, the Cross, and counter-PSYOP, 291–95
- recognizing deception in everyday life, 80–82
- Satan's ambitions, power, and fall, 270–71, 274–75
- Satan's pride and fall, 277, 281–82, 284–91
- Scripture alone as final authority, 87–88, 90–102
- Scripture as our final and sufficient authority, 173–76, 178–81
- Scripture as twisted and misused, 237
- strategic deception as burying lies in truths, 235
- strategic objectives of the enemy, 295–311
- the transformative power of Scripture, 119–26
- trusting the Bible, 135–36, 138, 140–44
- truth vs. falsehood, definitions of, 149–50
- understanding and resisting the enemy in your own life, 312–15
- the urgency of discernment, 226–27, 229–30
- word of as true, 83–147

Godhead, 13–14, 40, 54, 70, 142
Goebbels, Joseph, 239, 248–50, 252, 257, 278–81, 284
Goebbels, Magda, 279–80
Goering, Hermann, 278–79, 281
Good Shepherd, 17, 178
Gospels, the
- compromisers and man-pleasers in, 11–16
- distortion of, 208–10
- distortions in practice, 193
- preservation and historical confirmation of Scripture, 107–8, 110n47, 112, 116
- Satan's pride and fall, 285
- Scripture alone as final authority, 90
- Scripture as our final and sufficient authority, 176–77
- the transformative power of Scripture, 120–21

SUBJECT INDEX

Graham, Billy, 69, 169
Gratian, Emperor, 189
Great Britain, 39, 252
Great Commission, xii, xv, 14n22, 209, 302
Great Depression, 244
Great Fire of London, 271, 276
Great Isaiah Scroll, 134
Great Moon Hoax, 25
Great Schism, 168
Greco-Persian Wars, 138
Greece, 244
Gregor, Neil, 249
Gregory I, Bishop, 188
Gregory VII, Bishop, 188
Griffith, Frances Llewellyn, 103
Grove City College, 150
Grudem, Wayne, 78, 127
Guyana, 228

Habakkuk, Book of, 134
Habakkuk [biblical], 23
Habermas, Gary, 24n34, 42–43, 137
Hades [god], 125–26, 301
Haggai [biblical], 113–14
Haidt, Jonathan, 272n5
Hallowell, Edward, 274
Haman [biblical], 298
Hanks, Tom, 225
Harvard University, 41
Heartland International Film Festival, 223
Hebrews, Book of, 116, 177, 220
Hebrews [people]. *See* Israelites
Hefner, Hugh, 98
Hell, 24, 142, 157, 292n40, 300
Hellenism, 112
Henley, Don, 30n47
Henry, Carl F. H., 69
Hermon, Mount [historical], 292n40
Herod, King [biblical], 300
Herodotus, 137, 138n105
High Priest, 92, 130, 214
Hilary of Poitiers, 183
Himmler, Heinrich, 278–79, 281
Hinduism, 9, 63, 71, 157, 210
Hinn, Benny, 164
Hippo [historical], 177n45

Hippolytus of Rome, 165
Histories (Herodotus), 137–38
Hitler, Adolf
   defending truth in a postmodern age, 39
   from Eden to today's battlefields, 258
   the nature of deception, 153
   propaganda as on a national scale, 244, 248–53
   Satan's pride and fall, 278–81, 287
   trusting the Bible, 141
Hitler Youth, 280
Hittites, 128, 195
HIV/AIDS, 10, 236
Hodge, Charles, 119
Hodges, Donald A., 32
Hoffmeier, James, 103
Holocaust, 39, 129, 217, 240, 279
Holy Door, 174
Holy Ghost, 219n113
Holy Nails, 24
Holy Roman Empire, 246
Holy Spirit
   the biblical case against merit-based salvation, 154, 156, 163, 168, 170
   defending truth in a postmodern age, 17
   discerning truth from falsehood in your own life, 231
   distortions in practice, 190–91, 202, 204, 211, 224–25
   from Eden to today's battlefields, 256, 262
   Gospel compromisers and man-pleasers, 13–14
   guarding against strategic deception in your own life, 267–68
   inspiration and authority of God's word, 86
   preservation and historical confirmation of Scripture, 108, 111–15
   prophecy, science, and the Bible's enduring accuracy, 73
   Satan's ambitions, power, and fall, 274

SUBJECT INDEX

Scripture alone as final authority, 90, 92–93, 94n15, 97
Scripture as our final and sufficient authority, 173, 175–76, 178, 181
strategic objectives of the enemy, 302–4
the transformative power of Scripture, 123, 126
understanding and resisting the enemy in your own life, 312, 315
Holy Tradition, 93
Homer, 138
homosexuality. *See* LGBTQ+ movement
"Hotel California" [song], 30
Howell, Vernon Wayne. *See* Koresh, David (Vernon Wayne Howell)
Hoyle, Sir Fred, 58
humanism, 38, 50, 87
HUMINT (human intelligence), 102, 107
Hungary, 39
Hunt, Ethan, 10
Hus, Jan, 117, 202n87
Hussein, Saddam, 253

Iconium [historical], 74–75
Ignatius of Antioch, 116, 118, 201–3
Iliad (Homer), 138
imago Dei (image of God), 76–80, 296–97
IMF (Impossible Missions Force), 10
IMINT (imagery intelligence), 102
Immaculate Conception, 197
Imperial Government of Japan, 291
Inquisition, Roman Catholic, 151
Instagram, 275
Instructions for His Generals (Frederick the Great), 271
iPad, 273
Iraq, 148, 253
Irenaeus of Lyons, 116, 118, 176, 304–5
Iroquois tribe, 71
Isaac [biblical], 106, 128, 263
Isaiah, Book of, 281
Isaiah [biblical], 24, 131, 156, 179, 290
ISIS, 239
Islam, 9, 125–26, 158, 215

Isma'ilya, Egypt, 103
Israel, land of [historical], 66, 106, 113–14, 129, 288
Israel, land of [modern], 129
Israelites
the biblical case against merit-based salvation, 169
defending truth in a postmodern age, 25
distortions in practice, 200, 203
eradication of, 297–98
God's covenant promises and enduring word, 128–31
modern manifestations of spiritual deception, 8
preservation and historical confirmation of Scripture, 103–4, 110
prophecy, science, and the Bible's enduring accuracy, 66
Satan's pride and fall, 288
Scripture alone as final authority, 93
strategic objectives of the enemy, 295, 297–98
trusting the Bible, 134
Italy, 117, 141, 177

J'Accuse! (Zola), 152
Jackson, Gen. Thomas "Stonewall," 1, 3–4
Jacob [biblical], 67, 104, 106, 128, 263–64
James, Book of, 177
James, M. E. Clifton, 236
James [biblical], 101, 107, 185, 227
Januarius, Saint, 25
Japan, 195, 234
Jebusites, 128
Jeconiah (Jehoiachin, Coniah) [biblical], 299–300
Jehovah's Witnesses, xii, 13–15, 219
Jeremiah, David, 38, 40
Jeremiah [biblical], 131, 170
Jerome, 112–13, 203
Jerusalem [historical], 66nn115–116, 114, 178, 185, 200n84
Jerusalem [modern], 133
Jerusalem Council, 185

SUBJECT INDEX

Jesus Christ [biblical]
  affirmation of and archaeology, 105–19
  the biblical case against merit-based salvation, 154, 156–65, 167, 169–72
  biblical trust as your own foundation, 144
  deception as the art of misdirection, 3n4
  deception's roots as being in Scripture, xii, xv
  defending truth in a postmodern age, 17, 23–27, 32–33, 36–37, 42–43, 47, 50
  discerning truth from falsehood in your own life, 231–33
  distortions in practice, 181–216, 218, 220–26
  from Eden to today's battlefields, 257–58, 261–63, 266
  exclusivity of, 155–65
  God's covenant promises and enduring word, 127–31
  Gospel compromisers and man-pleasers, 11–15
  imago Dei as truth written into human design, 78
  inspiration and authority of God's word, 86
  modern manifestations of spiritual deception, 8–10
  the nature of deception, 153
  preservation and historical confirmation of Scripture, 105–11, 113–15, 116n57, 118
  propaganda as on a national scale, 239, 242, 245–46, 249–50
  prophecy, science, and the Bible's enduring accuracy, 62, 64–66
  protoevangelium, the Cross, and counter-PSYOP, 292–94
  Satan's ambitions, power, and fall, 270, 274
  Satan's pride and fall, 281, 286
  Scripture alone as final authority, 87–88, 91, 93, 95–101
  Scripture as our final and sufficient authority, 174–75, 178–79, 180n47
  Scripture as twisted and misused, 237
  in the shadows vs. saints in the spotlight, 192–98
  strategic objectives of the enemy, 296, 298–305, 307–11
  the transformative power of Scripture, 119, 121–26
  trusting the Bible, 135, 137, 139, 141, 144
  truth vs. falsehood, definitions of, 149
  understanding and resisting the enemy in your own life, 312–15
  the urgency of discernment, 226, 230
  vs. the papal command, 182–91
Jewish Agency, 129n83
Jewish Question, 39
Job, Book of, 70
Job [biblical], 286
Jobs, Steve, 273
John, Book of, 116n57
John [biblical], 115–16, 123, 131, 193, 199, 285
John the Baptist [biblical], 107, 196
Joint Resolution, 291
Jonah [biblical], 106, 111
Jonathan [biblical], 197
Jones, Alex C., 12
Jones, Jim, 228
Jonestown massacre of 1978, 228–29
Jordan, Michael, 90
Joseph [biblical], 104, 299
Josephus, 65, 107
Jubilee Years, 174
Jubilees, Book of, 112
Judah [biblical], 66
Judah [historical], 129, 299
Judaism
  the biblical case against merit-based salvation, 156, 169
  defending truth in a postmodern age, 39
  distortions in practice, 191, 193, 217
  from Eden to today's battlefields, 262
  God's covenant promises and enduring word, 129

350

SUBJECT INDEX

modern manifestations of spiritual deception, 8
preservation and historical confirmation of Scripture, 103–4, 107, 109, 112–14
propaganda as on a national scale, 240, 250
prophecy, science, and the Bible's enduring accuracy, 65, 75
Satan's pride and fall, 279, 285
Scripture alone as final authority, 95
Scripture as our final and sufficient authority, 179
strategic objectives of the enemy, 298
trusting the Bible, 134
Judas Iscariot [biblical], 300
Jude [biblical], 115
Judea [historical], 65
Judith, Book of, 113
Justin Martyr, 202–3

Kaaba, 125
Kadena, Japan, 234
Kadmonites, 128
Kant, Immanuel, 57n94
Keller, Tim, 99
Kenezzites, 128
Kenites, 128
Kennedy, D. James, 53
Kepler, Johannes, 44, 51, 71
KGB, 259
King James Version (KJV), 124, 281
Kirk, Charlie, 21
Koelsch, Stefan, 32n52
Koresh, David (Vernon Wayne Howell), 6–8, 20
Kuwait, 238

Lakota tribe, 278
Lamanites, 135
Lapine, Joshua, 73
Last Supper, 202
Latimer, Hugh, 230
Latter-day Saints (LDS). *See* Mormonism
Law of Human Nature, 40
Lazarus [biblical], 188
Lee, Alfred McClung, 235

Lee, Elizabeth Briant, 235
Lee, Gen. Robert E., 2–3, 17
Lenape tribe, 71
Leo XIII, Pope, 190
Lewis, C. S., 40, 45–46, 61, 120–22, 142, 157, 276
LGBTQ+ movement, 28, 38, 118
Library of Congress, US, 247
Libya, 253
Licona, Michael, 137
LifeWay Research, 12
Ligonier Ministries, 8, 12, 13n21
Little Ice Age, 29n43
Living Bible, 87
Locke, John, 41
Lodge, Henry, 100
London, England, 271
Lord. *See* God
Lord's Prayer, 202–3, 208
Lord's Supper, 88, 180n47, 198–99, 223
Louvre Museum, 270, 309
Lubyanka prison, 259
Lucifer, 277, 281, 288, 290–91
Lüdemann, Gerd, 65
Luke [biblical], 75, 115, 298
Luther, Martin
the biblical case against merit-based salvation, 169
distortions in practice, 181, 193, 202n87, 211–12, 220
preservation and historical confirmation of Scripture, 113, 116–17
strategic objectives of the enemy, 305–7
Lycaonia [historical], 74
Lyons [historical], 116, 176
Lystra [historical], 74–75

MacArthur, John, 4, 193, 241, 276, 290
Maccabees, Book of, 112–13
Magdalen College, Oxford University, 120
Magisterium, Roman Catholic, 89, 91–93, 171n33, 174, 179
"Make Room" [song], 172
Malachi, Book of, 112, 114
Malachi [biblical], 113–14, 200n83

SUBJECT INDEX

Marian dogmas, 91, 197n80, 216, 218, 223
Mariolatry, 192–93
Marshall, George C., 41
Marshall Plan, 41
Martin, Maj. William, 83, *83*, 140
Marx, Karl, 53
Marxism, 53
Mary [biblical]
    the biblical case against merit-based salvation, 157
    defending truth in a postmodern age, 25
    distortions in practice, 190, 192–93, 196–97, 212, 218, 223
    Scripture alone as final authority, 96
    strategic objectives of the enemy, 299
    trusting the Bible, 135
    understanding and resisting the enemy in your own life, 313
Mary Magdalene [biblical], 308
maskirovka (Soviet military deception), 155, 158
Masoretic Text, 118, 134
Mass, 12n19, 192, 198–201, 205, 211–12, 216
Massah [historical], 36
materialism, 11, 42–43, 45–46, 55, 60, 77
Matthew [biblical], 298
Mau Maus, 121
Maury, Matthew Fontaine, 71–73
Maxwell, James Clerk, 45
Mecca, 125
Medina, 125
Mein Kampf (Hitler), 39
Mere Christianity (Lewis), 276
Messiah
    distortions in practice, 183, 191
    preservation and historical confirmation of Scripture, 107
    prophecy, science, and the Bible's enduring accuracy, 66n115
    protoevangelium, the Cross, and counter-PSYOP, 292
    severing the line of, 298–300
    stopping at the cross, 300–301
    strategic objectives of the enemy, 295, 298–300
    trusting the Bible, 135
Metzger, Bruce M., 139
Meyer, Stephen C., 60
Micaiah [biblical], 67
Michael [angel], 25, 277, 310
Milan, Italy, 177
military deception (MILDEC)
    the biblical case against merit-based salvation, 155, 166
    deception and the reliability of Scripture, 85
    deception as the art of misdirection, 4
    deception's roots as being in Scripture, xii
    defending truth in a postmodern age, 18
    distortions in practice, 182, 192, 209
    propaganda as on a national scale, 241
military PSYOPs, xii, 18–19, 82, 158, 209, 229, 284
Miller, Christine, 228
Millerite movement, 156
Miracle Crusades, 164
Miracles (Lewis), 45
Mishnah, 114
misinformation as deception
    the biblical case against merit-based salvation, 172
    deception as beginning with truth, 2
    defending truth in a postmodern age, 52
    propaganda as on a national scale, 240, 242
    Satan's ambitions, power, and fall, 271
    Satan's pride and fall, 283–84
    strategic objectives of the enemy, 295
    trusting the Bible, 141
    truth vs. falsehood, definitions of, 150–51
    understanding and resisting the enemy in your own life, 313
Molokai Island, 100
Montgomery, Gen. Bernard, 236
Moody, D. L., 169
moral relativism, 17, 28, 34, 81–82

SUBJECT INDEX

moralism, 160, 164–65
Mormon, Book of, 63, 95, 123–24, 135–36
Mormonism, xii, 95–96, 101, 124, 136, 219
Moroni [angel], 124
Mosaic Law, 156
Moscow, Russia, 239, 259
Moses [biblical]
    defending truth in a postmodern age, 25
    from Eden to today's battlefields, 257, 263
    Gospel compromisers and man-pleasers, 15
    preservation and historical confirmation of Scripture, 103–4, 106, 110
    Scripture alone as final authority, 93
Mosiah, King [biblical], 135
Mother Earth, 98
Mr. T [character], 54
Muhammad, 125
Munich, Germany, 253
Muratorian fragment, 90, 177
Murphy, Audie, 223
Muslims. *See* Islam

National Aeronautics and Space Administration (NASA), 88, 226, 283
National Association of Evangelicals, 13n21
National Socialism, 279–80
Native Americans, 71, 278
naturalism, 42–45, 47–48, 52–55, 58, 61, 76
naturalistic evolution, 34, 38, 53, 296
Navy, US, xii, 71, 255
Nazir-Ali, Michael, 12
Nazism
    the biblical case against merit-based salvation, 162
    deception and the reliability of Scripture, 85
    defending truth in a postmodern age, 39, 41
    distortions in practice, 191, 217

    from Eden to today's battlefields, 258–59
    God's covenant promises and enduring word, 129
    guarding against strategic deception in your own life, 267
    propaganda as on a national scale, 238–41, 243–51, 255
    Satan's pride and fall, 279–81, 288
    trusting the Bible, 140
Nebuchadnezzar, King [biblical], 113, 287
Nehemiah, Book of, 134n93
neo-Darwinism, 48
Nero Decree, 278
New Age, 9, 172
New English Translation (NET), 281
New International Version (NIV), 281
New King James Version (NKJV), 281
New Testament
    the biblical case against merit-based salvation, 169
    defending truth in a postmodern age, 26
    distortions in practice, 184–85, 190, 192, 194, 196, 208, 214–15, 225
    God's covenant promises and enduring word, 130–32
    Gospel compromisers and man-pleasers, 13, 15
    knowing the enemy, 276
    preservation and historical confirmation of Scripture, 108, 110n47, 112–16
    prophecy, science, and the Bible's enduring accuracy, 74
    Satan's pride and fall, 277, 285
    Scripture alone as final authority, 90–93, 95
    Scripture as our final and sufficient authority, 173, 176–78, 181
    strategic objectives of the enemy, 298
    the transformative power of Scripture, 124n76
    trusting the Bible, 137–40
    the urgency of discernment, 226–27
New World Translation (NWT), 14n23
New York, 121, 210

The New York Sun [newspaper], 25
Newton, Sir Isaac, 2, 44, 51–52, 59, 71, 90
Nicaea [historical], 14
Nicene Creed, 96, 168, 180n47
Nicodemus [biblical], 211
Ninety-Five Theses (Luther), 117, 212, 305
Nineveh [historical], 106
Nirvana, 9
NIV (New International Version), 281
NKJV (New King James Version), 281
Noah [biblical], 105, 297n46
Normandy, France, 85, 153
Nuclear Navy, xiii, 4–5
Nuremberg, Germany, 240
Nuremberg Tribunal (Trial), 41, 240, 248
NWT (New World Translation), 14n23

Observe-Orient-Decide-Act (OODA) loop, 172
Okinawa, Japan, 234
Old Testament
    the biblical case against merit-based salvation, 156
    defending truth in a postmodern age, 23, 36
    distortions in practice, 199
    God's covenant promises and enduring word, 130
    preservation and historical confirmation of Scripture, 105, 109, 112–15
    Satan's pride and fall, 277, 285
    Scripture alone as final authority, 92
    Scripture as our final and sufficient authority, 175
    trusting the Bible, 134n93, 135, 139
On Fairy-Stories (Tolkien), 121
Operation Copperhead, 236
Operation Desert Storm, 237–38
Operation Fortitude, 85, 149, 153
Operation INFEKTION, 236
Operation Mincemeat, 83, 140–41, 162
Opticks (Newton), 2
Origen, 116, 118, 183, 186
The Origin of Species (Darwin), 60
Oxford University, 53, 120, 230

Packer, J. I., 90, 193
paganism, 131, 153–54, 188–90, 221, 292n40
papacy. *See* Rome [papacy]
Paradise, 211, 213
Paris, France, 151
Pas de Calais, France, 153
Pascal, Blaise, 44–45
Pasteur, Louis, 45
Pastor Aeternus (First Vatican Council), 185
Paul [biblical]
    the biblical case against merit-based salvation, 154, 156, 167, 169–70
    defending truth in a postmodern age, 18, 23, 40, 42
    discerning truth from falsehood in your own life, 231
    distortions in practice, 181, 185, 190, 194, 196–98, 204, 208, 213–15, 224
    from Eden to today's battlefields, 260
    God's covenant promises and enduring word, 131
    Gospel compromisers and man-pleasers, 11, 16
    preservation and historical confirmation of Scripture, 115
    prophecy, science, and the Bible's enduring accuracy, 74–75
    Satan's pride and fall, 282, 285
    Scripture alone as final authority, 91–93, 98–99, 101
    Scripture as our final and sufficient authority, 173, 179
    Scripture as twisted and misused, 237
    strategic objectives of the enemy, 307
    trusting the Bible, 142
    the urgency of discernment, 227, 229
Pauline letters, 90
Payne, J. Barton, 64
Pearl Harbor, 291
Pekharti [historical], 104
Penrose, Roger, 58
Pentateuch, 135
Pentecost, 170
Pentecostalism, 12

SUBJECT INDEX

People's Temple, 228
perception as deception
    the biblical case against merit-based salvation, 163, 165
    deception as beginning with truth, 2
    deception as the art of misdirection, 4–5
    defending truth in a postmodern age, 17–19, 25, 28–29, 32–33, 35, 43, 49–50
    distortions in practice, 209
    from Eden to today's battlefields, 257–58
    Gospel compromisers and man-pleasers, 16
    imago Dei as truth written into human design, 78, 80
    modern manifestations of spiritual deception, 5–7, 9
    the nature of deception, 152
    propaganda as on a national scale, 238–39, 241–42, 244, 246, 248, 250, 255
    prophecy, science, and the Bible's enduring accuracy, 62, 72–74
    Satan's ambitions, power, and fall, 271, 275–76
    Satan's pride and fall, 282, 284
    Scripture alone as final authority, 97
    strategic deception as burying lies in truths, 235
    the transformative power of Scripture, 124
    trusting the Bible, 137, 141
    truth vs. falsehood, definitions of, 148, 150
    why God's word is true, 84
Perizzites, 128
Persia [historical], 310
Peter, Book of, 116n57, 177
Peter [biblical]
    the biblical case against merit-based salvation, 169
    distortions in practice, 182n49, 183–87, 191, 196, 216, 220
    God's covenant promises and enduring word, 131

preservation and historical confirmation of Scripture, 115, 117
Satan's pride and fall, 281
strategic objectives of the enemy, 301, 303
the transformative power of Scripture, 122
Pew Research, 306
Pew Research Center, 28n43
Pharaoh [biblical], 103
Pharisees, 91, 93, 175, 178, 188
Philippians, 116
Philistines, 265
Pi-hahiroth [historical], 104
Piltdown Man, 192
"Pinball Wizard" [song], 31
Pisidian Antioch, 74
Pius XII, Pope, 217
Plantinga, Alvin, 57n94
Playboy Philosophy, 98
pluralism, 82, 136, 155
Poetics (Aristotle), 137, 138n105
Poland, 39
Polycarp of Smyrna, 116
Pontius Pilate, 65, 107
Ponzi, Charles, 84
Ponzi scheme, 84
Postman, Neil, 17
postmodernism, 16–62, 79, 82, 87
Powers, Francis Gary, 259–60
Presbyterianism, 119
Princeton Theological Seminary, 119, 139
Principia (Newton), 51
propaganda as deception
    the biblical case against merit-based salvation, 157, 160
    deception and the reliability of Scripture, 85
    defending truth in a postmodern age, 28, 32
    distortions in practice, 191
    from Eden to today's battlefields, 257–58, 264, 266
    guarding against strategic deception in your own life, 266–67
    how lies hide in truth, 236

SUBJECT INDEX

propaganda as deception (continued)
  modern manifestations of spiritual
    deception, 6
  on a national scale, 238–56
  the nature of deception, 152
  prophecy, science, and the Bible's
    enduring accuracy, 63
  Satan's pride and fall, 279–80, 288
  strategic deception as burying lies
    in truths, 235
  trusting the Bible, 137
  truth vs. falsehood, definitions of, 148
Protestantism
  the biblical case against merit-
    based salvation, 164, 167n21,
    169–70, 172
  deception's roots as being in
    Scripture, xi
  defending truth in a postmodern
    age, 26n40
  distortions in practice, 183, 193,
    199–200, 202n87, 206, 211–12,
    217, 220–21
  Gospel compromisers and man-
    pleasers, 11, 12n14
  preservation and historical
    confirmation of Scripture,
    112–13, 115–17
  propaganda as on a national scale,
    247
  Scripture alone as final authority,
    89–92
  Scripture as our final and sufficient
    authority, 179
  Scripture as twisted and misused, 237
  strategic objectives of the enemy,
    305–6
  truth vs. falsehood, definitions of, 149
The Protocols of the Elders of Zion, 191
Provine, William, 56
Pseudepigrapha, 112
PSYOPs (psychological operations)
  the biblical case against merit-
    based salvation, 157–60, 162–
    63, 165–66, 170
  counter-PSYOPs, xiv, 8, 18, 22, 52,
    56, 60, 69, 73, 75, 80, 88, 108,
    119, 180, 291–95

deception and the reliability of
  Scripture, 85
deception as beginning with truth, 2
deception as the art of
  misdirection, 4–5
deception's roots as being in
  Scripture, xii, xiv
defending truth in a postmodern
  age, 17–22, 27, 29, 32–33, 35,
  38, 40, 44, 46, 48–52, 55–57, 60
distortions in practice, 183, 187,
  191–93, 195, 198, 207, 209–11,
  216–20, 224–25
from Eden to today's battlefields,
  265–66
Gospel compromisers and man-
  pleasers, 11, 15–16
imago Dei as truth written into
  human design, 76, 78–80
inspiration and authority of God's
  word, 87
knowing the enemy, 276
military, xii, 18–19, 82, 158, 209,
  229, 284
modern manifestations of spiritual
  deception, 5–8
the nature of deception, 152–53
preservation and historical
  confirmation of Scripture, 108,
  119
propaganda as on a national scale,
  238, 242, 245, 247, 255
prophecy, science, and the Bible's
  enduring accuracy, 64, 67, 69,
  73, 75
protoevangelium, the Cross, and
  counter-, 291–95
recognizing deception in everyday
  life, 82
Satan's ambitions, power, and fall,
  275
Satan's pride and fall, 277, 284, 286
Satan's strategy in relation to, 276
Scripture alone as final authority,
  88, 97–98
Scripture as our final and sufficient
  authority, 174, 178, 180
Scripture as twisted and misused, 237

spiritual, xii, 7, 11, 216, 225, 235
strategic deception as burying lies
  in truths, 235
strategic objectives of the enemy,
  296–98, 300–301, 303, 311
truth vs. falsehood, definitions of,
  148–49
the urgency of discernment, 229
Ptolemaic period, 103, 112n49
Purgatory
  the biblical case against merit-
    based salvation, 157, 171
  discerning truth from falsehood in
    your own life, 231
  distortions in practice, 192, 210–14,
    216, 218
  Gospel compromisers and man-
    pleasers, 12
  the psychology of control, 211–16
  Scripture alone as final authority, 91
The Pursuit of Happyness [movie], 224

Qumran [historical], 133–34
Qur'an, 63, 124–26, 215

Raikes, Robert, 169
Ramsay, Sir William, 74–75
Ratey, John, 274
Rebekah [biblical], 263
Red Army, 155, 287
Reformation, Protestant
  the biblical case against merit-
    based salvation, 169–70, 172
  defending truth in a postmodern
    age, 26n40
  distortions in practice, 202n87, 206,
    211–12
  Gospel compromisers and man-
    pleasers, 11
  preservation and historical
    confirmation of Scripture,
    116–17
  Scripture alone as final authority,
    89
  Scripture as our final and sufficient
    authority, 179
  strategic objectives of the enemy,
    305–6

Reformers
  the biblical case against merit-
    based salvation, 167, 169
  distortions in practice, 193, 202n87,
    219–20
  preservation and historical
    confirmation of Scripture,
    113–15, 117
  Scripture alone as final authority,
    89, 94n15
  Scripture as our final and sufficient
    authority, 179
  the transformative power of
    Scripture, 119, 122
  truth vs. falsehood, definitions of, 150
Reich Chancellery, 279, 287
relativism
  the biblical case against merit-
    based salvation, 157, 165
  biblical trust as your own
    foundation, 147
  cultural, 16–22, 43, 232
  defending truth in a postmodern
    age, 16–17, 20–22, 28, 33–34,
    43–44
  discerning truth from falsehood in
    your own life, 231–32
  distortions in practice, 221
  evolutionary foundation of, 34–62
  imago Dei as truth written into
    human design, 79
  moral, 17, 28, 34, 81–82
  recognizing deception in everyday
    life, 81–82
  Scripture alone as final authority, 87
"Religion and Science" (Einstein), 84
Rephaim, 128
Retzsch, Moritz, 270, 309
Revelation, Book of
  biblical trust as your own
    foundation, 145
  defending truth in a postmodern
    age, 34
  distortions in practice, 219
  God's covenant promises and
    enduring word, 127

Revelation, Book of (continued)
  preservation and historical confirmation of Scripture, 115–16
  prophecy, science, and the Bible's enduring accuracy, 71
  Scripture as our final and sufficient authority, 177
  the transformative power of Scripture, 123
revisionism, 52, 140
Rickover, Adm. Hyman, xiii, 4–5
Ridley, Nicholas, 230
The Rise and Fall of the Third Reich (Shirer), 239
ROE (rules of engagement), 101, 111, 165, 171, 173, 175, 208
Roman Catholic Controversy (White), 206n93
Roman Catholicism
  the biblical case against merit-based salvation, 154, 157–58, 167, 169–71
  deception's roots as being in Scripture, xii
  defending truth in a postmodern age, 24, 26
  discerning truth from falsehood in your own life, 231–32
  distortions in practice, 182, 186–88, 190, 193–94, 196–202, 205–8, 211–12, 214–21, 223–25
  Gospel compromisers and man-pleasers, 11
  preservation and historical confirmation of Scripture, 112, 114, 116–18
  propaganda as on a national scale, 247
  Satan's ambitions, power, and fall, 271
  Scripture alone as final authority, 88–95, 101
  Scripture as our final and sufficient authority, 174–75, 177, 179
  Scripture as twisted and misused, 237
  strategic objectives of the enemy, 305
  truth vs. falsehood, definitions of, 149, 151
Roman Empire, 107, 246
Romania, 39
Romans and Roman culture
  distortions in practice, 184, 187–89, 199
  God's covenant promises and enduring word, 131
  preservation and historical confirmation of Scripture, 107
  propaganda as on a national scale, 244–46
  prophecy, science, and the Bible's enduring accuracy, 65, 66n115
  Scripture as twisted and misused, 237
  trusting the Bible, 137
Rome [historical], 131, 184, 187–89, 194, 244, 246
Rome [papacy]
  the biblical case against merit-based salvation, 167–69
  discerning truth from falsehood in your own life, 231
  distortions in practice, 182, 184–85, 191–94, 200, 206–7, 210, 216–20
  God's covenant promises and enduring word, 131
  Gospel compromisers and man-pleasers, 11–12
  preservation and historical confirmation of Scripture, 113, 115, 118
  propaganda as on a national scale, 245–46
  Scripture alone as final authority, 90, 94–95
  trusting the Bible, 137
Roosevelt, Franklin D., 291n38
Rosa Endowed Chairship of Molecular Biology, Biola University, 56
Rosetta Stone, 84
Royal Marines, 140
Royal Society Conference on Evolutionary Biology, 48
Rudy [movie], 223
Ruettiger, Daniel Eugene "Rudy," 223

SUBJECT INDEX

rules of engagement (ROE), 101, 111, 165, 171, 173, 175, 208
Run Baby Run (Cruz), 122
Russia, 191, 239, 259

Sabbath, 156, 169
sacramentalism, 160, 168–69
Samaritan Pentateuch, 135
Samaritans, 204
Samarkand codice, 125
Sanford, John C., 45
Satan
  ambitions of, 270–315
  the biblical case against merit-based salvation, 155–57, 163, 165, 170
  deception as beginning with truth, 2
  deception as the art of misdirection, 4–5
  deception's roots as being in Scripture, xi–xiv
  defending truth in a postmodern age, 18–19, 25, 29–32, 36, 38
  discerning truth from falsehood in your own life, 230–31
  distortions in practice, 208–10, 224
  from Eden to today's battlefields, 256–62, 264–66
  fall of, 270–315
  Gospel compromisers and man-pleasers, 13, 16
  guarding against strategic deception in your own life, 267–69
  how lies hide in truth, 236
  knowing the enemy, 276
  modern manifestations of spiritual deception, 6–8
  the nature of deception, 152–53
  power of, 270–315
  pride of, 277–91
  propaganda as on a national scale, 238–44, 247, 249–51, 253, 255
  protoevangelium, the Cross, and counter-PSYOP, 291–95
  recognizing deception in everyday life, 82
  scope of power as limited but lethal, 307–11
  Scripture alone as final authority, 98
  Scripture as twisted and misused, 237–38
  strategic deception as burying lies in truths, 235
  strategic objectives of the enemy, 295–304, 306–11
  subtle strategy of, 208–10
  trusting the Bible, 141
  truth vs. falsehood, definitions of, 149–50
  understanding and resisting the enemy in your own life, 312–14
  the urgency of discernment, 229
satispassio (suffering through sin), 213
Saul, King [biblical], 29, 265
Savonarola, Girolamo, 117
Schwarzkopf, Norman, 237
Science Speaks (Stoner), 64
Scientific Revolution, 44, 51
Scientology, 25
Scopes trial, 49
SCRIPTINT (scriptural intelligence), 102
Second Temple, 134
The Secret Thoughts of an Unlikely Convert (Butterfield), 118
Septuagint, 112, 114, 134–35
Seth [biblical], 299
Seventh-day Adventism, 156
Sheol, 288
Shirer, William L., 238–39
Shroud of Turin, 24
Sicily, Italy, 141
SIGINT (signals intelligence), 86, 184
Sikhism, 210
Silicon Valley, 273, 275
Simon (Cephas) [biblical], 186. *See also* Peter [biblical]
Simon bar Kokhba, 107
Sinai, Egypt, 118
Sirach (Ecclesiasticus), Book of, 112
smartphones, 250, 271–72
Smith, Joseph, 124, 135–36
Snapchat, 275
social media, 7, 29, 250, 272–73, 282–86, 288

SUBJECT INDEX

sola fide (faith alone)
    the biblical case against merit-based salvation, 154, 164–65, 167, 169
    distortions in practice, 193, 206–7, 213–14, 222
    Gospel compromisers and man-pleasers, 11
    Scripture alone as final authority, 101
    strategic objectives of the enemy, 305
    the urgency of discernment, 230
sola scriptura (Scripture alone)
    anchor in, 180–81
    the biblical case against merit-based salvation, 171
    distortions in practice, 181, 219–20
    as final authority, 87–102
    inspiration and authority of God's word, 87
    preservation and historical confirmation of Scripture, 117
    Scripture as our final and sufficient authority, 179
    Scripture as twisted and misused, 237
    strategic objectives of the enemy, 305
    the urgency of discernment, 229
SOPs (Standard Operating Procedures), 101
South Sea Company, 216
Soviet Union, 39, 152, 253, 259
Speer, Albert, 248
Spirit. *See* Holy Spirit
spiritual deception
    the biblical case against merit-based salvation, 155, 157, 162
    deception and the reliability of Scripture, 85
    deception as beginning with truth, 2
    deception's roots as being in Scripture, xii, xiv
    defending truth in a postmodern age, 50
    discerning truth from falsehood in your own life, 231–32
    distortions in practice, 186, 220
    from Eden to today's battlefields, 258, 261, 263
    guarding against strategic deception in your own life, 267
    modern manifestations of, 5–11
    the nature of deception, 152
    propaganda as on a national scale, 241–42
    protoevangelium, the Cross, and counter-PSYOP, 294
    recognizing deception in everyday life, 81
    Satan's pride and fall, 280, 283
    Scripture as our final and sufficient authority, 172, 175
    strategic objectives of the enemy, 306, 311
    understanding and resisting the enemy in your own life, 313
    the urgency of discernment, 226, 228
spiritual PSYOPs, xii, 7, 11, 216, 225, 235
Sproul, R. C., 8, 193, 242, 294
Spurgeon, Charles, 193, 227–28
SS, 279
St. Catherine's Monastery, 118
St. Peter's Basilica, 174, 187
Stalin, Joseph, 239, 253
Standard Operating Procedures (SOPs), 101
Stanford University, 49
State of Theology Survey, 12, 15
Steen, Jessica, 283
Stephen [biblical], 164n18
Stone-Campbell Restoration Movement, 124n76
Stoner, Peter, 64–65
Stormare, Peter, 283
Stott, John, 102
Strobel, Lee, 173
Stuart, J. E. B., 278
Sudeten German Free Corps, 252
Sudeten Mountains, 251
Sudetenland, 251–53, 255
suicide, 228, 272–73, 280
Sun Myung Moon, 191
Sun Tzu, xi, 276, 312
Syracuse University, 118
Syrian Antioch, 74

tabula rasa (blank slate), 41
Tacitus, 65, 107
Talmud (Gemara), 107, 114

SUBJECT INDEX

Taylor, Charles, 44
techniques, tactics, and procedures (TTPs), 166
Tefnut, Queen Mother, 103
Tel Dan Stele, 102–3
Tertullian, 177, 189
Tetelestai ("it is finished"), 199–200, 208
The Text of the New Testament: Its Transmission, Corruption, and Restoration (Metzger), 139
theistic evolution, 35–36, 46–49
Theology and Science (Henry), 70
theosis, 164
Thessalonica [historical], 75
Third Council of Constantinople, 185
Third Reich, 246, 248–49, 277–82
Thirtieth Dynasty, 103
Thor [god], 137
Thunberg, Greta, 98
Tiberius [historical], 65
Tillotson, John, 200n85
Time [magazine], 51
Timothy [biblical], 75, 170
To Hell and Back [movie], 224
Tobit, Book of, 113
Tolkien, J. R. R., 120–21
Tommy [album], 31
Tooth of Saint Apollonia, 25
Topkapi codice, 125
Torah, 104, 125–26
Treaty of Versailles, 244, 252
Trinity and Trinitarian theology
    the biblical case against merit-based salvation, 167, 168n25
    distortions in practice, 218
    Gospel compromisers and man-pleasers, 13, 14nn22–23, 15
    Scripture alone as final authority, 92
    trusting the Bible, 135
Triune God, 14
Trojan Horse, 149, 263
Trojans, 263
Troy [historical], 263
True Cross, 25
Trueman, Carl R., 150
Trump, Donald, 97
truth, absolute (universal)
    consequences of rejecting, 33–34
    defending truth in a postmodern age, 17, 20, 22, 29, 33–36, 38, 40, 42–44
    discerning truth from falsehood in your own life, 232
    imago Dei as truth written into human design, 79
    recognizing deception in everyday life, 80–82
    trusting the Bible, 140–41, 143
truth, biblical
    the biblical case against merit-based salvation, 170, 172
    biblical trust as your own foundation, 145–47
    deception as the art of misdirection, 4
    deception's roots as being in Scripture, xi, xv
    defending truth in a postmodern age, 36, 50
    discerning truth from falsehood in your own life, 232
    distortions in practice, 188, 201, 208
    Gospel compromisers and man-pleasers, 14
    guarding against strategic deception in your own life, 268
    imago Dei as truth written into human design, 76
    modern manifestations of spiritual deception, 8
    preservation and historical confirmation of Scripture, 105, 108
    propaganda as on a national scale, 243
    recognizing deception in everyday life, 82
    Scripture alone as final authority, 88, 95
    Scripture as our final and sufficient authority, 174–75, 178
    Scripture as twisted and misused, 237
    strategic objectives of the enemy, 304–5
    trusting the Bible, 143

TTPs (techniques, tactics, and
    procedures), 166
Turek, Frank, 141
Turkey, 74–75
Turning Point USA, 21
Turtle Island, 71
Tyler, Liv, 283
Tyndale, William, 202n87
Tyre [historical], 288, 290

Uganda, 253
Ukraine, 97
Ultra, 141
*Undeniable: How Biology Confirms Our
    Intuition That Life Is Designed*
    (Axe), 56
Unification Church, 191
Union, the, 3–4, 8, 278
United Kingdom, 306
United Nations (UN), 98
universal truth. *See* truth, absolute
    (universal)
universalism, 33
University of Cambridge, 60
University of Notre Dame, 223
Uthman, Caliph, 125

Vatican, 174, 185, 217, 222
Vedas, the, 63
Veil of the Virgin Mary, 25
Vermigli, Peter Martyr, 202n87
Victorian era, 124
Vietnam War, 157
Virgin Mary [biblical]. *See* Mary
    [biblical]
Virginia Military Institute (VMI), 1,
    3n4, 41, 71
Voice of America [news broadcast], 254
von Bismarck, Otto, 246
von Tischendorf, Constantin, 118
Vulgate, Latin, 112, 203

Wahlberg, Mark, 313
Waldorf School of the Peninsula, 273
Walker, Tommy [character], 31
Wannsee Conference, 39–40
War Guilt Clause, 244
Warfield, Benjamin, 219n113
Washington, George, 41, 254

Watch Tower Bible and Tract Society,
    14–15
Watts [character], 283
Webster, William, 206n93
The Weight of Glory (Lewis), 45
Weimar Republic, 244
Wesleyan University, 163
West Point, 277
"What Happens Here, Stays Here"
    campaign, 30
Whitaker, William, 219n113
White, James R., 206n93
White Fragility (DiAngelo), 98
The Who, 31
Why I Believe (Kennedy), 53
Wiersbe, Warren, 262
Wilhelm I, Kaiser, 246
Wilkerson, David, 121
Willis, Bruce, 283
Willmington, Harold, 288
Wittenberg, Germany, 305
World War I, 244
World War II
    deception and the reliability of
        Scripture, 85
    defending truth in a postmodern
        age, 41
    distortions in practice, 209, 217
    example of deception in, *234*
    how lies hide in truth, 236
    propaganda as on a national scale,
        238, 251
    protoevangelium, the Cross, and
        counter-PSYOP, 291
    truth vs. falsehood, definitions of, 149
    why God's word is true, 83
Wycliffe, John, 117, 202n87

Yahweh, 109–10
Yefuneh [biblical], 104
Younger Next Year (Lodge), 100
Youth Risk Behavior Survey, 272

al-Zarqawi, Abu Musab, 148, *148*
Zechariah [biblical], 106, 113–14
Zeus [god], 137
Zionism, 129n83
Zola, Émile, 151
Zwingli, Huldrych, 169, 202n87, 220

Scripture Index

OLD TESTAMENT

Genesis

1	35, 50, 237, 296
1:1–3	14n22
1:2	76
1:26	76
1:28	296
1:31	36, 296
2	35
2:7	48, 77, 296
2:16–22	260
3	36, 256, 307
3:1–3	258
3:1–5	251
3:1–6	256
3:4	36, 241
3:5	257, 258
3:6	256
3:13	259
3:14	292
3:15	258, 291, 292, 299
3:22	257
6:5–6	297
6:13	297n46
7:19	297n46
9:11	297n46
9:15	297n46
12	128
12:1–3	127–128, 297–298
15:4–5	128
15:18–21	128
18:25	159n13
23	195
25:29–34	263
27	263
48:16	104

Exodus

3:14	15, 110
13:19	104
14	103
14:2	104
14:9	104
15:20	29
16:4	203
20:4–5	195, 205
20:12	193n73
24	92

Leviticus

19:31	198

Deuteronomy

1:39	159n13
4:2	117
5:8–9	205
6:13	36
6:16	36
8:3	36
12:5–14	200n84
13:1–3	93
18:10–12	194, 198
18:15	66
18:21–22	67
21:17	193n73

Deuteronomy (continued)

25:4	115
29:29	119–120, 121
32:8	134
34:6	25

Ruth

4	193n73

1 Samuel

16:23	29
21:11	265
21:13	265

2 Samuel

1:26	197
6:14	29
12:22–23	159n13
23:2	111–112

1 Kings

8:27	205
22:28	67

2 Kings

6:17	310n62

1 Chronicles

17:11	299
17:14	299

Esther

3:12–14	298

Job

1	286
12:7–9	73
26:7	70

Psalms

8:8	72
14:1	53–54, 142
17:8	37
18:2	186
19:1	59, 205
19:1–4	72
22	62
22:1	63
22:7–8	63
22:12	292
22:12–13	63
22:16–18	63
22:29	63
27:1	265
27:2	206
34:18	119
53:1	142
69:21	199
90:2	120
103:20	308
107:23–24	72n123
119:105	17, 173, 181
119:160	21
145:17	159n13
149:3	29
150	29

Proverbs

1:7	54
3:5–6	145
4:23	275
12:22	265
15:3	120
29:25	246
31	119

Ecclesiastes

1:7	72n123
12:7	43

Isaiah

1:18	45
8:19–20	198
8:20	180
14	290, 290n35, 291
14:12	277
14:12–15	30n45, 288, 290n35, 314
14:12–21	288

14:13–14	312	10	310
14:14	277, 291	10:13	277, 310
40:26	70		
41	64	**Habakkuk**	
41:21	64	2:4	23
42:8	109, 195		
43:16	72n123	**Malachi**	
45	6n8	1:11	199–200
45:7	308		
46:9–10	67, 147		
53	135		
57:15	205		
59:1–2	261		
64:6	24, 156		
65:17	67		
66:1–2	204, 205		

DEUTEROCANONICAL BOOKS

1 Maccabees
9:27	113

2 Maccabees
12:45	212

Wisdom of Solomon
11:17	113

Judith
1:5	113

Jeremiah
17:9	21, 27, 42n67, 170, 171, 243
22	299
22:30	299
28:9	67
29:11	120
31:31	66
31:31–34	129–130
31:34	66

Ezekiel
28	288, 290, 290n35
28:12–17	314
28:12–19	290n35
28:13	289
28:13–17	30n45
28:13–19	289
28:15	289
28:17–19	289
36:25–27	211
36:26–27	170
37	129

ANCIENT JEWISH WRITERS

Josephus, Flavius
The Antiquities of the Jews
18.3.3	65n114, 107n41

RABBINIC WORKS

Babylonian Talmud

Yoma
9b:16	114n55

Sotah
12a	103, 103n34

Daniel
4:30	287
7	109
7:2–3	66
9:26	66, 66n115

NEW TESTAMENT

Matthew

1:1–17	298
2:16–18	300
3:7	292
3:16–17	14n22
4:1–11	294
4:9	300
5:17	199
5:17–18	86
5:18	140
6:5–15	190
6:11	203
7	23
7:13	22
7:16	162
7:21–23	169
7:23	11, 23
7:24–25	119
7:24–26	22–23, 80, 82
7:24–27	232
12:3	106
12:30	23, 101
12:40–41	106
13:19	282
13:55–56	193n73
15:1–6	178
15:3–9	93, 175
15:7–9	179
15:9	162
16:16	183
16:18	183, 184, 186, 187, 292n40, 301
16:19	95
16:24	10
18	92
18:3	27
18:18	95
19:4–5	105
19:4–6	47
19:14	159n13
20:25–26	190
23:9	194
23:35	106
24:4–5	170
24:15	106
24:30	201
24:37–38	105
25:14–30	302
28:19	14n22
28:19–20	xii, 37, 302

Mark

1:23–26	308
5:2–5	308
6:3	193n73
7:6–13	93
7:13	91
12:26	106
16:9	308

Luke

1:19	277
1:26	277
1:28	196, 197
1:43	197n80
1:46–47	196
3	47
3:23–38	298
3:31	299
4	36
4:25	106
9:23	10
10:7	115
10:18	286, 288
11:3	203
16:19–31	188
16:31	263
18:17	27
19:13	303
21	185
21:8	186
22:3	300
22:20	130
22:32	184, 218
23:42	213
23:42–43	211
23:43	211n101, 213
24:39–43	15
24:44	114

SCRIPTURE INDEX

John

1:1	14n23, 50, 110
1:1–3	14n22, 50
1:12–13	96
1:14	110
1:42	186
2:19–21	14
3:3	169
3:5	211
3:16–17	129
3:30	10, 196
4:23–24	204
4:24	195, 205
5:26	110
6	202, 206, 206n93, 237
6:35	202, 208
6:53–58	201
6:63	202
7:5	193n73
8:31–32	165, 231
8:32	ix
8:44	239, 241, 251, 257, 282, 307
8:56	105
8:58	14, 110
10:4–5	178
10:9	xii, 37, 202
10:10	30
10:27	17, 105, 178
10:28	315
10:33	109
10:35	127
12:31	282, 307
12:37	27, 263
13:27	300
14:6	xii, 10, 33, 43, 80, 82, 110, 155, 174, 194, 207
14:23	205
14:26	93, 191
14:30	307
15:5	202
15:26	168n25
16:7	168n25
16:13	93, 176, 315
16:23	190
17:3	109
17:5	109
17:8	176
17:11	190
17:17	122, 141, 147, 231, 232
19:25–27	193n73
19:26–27	197
19:28	199
19:30	199, 205, 214, 224, 301
20:23	94, 95
20:28	14
20:29	27
21:15–17	185

Acts

2	170
2:38	169
3:21	130
4:12	xii, 207
5:3	303
5:15	170
5:29	220
7	164n18
7:48–49	205
10:25–26	196
13	74
14	74
14:6–8	74–75
14:11–15	196
14:20	75
14:21	74, 74–75
14:21–26	74
14:26	74
15	185
15:19	185
16:1	75
16:31	37
17:6	75
17:11	93, 150, 162, 167, 169, 171, 186, 220, 231
17:24	261
17:24–25	204
20:28	185

Romans

1:7	194
1:17	23
1:17–19	23
1:18–21	142–143
1:18–25	142–143, 147, 232
1:19–22	40
1:20	54, 59, 70
1:23	196
1:24–25	142–143
1:25	43
2:14–16	42
2:15	119
3:10	158, 160
3:23	10, 27, 169
3:24	96
3:25	12n19
3:28	154, 156
5:8	122
5:12–18	257
6:6	243
6:16–23	261
6:23	154, 158, 264
8:3	243
8:5–8	10
8:9–11	224
8:11	14
8:13	224
8:20–23	256
8:37	313
10:9	222
10:17	27, 122
11:6	96, 98, 154, 224
11:26	66–67
12:1	10
12:2	145, 274
16:20	314

1 Corinthians

1:2	194
1:20	262–263
1:26	262–263
2:6–8	309, 310
2:12–13	86
3:11	184
3:16	205
4:15	194
6:9–10	227
10:4	186
10:13	243
11:2	88
11:23–26	198
12–14	170
14:22	170
15:14	137
15:20–23	15

2 Corinthians

4:4	240, 282, 307
4:7	10
4:8–9	132
5	214
5:8	43, 211n101, 212, 213
5:17	78, 119
11:3	181, 259
11:4	16
11:13–15	269
11:14	31, 208, 231, 251, 259
11:14–15	260
11:15	303
12:7–9	170
13:5	170, 171

Galatians

1:1	14
1:6–9	98, 99, 167
1:8	93, 124n76
1:10	11
1:11–12	115
2:5	16
2:16	96
2:20	10
2:21	156
3:3	156
3:8	128
3:11	23
3:28	8, 262
5:2	156
5:9	209
5:17–24	262
6:7	227

Ephesians

1:1	194
1:3	261–262
1:22–23	191
2:2	282, 307
2:8–9	95, 96, 99, 158, 180n47, 206, 213, 224
2:8–10	10
2:10	296
2:20	182–183, 184, 186
4:11	190
4:14	250, 266
4:24	78
5:11	294
5:19	29
6:10–12	282
6:10–18	267, 312
6:11	x
6:11–12	251, 266
6:11–17	269
6:12	227, 307, 312

Philippians

1:1	194
1:6	154
1:23	214
3:9	214
3:21	15
4:7	267
4:13	9

Colossians

1:2	194
1:16–17	v, 50, 121
1:18	190, 220
2:8	vi, 179
2:15	312
3:1	204
3:5	243
3:16	29

1 Thessalonians

2:13	173, 176
5:21	220

2 Thessalonians

1:10–11	197
2	92
2:9–12	163
2:15	88, 91, 215
3:6	215

1 Timothy

2:4	302
2:5	xii, 88, 190, 192–193, 196, 213, 223, 313
3:6	285
4:1	303
5:18	115
5:23	170

2 Timothy

2:15	37, 147, 162, 237
3:13	18, 82
3:15	91
3:16–17	86, 89, 140, 144, 171, 180, 180n47, 191, 229, 231

Titus

3:5	96

Hebrews

1:3	48
1:14	130
2:10	130
2:14–15	293
2:16	130
2:17	12n19
3:4	57
4:12	118
5:14	315
7:23–27	214
7:25	194, 197
7:27	199
9:24	204
9:24–28	199
9:26	211n101, 212, 213
9:28	201

Hebrews (continued)

10:10	23, 167, 167n21, 199, 205
10:10–14	12n19, 26, 198, 200, 210
10:12	200
10:12–14	205
10:14	200, 211n101, 212
10:38	23
11:1	196
12:1	197
12:2	197
13:15	200n83
13:17	220

James

1:5	81, 231, 312
1:13–18	227
1:14	243
2:17	224
2:24	101
3:9	78
4:7	314
4:8	222
5:16	194

1 Peter

2:5	215
2:9	215
3:15	45
5:1–4	191
5:2	185
5:8	150, 163, 281, 282

2 Peter

1:16–21	122–123
1:20–21	181
2:11	308
3:13	67
3:15–16	115

1 John

1:1–3	123
1:9	95
3:8	293

3:12	299
4:1	269
4:4	313

Jude

3	xii, 12, 93, 149, 173, 219, 302
9	25
17	115
18	115

Revelation

1:7	66, 66n116
1:17–18	125
2	115
2:10	303
3	115
3:20	222
5:8	197
5:9	8
9:11	281
12:7	277
12:9	251, 257
12:9–10	307
12:10	284, 285
12:17	303–304
13:8	78
20:1–3	163
21:1	67
21:27	212
22:18–19	117, 174, 176

ISLAMIC LITERATURE

Quran

Surah Al-Baqarah

2:85	126
2:256	126

Surah Al-Imran

3:3	125

Surah Al-Ma'idah

5:46	125

5:47   126

Surah Al-Anfal
8:12   126

Surah At-Tawbah
9:5   126

Surah Yunus
10:94   126

Surah Al-Mu'minun
23:102–3   216n108

Surah Al-Hadid
57:3   125

EARLY CHRISTIAN WRITINGS

Apostolic Fathers

Ignatius of Antioch
Smyrnaeans 7.1   203n91

Greek Fathers

Athanasius of Alexandria
Easter Letter   90
Festal Letters 39   90n9, 116, 177n44

Clement of Alexandria
Stromata 7.16   177n40

Eusebius of Caesarea
Ecclesiastical History 8.2.4–5   131n86, 131n87

Irenaeus of Lyons
Against Heresies   305n51
Against Heresies 3.11.8–9   116n56

John Chrysostom
Homilies on Matthew 19.5   208n96
Homilies on Matthew 54.3   183n51, 184n54

Justin Martyr
First Apology 66   203n91

Latin Fathers

Augustine of Hippo
Retractations 1.21.1   183n52, 184n54
Sermons 26   184n53
Tractates on John 124.5   184n54

Gregory the Great, Pope
Registrum Epistolarum 5.43   188n61

Hilary of Poitiers
Trinity 6.36   184n54

Jerome of Stridonium
Commentary on Matthew 1.6.11   203n89
Preface to Proverbs 6:492   113n52

Tertullian of Carthage
Apology 21   177n41
On Modesty   189n63
On Modesty 1   188n61

THE CHURCH OF JESUS CHRIST OF LATTER-DAY SAINTS

Book of Mormon

1 Nephi
11:18   135, 136n99
11:21   135

2 Nephi

25:23	95–96
30:6	135, 136n99

Mosiah

21:28	135, 136n99

Doctrine and Covenants

Official Declaration

2	136n99

Pearl of Great Price

Smith, Joseph
History of the Church 4:461

136n100

GRECO–ROMAN LITERATURE

Tacitus

The Annals of Imperial Rome

15.44	65n113, 107n40